Personalized Politics

The **Institute of Southeast Asian Studies** was established as an autonomous organization in 1968. It is a regional centre dedicated to the study of socio-political, security and economic trends and developments in Southeast Asia and its wider geostrategic and economic environment.

The Institute's research programmes are Regional Economic Studies (RES, including ASEAN and APEC), Regional Strategic and Political Studies (RSPS), and Regional Social and Cultural Studies (RSCS).

The Institute is governed by a twenty-two-member Board of Trustees comprising nominees from the Singapore Government, the National University of Singapore, the various Chambers of Commerce, and professional and civic organizations. An Executive Committee oversees day-to-day operations; it is chaired by the Director, the Institute's chief academic and administrative officer.

Personalized Politics

The Malaysian State under Mahathir

In-Won Hwang

ISEAS INSTITUTE OF SOUTHEAST ASIAN STUDIES, Singapore

First published in Singapore in 2003 by
Institute of Southeast Asian Studies
30 Heng Mui Keng Terrace
Pasir Panjang
Singapore 119614

E-mail: publish@iseas.edu.sg
http://bookshop.iseas.edu.sg

*The responsibility for facts and opinions in this publication rests exclusively
with the author and his interpretations do not necessarily reflect
the views or the policy of the Institute or its supporters.*

ISEAS Library Cataloguing-in-Publication Data

Hwang, In-Won.
    Personalized politics : the Malaysian state under Mahathir.
    1. Malaysia—Politics and government.
    2. Malaysia—Ethnic relations—Political aspects.
    3. Mahathir Mohamad, Dato' Seri, 1925-
    4. UMNO.
    I. Title.
    II. Title: Malaysian state under Mahathir
DS596.7 H98   2003   sls2002025517

ISBN 981-230-185-2 (softcover, ISEAS, Singapore)
ISBN 981-230-186-0 (hardcover, ISEAS, Singapore)

Typeset by International Typesetters Pte. Ltd.
Printed in Singapore by PhotoPlates Pte. Ltd.

Dedicated to my parents
Hwang Kwang-Yeon and Lee Yong-Soon
with love

Contents

List of Tables

Foreword

In 1955, when Malaya was still part of the British Empire, the colonial authorities held a general election as a step towards independence in 1957. That election was won by an alliance of three racially based parties headed by its Malay component, the United Malays National Organization (UMNO). Over the next decades, that alliance expanded to include other parties but its essential structure remains much the same — a dominant Malay party heading an alliance of parties representing smaller ethnic groups. The UMNO-dominated alliance won all but one seat in 1955 and has won overwhelming majorities in every election since then — usually occupying around 80 to 85 per cent of the seats in the national parliament and controlling almost all of the state governments. If, as Samuel Huntington has said, one of the marks of an institutionalized political party is adaptability in the face of changing circumstances, then UMNO and the Barisan Nasional (BN), as the alliance is now known, must be considered as very successful cases of institutionalization.

Malaysian society has undergone enormous change since the 1950s. The predominantly rural population of the 1950s has become increasingly urban. An economy based on the export of tin and rubber is now moving towards industrialization. An economy which was largely owned by foreigners is now largely in the hands of Malaysians. Malays, Chinese, and Indians who were concentrated in their own segments of a plural society are now all represented in the modern economy and have increasingly acquired a common "Malaysian" identity. And a society that appeared to be on the brink of national disintegration after racial rioting in 1969 has not witnessed major ethnic violence for more than thirty years. Most societies that have undergone the type of transformation experienced by Malaysia have also experienced considerable political upheaval and often drastic change in their political system. But in Malaysia the core framework of the political system has largely survived while adjustments have been implemented only gradually.

How has the political system, and particularly the dominant party institutions, UMNO and the BN, adjusted to social and economic change? Political scientists have always debated the nature of Malaysia's political system. Concepts such as consociationalism, limited democracy, semi-democracy, soft authoritarianism, and personal rule have all appeared in this debate and are used by Dr Hwang in this book. It is Hwang's argument that the nature of the political system has in fact changed quite radically despite the continuity in formal political institutions. In the 1960s the consociational model provided insights but by the 1970s and 1980s the system was moving from semi-democracy to a form of authoritarianism. By the 1990s, according to Hwang, Malaysian politics could be best understood as a form of personal rule. Although the main institutions remained in place, the long-serving prime minister, Datuk Seri Dr Mahathir Mohamad, exercised almost unfettered personal dominance.

The extent to which the Malaysian political system has adapted successfully to social and economic change was shown most clearly in its response to the economic collapse that hit Asia in mid-1997. Many had argued that Malaysia's political and social stability was simply a product of a rapidly growing economy and that the system would be very vulnerable to a major economic setback. But when the setback occurred in 1997–98, the much anticipated renewal of ethnic violence did not eventuate and the political system continued much as before.

This does not mean, however, that no challenges are looming. At the conclusion of his book, Dr Hwang discusses what he calls "the rise of new politics". He devotes particular attention to the extraordinary treatment meted out by the prime minister to his deputy, Anwar Ibrahim. Although public protest against Anwar's imprisonment was not sustained, it was clear in the 1999 election that Malay support for UMNO had declined sharply. On the other hand, non-Malay — especially Chinese — support for the BN had strengthened. At the turn of the century, many of the basic assumptions of political analysts about Malaysian politics were being undermined. UMNO's record of adapting itself to new challenges has been impressive but it remains a question whether it can successfully adapt to the post-Mahathir era.

In-Won Hwang is a young scholar who has spent many years studying Malaysian politics. His research led him to live in Malaysia for several years and to learn the Malay language. During his time in Malaysia he was able to meet and interview many members of the Malaysian political élite — both from the government parties and the opposition — as well as journalists, academics, and other observers of the political scene. His work, therefore, contains an authentic quality that can only be acquired through close association with the subjects of his study. Dr Hwang provides a fine analysis of Malaysian political trends and a valuable foundation for thinking about Malaysia's future.

Harold Crouch
Department of Political and Social Change
Research School of Pacific and Asian Studies
Australian National University

Acknowledgements

This book is based on my Ph.D. thesis entitled "Changing Conflict Configurations and Regime Maintenance in Malaysian Politics". With both an update and an elaboration of the thesis, the journey towards and preparation of this volume has been long.

I am indebted to numerous individuals for the completion of this book. First of all, I owe a great debt to Professor Harold Crouch, Professor Ben Kerkvliet, and Dr Ron May. I have been fortunate to have had these three people as my Ph.D. supervisors. I thank all three for their intellectual guidance, for their immeasurable support, and especially for their strong encouragement and great patience.

I must note my appreciation to Allison Ley. She was kind enough to spend invaluable time editing not only my earlier drafts of the Ph.D. dissertation but also the final revision of this book. My special thanks also go to Claire Smith, Bev Fraser, and Jill Wolf. They provided efficient administrative assistance and a conducive environment during my decade-long stay in the Department of Political and Social Change, the Australian National University. I would like also to extend my gratitude to other departmental colleagues and many Korean fellows for their warmth and hospitality. I sincerely regret being unable to name all of them here.

During the three-year long period of my fieldwork in Malaysia, I was greatly indebted to many people. I must note my appreciation of many Malaysian friends for their academic support and warm friendship, though I cannot thank them all by name. My special thanks go to Professor Lee Kam Hing, Professor Jomo, Dr Gomez, Lim Kit Siang, Datuk Rais Yatim, Datuk Kamarudin Jaffar, Tian Chua, Teresa Kok, Shamsul Akmar Musakamal, Ahmad Shabery Chik, Saifuddin Nasution Ismail, Soo Yew Thet, and Liew Chin Tong. Regardless of their different political orientations, they share a great enthusiasm and love for Malaysian people. My understanding of Malaysia has been immeasurably enhanced by formal and informal conversations with them.

I would also like to express my appreciation to the teachers I had when I was a graduate student in Korea: Professors Kim Sang-Joon, Oh Kie-Pyung, Rhee Sang-Woo, Chang Dal-Joong, Lee Kap-Yun, Park Ho-Seong, Kang Jung-In. My special thanks go to Professor Sohn Hak-Kyu and Professor Shin Yoon-Hwan. They advised me to study at the Australian National University and have continued to offer their encouragement. Now as then, my teachers, directly or indirectly, have continued to inspire me to continue to undertake research.

My greatest appreciation must go to my family. To my lovely wife Bo-Ai, thanks will never be enough for her sacrifice and love. She remains always there when I need her, full of trust. This book could not have been written without her complete support and encouragement. My son Jin-Ha and daughter Sun-Young are our most valued blessings of God. For the last decade, my mind has been at peace with their smiles and love.

My final and largest appreciation must go to my parents, Hwang Kwang-Yeon and Lee Yong-Soon. Their trust and patience towards their son gave me the strength and courage throughout the course of this study. I dedicate this book to my parents with love.

Glossary

ABIM	Angkatan Belia Islam Malaysia (Malaysian Islamic Youth Movement)
ADIL	Pergerakan Keadilan Sosial (Movement for Social Justice)
APU	Angkatan Perpaduan Ummah (Muslim Unity Movement)
AWSJ	*Asian Wall Street Journal*
BA	Barisan Alternatif (Alternative Front)
Berjasa	Barisan Jamaah Islamiah Se-Malaysia (Malaysian Islamic Council Front)
Berjaya	Bersatu Rakyak Jelata Sabah (United Common People of Sabah)
Bernama	the government-controlled national news agency
BMA	British Military Administration
BN	Barisan Nasional (National Front)
bumiputera	indigenous person (literally: son of the soil)
ceramah	a political meeting in a non-public place
CPM	Communist Party of Malaya
dakwah	Islamic revival (literally: call)

DAP	Democratic Action Party
DNU	Department of National Unity
DTCs	deposit-taking co-operatives
FAMA	Federal Agricultural Marketing Authority
fatwa	an authoritative legal ruling given by an authorized official interpreting Islamic law
FDD	Federal Development Department
FEER	*Far Eastern Economic Review*
FELDA	Federal Land Development Authority
FIDA	Federal Industrial Development Authority
GAGASAN	Gagasan Demokrasi Rakyat (Coalition for People's Democracy)
Gagasan Rakyat	People's Concept
GDP	gross domestic product
GERAK	Majlis Gerakan Keadilan Rakyat (Council of Malaysian People's Justice Movement)
Gerakan	Gerakan Rakyak Malaysia (Malaysian People's Movement)
GNP	gross national product
hudud	Koranic criminal punishment
Iban	indigenous community in Sarawak
IMF	International Monetary Fund
IMP	Independence of Malaya Party
ISA	Internal Security Act
JUST	Just World Trust
Kadazan	indigenous community in Sabah
kampung	village
KeADILan	Parti KeADILan Nasional (National Justice Party)
Ketuanan Melayu	Malay Supremacy
konfrontasi	Indonesia's confrontation campaign against the formation of Malaysia
korupsi	corruption
kronisme	cronyism
MARA	Majilis Amanah Rakyat (People's Trust Council)
MCA	Malaysian Chinese Association
MCS	Malaysian Civil Service

menteri besar	chief minister
merdeka	independence
MIC	Malaysian Indian Congress
MIDF	Malaysian Industrial Development Finance
MP	member of Parliament
MPAJA	Malayan People's Anti-Japanese Army
MPH	multipurpose holdings
MTUC	Malaysian Trade Union Congress
NCC	National Consultative Council
NDP	New Development Policy
NEAC	National Economic Action Council
NEP	New Economic Policy
nepotisme	nepotism
NGO	non-governmental organization
NOC	National Operations Council
NST	*New Straits Times*
NSTP	New Straits Times Press (Malaysia) Bhd.
OPP2	Second Outline Perspective Plan
OSA	Official Secrets Act
PAP	People's Action Party (see PMIP)
PAS	Parti Islam Se-Malaysia
PBB	Parti Pesaka Bumiputera Bersatu (United Bumiputera Pesaka Party)
PBDS	Parti Bansa Dayak Sarawak (Sarawak Dayak Party)
PBS	Parti Bersatu Sabah (United Sabah Party)
Pekemas	Parti Keadilan Masyarakat Malaysia (Malaysian Social Justice Party)
PERNAS	Perbadanan Nasional Berhad (National Trading Corporation)
PHEI	private higher educational institutions
PM	Prime Minister
PMIP	Pan-Malaysian Islamic Party
PPP	People's Progressive Party
PPPA	Printing Presses and Publication Act
PRM	Parti Rakyat Malaysia (Malaysian People's Party)

PSRM	Parti Sosialis Rakyak Malaya (Malayan People's Socialist Party)
reformasi	reformation
RIDA	Rural and Industrial Development Authority
Rukunegara	Basic Principles of the State (the National Ideology)
Sdn. Bhd.	Sendirian Berhad (Private Limited)
SEDC	State Economic Development Corporations
Semangat 46	Spirit of 46
SNAP	Sarawak National Party
SUPP	Sarawak United People's Party
SUARAM	Suara Rakyat Malaysia (Malaysian People's Voice)
surat layang	flying letter, photocopied letters, and political tracts, often containing unsubstantiated allegations and revelations
syariah	Islamic law
TARC	Tunku Abdul Rahman College
Tengku	prince
Tun	highest non-hereditary Malaysian title
Tunku	prince
UDA	Urban Development Authority
UEM	United Engineers (M) Berhad
UMNO	United Malays National Organization
UMNO (*Baru*)	New UMNO
USNO	United Sabah National Organization
wanita	woman
Wawasan 2020	Vision 2020
Yang di-Pertuan Agong	King

1

Introduction

Malaysia is generally described as a prime example of a society severely divided along ethnic lines and most observers agree that ethnic conflict has been, and still is, one of the most distinctive sources of political conflict. Malaysia, nonetheless, is one of the few plural societies that has achieved some measure of success in managing ethnic conflict and has enjoyed relative political stability since independence in 1957. Given this record, many studies of politics in Malaysia examine the development of political structures and processes which regulate conflict situations and achieve political stability. These approaches have analysed how ethnic-conflict management strategies have been applied to different situations but they have not given adequate attention as to how such strategies have changed to meet changing circumstances. This book examines how the ruling political élite in Malaysia, especially UMNO (United Malays National Organization) and Mahathir, has been able to maintain its political hegemony while achieving relative political stability in a severely fragmented society over the last few decades. In particular, this book is concerned with the link between a dynamic conflict structure and regime maintenance strategies in Malaysia.[1]

The study assumes that the conflict structure challenging or undermining the maintenance of the regime in Malaysia has been changing since independence in 1957. And, the period of changing conflict configurations provides opportunities for a fresh look at the nature of the ruling political élite's regime maintenance strategies. An assumption throughout lies in the nature of power politics, that those who enjoy positions of power in the apparatus of the state are unlikely to give up their power willingly. Although the UMNO-led ruling élite has adapted to the changing expectations of Malaysian society, the single most important motive for regime change and regime maintenance has been to sustain its own political power.

This book examines in detail what made the UMNO-led ruling élite transform its regime maintenance approaches (from consociational bargaining to authoritarian UMNO dominance, then to Mahathir's personal dominance) and what the essential elements of these changing regime maintenance strategies were. The findings on regime change as regime maintenance offer alternative perspectives on Malaysian politics that stress a question of "power" in determining the political behaviour of the hegemonic élite in accordance with changing conflict configurations.

Why Malaysia?

For many post-colonial plural societies, nation-building has been regarded as one of the most important tasks since World War II. Despite their aspirations, however, it has been a sobering experience to see ethnic hostilities and political instability in societies that are marked by major cultural cleavage. Evidence of ethnic conflict and political instability is abundant. For example, in recent decades there have been frequent and almost constant communal, religious, and regional disputes in Asia, as in Sri Lanka, Myanmar, Pakistan, Bangladesh, India, the Philippines, and Indonesia. Furthermore, the politics of contemporary Africa, as seen in such countries as the Sudan, Nigeria, Ghana, Burundi, and Uganda, provides the most vivid examples of communal hostilities and political instability in the newly independent countries of the post-colonial world. Ethnic conflicts have also occurred frequently in the Caribbean and South America.

In addition, this widespread phenomenon of cultural cleavage, with its unfortunate implications for political stability and political democracy, is by no means found only in the underdeveloped or developing countries in the Third World. Rather, the phenomenon of ethnic conflict can be found in almost every modern state in the world. If ethnic conflict and political instability were limited only to underdeveloped or developing countries, we could assume that economic development would eliminate ethnic tensions and facilitate stable democracy in general. However, this assumption is questionable, as seen in several industrialized countries. The growing expression of ethnic sentiment in the political processes of several industrialized nations, such as Canada, Northern Ireland, Switzerland, Belgium, and Spain, casts doubt on this.

Along with the ubiquity of ethnic conflict in the world, racial assertiveness has been widespread and has even intensified recently. The problem of ethnic conflict has become increasingly prominent in Eastern Europe since 1989 and the collapse of communist regimes in the early 1990s. The slaughters inside the former Yugoslavia and other ex-members of the Union of Soviet Socialist Republics (USSR) are the most dramatic manifestations of this contemporary development. As Rabushka and Shepsle assert "ethnic conflict is constrained neither by time nor space; the history of plural societies is replete with tragedies of civil strife dating over centuries and located in nearly every region of the globe".[2] One of the most distinctive, broadest, and long-lived phenomena to have developed since World War II is the persistent, even rising, communal assertiveness in scores of national political arenas. Many political scientists, therefore, assume that rising tensions and conflicts will inevitably occur in ethnically divided societies.

This view, however, is not necessarily shared by all analysts of countries with plural societies. Malaysia is only one of many nations in which ethnic conflict conditions daily life as well as politics. Like other plural societies, Malaysia has deep vertical cleavages, reflecting differences in race, religion, culture, language, and even ideology. The pluralistic character of Malaysia's population has come into being over the course of the last 150 years. Various culturally and ethnically differentiated groups can be found in Malaysia's population of just over 20 million. Religious groupings also tend to be along ethnic lines. In terms of culture, Malaysia is also particularly rich, being the home of four of the world's major cultures — Islamic, Chinese, Indian, and Western — as well as possessing a vigorous indigenous culture of its own. Though *Bahasa Melayu* (Malay Language) is the national language under Article 152 of the Constitution and must be used for official purposes, various ethnic groups use their own languages in daily lives. This ethnic mixture makes Malaysia a prime example of a plural society.

What makes Malaysia more unusual, however, is not only its highly variegated ethnic mix but also the large size of its ethnic minorities. In Malaysia, despite various differentiated groups, the most basic population division is that between *bumiputera* (son of the soil) and non-*bumiputera* people. Broadly speaking, Malaysia's ethnic groups fall into two main categories: those with cultural affinities indigenous to the region and to one another, classified as *bumiputera*; and those whose cultural affinities lie outside, classified as non-*bumiputera*. Malays constitute the principal *bumiputera* group and account for around 55 per cent of Malaysia's population. Together with other indigenous peoples they make up about 61.7 per cent of the population. Chinese constitute about 27.3 per cent of Malaysia's population and Indians about 7.7 per cent in Peninsular Malaysia.[3]

Malaysia, nonetheless, is one of the few plural societies that have achieved some measure of success in managing ethnic relations. The main measure of such success is the relative absence of violent racial conflict. Since independence in 1957, Malaysia has enjoyed political stability and relative racial harmony. Apart from an almost two-year period following racial riots after the 1969 general election, the parliamentary system of Malaysia has functioned continuously and general elections have been held regularly. Though not as a result of elections, there have been three consecutive changes of heads of government without violence and there have been ten uninterrupted general elections. In this sense, the political process of Malaysia has been regular and predictable for the last few decades. Its military, moreover, is clearly subordinate to the civil power and there has never been any threat of military intervention in the political process. This experience of political stability makes Malaysia a distinctive case among the newly independent countries of the post-colonial world.

The distinctiveness, however, does not only arise from the consistent experience of political stability in Malaysian society. Of further distinction is the UMNO-led ruling élite's successful overcoming of inter/intra-ethnic conflicts throughout a series of different conflict situations over the last few decades. Malaysian politics has gone through four different phases since independence in 1957 and the patterns of conflict configurations which confront regime continuity have also shifted at least three times during that period. Throughout the whole political process, however, the UMNO-led ruling élite has successfully adapted to these changes and has continued to maintain its own political hegemony with relative political stability. This makes Malaysia's experience of conflict management and regime maintenance more remarkable, providing a special incentive and rationale for the study of ethnic politics in a plural society.

Maintaining the Regime and Malaysian Politics

There is general consensus in the study of politics in plural societies that communalism is the most significant feature of the political system and that the theme of ethnic politics is tension between segmented ethnic communities. Much of this literature is concerned with the breakdown of communal relations but it also examines the development of political structures and processes which regulate conflict situations and achieve political stability. Most studies influenced by this perspective assume that plural societies are inherently prone to conflict and everything of political and economic significance is closely associated with communal interests. Political parties are organized communally and ethnic-based parties tend to represent communal interests. In ethnically divided societies, rising tensions and conflict are rarely resolved by orthodox democratic measures and, therefore, require special strategies to accommodate the nation's differing communal interests.

In particular, an intriguing solution to the puzzle of political stability in deeply divided societies has been proposed by scholars who have adopted "consociational analysis". Consociational analysts derive an empirical and normative model called consociational democracy from the study of stable Western European democratic regimes with severely fragmented societies, for example, the Netherlands, Switzerland, Belgium, and Austria. The empirical application of this approach has also covered the post-colonial plural societies of the Third World, for example,

Malaysia (1955–69), Lebanon (1943–75), and Fiji (1970–87).[4]

An excellent definition of consociational democracy is provided by Lijphart, who says it is defined in terms of four characteristics: (1) government by a *grand coalition* of the political leaders of all significant segments of the plural society; (2) the *mutual veto* or concurrent majority rule, which serves as an additional protection of vital minority interests; (3) *proportionality* as the principal standard of political representation, civil service appointments and allocation of public funds; and (4) a high degree of *autonomy* for each segment to run its own internal affairs.[5] The essential conceptual tools for the explanation of stability in fragmented societies are *compromise, bargaining, accommodation, coalition,* and *alliance*. In short, stability in a segmented society is said to be the result of the "co-operative efforts" of subcultural élites "to counteract the centrifugal tendencies of cultural fragmentation".[6]

Since Lijphart introduced the concept of consociational democracy, the literature dealing with consociational techniques for achieving and maintaining political stability in deeply divided societies has expanded rapidly, though not always conforming to Lijphart's approach.[7] The consociational approach has also been widely applied to the case study of conflict management in ethnically divided Malaysian society. The political science literature on consociational analysis in Malaysian studies is therefore not lacking.[8] Studies informed by this analysis in Malaysia basically suggest that what is required is greater attention to inter-ethnic accommodation, bargaining, and negotiation between ethnic élites in order to solve complex socio-political conflict. According to those studies, even under unpromising circumstances, consociational politics is still operative in Malaysian politics. Ethnic balancing in élite recruitment and the allocation of resources are essential indications of consociational politics. Since the 1970s, the notion of consociationalism as the primary way of analysing the nature of the Malaysian polity, however, has been challenged as the new generation of Malay leaders appeared to move away from the compromise and accommodative tradition. This was also because élite competition and division became more intra-ethnic during the 1980s. The consociational approach, nonetheless, has continued to be the dominant framework for the analysis of Malaysian political structures and processes.

Meanwhile, the consociational approach has been challenged by a theoretical discourse presented in "control" terms to provide an alternative mode of regime maintenance in deeply divided societies. Whereas the consociational approach focuses on the emergence and functioning of élite consensus as a key factor explaining stability in plural societies, the control approach primarily focuses on how a superordinate ethnic group can effectively manipulate/control subordinate or rival ethnic groups. In this theory, the terms *domination, repression,* and *hegemonic control* are the most common elements of managing ethnic conflict. The control approach as an alternative discourse to the consociational model was elaborated by Ian Lustick.[9] However, even before Lustick, the notion of control had long been illustrated by many other scholars as a means of explaining stability and conflict management in deeply divided societies, as shown in the studies of Furnivall (1939), Smith (1965), Rabushka and Shepsle (1972), and Esman (1973).[10]

Two implications of Furnivall's work on the plural society have been developed and elaborated by other scholars. One is that separate communities inherently incline towards conflict behaviour. The other is that the unity of plural societies is maintained through non-democratic means by an external force. The second notion of an "external force" to hold divided groups together is pertinent to the "control" approach. Similarly, Smith stresses the need for authoritative regulation to keep order in societies with rival communal groups. According to him, "given the fundamental differences of belief, value and organization that connote pluralism, the monopoly of power by one cultural section is the essential precondition for the maintenance of the total society in its current form".[11]

Esman even suggests "institutionalized dominance" as one of four paths to the effective management of communal conflict.[12] He asserts that regimes committed to the dominance of one communal group at the expense of another will always use three methods of conflict management. The three methods are: proscription or control of the political expression of collective interest among dominated groups; limitation of membership in the dominant community; and monopoly or preferential access for the dominant group to political participation, advanced education, economic opportunities, and symbols of status which reinforce the political, economic, and psychic control of the dominant group.[13] Similarly, Rabushka and Shepsle show that one way of resolving the tension between the plural character of a society and a democratic political ethos is through the dominant-majority configuration. According to them, the minority communities' democratic role is "politically significant only in the event of major splits in the dominant group".[14]

Perhaps, the most systematic introduction to the control approach is Lustick's study. He argues that the sustained manipulation of subordinate segments of a society by a superordinate segment better explains conflict resolution than mutual co-operation and bargaining of subnational élites. He stresses that consociational modes can only be applied effectively when an alternative means of control or domination is available for the dominant segment.[15] Empirically, he says, "there are at least as many deeply divided societies whose stability is accounted for by the effective exertion of the superior power of one sub-unit as by the 'co-operative efforts' of rival sub-unit élites".[16] Since the mid-1980s, Lustick claims that there has been a general slackening of interest in consociationalism as exemplary consociational countries collapsed or became destabilized.[17]

The experience of Malaysian politics since the 1970s conforms more to the control model than to the consociational one. A series of studies on classification of regimes also illustrates that Malaysia has moved closer to the authoritarian end on the liberal-authoritarian continuum over the last few decades. In 1965, Malaysia was evaluated as "near free" by an annual survey scoring political and civil liberties. It, however, moved towards a "partly free" status when the same survey was conducted in 1985. The classification of regimes at the end of 1997 shows that Malaysia had "non-liberal" status, in other words had moved closer to the authoritarian end.[18] The number of studies informed by the control perspective, nonetheless, is unimpressive compared with the amount of research devoted to consociational analysis. The most comprehensive introduction to the Malaysian political process from the control perspective is found in a study by Simon Barraclough. He argues that the regime has adopted coercion as the essential means of managing its political legitimacy and the use of coercion has not been confined to non-Malays but to all communal groups.[19] Though not directly related to the control approach, Diane Mauzy's notion of "coercive consociationalism" implies an increase in the non-consociational elements — centralized federalism, political dominance of one-party in cabinet and government, no constitutional establishment of mutual veto on the sensitive issues, a highly disproportionate electoral system, and authoritarian rule by a powerful prime minister rather than by a cartel of élites — in Malaysia's political structures and processes, especially under the Mahathir regime.[20]

Despite diverse interpretations in the study of stability in ethnic politics, some critical limitations are found in applying these approaches to the Malaysian case. Malaysia fits reasonably well into one or other of these two major theoretical approaches, but the theories cannot be applied to the whole political process in Malaysia. This is mainly because the existing theoretical traditions have not given adequate attention to the changing conflict configurations and the dominant political élites' subsequent modification of conflict resolution approaches. These limitations cause empirical over-extension when analysts apply them to the whole political structure to interpret the character of political stability and regime maintenance in deeply divided societies.

The consociational model, for example, would appear to suit the Malaysian political system in some respects. As described in Chapter 3, there are some characteristics of consociationalism in the Malaysian political system, especially in the first phase (1957–69). Nevertheless, notions of consociational power-sharing do not always seem to fit Malaysian ethnic politics. In fact, the Malaysian political system is backed by considerable authoritarian power and it demonstrates repeatedly characteristics of hegemonic control. From this perspective, the relatively strong consociational bargaining that occurred in the first stage is "aberrant". When it comes to interpreting the second phase of Malaysian ethnic politics (1969–87), the limitations of consociationalism are obvious. Because of the increasing political and economic discrimination in favour of the Malays in the 1970s, Lijphart himself notes that "it is doubtful that Malaysia after 1971 can be regarded as either fully democratic or fully consociational".[21] Furthermore, the authoritarian trend that began in the early 1980s after Mahathir Mohamad took political control cannot be sufficiently explained in terms of the concept of bargaining and consociationalism.

The control approach reveals the same limitation as the consociational approach to the issue of change in Malaysia. As an alternative approach to consociationalism, the control model seems more capable of analysing the second period after the 1969 racial riots. The period 1987–90 also illustrates that the necessary conditions for the practice of consociational democracy can be allowed only if the hegemonic political élite's power is not seriously undermined. However, in the years prior to 1969 and after 1990, the control approach has limited application to the Malaysian political system. Especially after 1990, the control model has difficulty explaining how the Malaysian state, after a period of strong state intervention, did not move in a more repressive and dictatorial direction, as has been the case in most Third World states. The control model has also been criticized for ignoring the mutual understanding of cultural values, growing factionalism within communal groups, and the development of multi-racial consciousness which enables convergence between segmented ethnic communities in a plural society. Ethnic identities in fact have by no means disappeared. As society modernizes, however, ethnic identities become less important and conflict tends to be reduced; in the case of Malaysia this is demonstrated by the restoration of conßsociational or accommodative practices in the 1990s.

Overall, the existing approaches have usefully analysed how ethnic-conflict management strategies have been applied in different situations, but they have not given adequate attention to how such strategies have changed to meet new circumstances. In Malaysia, the UMNO-led ruling élite has frequently changed its approach to society. The first stage of Malaysian politics (1957–69) was a period of Malay dominance, but with strong recognition of the non-Malay political role. This was mainly because inter-ethnic conflict was perceived as the main threat to regime stability in the process of nation-building after independence. Therefore, the terms "inter-ethnic bargaining" and "compromise" were most frequently used among the ruling élite of rival communal groups during the first twelve years of independence. The accommodation also served the UMNO-led ruling élite's interest more generally and allowed them to stay in power.

The conflict configuration, however, changed drastically as Malaysian society moved into its second decade of independence. Especially after the 1969 racial riots, the tradition of inter-ethnic élite accommodation became less important to preserve the political legitimacy of the UMNO-led ruling élite. The previous acquiescent attitudes of the segmental masses, especially the dominant Malays, towards their communal leaders were also replaced by open criticism. Given the more turbulent political environment, one of the most obvious features of the second stage of Malaysian politics (1969–87) was the shift in the UMNO leaders' attitude from moderate consociational bargaining to one of more hegemonic control. During that period, the modes and practices of ruling by the UMNO-led government moved closer to the control end on a consensus-control continuum, but in relative terms, political stability remained intact.

The year 1987 marked another significant change in the Malaysian political environment as intra-UMNO factional conflict became more and more intense. For the dominant Malay ruling élite led by Mahathir, the main sources of conflict undermining its hegemonic position came increasingly from within UMNO circles. This time the split within the ruling bloc seemed to provide the prospect of the transition from an authoritarian or semi-authoritarian regime towards a more competitive and accommodative political system. However, what actually happened in the post-1987 phase was the consolidation of Mahathir's authoritarian rule. The deepening UMNO factionalism and subsequent leadership crisis encouraged the Mahathir-led ruling élite to adopt a more assertive approach in order to curtail the political and civil liberties of its political opponents. Consequently, UMNO (*Baru*), a new ruling party, was formed around Mahathir. Since then, Mahathir has successfully maintained a political order and re-emerged as strong as ever.

In addition to the mid-1980s' authoritarian trend, there was another important change led by Mahathir's government in the 1990s. After the economic recession of the mid-1980s and the split of UMNO in 1988, various gestures by the Mahathir government were made to the non-Malay communities. During this period, the control mode was not completely abandoned. The political dominance of the ruling élite was indeed further consolidated, especially around Mahathir's personality.

It was, however, during this period that political sensitivity towards the non-Malays was reduced remarkably. Among the important changes were: liberalization of language and education policies; promotion of nation-building in the society, such as *Bangsa Malaysia* and *Wawasan 2020*; and re-definition of the Malay community's traditional concerns, such as the position of the Malay rulers, the Malay language, and Islam. These changes were initiated by UMNO leaders and Mahathir in particular. These ambivalent "repressive-responsive" features, however, were not contradictory but "mutually supportive" for Mahathir's dominance in the processes of power throughout the third period of Malaysian politics (1987–98).

The period from 1998 onwards can be regarded as the fourth phase of regime maintenance and it is closely related to another shifting pattern of conflict configuration in the Malaysian society. After several years of speculations of a leadership tussle between Mahathir and his deputy Anwar Ibrahim, Anwar was abruptly dismissed from office, expelled from the ruling party, beaten while in police custody, and eventually charged in court on several counts of sodomy and corruption in September 1998. Anwar's sudden discharge and its dramatic aftermath shocked the nation and Malaysian civil society became increasingly politicized. The brutal treatment of Anwar tarnished Mahathir's national image and anti-Mahathir sentiment became widespread, especially among the Malay community. What was more significant was that the Anwar episode promoted the emergence of multi-ethnic consciousness in Malaysian civil society, and anti-Mahathir sentiment translated into serious disenchantment with the UMNO-led ruling élite as a whole. This time the most crucial elements threatening the Mahathir regime's political hegemony arose from the resurrection of multi-ethnic civil society and enhanced prospects for political liberalization. Until recently, the Mahathir regime appeared to have effectively managed the ongoing crisis situation and Mahathir's personal grip on power seemed intact. Malaysian politics beyond Anwar, nonetheless, provides another opportunity to return to the nexus between factional conflict in the ruling bloc and the breakdown or erosion of authoritarian rule. The future prospects of "regime change" or "regime maintenance" are still uncertain.

A Question of Power as an Alternative Approach

Rothchild suggests that the various élite power-sharing regimes represent "amalgams of authoritarian control and consociational democracy". He argues that "élite power-sharing regimes can be either moderately authoritarian or moderately democratic systems ... Either way, such regimes unite the competing thrusts of political control and bargaining among the state and various societal notables".[22] In the study of politics in Malaysia, Case notes that Malaysia has displayed both Lijphart's consociationalism and Lustick's control in élite relations and ethnic alignments. These characteristics made the Malaysian polity a "semi-democracy" in nature.[23] Likewise, Crouch characterizes the ambiguous Malaysian political system as a "repressive-responsive regime".[24] Studies informed by this perspective help us to understand the Malaysian political structures which combine some key elements of liberal political processes with considerable levels of state control.

This study also begins by locating the admixture of consociational and control features of the Malaysian political structures at the centre of the analysis. Nonetheless, in response to the weaknesses of the existing theoretical approaches, a series of questions arises: in which circumstances do super-ordinate groups exercise consociational modes of ruling over sub-ordinate groups? What motivates the political ruling élite to transform, or modify, its regime maintenance strategies into ones which are more hegemonic? Or, under which conditions is the political ruling élite likely to incorporate consociational and control features in managing conflict situations? Why does this mixture take place? These are key questions in interpreting the nature of the UMNO-led ruling élite's political behaviour in containing conflict and maintaining regime stability. The main interest of this study lies in how the political behaviour of the ruling élite has adapted to changing socio-political configurations to maintain regime stability.

Nordlinger emphasizes the critical role of conflict group leaders in the process of conflict regulation in deeply divided societies.[25] However, in circumstances of uneven power distribution, the various conflict group élites or conflict organizations, namely political parties, are not always treated equally. Rather, we need to highlight the critical role of *a hegemonic political party and its dominant leaders*. In this study, the UMNO-led ruling élite, therefore, will be considered a primary political actor, though the role of the ruling coalition and the opposition will be considered also. The rationale behind this is that UMNO, as the dominant group in the government, has played a crucial role in post-colonial Malaysian society by substituting for colonial rule as a force ensuring a stable political order. Especially since the mid-1980s, the capacity of the UMNO-led ruling élite for adaptability and responsiveness to the changed conflict circumstances has been prominent.

In analysing the nature of the political behaviour of the UMNO-led ruling élite in containing conflict and maintaining regime stability, this study will be considering the *motives, incentives,* and *timing* of the changing regime maintenance strategies by the UMNO-led ruling élite as major analytical concepts. The presence of strong conflict-regulating motives, according to Nordlinger, is a necessary condition if the political ruling élites are to engage in conflict-regulating behaviour.[26] In a similar vein, Horowitz notes that:

> … since élite competition is one of the sources of ethnic conflict, it is a mistake to impute good intentions to leaders without good political reasons for thinking they in fact entertain such intentions. What is needed is a theory of *timing* and *incentives* for élite co-operation [and élite competition].[27]

Neither Nordlinger's motivations nor Horowitz's incentives are directly related to conceptual and empirical issues in the study of regime change and regime maintenance in an ethnically divided society. The concepts of "motive" or "incentive", nonetheless, provide meaningful insights into the nature of the UMNO-led ruling élite's initiating role in modifying its regime maintenance strategies over the last few decades: from moderate consociational arrangements (1957–69) and then authoritarian Malay dominance (1969–87) to Mahathir's personal dominance but with an ambivalent repressive-responsive admixture (1987–98).

From the perspective of the hegemonic political party and its critical role in initiating change in specific ruling patterns, this study will draw special attention to the notion of relative leadership autonomy. The capacity of the political élite is always limited. Especially in ethnically segmented societies, the limitations are mostly imposed by cultural cleavages and other communal factors. The notion of relative autonomy, nonetheless, suggests that the hegemonic political party and its dominant leaders may pursue their own interests without needing to take account the interests of the classes or certain segmented groups in the society at large. Among conflict-regulating motivations, this study gives primary emphasis to *a question of power* in determining the political behaviour of the hegemonic political élite in accordance with the changing conflict configurations. Although the UMNO-led ruling élite has adapted to changing expectations of Malaysian society to meet new social and political conflict circumstances, the single most important motive for the adaptability and responsiveness has been to acquire or retain its own interests defined in terms of power. In some situations, this motivation may lead the ruling élite to act or establish more moderate co-operative behaviour. Not surprisingly, the ruling élite seeks the possibility of political alternatives which combine moderate levels of public participation with moderate levels of state domination. A concern throughout, however, will be the nature of power politics, that those who enjoy positions of power in the apparatus of the state are unlikely to give up their power willingly.

The notion of power politics, or political realism, has been closely linked to traditional theories of the state and international relations. Studies influenced by the realist tradition basically assume that states are the most important actors in world politics and most states are indeed strongly inclined to seek power. The power assumption in political realism, however, provides further insight in the domestic domain. Locating the aspiration for power principally in human nature, Morgenthau, one of the leading realists, also argues that "domestic and international politics are but two different manifestations of the same phenomenon: the struggle for power ... The difference between domestic and international politics ... is one of degree and not kind".[28] Accordingly, the question of power as a general trend in politics may offer an alternative to the understanding of the hegemonic political élite's behaviour in containing conflict and maintaining regime stability in Malaysia.

Malaysia alone has been chosen as a case study because it is a prime example of successful conflict resolution in a society that continues to be characterized by deep vertical cleavages. This research uses an in-depth historical, descriptive-analytical approach. It also compares some of the empirical aspects of transitions from authoritarian regimes, especially under Mahathir's rule. The primary sources of empirical data are newspapers, news magazines, government documents, and other academic publications. Another important source of information is interviews with main political actors, journalists, academics, and other knowledgeable persons. Approximately sixty interviews were held in three different time periods between December 1997 and May 2000. Further e-mail correspondence with some of the interviewees was also conducted.

Outline of Chapters

This study is composed of eight chapters. Chapters are organized in chronological and thematic order. Chapter 1 is introductory. It contains research background, reviews of theoretical traditions, research questions and an alternative perspective on the study of politics in Malaysia.

Chapter 2 presents a historical and political overview of the roots of conflict in Malaysian society. The main purpose of this chapter is to provide the background analysis of which conditions and by which processes different ethnic identities become activated and transformed into political opponents prior to independence in 1957.

Chapter 3 deals with the first twelve years of post-colonial Malaysian politics (1957–69) as a trial period of regime maintenance through consociational power-sharing arrangements. In analysing the relevance of consociationalism in this period, the chapter will trace the kinds of factors which have motivated the UMNO-led ruling élite to choose consociational strategies to maintain its power. The chapter will detail the main consociational elements of élite bargaining and analyse the outcomes of consensual élite bargaining.

Chapter 4 focuses on the period of authoritarian Malay dominance during the second phase of Malaysian politics (1969–87). The first part of the chapter discusses UMNO and its dominant leaders' motives for changing the regime maintenance approach from one of consociational bargaining to one characterized by hegemonic control. The second and third sections of the chapter focus on the key elements of hegemonic control in the 1970s and 1980s and the growing intra-élite conflict within UMNO as a consequence of the power struggle.

Chapter 5 deals with the relations between UMNO's leadership split and the transition from authoritarian rule, especially during the period

1987–90. The main question of this chapter is how rivalries within the hegemonic ruling élite affect political behaviour and what is the extent of consensual unity in multi-racial Malaysian society. This chapter provides an analysis of Mahathir's regime maintenance strategies in circumstances where the threats came increasingly from within the hegemonic ruling bloc.

Chapter 6 explores the consolidation of Mahathir's supremacy within and outside the ruling party and the repressive-responsive Malaysian political structure and process in the 1990s. Since 1990, the Mahathir-led ruling élite has shown greater tolerance in ethnic politics while at the same time further restricting "limited democracy" through hegemonic state control. What are the motives behind such ambivalent levels of tolerance for political and cultural expression? This chapter traces the background, context, and outcomes of Mahathir's dominance and the repressive-responsive Malaysian political system in the period 1990–98.

Chapter 7 deals with the lead-up to, and the consequences of, Anwar Ibrahim's downfall in the years after 1998. It examines the context in which the leadership conflict took place and how Mahathir responded to a second crisis within the ruling bloc. The Mahathir-Anwar leadership tussle presented another opportunity to transform the Malaysian political landscape. Consequently, this chapter focuses on a comparative analysis of the 1987 and 1998 UMNO factional split and its consequences for the changing nature of authoritarian rule in Malaysia.

Chapter 8 concludes the book with a summary of the major findings of the study. In concluding the book, this chapter also deals with the prospects for Malaysian politics in terms of regime change and regime maintenance.

NOTES

1. The notion of regime is situated in a different context of relationships in the international and the domestic arena. Regime maintenance or regime continuity, in this study, implies the persistence of the modes and practices of ruling by the particular personnel or social group who has access to political power in a state. For more detail on the definition and account of regime, see Stephanie Lawson, "Some Conceptual and Empirical Issues in the Study of Regime Change", *Regime Change and Regime Maintenance in Asia and the Pacific*, Discussion Paper Series Number 3 (Canberra: Research School of Pacific and Asian Studies, Australian National

University, 1991) and Robert M. Fishman, "Rethinking State and Regime: Southern Europe's Transition to Democracy", *World Politics* 42, no. 3 (1990): 422–40.

2. Alvin Rabushka and Kenneth A. Shepsle, *Politics in Plural Societies: A Theory of Democratic Instability* (Columbus, Ohio: Charles E. Merrill Publishing Company, 1972), p. 7.

3. Government of Malaysia, *Seventh Malaysia Plan 1996–2000* (Kuala Lumpur: Percetakan Nasional Malaysia Berhad, 1996), p. 106.

4. Arend Lijphart, "Consociational Democracy", *World Politics* 21, no. 2 (1969): 207–25; Arend Lijphart, *Democracy in Plural Societies* (New Haven and London: Yale University Press, 1977); and Gerhard Lehmbruch, "Consociational Democracy in the International System", *European Journal of Political Research* 3 (1975): 377–91.

5. Lijphart (1977, pp. 25–52).

6. Arend Lijphart, "Cultural Diversity and Theories of Political Integration", *Canadian Journal of Political Science* 4 (March 1971): 9.

7. Donald Rothchild, "Review Article: Ethnicity and Conflict Resolution", *World Politics* 22, no. 4 (1970): 597–616; Eric A. Nordlinger, *Conflict Regulation in Divided Societies* (Cambridge, Mass.: Center for International Affairs, Harvard University, 1972). Articles by Daalder, Lehmbruch, Steiner, Lorwin, Noel, Ormsby, and other scholars on the consociational approach published in a volume by Kenneth McRae, ed., *Consociational Democracy: Political Accommodation in Segmented Societies* (Toronto: McClelland & Stewart, 1974).

8. J.M. Gullick, *Malaya* (London: Longmans, 1964); K.J. Ratnam, *Communalism and the Political Process in Malaya* (Singapore: University of Malaya Press, 1965); R.S. Milne, *Government and Politics in Malaysia* (Boston: Houghton Mifflin, 1967); Karl von Vorys, *Democracy Without Consensus: Communalism and Political Stability in Malaysia* (New Jersey: Princeton University Press, 1975); Diane K. Mauzy, *Barisan Nasional: Coalition Government in Malaysia* (Kuala Lumpur: Marican & Sons Sdn. Bhd., 1983); James P. Ongkili, *Nation-Building in Malaysia, 1946–1974* (Singapore: Oxford University Press, 1985); and William Case, *Elites and Regimes in Malaysia: Revisiting a Consociational Democracy* (Clayton: Monash Asia Institute, 1996).

9. Ian Lustick, "Stability in Deeply Divided Societies: Consociationalism versus Control", *World Politics* 31, no. 3 (1979): 325–44.

10. J.S. Furnivall, *Netherlands India: A Study of Plural Economy* (Cambridge: Cambridge University Press, 1939); M.G. Smith, *The Plural Society in the British West Indies* (Berkeley and Los Angeles: University of California Press, 1965); Rabushka and Shepsle (1972); and Milton J. Esman, "The Management of Communal Conflict", *Public Policy* 21 (1973): 49–78.

11. Smith (1965, p. 86).

12. The other three are induced assimilation, syncretic integration, and balanced pluralism. See Esman (1973, pp. 57–63).

13. Esman (1973, pp. 56–57).

14. Rabushka and Shepsle (1972, p. 89).

15. Lustick (1979, p. 326).

16. Lustick (1979, p. 330).

17. For the most critical review of the consociational model, see Ian Lustick, "Lijphart, Lakatos, and Consociationalism", *World Politics* 50, no. 1 (1997): 88–117. For other effective critiques, see Brian Barry, "Consociational Model and Its Dangers", *European Journal of Political Research* 3 (1975): 393–412; and Sue M. Halpern, "The Disorderly Universe of Consociational Democracy", *West European Politics* 9, no. 4 (1986): 181–97.

18. For more detail on the classification of regimes by country, see Larry Diamond, Juan J. Linz, and Seymour Martin Lipset, eds., *Democracy in Developing Countries: Asia* (Boulder, Colorado: Lynne Rienner Publishers, 1989), pp. 36–37 and Larry Diamond, *Developing Democracy: Toward Consolidation* (Baltimore and London: Johns Hopkins University Press, 1999), pp. 279–80.

19. Simon Barraclough, "The Dynamics of Coercion in the Malaysian Political Process", *Modern Asian Studies* 19, no. 4 (1985): 797–822.

20. Diane K. Mauzy, "Malay Political Hegemony and Coercive Consociationalism", in *The Politics of Ethnic Conflict Regulation*, edited by John McGarry and Brendan O'Leary (London: Routledge, 1993), pp. 106–27.

21. Lijphart (1977, p. 153).

22. Donald Rothchild, *Managing Ethnic Conflict in Africa: Pressures and Incentives for Cooperation* (Washington: Brookings Institution Press, 1997), pp. 13–14.

23. William Case, "Semi-Democracy in Malaysia: Withstanding the Pressures for Regime Change", *Pacific Affairs* 66, no. 2 (1993): 183–205. A similar conceptualization of Malaysian polity can be found in Zakaria Haji Ahmad, "Malaysia: Quasi Democracy in a Divided Society", in *Democracy in Developing Countries: Asia*, edited by Larry Diamond, Juan J. Linz, and Seymour Martin Lipset (Boulder, Colorado: Lynne Rienner Publishers, 1989), pp. 347–81.

24. Harold Crouch, *Government and Society in Malaysia* (Ithaca and London: Cornell University Press, 1996), especially pp. 236–47.

25. Nordlinger (1972, pp. 39–41).

26. For more detail on conflict-regulating motives, see Nordlinger (1972, pp. 42–53).

27. Donald L. Horowitz, *Ethnic Groups in Conflict* (Berkeley: University of California Press, 1985), pp. 573–74; italics added.

28. Hans Morgenthau, *Politics Among Nations: The Struggle for Power and Peace* (New York: Alfred A. Knopf, 1985), p. 52.

2

The Origins and Patterns
of Conflict in Malaysia

> ... ethnicity is a product of modern politics. Although people have had identities — deriving from religion, birthplace, language, and so on — for as long as humans have had culture, they have begun to see themselves as members of vast ethnic groups, opposed to other such groups, only during the modern period of colonization and state-building. (John R. Bowen 1996)[1]

Since independence in 1957, ethnicity has been one of the prime sources of conflict in multi-ethnic Malaysian society and this conflict and its resolution have been a primary concern in the study of politics in Malaysia. This chapter provides a historical and political overview of the roots of ethnic relations in Malaysian society. To understand why "ethnic differences" became "ethnic contrast", which in turn became "ethnic antagonism", it is necessary to trace the colonial origins of communal-group contrast in Malaya. In doing so, this chapter examines the conditions under which, and the processes by which, ethnic identities and differences become activated and converted to political conflict.

This chapter is divided into four sections. The first summarizes the creation of a pluralist society in Malaysia. The second focuses on the specific question of the non-assimilation of the main ethnic communities in Malaysia and considers factors which have made the assimilation of the Malayan peoples difficult, despite their proximity within the same political unit. The third part is about the deepening of inter-ethnic conflict and why inter-ethnic relations deteriorated. In other words, what kinds of factors have catalysed the deepening of inter-ethnic conflict in Malaysia? The final section deals with the institutionalization of an ethnic-conflict configuration in Malaysia's modern political system.

The Origins of a Multi-Ethnic Malaysian Society

Numerous ethnic groups exist in Malaysia. Ethnic relations in Malaysia, however, generally revolve around the relations between the Malays and the non-Malays (including the Indians) in Peninsular Malaysia, or more specifically the complex Malay-Chinese relationship.

Since the early Christian era there has been continuous contact between various ethnic and nationality groups on the Malay Peninsula. The interplay of these main ethnic groups, especially the Malays and the Chinese, on the Malay Peninsula goes back to the time of the earliest Chinese settlement in Malaya in the fifth century. Most of the early contact arose from trade relationships. During the Malacca sultanate, a number of small Chinese communities was established in Malacca as the result of this contact.[2] However, it was only after the tremendous influx of Chinese immigrants under British colonial rule, in the period from the 1870s to the outbreak of World War II, that serious friction between the Malays and the Chinese began to develop in Malaya. Consequently, the origins of ethnic conflict in this country were by-products of British colonialism.

Table 2.1 illustrates how, after the beginning of British colonial rule in 1874, the pattern of population distribution changed due to the influx of migrants from China and India. After the beginning of British colonial rule, in other words, the trend was towards a complex type of pluralism, which manifested itself in the multi-ethnic composition of the Malayan population. The Malay proportion declined from 85.9 per cent in 1835 to 49.5 per cent in 1947. On the other hand, the Chinese proportion grew from 7.7 per cent in 1835 to 38.4 per cent in 1947. The Indian population grew more than 100 per cent during this period. Not until the 1930s when the colonial government put restrictions on migration and the demand for labour began to decrease as a result of the depression, did the flow of migration slow down.

TABLE 2.1
Racial Composition of Malaya, 1835–1947[a]
(In percentages)

	1835	1884	1921	1931	1947
Malays[b]	85.9	63.9	54.0	49.2	49.5
Chinese	7.7	29.4	29.4	33.9	38.4
Indians[c]	—	—	15.1	15.1	10.8
Others[d]	6.3	6.7	1.5	1.8	1.3
Total	376,000	1,401,000	2,906,000	3,787,000	4,908,000

[a] The figures for 1921, 1931, and 1947 refer to Peninsular Malaysia only.
[b] "Malays" includes Malays, Indonesians, and aborigines.
[c] Pakistanis and Ceylonese are counted with "Indians".
[d] "Others" in 1835 and 1884 are made up mainly of Indians and Pakistanis.

Sources: Compiled from Alvin Rabushka, *Race and Politics in Urban Malaya* (California: Hoover Institution Press, 1973), p. 21; and Syed Husin Ali, *Malay Peasant Society and Leadership* (Kuala Lumpur: Oxford University Press, 1975), p. 23.

The Malays were not the earliest inhabitants of the Malay Peninsula. However, their migration to this area occurred far enough back in history for them to be generally considered the indigenous people of this country. Their initial arrival on the peninsula was probably between 2500 BC and 1500 BC.[3] These peoples were known as the proto-Malays. It was believed that the descendants of these proto-Malays, together with the later immigrants who entered from Indonesia, constituted the ancestors of the modern Malays. They displaced the various aboriginal peoples to the jungle interior and gradually settled in the coastal areas and plains. However, many of the Malays now living in Malaysia migrated relatively recently from various parts of insular Southeast Asia, especially from Indonesia. Despite the diversity of their geographical origins and their length of residence, nowadays the Malays have a strong sense of common communal and cultural identity.

The Chinese from the southeastern provinces of China — Kwangtung, Fukien, and Kwangsi — had been coming to the Malay Peninsula to trade since as early as the fifth century. The Chinese immigration took place in two phases. The first significant Chinese immigration to Malaya began after the Portuguese captured Malacca in the sixteenth century. During this period, however, the Manchu government in China actively discouraged emigration and this meant that emigrants could not return but had effectively cut themselves off completely from China. At the time, few Chinese women undertook these dangerous journeys, and so male immigrants tended to marry into local Malay families. Today their descendants are known as the Babas and they are found mainly in Penang and Malacca. Although in general they have retained the old Chinese traditions in dress, religion, and customs, they speak a language which is a Chinese version of Malay and have assimilated many Malay customs and habits. For centuries they have looked on Malaysia as their home.[4]

The second and more substantial phase of Chinese emigration began in the second half of the nineteenth century. During this period, China abolished her laws forbidding emigration and so not only men but an increasing number of women came to the Malay Peninsula. At the same time, the huge influx of immigration to Malaya was stimulated by the growing demand for labour which was encouraged by the British colonial government. Both the Chinese and the British began to exploit local resources, especially tin, as well as engage in trade relationships. Among other economic ventures were the planting of various cash crops such as pepper, spices, sugar cane, and coffee.

Most Chinese came as indentured labourers, working to pay off their debt to whoever paid their passage to Malaya. Having paid off this debt, they worked the tin mines or opened up shops and business ventures. The tin mines had attracted the Chinese for centuries and until the nineteenth century tin-mining was predominantly a Chinese enterprise. The Malay rulers were willing to let the Chinese work the tin mines for a fee, but it was only when the British took control of the Malay states that Chinese participation in commerce expanded rapidly.

The Indians, too, first came as traders — even before the Chinese. However, the major wave of Indian emigration came after the British had established bases in Malaya. In the late nineteenth and early twentieth centuries, rubber, which was to become the largest single source of income for the British in Malaya, was introduced. The major flow of Indian migration began in the 1880s and increased sharply in the second decade of the twentieth century when the rubber plantation sector began to expand very rapidly. The British systematically recruited labour from

India to work on the rubber plantations in the Malay Peninsula, and the number of Indians increased considerably. They were mainly indentured labourers, like the Chinese, bonded by contract to work for a specific period. Many of their descendants are still rural-based, mainly on rubber estates.

The introduction of these immigrants on such a large scale greatly upset the ethnic balance in the country. As a result of this immigration, before World War II Malaya was the only country in Southeast Asia where the immigrant races outnumbered the indigenous people. The 1931 Census shows that the number of Malays was 1,644,173 (37.5 per cent), if the indigenous peoples are included 1,962,021 (44.7 per cent), Chinese 1,709,392 (39.0 per cent), and Indians 624,009 (14.2 per cent).[5] When the 1931 Census revealed for the first time that the Malays were outnumbered in their own country by the non-Malays, it came as something of a shock to both the Malays and the British colonial authorities. The Malays, "*who had now become a numerical minority within their own country*", were concerned with preserving their birthright as the indigenous people of the country.[6] Therefore, restrictions were imposed on further immigration, especially from China, not only "to prevent unemployment or economic distress" but also "to control the political unrest".[7]

The problem of outnumbered Malays was not too apparent at first because both Chinese and Indian workers came on contract and had every intention of leaving. The great majority of Chinese initially had no desire to settle in Malaya but only of seeking their fortune there and returning to their villages in China. Wilson, the Permanent Under-Secretary of State for the Colonies, describes the situation in Malaya, based on the 1931 Census, in his report:

> ... the number of the Chinese population which has been for a long time in the country is relatively very small and the number of those who were born there and expect to end their days there is smaller still ... the same is true of the Indian immigrant, so that the number of non-Malays who have adopted Malaya as their home is only a very small proportion of the whole population of the territory.[8]

Over time, however, many of the immigrants became permanent settlers in the country. They married within their ethnic groups, and a

TABLE 2.2
Proportion of the Population Locally Born,
by Race, in the Federation of Malaya
and Singapore, 1921–57 (In percentages)

	1921	1931	1947	1957
Malays	—	—	96.0	97.4
Chinese	20.9	29.9	63.5	75.5
Indians	12.1	21.4	51.6	65.0
Total	56.4	58.9	78.3	84.8

Source: Federation of Malaya, *1957 Population Census of the Federation of Malaya, Report No. 14* (Kuala Lumpur: Department of Statistics, 1960), p. 15.

new generation of Chinese was born in Malaysia. As the twentieth century progressed there was a growing number of local-born Chinese and Indians who began to think of Malaya as their home, still keeping their cultural heritage but having no intention of returning to their original countries.

As shown in Table 2.2, the proportion of locally born among the non-Malay communities sharply increased from 1921 to 1957. The major increase in the number of locally born occurred between 1931 and 1947. By 1957 over three-quarters of the Chinese and two-thirds of the Indians had been born locally. It was this section of the immigrant communities that began to demand citizenship rights in Malaya, and according to Parkinson "the inter-racial problem began, not when people arrived, but from the date when they began to settle".[9] The problem of claims to citizenship from immigrants became apparent in the early twentieth century in Malaya, as shown in the report by Wilson:

> Those who have been born in Malaya themselves, or whose children have been born there ... state that in a great many cases those concerned have never seen the land of their origin and they claim that their children and their children's children should have fair treatment.[10]

The Non-Assimilation of the Main Ethnic Communities

Compared with many other multi-ethnic countries, one of the most unusual features of Malaysian society is the non-assimilation of the main ethnic communities, in terms of intermarriage or amalgamation. While intermarriage is certainly not unknown in the Malay Peninsula, as shown most obviously in the case of the Babas, it is not common, especially between the Malays and the Chinese. What were the key factors contributing to the non-assimilation of the main ethnic communities in Malaya?

First of all, the attitude of immigrant peoples should be considered one of the key internal factors resulting in the non-assimilation of the main ethnic groups. Unlike the earlier immigrants who had assimilated into the local Malay community, the later Chinese and Indian immigrants rarely considered Malaya their homeland. Rather they identified themselves as "transients" or "birds of passage". While the Malays, along with some aborigines and the natives of Sabah and Sarawak, are regarded as indigenous people, the Chinese and the Indians were brought to the country as "aliens" or "guest workers". Their primary objective in coming to Malaya was to amass sufficient wealth and return to their home countries. Therefore, as Tregonning notes, "they felt little necessity to adapt themselves in any way to their temporary environment, and conscious of their difference they kept apart from their fellow inhabitants of the peninsula".[11] The attitude of most migrants would not have mattered had they left the Malay Peninsula but an increasing number stayed on and by settling they contributed to the inter-racial problem.

As the second internal factor, and more seriously, there were a number of fundamental socio-cultural differences that made assimilation more difficult between the major ethnic communities. In brief, the main ethnic communities, especially the Malays and the Chinese, were, and still are, extraordinarily different in almost every aspect of their lives, such as religion, language, foods, customs, and world-views. These fundamental differences hindered their assimilation into a common cultural society.

Most of all, language has been the major barrier to the assimilation of the main ethnic communities. The different ethnic communities have kept their own languages as their mother tongue. In addition, there have also been various sub-communities of Chinese and Indians who continue to speak the dialects or languages of their original provinces in China and India. According to the census of 1957, only 3 per cent of Chinese aged ten and over, and only 5 per cent of Indians in the same age group were literate in the Malay language, while 46 per cent of Malays, in the same age group, were literate in Malay.[12] The ethnic communities also have different dietary restrictions. For example, the Chinese eat pork, which is not *halal* and therefore forbidden in the Malay Muslim community. Similarly, for religious reasons the Hindu Indians do not eat beef. Furthermore, the Chinese often keep dogs at home, while Malays regard contact with dogs as unclean, requiring ritual ablution.

Along with these differences, the world-views of the two communities are poles apart. Practically all Malays are Muslims and, as such, are not allowed to marry non-Malays who do not convert to Islam. Thus, the social and religious structure of the Malay community makes it extremely difficult for other religious or ethnic groups, with the exception of Arabs or Indian Muslims, to integrate with them. On the other hand, Chinese follow a variety of religious traditions, including Buddhism and Taoism, and are generally sinocentric. In addition, the majority of Indians are Hindu. For ethnic communities with strong national, cultural, and religious traditions, conversion to another religion is not a common event. In this respect, intermarriage between the three communities, which may have helped to break down racial barriers, was difficult, though not all that unusual.

Thirdly, the role of "secret societies" inhibited immigrant Chinese from assimilating into the existing Malay society. Traditionally, Malay rulers dealt with the Chinese as a whole through the Kapitan China System in which the leader of the Chinese was appointed by the Malay sultan to adjudicate community affairs. However, as the Chinese population expanded during the British administration of the late nineteenth and early twentieth century, the Kapitan China System became ineffective. Furthermore, the increasing diversity within the Chinese community required more than one individual to protect and represent their interests. Therefore, when the Chinese migrants came to the Malay Peninsula, societies based on clan or dialect associations were often indispensable organizations affording protection and assistance in an alien and often hostile environment. The secret societies came to play an increasingly important role as the Chinese population expanded in the early twentieth century. The strength and importance of secret societies are well explained by the fact that the British government believed that "the best way of governing the Chinese was through the

Chinese themselves".[13] Indeed, it had been estimated that "sixty per cent of the Chinese in the Straits were sworn members and most of the remaining forty per cent were under their influence" in the early twentieth century.[14] In this context, the secret societies were of fundamental importance in maintaining links with China and in preserving Chinese values and culture. Thus, the absorption of the Chinese into the existing Malay political and social system was hindered by the secret societies.

With these internal factors inhibiting assimilation of the main ethnic communities, the British government policy towards the Malay Peninsula, as a key external factor, also helped keep them separate. In particular, "a policy of active intervention and indirect rule" from 1867 until the Japanese occupation of Malaya had its roots in the division of Malayan society on a communal basis between the main ethnic communities. Joginder Singh Jessy mentions the effects of British policy on Malay society as follows:

> The primary result of the British policy ... was to keep Malay society and institutions intact. But this was achieved at the expense of excluding the Malays from participating in the modern economy in any effective manner. The political position of the Malays which was preserved put them in a good position when the politics of independence drew near. But economically, Malay society was generally impoverished. The educational policy helped to make for a placid peasantry but denied opportunities for the Malays in other fields.[15]

Since 1867 when the administration of the Straits Settlements was transferred to London, the British government extended its influence to the Malay sultanates, motivated especially by economic interest.[16] British rule in the nine Malay states had been extended gradually and indirectly by means of what came to be known as "the Resident System". Each of the sultans of Perak, Selangor, Pahang, and Negeri Sembilan agreed to accept the British Resident as "adviser" in the administration of the states except in matters of Islamic religion and Malay customs. These states eventually formed the Federated Malay States (FMS). Though the remaining five Malay states, which formed the Unfederated Malay States (UMS), retained greater autonomy, they had also gradually come under British protection by 1930.

In fact, the Resident System became the precursor of direct British rule in Malaya. Although the legal position of the sultans was safeguarded under the Resident System, the "advice" given to the sultans by the British Residents had to be "acted on" so that the British in practice exercised nearly complete control of the decision-making powers of the Malay states. This reduced the position of the sultans to the level of dependents on British protection, encouraged an uncontrolled flow of immigrant labour from China and India, and isolated Malays from the economic mainstream. It was during this period that the British had encouraged Chinese and Indian migration to the Straits Settlements to fulfil their own economic needs.

Of the many differences — such as occupation, income, education, and ownership of share capital — between the ethnic communities, perhaps none was more significant than patterns of residence in rural and urban areas. In terms of demographic distribution, in 1957 four-fifths of the Malays were in the rural areas, while over half of the Chinese population lived in the towns, and a majority of the Indians was concentrated in the estates. Thus, as shown in Table 2.3, in 1957 almost three-quarters of the Chinese population lived in towns of 1,000 and more, while only one-fifth of Malays did. The dramatic rise of the proportion of Chinese in urban areas from 1947 to 1957 (from 43.1 to 73 per cent) is usually attributed to the forced relocation of rural Chinese squatters into "new villages" by the British colonial government during the "emergency" in the early 1950s. Over a half million rural settlers, mostly Chinese, were resettled into "new villages", many of which became

TABLE 2.3
Urban Concentration* of Each Ethnic Group,
West Malaysia, 1931–57 (In percentages)

	1931	1947	1957
Malay	8.6	11.3	19.3
Chinese	38.8	43.1	73.0
Indian	25.9	33.8	41.1

* Urban areas with a population of 1,000 and above.

Source: Federation of Malaya, *1957 Population Census of the Federation of Malaya, Report No. 14* (Kuala Lumpur: Department of Statistics, 1960), p. 11.

small towns. The "emergency" was the popular name of a period of warfare between guerrilla forces and the government which officially lasted from 1948 to 1960, although most of the active fighting had ended by the mid-1950s.

The sudden influx of immigrants to tin mining and rubber factories and the pro-Malay policies of the British government also created a serious ethnic imbalance in the economic distribution of wealth. Tin mining and trading, for example, brought in the most wealth and these were also urban pursuits. On the other hand, the pro-Malay policies of the British government "helped to preserve the traditional patterns of Malay society and its peasant-based economy".[17] Though these policies seemed appropriate, especially in terms of avoiding political controversy between different racial groups, they "did not help the Malays to come to terms with the modern world or adapt themselves to a competitive economic system".[18] Since the Malays were encouraged to remain in rural areas, many were therefore denied access to urban amenities and to the wealth available to non-Malays. According to the 1947 Population Census, nearly three-quarters of the total male Malay working population was engaged in agriculture and fishing. On the contrary, although one-third of the male Chinese working population was engaged in agriculture, over 50 per cent of the population were mainly shop assistants, tin mining labourers, construction workers, traders, businessmen or were engaged in the various professions.[19] As for the Indians, the majority of them were estate workers. This meant that the majority of the Malays was generally found in the lower-income economic activities while the non-Malays were found in the higher-level economic activities.

Moreover, certain specific policies of British colonialism made it more difficult for the various ethnic groups to integrate. One of the key policies maintaining communalism was the colonial education policy. In brief, prior to 1952, there was no national system of education in Malaya. Rather, the British policy on education for the three main ethnic communities "ranged from token paternalism (towards the Malay peasantry) to complete neglect (of the Chinese); the Tamil labourers were presumed not to require any education at all".[20]

While the traditional Malay rulers' children were educated in public school-type English-medium schools, most of the Malay masses were given only minimal vernacular education suitable for the rural way of life. Although Malay education after 1920 was free and compulsory, it did not go beyond primary level. As for the Chinese, they were left largely to their own devices as far as Chinese-medium education was concerned. It was the local Chinese community which provided the necessary impetus to education by setting up Chinese schools for their own children. The Indians were also left to their own devices. As a result of this policy and the attitude of the British colonial government, there was a clear "educational division of each community" during this period.[21] More seriously, the educational division of the main ethnic communities further intensified the division of labour between the different sectors in the society.

In sum, along with some internal inhibiting factors resulting from fundamental differences in almost every area of the life-styles of the Chinese, Indian, and Malay communities, the limited social contact between and amongst the various ethnic groups, mostly induced by the British colonial policy, made assimilation of the separate Malayan peoples extremely difficult during the colonial period and helped shape inter-communal relations after independence.

The Deepening of Inter-Ethnic Conflict

Although British colonial policies before World War II resulted in the segregation and non-assimilation of the main ethnic communities in Malaya, the relations between the Chinese and the Malays were relatively peaceful. However, serious inter-racial animosities broke out after the Japanese came to the Malay Peninsula. As Clutterbuck notes "the relations between Chinese and Malays, which had been good before the war, were ruined" during World War II.[22] Funston also stresses the distinct impacts of the British rule and subsequent Japanese occupation on Malayan ethnic relations:

> Social dislocation, though widespread, was not so severe that it forced the masses into the political arena; [the] British ostensibly pursued a pro-Malay policy and had some success in convincing Malays that it was acting as their protector *vis-à-vis* the non-Malays; and when Malay political activity nonetheless surfaced repressive action was quickly taken. The Japanese occupation upset this fine balance and brought into being a politicized mass

that could link up with the existing political élite. It was not to be long before
the accumulated tensions of two colonial regimes gave rise to the first direct
participation of the Malay masses in the political field.[23]

Indeed, it was the colonial policies of the Japanese Military Administration
towards Malayan peoples, along with the post-war British policies, that
played a substantial role in deepening and reinforcing inter-ethnic
cleavages, particularly between the Malays and the Chinese, in Malaya.

With the aim of establishing "the Greater East Asia Co-Prosperity
Sphere" encompassing East and Southeast Asia, the Japanese invaded
several towns on the northern coast of Malaya on 8 December 1941.
Through rapid military conquest, the Japanese completely replaced the
pre-war British colonial administration after the capitulation of Singapore
(renamed Shonan, the Light of the South) on 15 February 1942. After
that, the Japanese Military Administration ruled Malaya until 15 August
1945.

In contrast to the British practice of having a dual form of government
in Malaya, the Japanese governed Malaya as a single integrated colony
under one supreme government headed by the Japanese Military
Administration. Like the British, however, the Japanese Military
Administration treated the three main ethnic groups of Malaya
"separately", or to use the more exact term "differentially". As a result, as
discussed later, this differential approach by the Japanese encouraged
and catalysed inter-ethnic hostility among Malayan peoples.

Towards the Malays, the Japanese Military Administration adopted
a moderate policy, encouraging Malay nationalism, to gain Malay mass
co-operation. For their own purposes, the Japanese generated various
intensive political activities at all levels of Malay society.[24] In this context,
"mass demonstrations, slogan competitions and lecturing contests were
frequently held; pan-Malayan conferences and training programmes were
arranged".[25] Administratively, the Japanese retained the sultans, but
reduced their powers considerably. Andaya mentions that "the weakened
status of the traditional rulers in the Occupation, combined with Japanese
encouragement of Malay nationalism, contributed to the growing
importance of a new Malay élite who had arisen in the 1920s and
1930s".[26] In addition, distrusting the political reliability of the Chinese,
the Japanese deliberately recruited Malays into the police and armed

forces to maintain security against the Malayan Peoples' Anti-Japanese Army (MPAJA), which was dominated by the Malayan Communist Party (MCP). Some Malays were also promoted to higher posts in the administration.

With regard to the Indians, the Japanese did not treat them as well as the Malays but the Indians were never brutalized as were the Chinese. Rather, the Japanese used the appeal of nationalism to win over the support of the Indians, many of whom were extremely anti-British because of the struggle for independence that was in progress in India at this period. In this context, the Japanese Military Administration allowed the existence of Indian Independence League Movements which called for the liberation of India from British rule. Though Indians focused on their homeland, the very fact of the existence of the Indian Independence Leagues and their activities generated political consciousness amongst them in Malaya.

However, co-operation from the Chinese was almost impossible to obtain. The Chinese in Malaya were more inclined to aid their countrymen fighting the Japanese in China. Even prior to the Japanese invasion in 1942, anti-Japanese activities among the Chinese community in Malaya had already begun, as shown in the anti-Japanese activity of the MCP. The MCP, formally organized in April 1930, had led anti-Japanese activities with the Japanese invasion of China in 1937. Thus, the Japanese attitude towards the Chinese was generally one of ruthless repression. Of all the main ethnic groups in Malaya, the Chinese received the harshest treatment from the Japanese, mainly because of the Sino-Japanese War and their continuing co-operation with China.

One of the first and cruellest acts of retaliation committed by the Japanese Military Administration after the fall of Singapore was the infamous *sook ching* (purge through purification) aimed at the suppression of hostile Chinese. This was the biggest massacre of the Chinese during the Japanese occupation in Malaya, with a death toll estimated to be between 6,000 and 40,000.[27] Although such a large-scale massacre against the Chinese was not repeated, "smaller but equally brutal atrocities were committed against the Chinese throughout the Occupation".[28]

In response to the hostile policies of the Japanese, the main anti-Japanese activities came from the ranks of the Chinese. An underground anti-Japanese movement called the Malayan Peoples' Anti-Japanese Army (MPAJA) was largely Chinese in composition, although its members also included a few Malays. Its leaders were from the Malayan Communist Party (MCP). With British aid in the form of supplies, intelligence, and training, the MPAJA provided the backbone of the resistance movement against the Japanese in Malaya. Although the Japanese Military Administration changed its policies towards the Chinese from repression to moderation from late 1943 onwards, by integrating them with other races in advisory councils, business, education, and government, the Chinese were never forgiven for their support of the anti-Japanese struggle until the war was over.

Although the Japanese did not deliberately promote racial animosity between the Malays and the Chinese, the differential policies followed by the Japanese Military Administration for their own reasons had different repercussions on different ethnic communities in Malaya. In other words, the divisive and differential Japanese policy created pervasive social tensions in Malayan society and local interpretations of these policies by Malay and Chinese communities naturally led to bitter inter-racial conflicts. Such sensitive racial responses are well described in two different studies by Andaya and Zainal Abidin as follows:

> During the Occupation the anti-Chinese feeling among Malays was further encouraged by the Japanese who used paramilitary units composed mainly of Malays to fight Chinese resistance groups. The communal violence of the post-war years can thus be regarded as a logical outcome of divisive ethnic policies and attitudes ... [29]

> The Japanese hostile acts against the Chinese and their apparently more favourable treatment of the Malays helped to make the Chinese community feel its separate identity more acutely ... it was also the beginning of racial tension between the Malays and the Chinese. [30]

Indeed, though the Japanese Military Administration reigned over Malaya for only a relatively short period of three-and-a-half years, the effects of Japanese rule on Malaya were much more harmful than the British rule as far as ethnic relations were concerned. Most particularly, the Japanese occupation brought about profound changes among peoples in Malaya. It awakened a keen political awareness among Malayan peoples by intensifying communalism and racial hatred. Especially, it acted as a catalyst for the emergence and development of Malay nationalism in Malaya. As Hall states, political consciousness among the Malays was weak prior to the Japanese invasion. And, Malay nationalism was only in an incipient stage and was confined to a small group of intellectual radicals.

> Before the war the Malays had been the least politically minded of all the peoples of South-East Asia ... During the occupation period, however, Malay national sentiment had become a reality; it was strongly anti-Chinese, and its rallying cry, "Malaya for the Malays" ...[31]

What was more significant about Malay national sentiment was the unity among Malays, who had been politicized during the war, to resist an expected Chinese bid for power which would threaten Malay sovereignty. This meant that political awareness among Malays was no longer limited to a small group of educated intellectuals or in the urban areas, but became a real concern even for uneducated *kampung* (village) Malays as well. In this context, the Japanese occupation "politicised the Malay peasantry to the extent that they were available for mass mobilisation immediately after the war".[32] The activities of the Chinese-dominated MPAJA in Malay villages during the Japanese occupation especially heightened Malays' political consciousness and accounted for the rapid rise in Sino-Malay racial strife after the war.[33]

Substantial changes also occurred in non-Malay communities as a whole, especially in the Chinese communities. As mentioned earlier, like the Indians, the nationalism of the Chinese, as "aliens", was not directed towards Malaya but towards China. In fact, the politically active Chinese were in a minority, although their vitality made them seem dominant. Indeed, the majority of Chinese remained uninterested in the political situation both at home and abroad. However, the hostile and discriminatory policies of the Japanese against the Chinese aroused resentment among most Chinese towards Malays, and the political interests of the Chinese eventually turned towards Malaya instead of China.

Furthermore, the political influence of the Chinese increased throughout the war. The MCP, in particular, increased its influence through its propaganda and the MPAJA's guerrilla activities against the Japanese. When the Japanese occupation ended in 1945, the MPAJA was the only armed, and the best organized, force within Malaya. In the chaos of the post-war years, the MCP-MPAJA immediately took over local governments and used this opportunity to deal harshly with the Chinese "traitors" and Malay "collaborators" of the Japanese occupation. They took bloody revenge against these traitors and collaborators. However, their main targets after the war were, in fact, Malay officials who were thought to have co-operated treacherously with the Japanese. This had serious effects on ethnic relations in Malayan society as a whole, as Andaya notes:

> ... the violence initiated by ideology ... quickly became interpreted as an inter-ethnic conflict. The Malays organized themselves under their village secular and religious leaders to fight what they saw as the "Chinese" MPAJA/MCP.[34]

The Institutionalization of the Inter-Ethnic Conflict Configuration

Wartime Japanese policies towards Malaya, as mentioned in the previous section, awakened a keen political consciousness of the Malayan peoples, which resulted in the politicization of Malayan society. However, the post-war British approach towards Malaya stimulated and accelerated the institutionalization of political consciousness among Malayan peoples. During this period, the Malay masses collectivized their political demands into an organized political front against the non-Malay communities as well as the British government.

When the British reoccupied Malaya in September 1945, it was placed under the British Military Administration (BMA) and the BMA, with central authority, continued to use the Japanese-type integrated government for Malaya. Despite traditional pro-Malay policies, the British, however, felt obliged to the Chinese for their wartime effort and introduced the concept of the Malayan Union which greatly improved the status of non-Malays. The Union was designed to effect constitutional changes to unite all the Federated Malay States, Unfederated Malay States, and the Straits Settlements of Penang and Malacca into one entity.[35]

The proposed Malayan Union would not only force the nine sultans to surrender their sovereignty to the British government but also to change the conditions of citizenship. The BMA introduced the principle of *jus soli* which conferred citizenship on any persons born in Malaya and Singapore after the establishment of the Malayan Union. It also devised liberal citizenship provisions for other domiciled immigrants. Furthermore, all citizens of the new Malayan Union were to have equal rights, including admission to the administrative civil service. Thus, Malayan citizenship was to be extended to all without racial discrimination under the Malayan Union.[36]

With the concept of the Malayan Union, in short, the British had rejected their pre-war policy of recognizing the sovereignty of the Malay sultans, the autonomy of the Malay states, and Malay special privileges. One of the distinguishing features of the Malayan Union proposal was the absence of any distinction between Malays and non-Malays. According to the conditions of Malayan Union Citizenship, it was estimated that 83 per cent of Chinese and 75 per cent of Indians in Malaya would qualify for citizenship.[37] The effect of these new citizenship qualifications on Malayan peoples, especially on Malays, was quite significant, considering the predicted numbers of non-Malay citizens in Malaya under the Malayan Union scheme.

When the Malayan Union proposal was formally outlined by the Secretary of State for the Colonies in Parliament on 10 October 1945, the Malay reaction was unexpectedly serious and widespread.[38] The Malay press carried a considerable number of letters and reports criticizing and opposing the Malayan Union proposal. There was also great resistance among the ordinary Malay people to this new proposal. There were demonstrations running to thousands of people in almost every town. For example, in Kedah, 50,000 people took part in a demonstration and in Kelantan 36,000 people participated.

Furthermore, throughout the country, many organizations voiced their protest in local newspapers, accusing the British government of using "'methods of intimidation' to obtain the Malay Sultans' agreement to the new treaties".[39] On 20 November 1945, eight Malay associations in Johor joined to form the Malay League of Johor and on 3 January 1946, the Peninsula Malay Movement of Johor was organized under the leadership of Dato' Onn bin Jaafar, a Malay district officer in the state of Johor and a leading figure of the protest group. Finally, on 1 March 1946, about 200 Malay delegates representing forty-one Malay associations met in Kuala Lumpur for a Pan-Malayan Malay Congress to discuss the idea of forming a centralized organization. The main objective of this congress was to unite the Malays into a strong association so as to obtain a repeal of the constitution of the proposed Malayan Union.

The gathering of these various associations was particularly significant in terms of the institutionalization of political consciousness among Malays because the Pan-Malayan Malay Congress was the forerunner of the Pertubuhan Kebangsaan Melayu Bersatu, or the United Malays National Organization (UMNO). With the formation of UMNO to oppose the Malayan Union, the Malays finally had their own united political force, whereas, before this, they were having difficulty organizing themselves into a united political front. In fact, they were politically fragmented between socialist, conservative, radical, religious, and royalist elements.

At the next Pan-Malayan Malay Congress held in Johor Baru later on 11 May 1946, UMNO was inaugurated. Dato' Onn bin Jaafar was elected as its first president. UMNO defended the traditional power of the sovereignty of the sultans and rejected the Malayan Union. Though the British government initially refused to withdraw the proposal for the Malayan Union, UMNO kept protesting and, together with the nine sultans, boycotted all activities organized by the British government. The political situation in Malaya during this period was described accurately in a secret telegram to Hall, Secretary of State for the Colonies, from Gent, an original proponent of the Malayan Union, on 11 May 1946:

> ... almost universal Malay political opinion here gives no basis for expecting effective operation of constitution on Union ... Strength and organisation of Malay opinion and their free criticism of their own Rulers has surprised all who have experience of Malaya, including especially the Rulers themselves.[40]

In contrast to the Malays' widespread response, curiously, non-Malays initially showed little enthusiasm for the Malayan Union proposal even though it had the potential to improve their position and give them political rights which they had been previously denied. The Chinese were more interested in the restoration of their businesses damaged by the war, than in politics.[41]

In circumstances of mounting agitation from the Malays and lack of support from the non-Malays, the constitution of the Malayan Union was reviewed at a conference between the sultans, representatives of UMNO, and representatives of the British government. Finally, a new constitution based on the concept of federalism was agreed upon by the British government. As a result, on 1 February 1948, the Federation of Malaya Agreement was signed by the sultans and the British High Commissioner.

The Federation of Malaya Agreement stated that the high commissioner would be responsible for safeguarding the "special position" of the Malays and the "legitimate interests" of the non-Malays. Meanwhile, under the Federation scheme, sensitive issues that had dominated Malaysian politics to the present, such as the special rights and privileges of the Malays, the position of the sultans, and the place of the Chinese in Malaya, were brought out into the open and upheld. The conditions of citizenship were made more restrictive than in the earlier Malayan Union scheme, requiring residence of at least fifteen years over the previous twenty years, a declaration of permanent settlement, and a certain level of competence in Malay and English.[42]

In contrast to their earlier indifference to the Malayan Union proposal, non-Malays were aggrieved at the restoration of Malay constitutional privileges when the Federation scheme proposed to replace the Malayan Union proposal. The non-Malays, especially the Chinese, protested and threatened to walk out of the various councils. Again, the new constitutional proposal accelerated the institutionalization of political movements among the Malayan peoples. For example, on 22 December 1946, two days before the new constitutional proposal, the All-Malaya Council of Joint Action (AMCJA) was formed, with the wealthy Baba businessman, Tan Cheng Lock, as its chairman. On 22 February 1947, the Pusat Tenaga Ra'ayat (People's United Front or PUTERA), consisting of the Malay National Party, the Angkatan Pemuda Insaf, the Peasants' Union, and the Angkatan Wanita Sedar, was established by radical Malays. The continuing political activities against the Federation scheme were supported by these political organizations. However, these nascent political movements were mostly ineffectual and even AMCJA was unable to play an effective role in the course of events due to internal divisions. In the end, opposition against the Federation scheme failed to achieve its purpose.[43]

Following the implementation of the Federation of Malaya in February 1948, Malaya underwent a serious armed insurrection led by the MCP. In response, the British declared "the emergency", which lasted for twelve years. One of the critical consequences of the emergency was the intensification of racial rivalry between the Malays and the Chinese. The MCP's main aim was to wrest control of the country from the British. And their main targets were mainly Malays and British personnel. The Chinese-dominated MCP obtained most of its supplies from the Chinese, in particular those squatters who lived near the jungle fringes. On the other hand, most members of the government security forces were Malays. Thus, an ideologically originated struggle between the British and the MCP soon evolved into intensified ethnic rivalry in Malaya.[44]

When the emergency began in mid-1948, moderate Chinese leaders were at a loss. To make matters worse for the Chinese, the British government was also concerned with the possibility of the MCP gaining greater influence over the Chinese community. Therefore the British government encouraged the formation of an alternative political association amongst the Chinese. As a result, on 27 February 1949 the Malayan Chinese Association (MCA) was formed under the leadership of Tan Cheng Lock, a moderate Chinese leader, to represent the interests of the Chinese community. Though the MCA was not a mass party, rather a businessman's pressure group, "it did provide a means by which moderate Chinese activists could participate in the evolving political process".[45]

In the mean time, in August 1946, the Malayan Indian Congress (MIC) was formed to look after the welfare of Indians in Malaya. Initially the MIC was not a significant movement, attached as it was to the politics of India rather than Malaya. However, the MIC gradually began to play a role representing the interests of the Indian community as the Indians in Malaya, like the Chinese, tended to show their interest towards Malaya in the process of political development during the post-war British period. Meanwhile, there were several other forces transformed into political parties in the early 1950s. Few parties were politically influential.

However, they were clearly divided along ethnic lines. Those established before the independence of 1957 were: Pan Malayan Islamic Party (PAS), People's Progressive Party (PPP, from 1952 to 1956 known as the Perak Progressive Party), Labour Party, and Party Rakyat.

Summary

It is clear that ethnic identities belong to times long past and antedate the colonial arrival. Different ethnic groups also have a propensity to split and the ethnic diversity itself tends to lead towards ethnic conflicts. However, as Horowitz has stressed, it was the colonial powers that helped shape how ethnic groups compare and contrast each other. The colonial governments often promoted ethnic disparities by favouring certain groups over others for effective rule over the colonies.[46] And it was this colonial experience, or discrimination, that has fostered the determined ethnic identities in many post-colonial nation-states.

In Malaysia, the legacies of colonialism created new functions for ethnic groups thereby shaping the quality of inter-ethnic interactions. These relations could be perceived as a by-product of British colonial rule in that the segmental plurality of ethnic groups was transformed into a "backward-advance dichotomy", especially between the Malays and the Chinese. The political antagonism that arose as a result of wartime Japanese policies towards Malayan society tended to deepen ethnic divisions and sharpen inter-ethnic conflict. It was during the post-war British administration and in reaction to the British-proposed Malayan Union that the lines of ethnic contrast were replicated as ethnically based parties in the modern political system.

The formation of ethnically based parties does not necessarily mean a further exacerbation of ethnic conflict since those parties can act as agents of inter-communal co-operation. As Huntington asserts, the presence of institutionalized political parties is a crucial condition for bringing a stable political order to newly independent countries in the post-colonial world.[47] Nevertheless, there might be some doubt about how far an ethnically based political party system can sustain favourable conditions for successful management of communal conflict. It must be noted that mono-ethnic parties tend to mobilize ethnically oriented mass discontent to derive their support from their ethnic communities.

Furthermore, the formation of ethnically based political parties in Malaysia, especially the politically dominant UMNO, was a by-product of increasing pressure to redress immediate grievances over nationalistic as well as communal identities. Therefore, the creation of exclusive political organizations in Malaysia along ethnic lines can be perceived as a modern attempt to consolidate a segmental plurality of ethnic configuration rather than to resolve it. To a certain extent, the presence of institutionalized political parties can contribute to socio-political stability in a plural society. However, circumstances where ethnic cleavages are woven into an exclusive political framework may provide long-term obstacles to integration of diverse ethnic groups in the process of nation-building. Ethnically based political parties, indeed, played a substantial role as institutional mechanisms for political manifestations of the communal rivalries in Malaysia's post-colonial era.

NOTES

1. John R. Bowen, "The Myth of Global Ethnic Conflict", *Journal of Democracy* 7, no. 4 (1996): 4.

2. On the early history of Malaya, see B.W. Andaya and L.Y. Andaya, *A History of Malaysia* (London: Macmillan Press, 1982); D.J. Steinberg, ed., *In Search of Southeast Asia: A Modern History* (Sydney: Allen & Unwin, 1987); and D.G.E. Hall, *A History of South-East Asia* (fourth edition) (London: Macmillan Press, 1981).

3. B.W. Hodder, *Man in Malaya* (London: University of London Press, 1959), p. 22. On the origins of the Malays in the Malay Peninsula, see M.W.F. Tweedie, "The Stone Age in Malaya", *Journal of the Malayan Branch of the Royal Asiatic Society* 26, part 2 (1953): 1–100.

4. For a more detailed analysis of Baba Chinese, see Tan Chee Beng, "Baba and Nyonya: A Study of the Ethnic Identity of the Chinese Peranakan in Malacca", unpublished Ph.D. thesis, Cornell University, 1979.

5. These figures includes the Straits Settlements (Singapore, Malacca, and Penang), the Federated Malay States (Selangor, Perak, Pahang, and Negeri Sembilan) and the Unfederated Malay States (Johor, Perlis, Kedah, Kelantan, and Terengganu). For more detailed data, see British Malaya, *A Report on the 1931 Census and on Certain Problems of Vital Statistics* (Westminster: Crown Agents for the Colonies, 1932), pp. 120–26.

6. Collin E.R. Abraham, *Divide and Rule: The Roots of Race Relations in Malaysia* (Kuala Lumpur: INSAN, 1997), p. 201, italics in original.

7. Abraham (1997, p. 200). For more detailed contexts of *The Immigration Restriction Ordinance of 1928* and *The Aliens Ordinance of 1933*, see Abraham (1997, pp. 199–201).

8. Samuel Herbert Wilson, *Report of Brigadier-General Sir Samuel Wilson, Permanent Under-Secretary of State for the Colonies on His Visit to Malaya 1932* (London: His Majesty's Office, 1933), pp. 26–27. According to Parmer, the average length of stay of immigrants was two to three years. See J.N. Parmer, *Colonial Labor Policy and Administration* (New York: Association for Asian Studies, 1960), p. 17.

9. C.N. Parkinson, *A Short History of Malaya* (Singapore: D. Moore, 1954), p. 18.

10. Wilson (1933, p. 27).

11. K.G. Tregonning, *A History of Modern Malaya* (London: Eastern Universities Press, 1964), p. 182.

12. Federation of Malaya, *The 1957 Population Census of the Federation of Malaya, Report No. 14* (Kuala Lumpur: Department of Statistics, 1960), pp. 94–95.

13. R.N. Jackson, *Pickering, Protector of Chinese* (Kuala Lumpur: Oxford University Press, 1965), p. 50.

14. Jackson (1965, p. 51).

15. Joginder Singh Jessy, *History of South-East Asia (1824–1965)* (Kedah: Penerbitan Darulaman, 1983), p. 380.

16. For more detailed analysis of the British colonial policy, see Archana Sharma, *British Policy towards Malaysia, 1957–1967* (London: Sangam Books Limited, 1993); Nicholas Tarling, "Intervention and Non-Intervention in Malaya", *Journal of Asian Studies* 21, no. 4 (1962): 523–27; and Rupert Emerson, *Malaysia: A Study in Direct and Indirect Rule* (Kuala Lumpur: University of Malaya Press, 1964).

17. Gordon P. Means, *Malaysian Politics* (London: Hodder and Stoughton, 1976), p. 43.

18. Means (1976, p. 43).

19. British Malaya, *A Report on the 1947 Census of Population* (London: Crown Agents for the Colonies, 1949), p. 106.

20. Hua Wu Yin, *Class and Communalism in Malaysia: Politics in a Dependent Capitalist State* (London: Zed Books, 1983), p. 59.

21. Tregonning (1964, p. 183).

22. Richard Clutterbuck, *Conflict and Violence in Singapore and Malaysia 1945–1983* (Boulder: Westview Press, 1985), p. 38.

23. N.J. Funston, *Malay Politics in Malaysia: A Study of the United Malays National Organisation and Party Islam* (Kuala Lumpur: Heinemann Educational Books, 1980), p. 36.

24. A.J. Stockwell, *British Policy and Malay Politics during the Malayan Union Experiment,*

1945–1948 (Kuala Lumpur: Malayan Branch of the Royal Asiatic Society, 1979), pp. 1–16.

25. Stockwell (1979, p. 9).

26. Andaya (1982, p. 248). For a detailed analysis on the rise of nationalism in Malaya before the 1941, see Joginder Singh Jessy (1985, pp. 377–88); William Roff, *The Origins of Malay Nationalism* (New Haven: Yale University Press, 1967); and Radin Soenarno, "Malay Nationalism, 1896–1941", *Journal of Southeast Asian History* 1, no. 1 (1960): 1–28.

27. The figures for the total number of Chinese massacred differ between Japanese and Chinese sources. See Cheah Boon Kheng, "The Social Impact of the Japanese Occupation of Malaya (1942–1945)", in *Southeast Asia under Japanese Occupation*, edited by Alfred W. McCoy (New Haven: Yale University Press, 1980), p. 119, note 16. Andaya, however, estimated the number of deaths to be between 5,000 and 25,000. See Andaya (1982, p. 251).

28. Andaya (1982, p. 251).

29. Andaya (1982, p. 253).

30. Zainal Abidin bin Abdul Wahid, "The Japanese Occupation and Nationalism", in *Glimpses of Malaysian History,* edited by Zainal Abidin bin Abdul Wahid (Kuala Lumpur: Dewan Bahasa dan Pustaka, 1970), p. 97.

31. Hall (1981, p. 871).

32. Funston (1980, p. 35).

33. Cheah Boon Keng (1980, pp. 110–11).

34. Andaya (1982, p. 252).

35. For more detail on the Malaya Union, see J.D.V. Allen, *The Malayan Union* (New Haven: Yale University Press, 1967); Mohamed Noordin Sopiee, *From Malayan Union to Singapore Separation: Political Unification in the Malaysia Region 1945–1965* (Kuala Lumpur: Penerbit Universiti Malaya, 1974); and A.J. Stockwell 1979.

36. Great Britain, *Malayan Union and Singapore: Summary of Proposed Constitutional Arrangement* (London: HMSO, 1946).

37. K.J. Ratnam, *Communalism and the Political Process in Malaya* (Kuala Lumpur: University of Malaya Press, 1967), p. 75.

38. About the reaction to the Malayan Union and political activity of the Malays, see Stockwell (1979, especially pp. 42–94).

39. Andaya (1982, p. 256).

40. A.J. Stockwell, ed., *Malaya, Part I: The Malayan Union Experiment 1942–1948* (London: HMSO, 1995), p. 229.

41. Richard Hugh Sedley Allen, *Malaysia, Prospect and Retrospect: The Impact and*

Aftermath of Colonial Rule (London: Oxford University Press, 1968), p. 84.

42. For citizenship regulations in greater detail, see Federation of Malaya, *The Federation of Malaya Agreement, 1948 as Amended* (Kuala Lumpur: Government Press, 1956), pp. 40–43. See also Federation of Malaya, *The Federation of Malaya Agreement (Amendment) Ordinance* (Kuala Lumpur: Government Press, 1952).

43. About the political activity against the Federation and the claims of the AMCJA and the PUTERA, see PUTERA and AMCJA, *The People's Constitution for Malaya* (Kuala Lumpur: Ta Chong Press, 1947).

44. Victor Purcell, *Malaya: Communist or Free?* (London: Victor Gollancz, 1954), pp. 59–97; Richard Clutterbuck (1985, pp. 167–260); and Robert Jackson, *The Malayan Emergency* (London: Routledge, 1991).

45. J.M. Gullick, *Malaysia: Economic Expansion and National Unity* (London: Ernest Benn, 1981), p. 93.

46. Donald L. Horowitz, *Ethnic Groups in Conflict* (Berkeley: University of California Press, 1985), pp. 108–13.

47. Samuel P. Huntington, *Political Order in Changing Societies* (New Haven: Yale University Press, 1968).

Regime Maintenance through Consociational Bargaining

3

The case of Malaysia [1955–69] provides the ... example of reasonably successful consociational democracy in the Third World, although the nature of its plural society and the kind of consociational institutions it developed differ considerably both from Lebanon and from the European cases. (Arend Lijphart 1977)[1]

Kuala Lumpur was a city of fire; I could clearly see the conflagrations from my residence at the top of the hill and it was a sight that I never thought I would see in my life-time. In fact all my work to make Malaysia a happy and peaceful country through[ou]t these years, and also my dream of being the happiest Prime Minister in the world, were also going up in flames. (Tunku Abdul Rahman Putra 1969)[2]

Many scholars of conflict resolution argue that intense ethnic conflicts in deeply fragmented societies are rarely resolved by orthodox democratic means such as pure majoritarianism, ordinary parliamentary opposition, political campaigning, and winning elections.[3] Therefore, scholars have proposed the alternative "consociational" model, probably best defined by Lijphart in terms of "grand coalition", "mutual veto", "proportionality", and "autonomy". Lipjhart argues that through government by an élite cartel, a democracy with a fragmented political culture is stabilized. This model is used to deal with intense conflicts, both in the smaller developed European countries and the post-colonial plural societies of the Third World. This chapter explores the relevance of consociational conflict resolution for regime maintenance, to the first period of Malaysian ethnic politics, 1957–69.

The intense ethnic and societal cleavages in Malaysia have inclined many scholars to view consociational élite bargaining as the most useful theoretical approach to analysing regime maintenance in the Malaysian political system. Much of the consociational writing regarding Malaysia, therefore, has been oriented towards exploring how the élites of the various ethnic groups are able to reach some measure of consensus to achieve and preserve socio-political stability, within a relatively democratic political system. These studies show that some of the features of consociationalism are exhibited by the Malaysian political system, especially in the years shortly before and immediately after Malaysian independence. Moreover, most of these works conclude that the Malaysian government's efforts at achieving conflict resolution were praiseworthy. Arend Lijphart, as the original proponent of consociationalism, also claims that the case of Malaysia especially in the 1957–69 period provides a reasonably successful example of consociational democracy in the plural societies of the Third World.[4]

This chapter first examines the motives for a consociational power-sharing arrangement during the 1957–69 period. The main concern is to assess what kinds of factors have motivated the segmental ethnic élites, especially UMNO leaders, to choose consociational methods as major regime maintenance strategies. The second part explores major features of consociational conflict management during the first period of Malaysian ethnic politics. The third part focuses on the breakdown of the May 1969 racial riots as a failure of consociational politics.

Consociational Power-Sharing Motives

According to Lehmbruch and Lijphart, the possibility of consociational democracy increases when certain conditions exist in a deeply fragmented society, despite intrinsic attributes of the society that obstruct democratic political stability. They identify favourable conditions for consociational élite-co-operation among conflict groups. These include: multiple party systems, a relatively even balance of power among the segmental parties, prior traditions of élite accommodation, a high degree of segmental isolation, small country size, the presence of cross-cutting cleavages and overarching loyalties.[5] As Lijphart noted, these conditions are neither necessary nor sufficient conditions for guaranteeing the success of consociational politics. Lijphart points out these conditions are considered helpful factors. Therefore, "even when all of the conditions are unfavourable, consociationalism, though perhaps difficult, should not be considered impossible. Conversely, a completely favourable ... condition ... does not guarantee consociational choices or success".[6] Nonetheless, the likelihood of consociational power-sharing arrangements increases when a number of these conditions are satisfied simultaneously in a deeply divided society.[7]

The Malaysian political system conformed to some of these favourable conditions especially before and at the point of independence. As described in the previous chapter, a very small degree of social interaction occurred among the main ethnic communities. Even residence of ethnic group was, to a large extent, segregated and the groups were, and still are, quite different in many aspects of daily lives, such as dietary habits, customs, religion, language, and world-views. It is still a moot point to what extent such highly segmented isolation enhanced political autonomy among the segmental leaders in their relations with leaders of other groups. However, there is little doubt that this facilitated the winning of political loyalty or public support from their own communities as long as they appeared to be working for their own segments of society. Moreover, prior traditions which contributed to co-operative decision-making among communal leaders were by no means rare, though not prominent, in the Malayan political process. In line with Lijphart, Malaysia is also a relatively small country, although it is hard to assess to what extent the coalescence of ethnic group leaders is affected by the size of the country. At the point of independence the Malaysian population was estimated at less than seven million, even smaller than those of the successful European consociational democracies.

However, the Malaysian context did not contain some of the major favourable conditions for consociationalism. According to Lijphart, the presence of segmental political parties is favourable "only on the condition that all parties are minority parties".[8] He continues that "a multiple balance of power among the segments of a plural society is more conducive to consociational democracy than a dual balance of power or a hegemony by one of the segments".[9] There is no doubt that the consociational resolution of conflict can be facilitated in Malaysia as the salient ethnic cleavages are expressed through political parties which represent the segmental groups. Nonetheless, as shown in Table 2.1 of the previous chapter, at the point of independence the Malays made up about half the whole population and the Chinese were roughly 40 per cent. The numerical superiority of the Malays was threatened by the minority ethnic groups soon after independence during the brief period of political union with Singapore, as shown in Table 3.3. For that reason, the Malaysian political system should be characterized as a near-majority configuration and, in Lijphart's theory, quite unfavourable for consociational bargaining.[10] More importantly, the political paramountcy of the Malays was, and still is, a special feature of Malaysian politics. The Malays claimed an intrinsic privileged position in political power as an indigenous people whereas the Chinese and the Indians were considered as transient or alien in the country. Although the superior economic position of the non-Malays was generally recognized by the Malays, the political paramountcy of the Malays was not negotiable from the Malay perspective. Malay political supremacy can be viewed as a crucial barrier to consociationalism in Malaysian politics.

Lijphart also assumes that the more societal cleavages cross-cut each other, the more cross-pressures are enhanced in a plural society. The enhancing of cross-pressures within the various segments will encourage moderate attitudes and affect the chances of a consociational power-sharing arrangement.[11] Similarly, the "basic national symbols" accepted by all segmental group members will increase the probability of inter-élite co-operation in a deeply divided society.[12] However, the conditions of cross-cutting cleavages and overarching loyalties hardly fit the Malaysian case. The main ethnic communities were extraordinarily different in almost every aspect of their lives. Furthermore, all of the national symbols in Malaysia were derived from the Malay tradition and this hardly produced cohesion for the society as a whole. Rather, the fundamental differences among the main ethnic communities mutually reinforced the societal cleavages in Malaysian ethnic society. The highly segmental isolation might have provided political leaders with the advantage of a high degree of autonomy in bargaining with other communal group leaders. However, over-emphasis on élite-level bargaining could result in loss of support from their own community in the long run, especially in circumstances where the societal cleavages hardly cross-cut each other at the grassroots level.

In sum, although some favourable conditions for consociationalism appeared to be present in Malaysia, these did not necessarily guarantee that élites would choose consociationalism or that it would be successful. In other words, the consociational power-sharing arrangement should not be perceived as the inevitable conflict-regulating choice by Malaysia's communal political élites. We have to ask therefore what motivated the leaders, especially UMNO leaders, to choose a consociational means of regime maintenance in a situation where conditions for consociational strategies were not overwhelmingly favourable.

The Presence of Perceived External Pressure or Threat

Nordlinger argues that "an external threat or danger" is often the most effective binding force that holds centrifugal tendencies together in a single political unit.[13] As well as an external threat, "an external pressure" also can be a positive facilitator for successful power-sharing arrangements. In Malaysia, the presence of perceived external pressure or threat occurred a few years before and just after independence, as the country came under pressure from the British to establish inter-ethnic co-operation and later as it faced the threat of Indonesian "Confrontation" respectively.

During the period 1955–57, the primary task of nationalist leaders was the achievement of independence. Independence from British colonial rule was perceived as a common goal among the major ethnic groups in Malaya, although there were differences about how that goal could be achieved.[14] And, the Chinese-dominated Communist insurgency was perceived as a threat to both the Malay community and much of the Chinese and Indian communities as well. For this reason, the British colonial government emphasized the necessity of "active co-operation from the Chinese — not only from the leaders but from people of all classes".[15] Therefore, the British administration encouraged the MCA to provide "an alternative standard [to the MCP] to which loyal Chinese could rally".[16] After World War II in a situation where there was little political co-operation between the Malays and the Chinese, the British colonial government insisted, particularly to Malay political leaders, that independence would be granted only to a multi-racial government and not to a government dominated exclusively by one race. In the process of struggle for independence, the prominent leaders of UMNO realized that independence was unlikely to be achieved unless they had the support of non-Malays, especially the Chinese. So, a grand coalition of three distinct communal parties, UMNO, MCA, and MIC, provided a visible arrangement to demonstrate multi-racial co-operation and meet the stipulations of the British administration. Whatever the British colonial government's motives, their determined policies acted as a catalyst for multi-racial political co-operation in Malaya.

Meanwhile, "Confrontation" with Indonesia after independence demonstrated how a credible external threat motivated inter-racial co-operation and increased multi-ethnic support for the Alliance regime in Malaysia. The perception of "external threat" appears to have been a uniting force in the parliamentary elections held in 1955 and 1964. "Independence" from the British was a national issue in 1955, as was "Confrontation" with Indonesia in 1964. In 1955 the Alliance achieved its overwhelming victory campaigning as the party best equipped to gain independence from the British. The second important issue in 1955 was the ending of the "emergency", the common desire for a return to normalcy. Later, the 1964 election was dominated by the national issue of Indonesian "Confrontation". In the 1964 election, the voters rallied behind the Alliance in response to an external threat posed by "Confrontation" with Indonesia.[17]

The poor results for the Alliance of the 1959 election showed how the presence of perceived external pressure or threat played an important role in the Alliance regime's obtaining multi-ethnic electoral support. Whenever national issues, originating from external pressure and/or threat, had not come to the fore, the most salient issues had taken on a communal character. Indeed, in the absence of a national threat following the end of the emergency and the achievement of independence, the major concerns of the 1959 elections were sensitive domestic issues of language, education, and culture. The 1959 election results for the Alliance were the poorest yet. This phenomenon appeared more clearly in the 1969 election. Following the end of Confrontation with Indonesia, the attention of the Malaysian people was again redirected to crucial domestic problems associated with the political position of the non-Malays and the role of their language and education, just as they had in the 1959 election. In short, the campaigns and results of the 1969 election revealed how the Alliance framework was vulnerable to racial sensitivity. Even though there is no clear data to prove a direct relationship between external pressure and high probability of élite co-operation, at the very least the presence of the external pressure or perceived threat seems to have been translated into votes for the Alliance coalition, as shown in the results of elections in the period 1955–69 (see Table 3.1).

TABLE 3.1
Parliamentary Elections, 1955–69: Seats Won by Political Parties

	1955	1959	1964[a]	1969[b]
Alliance	51 (81.7%)	74 (51.8%)	89 (58.4%)	66 (48.4%)
Democratic Action Party	—	—	—	13 (13.7%)
Gerakan Rakyat Malaysia	—	—	—	8 (8.6%)
People's Action Party	—	—	1 (2.1%)	—
People's Progressive Party	—	4 (6.3%)	2 (3.6%)	4 (3.9%)
Pan-Malaysian Islamic Party	1 (4.1%)	13 (21.3%)	9 (14.4%)	12 (23.7%)
Socialist Front	—	8 (12.9%)	2 (16.2%)	—
United Democratic Party	—	—	1 (4.3%)	—
Party Negara	0 (7.9%)	1 (2.1%)	—	—
Malayan Party	—	1 (0.9%)	—	—
Independents	0 (2.2%)	3 (4.8%)	0 (0.7%)	0 (0.3%)
Total	52	104	104	103

[a] The 1964 election excludes Singapore, Sabah, and Sarawak.
[b] The 1969 election excludes Sabah and Sarawak. Election in one constituency postponed.
— = Data not available.

Source: Compiled from NSTP Research and Information Services, *Elections in Malaysia: A Handbook of Facts and Figures on the Elections 1955–1986* (Kuala Lumpur: Balai Berita, 1990).

Unstable Political Hegemony and Weak Economic Position

Nordlinger noted that "economic factors" induced the dominant political élites to engage in co-operative conflict-regulating behaviour.[18] It seems that economic necessity provided an important motive for UMNO leaders to co-operate with the MCA leaders. The Chinese were in control of all trade and commerce in Malaya/Malaysia that was not under foreign, mostly British, control. As a result of the economic superiority of the Chinese, it was widely recognized that the MCA provided a large share of finance to the Alliance regime, while UMNO provided more voting power.[19] UMNO's early moves towards financial self-sufficiency, including a party lottery, soon after its formation failed.[20] Therefore, UMNO leaders aligned themselves with the MCA not only to win electoral support, but also to finance the Alliance's political campaigns, such as payment of helpers, financial support for the candidates, printing of posters and other propaganda material. Apart from the financial support for the Alliance's election campaigns, UMNO needed to gain financial co-operation with Chinese businessmen-politicians to open up economic opportunities in the modern sector for the under-privileged Malays in the earlier period of independence.

As well as UMNO's economic dependence on the cash-rich MCA, long-term political considerations also motivated the UMNO leaders to take part in consociational power-sharing with the MCA. Apart from the special political position of the Malays originating from their indigenous status, the more substantial political power of the Malay community derived from their numerical superiority in the electorate and the nation-wide distribution of those numbers. However, in the years after independence, the numerical superiority of the Malays was threatened. In detail, the numerical superiority of the Malays before and up to independence was mostly due to the special citizenship conditions based on the 1948 Federation of Malaya Agreement. This required residence of at least fifteen years during the previous twenty-five years in the Federation for acquiring citizenship of Malaya, which gave considerable advantage to the indigenous Malays.[21] Therefore, the Chinese and Indians were absolutely weak in terms of political power due mainly to the lack of numbers of registered voters in the electorate. However, as shown in Table 3.2, the superior communal composition

TABLE 3.2
Communal Composition of the Electorate in the
Parliamentary Elections, 1955–69 (In percentages)

	Malays	Chinese	Indians
1955	84.2	11.2	4.6
1959	57.1	34.5	8.4
1964[a]	54.4	37.5	8.1
1969[b]	55.7	36.3	8.0

[a] The 1964 election excludes Singapore, Sabah, and Sarawak.
[b] The 1969 election excludes Sabah and Sarawak.

Source: Mohammad Agus Yusoff, *Consociational Politics: The Malaysian Experience* (Kuala Lumpur: Perikatan Pemuda Enterprise, 1992), p. 24.

of Malays markedly decreased with the increased number of the non-Malay electorates.

Furthermore, the overall racial composition of Malaya itself by no means provided a stable numerical superiority for Malays, as shown in Table 3.3. In particular, the numerical superiority of Malays in Peninsular Malaysia was dramatically reversed during the brief period of political

TABLE 3.3
Ethnic Composition of Malaya/Malaysia, 1947–64
(Population in thousands)

	Malays[a]	Chinese	Indians[b]	Others
1947	2,428 (49.5%)	1,885 (38.4%)	531 (10.8%)	65 (1.3%)
1957	3,125 (49.8%)	2,334 (37.2%)	707 (11.3%)	112 (1.8%)
1964[c]	3,963 (50.1%)	2,918 (36.8%)	884 (11.2%)	153 (1.9%)
1964[d]	4,226 (43.3%)	4,301 (44.1%)	1,036 (10.6%)	200 (2.0%)
1964[e]	5,116 (46.1%)	4,680 (42.2%)	1,042 (9.4%)	251 (2.3%)
1964[f]	4,853 (52.3%)	3,297 (35.7%)	890 (9.6%)	204 (2.2%)

[a] "Malays" includes Malays, Indonesians, and aborigines.
[b] "Indians" includes Pakistanis and Ceylonese.
[c] 1964 refers to Peninsular Malaysia only (excluding Singapore).
[d] 1964 refers to Peninsular Malaysia only (including Singapore).
[e] 1964 refers to the Federation of Malaysia (including Singapore, Sabah, and Sarawak).
[f] 1964 refers to the Federation of Malaysia (excluding Singapore).

Source: Compiled from Means (1976, p. 12, table 1; and p. 294, table 12).

integration with Chinese-dominated Singapore as revealed in the figure
1964^d in Table 3.3. Therefore, at least before the expulsion of Singapore,
it appeared that UMNO leaders needed to co-operate with the MCA
for electoral reasons. In fact, one important reason behind the decision
to force Singapore out of the Federation of Malaysia in 1965 was the
immediate desire to restore the former numerical superiority of the
Malays. As shown in the figure 1964^f of Table 3.3, the Malays regained
a higher percentage population than the Chinese after the separation of
Singapore.

For the Chinese, the acquisition of political power was necessary for
ensuring their strong economic position. The MCA was largely founded
as a businessmen's pressure group rather than a mass-based political party.
Therefore, MCA leaders were more concerned with the maintenance of
Chinese economic predominance. MCA leaders, however, realized that
no exclusively Chinese party could ever win a legislative majority in an
election. Therefore, while UMNO was heavily dependent on the MCA's
financial contributions to the Alliance, the MCA needed UMNO's voting
power to win seats in the election. As shown in Table 3.2, although they
comprised about 40 per cent of the population, the Chinese constituted
only about 11 per cent of the electorate in the 1955 election, compared
with 84 per cent of the Malay electorate. In sum, both UMNO and the
MCA had political and economic assets which induced them to offer
trade-offs to each other.

Élite Accommodation Tradition and Inter-Racial Co-operation Experience

Lehmbruch argues that successful co-operative experiences among
segmental political leaders may induce them to internalize consociational
strategies as routine patterns of conflict regulation.[22] That is to say, rival
groups may consistently employ consociational strategies, thereby
institutionalizing them. It follows then that a prior coalescent decision-
making tradition among the conflict group leaders increases the
possibility of co-operative power-sharing arrangements in a deeply
divided society.[23]

Even before the British colonial administration in Malaya, there
were forms of inter-racial co-operation between the Malays and the

Chinese, especially at the élite level. One example was the Kapitan China System. Traditional Malay rulers, the sultans, dealt with the Chinese through this system. Malay sultans managed communal disputes in consultation with the Kapitan China, who was the recognized leader of local Chinese communities. Though the Kapitan China played no formal political role, the Kapitan China System was an essential form of inter-ethnic co-operation especially when the Chinese were numerically small compared with the Malays.

In terms of managing the Chinese immigrants, the role of the secret societies during the British rule is also worth noting. These secret societies based on clan or dialect associations were essential organizations affording protection and assistance to Chinese immigrants when they came to the Malay world, a new and often hostile environment. Though these societies had existed before the British administration, they played an increasingly important role in the Chinese immigrant community as a whole, as Chinese immigration expanded in the early twentieth century. The British administration also recognized the essential role of the secret societies in regulating immigrant community affairs in Malaya. In fact, the Kapitan China himself was usually a leading member of a secret society and was himself subject to the loyalties and obligations of his own secret society. The Kapitan China System became less relevant to inter-racial co-operation as Chinese immigrants increased significantly during the British administration and activities of the Chinese were gradually extended to the political sphere.[24]

After the Japanese occupation, a similar experiment of inter-communal consociational practice among the segmental groups in Malaya occurred. The British-sponsored Communities Liaison Committee consisting of six Malays, six Chinese, one Indian, and three other minority representatives (Eurasian, Ceylonese, and European) was established in 1949 and met in August and September of that year to alleviate the immediate problem of inter-communal tension after the outbreak of the communist revolt. The representatives published a statement of "Agreed Views" as a memorandum of the committee's unanimous opinions on long-term political problems of Malaya.[25] Although the Communities Liaison Committee was originally initiated by the British administration and was never embodied in a continuing non-communal organization, prominent leaders of all ethnic communities viewed its style as appropriate for the negotiation of compromise solutions. Furthermore, the experience of the committee taught the communal leaders a lesson in terms of methods of inter-ethnic bargaining. In other words, the committee showed that a significant racial compromise was more likely to emerge from "semi-secret and 'off-the-record' negotiations conducted by communal leaders".[26]

The UMNO-MCA alliance in the 1952 election further encouraged the institutionalization of co-operative strategies in the Malayan political party system. It seemed that, particularly for the Malays, there were three alternatives in the Malayan political party system: a model of ethnic separatism (Pan-Malayan Islamic Party, PAS), a non-communal integration formula (Independence of Malaya Party, IMP), and inter-communal co-operation (Alliance). Of these three alternatives, the inter-communal bargaining model provided a winning formula for the explicitly separate ethnic parties as shown in elections since 1952.

The first election in Malaya was for the Municipal Council of George Town on Penang held on 1 December 1951. Of the three contestant parties — the Radical Party of Penang, the Penang Labour Party, and UMNO — the Radical Party of Penang, campaigning on a "non-communal" platform, won six of the nine seats. Though the 1951 election did not indicate conclusively future trends in Malayan politics, the result suggested a significant lesson at least for UMNO facing the Kuala Lumpur Municipal Council election just two months later. Facing the immediate challenge of the IMP led by Onn bin Jaafar, campaigning against communalism in politics, UMNO had no effective election strategies but to co-operate with the MCA. The MCA, as a communally based political party, also had a reason for joining a common election front with UMNO against the non-communal IMP. IMP was established by UMNO's first president Onn bin Jaafar on 16 September 1951. Onn bin Jaafar initially tried to open UMNO membership to non-Malays and convert the party into a non-communal national party. But his plan was rejected by the other UMNO leaders and he formed a new multi-racial political party IMP. The Kuala Lumpur Municipal Council Election of 1952 was of crucial importance to both the non-communal IMP and the inter-communal Alliance. Apart from its symbolic position as the capital of Malaya, the mixed communal constituencies of Kuala Lumpur revealed that no communal party could win a majority with a strictly communal appeal in the election. So, this election provided a significant empirical test for alternative integrative options in Malaysian politics.[27]

The election results showed that the UMNO-MCA coalition won nine of twelve seats contested. The IMP took only two seats while an independent candidate won the remaining seat. Interestingly, the two elected candidates of the IMP were both MIC members.[28] At this election, the term "Alliance" was not used. Both parties, however, deliberately avoided political and communal issues, effectively depriving the non-communal IMP of a campaign issue. This inter-communal electoral front plainly revealed which formula was the most effective of the three alternative integrative options mentioned above. Soon after the Kuala Lumpur Municipal Council election, Tunku Abdul Rahman said that UMNO "will co-operate with other organizations, but we certainly want to preserve our identity [as a communal party]".[29] Again, at the following municipal elections between December 1952 and December 1953, the Alliance captured eighty-five seats out of the 107 seats contested in fourteen cities of the Federation. Meanwhile, the IMP won only one seat when one of its members was re-elected in the Kuala Lumpur Municipal Council election in December 1952.[30] The successive electoral victories of the Alliance provided evidence of the value of the inter-communal co-operative strategy and consequently led to the idea of institutionalizing the inter-communal power-sharing arrangement. At a National Convention on 23 August 1953, therefore, both parties decided to establish a national Alliance, and a National Executive Council was installed as the supreme authority in September 1954. Then in October 1954, the MIC joined the Alliance. Indeed, the UMNO-MCA common election front and its successful experience brought Malayan ethnic politics into a distinctly new stage of inter-communal grand coalition.

The Relevance of Consociational Politics to the 1957–69 Period

One of the most essential elements of consociational conflict regulation is a grand coalition of the leaders of all significant segment groups to govern the country.[31] In addition, in circumstances where the political risks are high and mutual confidence is uncertain, a larger (and longer-term) coalition is more appropriate than a minimum winning coalition (or government versus opposition). This larger, longer-term coalition is the very feature many scholars have focused on in consociational writings on Malaysian politics.

The Alliance as a political party was officially registered in 1958. However, the leaders of different groups in Malaysia had already established a pattern of grand-coalition co-operation prior to independence. The Alliance of the three main communal parties won a remarkable victory in the first federal election in 1955 by taking all but one of the elected seats. It then formed a cabinet in which all three communal political parties participated. After establishing a stable governing coalition, the Alliance contested two more federal elections in 1959 and 1964. For three consecutive federal elections, the Alliance showed the strength and efficiency of the inter-communal grand coalition in an ethnically divided society by winning convincingly.

As well as the grand coalition, the other key features of consociationalism mentioned by Lijphart are: the mutual veto rule, which serves as an additional protection of vital minority interests; proportionality as the principal standard of political representation, civil service appointment, and allocation of public funds; and a high degree of autonomy for each segment to run its own internal affairs.[32] Although the 1957–69 Malaysian political system did not fully conform to all of these consociational elements, it nonetheless involved the articulation of the main features of consociationalism. The following section will discuss the extent to which the Malaysian political system conformed to the features of consociational arrangement during this period. Major consociational features will be described in two aspects: the formal organization of the Alliance regime and substantial inter-ethnic conflict-regulating practices.

The Structure of the Alliance Regime:
Proportionality and Mutual Balancing

The principle of proportionality means that "all groups influence a decision in proportion to their numerical strength".[33] The proportionality principle can be applied in various fields, such as the allocation of parliamentary seats, administrative positions, and distribution of scarce resources. In so far as the principle decreases the potential for communal tension in the allocation of resources, it appears to serve as an effective conflict-regulating practice.[34]

The Alliance regime can be said to have adhered roughly to the rule of proportionality as far as the formal structure of its decision-making body is concerned. The Alliance had two supreme bodies, the National Council and the National Executive Committee, which comprised representatives from the three communal parties. The National Executive Committee consisted of six UMNO members, six MCA members, and three MIC members. As a primary decision-making body, the National Executive Committee exercised the formal power of selecting candidates and chief party administrators, initiating party policies, and recommending disciplinary actions. The National Council was also composed of proportionally balanced representatives from each party. It was made up of sixteen representatives each from UMNO and MCA and six from MIC. In fact, MCA and MIC were over-represented in these bodies. The proportionality principle, however, disguised the reality that UMNO exercised far more influence than its numerical representation would suggest. The principle of proportionality can also be applied to a special "Alliance Action Committee". This special committee was set up in the aftermath of Singapore's separation in mid-1965 to handle mutual differences and internal conflict within the Alliance. The committee discussed: education and the role of the Chinese language; the Malaysian Malaysia concept, which includes the issues of second-class citizenship and Malay privileges; and the relationship of the three constituent parties within the Alliance structure. This special committee was composed of eight members from UMNO, nine from the MCA, and four from the MIC. The reason for allocating only eight positions to UMNO was to quash the charge that the Alliance and the federal regime were Malay-dominated after Singapore's expulsion.[35]

In addition to the structure of the Alliance's decision-making organization, the governmental power-sharing in the cabinet seems to provide another example of proportionality, though in reality UMNO wielded disproportional influence. In fact, UMNO leaders held most of the important cabinet posts — Prime Minister, Deputy Prime Minister,

Foreign Minister, the Ministries of Education, Interior, and Rural and Economic Development. The limited number of MCA cabinet members, however, was compensated by some members holding key cabinet posts, such as the Ministries of Finance, and Commerce and Industry.[36] Furthermore, MCA played an important role in deciding the composition of the cabinet during this early period. According to Funston, for example, MCA sometimes exercised a veto (or at least significant influence) on the nomination of UMNO figures for cabinet posts. For instance, some UMNO figures could not obtain full cabinet posts or were removed from their post because of direct and indirect opposition or influence from MCA. According to Funston, two prominent UMNO figures, Syed Jaafar Albar and Syed Nasir Ismail, could not obtain full cabinet posts because of MCA's opposition. Similarly, it was because of MCA's intervention that the outspoken Khalid bin Awang Osman, Assistant Minister of Commerce and Industry, was transferred to an ambassadorship in West Germany in late 1965.[37] However, such influence or veto by MCA only operated in a limited and informal manner within the Alliance circle and did not amount to the mutual veto discussed in consociational theory.

At first glance, the figures of the federal public service also support the principle of proportionality in the Alliance government. As shown in Table 3.4, in 1957, federal public service Division I positions, which

TABLE 3.4
Ethnic Composition of Federal Public Service
(Division I), 1957–68 (In percentages)

	1957	1962	1968
Malays	14.1	29.3	36.3
Chinese	13.2	34.0	36.1
Indians	7.0	15.9	21.5
Expatriate	61.0	14.1	0.9
Others	4.6	6.7	5.2

Source: D.S. Gibbon and Zakaria Hj. Ahmad, "Politics and Selection for the Higher Civil Service in New States: The Malaysian Example", *Journal of Comparative Administration* 3, no. 3 (1971): 336.

TABLE 3.5
Ethnic Composition in Selective Public Service
(Division I), 1968 (In percentages)

	Medical	Telecom	Education	MCS	Police	Customs	Immigration
Malays	10.1	17.9	32.2	86.7	43.2	63.4	50.0
Chinese	40.7	44.3	40.3	6.4	30.8	32.7	41.7
Indians	44.6	31.1	24.0	6.4	21.7	4.9	—
Others	4.6	6.7	3.5	0.5	4.3	—	8.3

MCS = Malaysian Civil Service.

Source: Milton J. Esman, *Administration and Development in Malaysia: Institution Building and Reform in a Plural Society* (Ithaca and London: Cornell University Press, 1972), p. 76, tables 5 and 6.

covered professional and administrative works, were dominated by expatriate officers, mostly British. The percentages of positions held by three ethnic communities doubled by 1962. The greatest increase occurred in the Chinese communities. In 1968 the number of positions occupied by expatriates was no longer significant as they had mostly been replaced by Malays. However, the Chinese still enjoyed large numbers in the federal civil service compared with their overall proportion of the population during this period. Especially among Division I posts, the professional and technical services — medicine, health, engineering, statistics, telecoms — were predominantly held by non-Malays, while the Malays were more concentrated in semi-professional or administrative services — customs, prisons, forest, immigration (see Table 3.5).

However, in reality, proportionality did not really give non-Malays matching power in the government. As mentioned earlier, the key posts in cabinet were dominated by UMNO leaders. And in relation to the appointment to the public service, the Malays predominated in the top policy-making positions in the public service and substantially controlled government and administrative organizations, as shown in Table 3.6. In short, while statistics might suggest that the Malays and non-Malays were more or less proportionately distributed throughout the government and administrative services, the key question is whether numerical proportionality resulted in a matching degree of influence. The answer to that question was clearly in the negative.

TABLE 3.6
Ethnic Composition of Higher Administrative Officials in the
Malayan/Malaysian Civil Service,* 1957–68 (In percentages)

	1957	1962	1968
Malays	35.5	79.0	85.1
Chinese	2.5	6.1	7.4
Indians	0.8	5.4	6.4
Expatriate	61.1	9.4	0.2

* The Malayan Civil Service (MCS) was the administrative élite of the public service and the super-ordinate positions were held by members of the MCS.

Source: Gordon P. Means, "Special Rights as a Strategy for Development: The Case of Malaysia", *Comparative Politics* 5, no. 1 (1972): 47.

Consociational Practices of the Alliance Regime: Compromise and Concession

The practice of inter-communal bargaining by the Alliance largely depended on the autonomy of political leaders and their ability to convince the rank and file to follow decisions made at the élite level. Within the Alliance, communal issues were decided by consensus rather than by vote. Sometimes there was intense bargaining behind closed doors; however, once they came to a final decision then it was the responsibility of each party's leaders to obtain compliance from their own rank and file. To achieve this, Malay leaders often went on nation-wide tours to persuade UMNO members and the Malay community at the grass-roots level. In addition, decisions reached between the communal leaders were, in general, not publicly explained to avoid the politicizing of communal issues. In this way, a "purposive de-politicization" was deliberately (and consistently) practised by the Alliance leaders to minimize possible differences among the rank and file.[38] As far as possible, therefore, public discussion of controversial communal issues was deliberately avoided. Esman has described how in Malaysia before May 1969 the Alliance regulated communal conflict according to what has been called an "avoidance model" of conflict management.[39] Two remarkable examples of consociational practice are shown in the package deals of the 1957 constitutional contract and the national language bill of 1967.

The Package Deals of the 1957 Constitutional Contract

The Alliance victory in the 1955 Federal Legislative Council election was followed by a Constitutional Conference held in London from 18 January to 8 February in 1956. At this conference, representatives of the Alliance and Malay rulers agreed that Malaya would become an independent state within the Commonwealth by August 1957, with an independent Constitutional Commission to be appointed to draw up a draft constitution. The Constitutional Commission, as a non-communal and non-partisan body, was composed of an English chairman, Lord Reid, and one member each from Britain, Australia, India, and Pakistan. However, the Alliance submitted its memorandum, the result of the tough bargaining over the relative constitutional position of Malays and non-Malays, to the Reid Constitutional Commission.[40] In February 1957, the Reid Constitutional Commission published *Report of the Federation of Malaya Constitutional Commission*. The Report, however, was not entirely accepted in the 1957 Federation of Malaya Constitution. Consequently, the Alliance's proposals, especially UMNO's views, were subsequently incorporated into the 1957 Federation of Malaya Constitution. One of the most essential differences between the Constitutional Commission's Report and the 1957 Federal Constitution was the constitutional guarantee of Malay special rights. The Commission's Report did not recognize the constitutional status of Malay special rights. According to the Report, "the Malays should be assured that the present [special] position will continue for a substantial period, but that in due course the present preferences should be reduced and should ultimately cease so that there should then be no discrimination between races or communities".[41] However, the recommendation of the Constitutional Commission on this issue was firmly rejected in the end. In the 1957 Federation Constitution, all provisions for their future re-evaluation or eventual abolition were deleted and Malay special rights received specific constitutional status as mainly defined in Article 153.[42]

The original agreement on the constitutional contract was a trade-off between Malays and non-Malays, in particular UMNO and the MCA. As a major concession from the Malays, the constitutional package gave non-Malays liberal citizenship regulations. In return, non-Malays had to accept the constitutional status of Malay special rights in various fields, such as language, religion, and the status of the Malay rulers.

In detail, the constitutional contract further relaxed citizenship regulations for non-Malays and, more importantly, accepted the concept of *jus soli* for those born after independence as stated in Article 14, that is, citizenship was obtainable, subject to Clause (2) of Article 14, to all those born in the Federation on or after *Merdeka* (that is, after "freedom" or independence).[43] In addition, provisions for acquiring citizenship by other means were made easier. For instance, any person of or over the age of eighteen years who was a resident of the Federation at independence was eligible to be registered as a citizen if he had an elementary knowledge of the Malay language, "except where the application is made within one year after Merdeka Day and the applicant has attained the age of forty-five years at the date of the application".[44] Consequently, these liberal citizenship requirements would — in the long run — increase the voting strength of the non-Malays, and therefore the potential political power of the non-Malays. Though the Reid Commission's recommendations to create Malayan citizenship on the principle of *jus soli* was highly controversial, all of the citizenship recommendations were incorporated into the constitution with the backing of the Alliance.[45]

According to the constitutional contract, Malay was to become the sole official language from 1967 unless Parliament decided otherwise (Article 152). However, the using, teaching, or learning of Chinese and Tamil languages were not prohibited. For a period of ten years after Merdeka Day, along with Malay, the continued use of English as an official language in any legislative or court was guaranteed. But no other languages were permitted in legislative proceedings.[46] Islam was to become the official religion of the Federation, but the freedom of other religions was to be guaranteed (Article 3). The symbolic position of Malay rulers was to continue and rotate among the nine sultans who also headed their respective states (Article 153). In particular, Article 153 of the Federation Constitution empowered the Yang di-Pertuan Agong, the King, to protect the special position of the Malays and specified the sphere of privileges. One crucial means of protecting the Malay special position was through the practice of a quota (or preference) system. These included: the operation of quotas within the public service reserving a certain portion for the Malays, especially in the administrative and diplomatic areas; the operation of preferences for permits and licences for certain trades and businesses; special quotas or preferences for scholarships, exhibitions, and other educational or training privileges; reservation of certain lands for exclusive ownership and use by Malays only (Article 153).[47]

The National Language Bill 1967

Communal disputes over language and education continued for ten years, and many Chinese were apprehensive as the day for the adoption of Malay as the sole national language approached. For instance, the *Razak Report* (Report of the Education Committee) was published in 1956 to set the guidelines for the development of Malayan education. The *Razak Report* was clearly directed towards the achievement of nation-building through a common educational system. The Malays demanded that the government implement the *Razak Report*'s recommendations swiftly. This led to the formation of the National Education Policy, as spelt out in the Education Act 1961. It clearly stressed the establishment of a common curriculum with the main medium of instruction, Bahasa Malaysia.[48] In these circumstances, the Chinese community was reluctant to accept the clause in the 1957 Federal Constitution which had delayed the implementation of the national language provisions for ten years until 1967. Most vocal were the Union of Chinese Teachers, Chinese guilds and associations, and the MCA Youth Organization who initiated protests against the implementation of the national language provision. These groups also demanded the establishment of a Chinese-medium Merdeka University.[49] While the Central Working Committee of the MCA was not in a position to support these movements because of its alliance with UMNO, they asked "for the more liberal use of Chinese language in selected fields and in Government notices, forms and so on".[50]

On the initiative of Tunku Abdul Rahman, then Prime Minister and President of UMNO, a new compromise was therefore worked out within the Alliance, which resulted in the National Language Bill being introduced in Parliament on 24 February 1967. The Bill provided for the implementation of Malay as the sole official language, but it made provision for the continued use of English for official purposes and a liberal use of the non-Malay languages for non-governmental and non-official purposes. The Alliance government described the Bill as "a course guaranteeing peace" because it was "opposed to that [attitude] of the chauvinists, as represented by the non-Malay opposition parties, and the 'ultras' as represented by the Pan Malayan Islamic Party".[51]

In addition to the written constitutional contract between the Malays and the non-Malays, inter-communal bargaining consisted of another, widely acknowledged, feature. That was the guaranteeing of political and governmental superiority for the Malays on the one hand and the continued role of the Chinese in the economy (with liberal political participation) on the other. At the élite level, non-Malays recognized that Malays were politically superior by virtue of their indigenous status and that the Malaysian polity would have a Malay character by means of the constitutionally guaranteed special positions. In particular, Malays were to be assured of safe majorities in both the state and federal parliament by the delineation of constituency boundaries, which favoured the predominantly Malay rural areas. Therefore, Malays would control the highest positions of the government and they would dominate members of the federal cabinet. In return, the Malay élites were to agree that the non-Malays would not be unduly subject to restrictions on their economic activities. While the non-Malays were to assist Malays to catch up economically, they were assured of free participation in the entire modern economy. Esman describes the inter-ethnic compromise of the Alliance government as follows:

> ... [the] political bargain realized great benefits for all parties, in many cases more than the original participants had expected to achieve. The Malays gained political independence, control of government, and a polity which was to be Malay in style and in its system of symbols. In return the Chinese gained more than overseas Chinese in Southeast Asia had dreamed of — equal citizenship, political participation and office holding, unimpaired economic opportunity, and tolerance for their language, religion, and cultural institutions.[52]

These arrangements clearly deviated from a strict reading of the consociational concept but were integral parts of the Malaysian constitutional bargain.

Towards the Undermining of Consociationalism

From 1955 to 1963, Malays felt secure in their special position in Malaya. By virtue of the numerical superiority of the electorate and the constitutional guarantee of Malay special rights, the political paramountcy of Malays had not been threatened in any serious manner by non-Malays. Singapore's entry into the new federation, however, had a huge impact on Malaysian society as a whole.[53] Again, mutual fears and suspicions between the Malays and the Chinese were to spread in the rank and file as well as in the communal élites.

Firstly, the overall ethnic composition of Malaysia dramatically changed after Singapore joined the Federation. The former numerical superiority of the Malays in Peninsular Malaysia was overtaken by the increased number of non-Malays, due to the inclusion of the Singapore Chinese, as shown in Table 3.3. In addition, even though the electorate of Singapore was not counted in the 1964 federal election, the difference in the number of voters between the Malays and the Chinese had further narrowed from 22.6 per cent (1959) to 16.9 per cent (1964), as shown in Table 3.2. Obviously, this electoral gap between the Malays and the Chinese would have been even narrower if the electorate of Singapore were considered. Therefore, UMNO leaders were immediately concerned with restricting Singapore's role in federal politics. This was done by allocating Singapore, which made up 16.6 per cent of the population, only fifteen seats of the total 159 parliamentary seats of Malaysia (9.4 per cent). On the contrary, Sabah and Sarawak, where *bumiputera* formed a large part of the population, were allocated sixteen and twenty-four seats (10.1 per cent and 15.1 per cent respectively), although their population made up of only 4.6 per cent and 7.4 per cent of the total population.[54]

To limit the role of Singapore in federal politics, a special Singapore citizenship provision was also created which barred Singapore citizens from voting and contesting elections in Malaya.[55] This was because the approach of the Singapore-based People's Action Party (PAP) to federal politics threatened both the Alliance regime and Malay society as a whole. In the first Singapore Legislative Assembly election after the formation of Malaysia, held on 21 September 1963, the PAP captured a majority of thirty-seven out of a total of fifty-one seats. The Singapore Alliance

(UMNO, MCA, and Singapore People's Alliance) failed to take any seats while the Barisan Socialis won thirteen seats. More importantly, UMNO's Singapore branches lost to the PAP in all the Malay-majority constituencies where the latter had fielded their own Malay candidates.[56] As the only body to achieve a genuine multi-racial social base without losing the confidence of the non-Malay masses, the PAP gave the impression that they sought to replace the MCA in the Alliance. For this reason, perhaps, the PAP decided to contest the federal election in 1964.[57] Even though the PAP leadership was very keen to establish a partnership with UMNO in the Alliance, UMNO leaders, especially "ultras", considered the participation of the PAP in the federal election as evidence of Lee Kuan Yew's ambition to extend his influence across the causeway.

Eventually, the intense mutual suspicion between UMNO and the PAP resulted in considerable intensification of racial antipathy in Malaysian society. One manifestation was the 1964 Singapore racial riots. Following the miserable defeat in the 1963 Singapore Legislative Assembly elections and the victory in the 1964 federal elections, UMNO organized a mass protest rally of about 12,000 Malays and formed an "Action Committee" to demand special privileges for the Malays in Singapore. The Action Committee demanded special privileges for the Singapore Malays in job quotas, scholarship stipends, land reservations, and exclusive Malay occupancy rates at a special reduced price in certain government-built housing projects.[58] The PAP strenuously rejected the desirability of preferred treatment based on race and a bitter confrontation between the two parties escalated into several racial riots during July and September 1964.[59] It was reported that thirty people were killed, 260 injured, and over 1,130 arrested during the racial riots.[60] Closely related to these political processes, in fact resulting from them, was the PAP's idea of "Malaysian Malaysia". The essence of the idea was that "Malaysia was conceived as belonging to Malaysians as a whole and not to any particular community or race".[61]

In brief, Singapore's entry into, and the PAP's approach to, the Federation substantially and simultaneously threatened the two pillars of Malay political hegemony in Malaysia, specifically numerical superiority and constitutional special rights. Consequently, extreme antagonism among Malays began appearing at both the élite and grassroots levels. Finally, this series of events was followed by Singapore's expulsion from Malaysia on 9 August 1965.

Although Singapore was removed from the Malaysian political scene after only two years of merger, its impact continued to be felt. Singapore's secession immediately eliminated the internal threat which had challenged Malay political paramountcy. After Singapore's removal, the Malays restored their former numerical superiority. For the Malay community as a whole, however, the PAP's activities sharply intensified Malay suspicion and fear of the Chinese. On the other hand, the Chinese community became increasingly aware of the danger that the Chinese would be reduced to an insignificant minority in the Federation. The Chinese were shaken by the reasons for Singapore's expulsion and consequently the PAP had an impact on the awakening and articulating of the Chinese political consciousness.[62] It was in this context that the Democratic Action Party was inaugurated on 19 March 1966. There had not been a major non-Malay opposition party, communally based, until the DAP was established. Due to the intensification of communal fears, the DAP was soon able to establish itself as the main Chinese opposition party in Peninsular Malaysia.

Meanwhile, towards the end of August 1967, full diplomatic relations were resumed between Malaysia and Indonesia. As did the expulsion of Singapore, the end of the "Confrontation" had a great effect on Malaysian ethnic politics too. Improved relations between Malaysia and Indonesia eventually removed the external threat which had provided strong motivation for inter-ethnic co-operation within the Alliance system over the last few years. Coincidentally, the tenth anniversary of Malayan independence approached. Again, the Alliance leaders were forced to face crucial issues of national language and education just as they had before independence. However, the political situation at this time was totally different from the years before and immediately after independence. In short, mutual fear and suspicion within the Alliance did not come out very strongly when the main preoccupation was obtaining independence, or when Singapore and Indonesia seemed to pose significant threats — although of different types. The major political issues, however, were totally different in the absence of immediate external threats.

Since the expulsion of Singapore from the Federation, racial tension in Malaysia had intensified as a result of the controversy during late 1966 and early 1967 in connection with the National Language Bill, as discussed above. Mutual fear and antipathy were generated during the process of compromise over the National Language Bill between the Malays and the non-Malays. Furthermore, the compromise over the national language issue led to serious divisions among Malay intellectuals, within UMNO as well as within the Malay community itself.[63] After the passage of the Bill, dissatisfaction grew among many Malays within and outside UMNO. Mass demonstrations were held by various groups including the Malay Teachers' Associations, the Malay Language Society of the University, and the National Writers Association. All of these groups united under the leadership of the National Language Action Front to get the Bill changed. Within UMNO itself there was some discontent, not just with the Bill but also with the leadership of the Prime Minister, Tunku Abdul Rahman.[64] More importantly, however, this controversy reopened and intensified the emotive issues of language, education, the political position of the non-Malays, and the Malays' economic status.

In sum, one of the crucial conditions for successful consociationalism is that segmental leaders be recognized by the masses. However, one of the most important aspects of the post-1963 period in Malaysia was the increased politicization of both Malays and Chinese, with the result that segmental leaders no longer exercised sufficient authority over their own communities. And the gradual polarization of communities during the period 1963–69 was heading towards the breakdown of inter-ethnic consociational conflict management.

Consociational Regime Maintenance Breaks Down

When the 1969 election results were released, both the Alliance and opposition parties were surprised at the strong performance of Chinese opposition parties and the losses suffered by the Alliance. To celebrate their election success, the Democratic Action Party (DAP) and the Gerakan Rakyat Malaysia (Malaysian People's Movement or Gerakan) held "victory parades" in Kuala Lumpur on 11 and 12 May. Subsequently, on the evening of 13 May, a "counter-demonstration" by Malays in response to the opposition's victory processions was organized by local UMNO branches in the courtyard of the Selangor Menteri Besar's residence. Two Chinese passing by in a car were attacked and killed. And so the May 13 racial riots began.[65]

The May 13 racial riots were the single most intensive case of inter-racial violence Malaysia had undergone since independence. Although racial violence was nothing new to Malaysia during the years before and after independence, outbreaks were usually relatively small in scale and localized. The May 13 racial riots, however, resulted in an extensive loss of life and property. What was worse was that they erupted in the nation's capital, Kuala Lumpur. According to official figures, 196 people were killed from 13 May to 31 July and some 6,000 residents of Kuala Lumpur, 90 per cent Chinese, were made homeless.[66] However, informed observers, such as journalists and non-government sources, claimed that the actual number was much higher.[67] More seriously, the immediate cause of the racial riots was a very sensitive issue in Malaysian ethnic politics — Malay special rights. The May 13 racial riots constituted a huge challenge to the Malaysian political system and penetrated deeply into the national consciousness.

The government initially blamed communists for the racial violence. Soon after the riots, Tunku Abdul Rahman claimed that "the terrorist communists [had] worked out their plan to take over power. They [had] managed to persuade voters by threat, by intimidation, and by persuasion to overthrow the Alliance through the process of democracy."[68] Tunku Abdul Rahman claimed that the combination of communists, especially the Labour Party, and the provocative Chinese opposition parties was the fundamental cause of the racial riots. As evidence, he drew upon the development of the situation initiated by the Labour party shortly before the 1969 elections. On 3 December 1968, the Labour Party announced its boycott of the election. The rationale for the Labour Party's election boycott was the arrest of a number of people on 9 November 1968, including prominent Labour Party members accused of working with the illegal Malayan Communist Party. While painting anti-election slogans, a Labour Party activist was shot by the police on 4 May 1969. The Labour Party held the funeral procession on 9 May and *darah bayar darah* (blood will be paid by blood) was among the many slogans. Tunku

Abdul Rahman linked this Labour Party–sponsored funeral procession with the Chinese opposition victory parades.[69]

However, it was later acknowledged that the influence of communism was not directly responsible for the 1969 racial riots. Ismail, Minister of Home Affairs, admitted later: "We found they [the communists] were as much surprised as we were [at the outbreak of the racial violence]".[70] Even before this, in a separate statement, Ismail claimed: "Democracy is dead in this country. It died at the hands of the opposition parties who triggered off the events leading to this violence".[71] In fact, the appeal of the Chinese opposition parties, especially the DAP, to Chinese communal interest during the elections proved more attractive than the Labour Party's call for a boycott of the elections. The official report of the National Operations Council (NOC) viewed the fundamental cause of the racial riots in terms of communal polarization and animosity between the Malays and the Chinese. The NOC's analysis of the roots of the May 13 racial riots emphasized: (1) Malay dissatisfaction over the non-implementation of long-standing policies, such as language policy and education policy; (2) the non-Malay provocation of Malay sensitivities by challenging their special rights or privileged position guaranteed under Article 153 of the Constitution; and (3) a growing sense of insecurity felt by the Malays due to racial imbalance particularly in the economic field.[72]

Growing Racial Sentiment and the Loss of Segmental Mass Support

Why was the 1969 general election so special that it caused unprecedented racial violence and led to the collapse of the Alliance system? When the Alliance system was established in 1955, the drive for *Merdeka* dominated Malayan society. Therefore, the general election in 1955 was seen as a test of the possibility of independence for both the Malays and non-Malays. In addition, neither the 1959 election nor the 1964 election fully tested the viability of the Alliance system. The 1959 election was held in a general mood of "the freshness of independence" and, furthermore, the non-Malay communities were to a large extent on the "defensive" during the years shortly after independence.[73] Although the sensitive issues of language and education were raised in the 1959 election, the non-Malay political parties were too weak and lacked the mass support to mobilize these sensitive issues for a full-scale election campaign. In the 1964 election, the immediate external threat of the Indonesian Confrontation distracted the election campaigning from the sensitive issues of Malaysian ethnic politics — Malay special rights, language, and education. It should also be remembered that states of emergency were in place in both 1959 and 1964. Therefore, the Alliance was able to recover losses it had suffered in the 1959 general election.

The political mood of 1969, however, was entirely different. Although the emergency had not been formally lifted, the end of "Confrontation" with Indonesia had been followed by considerable relaxation. Up to 1968, the main opposition to the Alliance had come from the Malay party PAS while the non-Malay opposition had been divided between the People's Progressive Party (PPP) and the Socialist Front. Besides, PPP was strong only in Perak and PAS showed its strength only in the predominantly Malay states of Kelantan, Terengganu, and Kedah. None of these opposition parties ever obtained significant nation-wide support in the elections before 1969.

Two new non-Malay opposition political parties, however, were extensively involved in the 1969 election campaign. One was the DAP. Being perceived as a successor of the Singapore-based PAP, the DAP was well-known and became the first nation-wide Chinese opposition party in Malaysia. The other was Gerakan. Although Gerakan put forward a more or less moderate non-communal platform, it also strongly appealed to the Chinese vote, especially in Penang. Accordingly, its policies on the sensitive issues of language and education were similar to, though more moderate than, those of the DAP.[74] In particular, the DAP introduced a new element into the Malaysian political scene as the party revived the "Malaysian Malaysia" issue, which had led to the expulsion of Singapore, during election campaigning. This aroused strong communal sentiment in the Chinese community.[75]

For the first time the Alliance was faced with well-organized, nation-wide Chinese opposition parties as well as its old foe, the Malay opposition party PAS in the 1969 elections. Both Malay and non-Malay opposition parties appealed to sensitive communal issues in the absence of over-arching national issues. On the Malay side, PAS instigated Malays to abandon UMNO because it was selling out Malays' indigenous rights to the immigrant races. On the Chinese side, the DAP mobilized the Chinese by accusing the MCA of selling out their political rights to the Malay hierarchy. Consequently, towards the end of the 1960s in Malaysia the principle of "de-politicization", one of the key elements for consociationalism, no longer applied. Even before the election campaign had begun, both the major partners in the Alliance, UMNO and the MCA, were threatened by the more open and volatile communal situations. As a result of the deepening of communal differences initiated by Lee Kuan Yew's concept of a Malaysian Malaysia, the MCA, as a component of the Alliance, had been put under pressure by those who accused it of selling out Chinese political rights to the Malays. The compromising attitude of the conservative UMNO leaders over sensitive issues, as shown in the fairly liberal National Language Act in 1967, meant that UMNO was also vulnerable to an increasing threat from PAS who were appealing to the Malay rural electorate.

The results of the 1969 election were a shock to the Malay community. Although the Malay opposition PAS increased its influence, what was apparent from the election results was a massive gain for the Chinese opposition parties at the expense of the Alliance, especially the MCA. As Table 3.7 shows, the Alliance lost control of Penang, Perak, and Kelantan, while it gained only half of the state seats in Selangor, creating a potential deadlock with the combined opposition parties. In Selangor, out of the total twenty-eight contested seats, DAP took nine seats, Gerakan four, and independents took one. Furthermore, in most states the Alliance recorded poorer results at both the federal and state levels. As shown in Table 3.8, Gerakan gained control of the Penang state legislative assembly. PAS retained control of the Kelantan state legislative assembly. In the Perak state election, PPP obtained twelve seats, DAP six, Gerakan two, and PAS one, while the Alliance won fewer than half of the seats (nineteen out of forty). In sum, the Alliance obtained the majority of votes in only four states — Johor, Kedah, Pahang, and Perlis.

Why then did the racial crisis occur in Selangor but not in Penang and/or Perak where the UMNO-led Alliance government actually lost control of state power? It is necessary to consider this question in order

TABLE 3.7
Federal and State Elections: Seats Won, Contested,
and Percentage of Votes Won by the Alliance in 1964 and 1969

	Federal		State	
	1964	1969	1964	1969
Johor	16/16 (71.7%)	16/16 (67.6%)	32/32 (67.5%)	30/32 (65.0%)
Kedah	12/12 (68.6%)	9/12 (53.5%)	24/24 (67.8%)	14/24 (53.5%)
Kelantan	2/10 (42.9%)	4/10 (47.5%)	9/30 (42.9%)	11/30 (47.5%)
Malacca	4/4 (66.2%)	2/3 (45.2%)*	18/20 (65.1%)	15/20 (48.3%)
Negeri Sembilan	6/6 (58.9%)	3/6 (46.4%)	24/24 (58.7%)	16/24 (46.2%)
Pahang	6/6 (71.3%)	6/6 (60.8%)	24/24 (68.4%)	20/24 (55.1%)
Penang	6/8 (47.3%)	2/8 (36.9%)	18/24 (47.2%)	4/24 (33.6%)
Perak	18/20 (55.4%)	9/20 (43.2%)	35/40 (54.7%)	19/40 (43.6%)
Perlis	2/2 (68.9%)	2/2 (51.2%)	11/12 (60.9%)	11/12 (53.5%)
Selangor	12/14 (53.9%)	9/14 (44.0%)	25/28 (55.5%)	14/28 (41.6%)
Terengganu	5/6 (56.5%)	4/6 (49.99%)	21/24 (55.3%)	13/24 (49.3%)
Total	89/104	66/103	241/282	167/282
	(58.4%)	(48.4%)	(57.6%)	(48.0%)

* Election of one constituency in Malacca was postponed.

Sources: Compiled from Vasil (1972, pp. 73–96); NSTP Research and Information Services, *Elections in Malaysia: A Handbook of Facts and Figures on the Elections 1955–1990* (Kuala Lumpur: New Straits Times Press, 1994).

TABLE 3.8
State Elections: Seats Won, Contested, and
Percentage of Votes Won by the Opposition in 1969

	Penang	Perak	Kelantan	Selangor
DAP	3/3 (8.4%)	6/8 (9.5%)	—	9/12 (31.1%)
Gerakan	16/19 (46.8%)	2/2 (3.8%)	—	4/8 (16.5%)
PPP	0/3 (0.4%)	12/13 (24.6%)	—	—
PAS	0/5 (7.0%)	1/28 (18.4%)	19/30 (52.2%)	0/12 (9.6%)
Party Rakyat	1/1 (1.2%)	—	—	—
Independents	0/3 (1.7%)	0/1 (0.1%)	0/6 (0.3%)	1/2 (1.3%)

— = Data not available.

Source: Compiled from Vasil (1972, pp. 76, 80, 81, and 83).

to understand the political background of the breakdown of consociational conflict resolutions.

Although the Malay population in Selangor was smaller than the Chinese, its political significance was very different from that of Penang and Perak. In the state of Selangor, one of the Malay sultanates, the Malays had traditionally dominated elections since 1955. Unlike Penang where election results were not perceived as the transfer of power from the indigenous to the immigrant faction, a power shift in Selangor would have been regarded as a shift in political control from the UMNO-led Alliance to the DAP-led Chinese opposition. In Perak, though it is also a Malay sultanate, racial tension between the Chinese and the Malays was not as severe as in the state of Selangor.[76]

However, anger and anxiety were stirred up because pro-government Malays perceived the pattern of voting in the Selangor state elections as a betrayal of the consociational bargain by the Chinese. While the Malays voted solidly for UMNO as shown in UMNO's overwhelming win in twelve out of the thirteen state seats it contested, many Malays viewed the enormous losses of the MCA (eleven out of twelve contested seats) to Chinese opposition parties as evidence that "the Chinese had betrayed the Alliance formula by voting for an [Chinese] opposition that had revived fundamental questions of language and Malay special rights".[77] Malays considered that the Chinese no longer respected the promises (or compromises) made at the time of independence between UMNO and the MCA, regarding language and Malay special rights. Frustration and anxiety amongst Malays thus arose from the uncertain situation in Selangor where fourteen Alliance candidates and opposition members were elected respectively. To break the deadlock, UMNO tried to persuade Gerakan to join in the formation of a coalition state government. Gerakan rejected this, as Gerakan's secretary-general Tan Chee Khoon put it: "I have said many times that I will not sleep with Alliance partners. ... Now more than ever when they are castrated, how can I do so?"[78] Meanwhile, the DAP announced its intention of forming a coalition government in Selangor with other opposition parties. In addition, the DAP's secretary-general Goh Hock Guan indicated that the party would look into the legal implications of the constitutional provision that only a Malay could be appointed Menteri Besar in Selangor.[79] However, according to the Selangor state constitution, there was no provision that the *menteri besar* must be a Malay or a Muslim. What was worse for the Malays, there was no Malay assembly person among the Selangor opposition members who could be put forward as a possible *menteri besar*.

With racial tensions already running high, the Chinese opposition-organized "victory" parades on 11 and 12 May exacerbated "the darkest Malay fears of being turned into 'aborigines' in their own country".[80] The slogans carried in the victory processions by the Chinese suggested just this: *Kuala Lumpur sekarang China punya* (Kuala Lumpur now belongs to the Chinese); *Orang Melayu balek kampong* (Malays go back to the villages); *Melayu sekarang tidak ada kuasa lagi* (Malays now no longer have power); and *Semua Melayu kasi habis* (Finish off all Malays). Tunku Abdul Rahman blamed the victory parade as the immediate cause of the racial riots, as follows:

> That this victory procession should be followed up by another by UMNO on May 13th was inevitable, as otherwise the party members would be demoralized after the show of strength by the Opposition and the insults that had been thrown at them.[81]

The NOC's official report also implies that the primary cause of the racial violence was the fear of Chinese dominance: "The Malays who already felt excluded in the country's economic life, now began to feel a threat to their place in the public services [that is, political control]."[82]

Ethnic Polarization Undermining Consociational Framework

In analysing the more fundamental causes of the disintegration of consociational élite co-operation, the concepts of "group comparison" and "group entitlement" are worth noting.[83] According to Horowitz, ethnic differences have produced an extraordinary amount of ethnic conflict in many post-colonial nation-states. Specifically, he highlights the "backward-advanced dichotomy" between indigenous and immigrant groups as the most common source of ethnic conflict in many African, Asian, and Caribbean post-colonial plural societies.[84] In a situation where socio-economic backwardness and indigenousness are combined, the claims and responses of the backward-indigenous groups are likely to be demands for preferential treatment in the socio-economic arena (for example, education, employment, or business), as well as political dominance. On the contrary, the advanced-immigrant groups are reluctant to accept the legitimacy of such demands by the backward-indigenous groups since they can be considered politically backward in comparison with the indigenous groups.[85] Consequently, when the backward-indigenous groups are dissatisfied with the progress of the so-called "catch up" programmes and "feel under siege in their own home" even in the political arena, violent political activity can be aroused.[86]

In Malaysia, the years after 1960, especially during the First Malaysia Plan, 1966–70, saw extensive development activities. As the long MCP-inspired emergency came to an end, the Alliance government was able to concentrate more on development than security. A new Ministry of National and Rural Development was formed to ensure the speedy and efficient implementation of the rural development programme. More emphasis was placed on development and progress of rural areas, which presumably benefited the Malays more than anyone else. However, under the Alliance rule in the 1960s, ethnic inequalities were mostly addressed indirectly, without undertaking any vigorous preferential programmes to improve the economic status of the Malays. The Alliance government hoped that economic imbalance among the ethnic communities would fade away through policies aimed at rapid economic growth and assistance to the rural poor, who were mostly Malays.

Through these developments, various quasi-government institutions came into existence. For example, the Federal Land Development Authority (FLDA, later FELDA) began as a scheme for land settlement in 1956.[87] Another body, the Rural and Industrial Development Authority (RIDA) was established in 1950 and reorganized fifteen years later as the Majlis Amanah Ra'ayat (Council of Trust for the Indigenous People, MARA).[88] Other organizations were also created, including the Federal Agricultural Marketing Authority (FAMA) established in 1952 and the Bank Bumiputera formed in 1965.[89] The achievements of these statutory bodies, however, were limited during the Alliance government's fifteen-year rule. For example, in 1969 the total commercial bank loan in Malaysia was RM1,801 million.[90] In contrast to this, during 1951–70, the total loan from RIDA and MARA, the only major sources of credit to Malays before 1965, was only RM70 million. This meant that over a twenty-year period, total loans to Malays amounted to less than 4 per cent of the loans from commercial banks during one year.[91]

Various figures show that the Malays were in danger of falling further behind non-Malays, especially the Chinese, regarding ownership of the Malaysian economy, especially in terms of patterns of ownership, distribution of wealth, and participation in the modernization and development processes. The Malay perception of the problem of economic imbalance is demonstrated in the *Second Malaysia Plan 1971– 1975,* as follows:

> Despite the significant progress made in improving the economic well-being of the have-nots, *the problem of economic imbalance* remained. ... Indications are that wide gaps in income and living conditions between the traditional sector (both rural and urban) and the modern sector continued to exist. They arose from differing opportunities for education, employment and ownership of or access to entrepreneurial resources. These differences were accentuated by the concentration of Malays and other indigenous people in the low-income activities.[92]

The extent of economic imbalance among ethnic communities can be clearly illustrated in the field of ownership. As shown in Table 3.9, only 1.5 per cent of limited companies' share capital in Peninsular Malaysia was owned by Malays at the end of 1969, whereas 22.8 per cent was held by the Chinese and 62.1 per cent by foreign-controlled companies or branches of companies incorporated overseas.

TABLE 3.9
Ownership of Share Capital of Limited Companies
in Peninsular Malaysia, 1969

Companies Incorporated in Peninsular Malaysia	RM ('000)	Percentage
Malays and Malay interests	70,633	1.5
Chinese	1,064,795	22.8
Indians	40,983	0.9
Federal and state governments	21,430	0.5
Nominee companies	98,885	2.1
Other individuals and locally controlled companies	470,969	10.1
Total foreign ownership	2,909,845	62.1
Total	4,677,540	100.0

Source: *Second Malaysia Plan 1971–1975,* p. 40.

In fact, this figure shows that the predominant power and perhaps ultimate control of the Malaysian economy was in non-Malaysian hands, not the Chinese. However, as noted by Mauzy, "perceptions and myths [of relative economic deprivation] are as important as the objective truth" in an ethnically divided society.[93] In the early period of independence, the widespread perception was that the Chinese dominated the economy and, through various means, inhibited Malay participation in the modern economy. Furthermore, it could not be denied that many more Malays fell below the poverty line than did Chinese. The employment pattern in Malaysia until 1970 showed that the Malays were predominant in agricultural sectors, whereas non-Malays were predominant in mining, plantations, manufacturing, construction and commerce. For example, the tin mining industry, which is highly capital-intensive, was over-whelmingly dominated by non-Malays. Although the National Land Council recommended the government prospect for tin in Malay Reservation Land and encouraged Malays to take up mining leases, only 2 per cent of mining land was leased to Malays.[94] At any rate, towards the end of the 1960s, in terms of economic power the Malays had fallen behind the immigrant peoples and the need to address the economic imbalance inevitably led to growing ethnic conflict.

Another serious imbalance appeared in the field of education, showing a frustrating economic pattern for the Malays. Mainly due to the admission quotas, as shown in Table 3.10, the overall enrolment percentages of Malay students gradually increased from twenty-two to thirty-one to forty-five during the 1961/62, 1965/66, and 1969/70 sessions at the University of Malaya. However, despite preferential treatment in admission, the Malays were greatly under-represented in the professional and technical areas. As shown in the 1965/66 period, Malay students' enrolment in the faculties of engineering, science, and medicine at the University of Malaya were only 3, 7, and 12 per cent respectively. Furthermore, the relatively high proportion of Malay students in the faculties of medicine, economics, and administration during the 1965/66 and 1969/70 sessions concealed the higher drop-out rates for Malays, thus giving an inflated sense of their educational achievements.[95] Though there was a gradual improvement in Malay enrolment in general, the overall difference between the Malays and

TABLE 3.10
Student Enrolment, by Faculty, at University of Malaya

	Malay	Non-Malay
1961/62		
Agriculture	4 (16.0%)	21 (84.0%)
Arts	91 (35.4%)	166 (64.6%)
Engineering	1 (1.2%)	81 (98.8%)
Science	7 (7.4%)	88 (92.6%)
1965/66		
Agriculture	21 (44.7%)	26 (55.3%)
Arts	294 (45.0%)	359 (55.0%)
Engineering	3 (3.0%)	98 (97.0%)
Science	13 (7.1%)	169 (92.9%)
Medicine (pre-medic and first-year)	15 (12.3%)	107 (87.7%)
1969/70		
Agriculture	25 (26.3%)	70 (73.7%)
Arts	722 (58.8%)	505 (41.2%)
Engineering	5 (4.4%)	109 (95.6%)
Science	79 (25.7%)	228 (74.3%)
Medicine (pre-medic and first-year)	50 (30.1%)	116 (69.9%)
Economic and Administration	197 (39.0%)	308 (61.0%)

Source: Government of Malaysia, *Towards National Harmony* (Kuala Lumpur: Government Press, 1971), pp. 11–12.

non-Malays, especially the Chinese, in the professional and technical fields was profound.[96] Many (well over half) Malay students were studying in non-professional subjects, such as Malay Studies or Islamic Studies. It was therefore apparent that Malays were hardly "keeping pace with the rapidly expanding professional and technical ranks of the other communities".[97]

There might be some doubt about the Alliance consociational framework being a major factor sustaining socio-economic ethnic polarization in the Malaysian society. Nonetheless, it was widely believed that the government's efforts to eliminate ethnic imbalances were far from effective during the fifteen years of Alliance rule. And towards the end of the 1960s, it became clear that many Malays were increasingly dissatisfied with the Alliance-type consociational arrangement which had demonstrated little efficacy regarding Malay economic concerns.

Summary

In a study analysing the political behaviour of eighteen multi-ethnic states scattered throughout the world, Rabushka and Shepsle conclude that the correlation was, and still is, weak between political stability and cultural diversity in the post-independence politics of many post-colonial plural societies. Rather, they argue that "intense ethnic conflict frequently erupts shortly after native peoples obtain their independence".[98] However, the newly independent multi-ethnic Malaysian society did not seem to fit this picture. Until the late 1960s, the Alliance regime appeared stable enough to manage various controversial inter-racial tensions and was able to maintain a relatively successful democratic stability. At least for the first twelve years of independence, the newborn multi-ethnic Malaysian state seemed to provide evidence that peaceful racial harmony, or co-existence, was possible in a relatively competitive democratic framework. During this period, the Malaysian political system demonstrated some of the main features of consociational politics. In particular, the presence of inter-ethnic élite co-operation within the Alliance government and the sufficient rank and file support made Malaysian politics consociational in the earlier period of independence. In the course of élite co-operation, the segmental leaders employed some basic elements of consociationalism — such as the proportionality principle, mutual balancing, compromises and concessions — although they had rather limited application in practice.

Nonetheless, the consociational arrangement did not always maintain the political legitimacy of the Alliance regime. After the mid-1960s, the Alliance regime faced greater challenges from both Malays and Chinese demanding greater economic benefit and political rights respectively. Ethnically based political forces, especially opposition parties, increasingly challenged the Alliance framework of compromise and bargain by instigating growing racial sentiment. Especially after 1965, this resulted in the increased politicization of Malaysian ethnic society. It became clear that the Alliance's segmental leaders no longer exercised sufficient authority over their own masses.

According to the Malay perspective in particular, the consociational Alliance regime did not seem to guarantee their intrinsic privileged political hegemony as an indigenous people, even though Malays recognized the superior economic position of non-Malay immigrants. The non-Malays, especially the Chinese, increasingly challenged Malay political hegemony, which was an essential part of the Alliance bargain. For Malay élites, the 1969 election results were enough to prove the inadequacy of the consociational model as regime maintenance because their main counterpart Chinese élites were no longer fully recognized by the segmental masses. The consociational Alliance regime eventually collapsed when escalating Malay grievances over the undermining of their special political position turned into serious inter-racial riots in 1969. For UMNO leaders, it was therefore a natural step to renegotiate the consociational arrangement, or to find an alternative, in order to maintain their own political security in a situation of deepening ethnic conflict.

NOTES

1. Arend Lijphart, *Democracy in Plural Societies: A Comparative Exploration* (New Haven and London: Yale University Press, 1977), p. 150.

2. Tunku Abdul Rahman Putra, *May 13: Before and After* (Kuala Lumpur: Utusan Melayu Press, 1969), pp. 91 and 94. Tunku Abdul Rahman was the first Prime Minister of Malaysia.

3. Eric A. Nordlinger, *Conflict Regulation in Divided Societies* (Cambridge, Mass.: Center for International Affairs, Harvard University, 1972), pp. 33–39; Alvin Rabushka and Kenneth A. Shepsle, *Politics in Plural Societies: A Theory of Democratic Instability* (Columbus, Ohio: Charles E. Merrill Publishing Company, 1972).

4. Lijphart (1977, pp. 150–53).

5. Lijphart (1977, pp. 53–103) and Grehard Lehmbruch, "Consociational Democracy in the International System", *European Journal of Political Research* 3 (1975): 377–91.

6. Lijphart (1977, pp. 54–55).

7. Lehmbruch (1975, p. 380).

8. Lijphart (1977, p. 64).

9. Lijphart (1977, p. 55).

10. Lijphart claims that the presence of a majority or near-majority segment is the most unfavourable configuration for consociational democracy. For more details, see Lijphart (1977, pp. 55–61).

11. Lijphart (1977, pp. 71–83).

12. Lehmbruch (1975, p. 380).

13. See Nordlinger (1972, pp. 43–46). Also see Lehmbruch (1975, p. 382).

14. The huge number of British documents during this period shows the influence of the British colonial government on Malayan politics in the years 1942–57. For a complete collection of these British documents, see A.J. Stockwell, ed., *Malaya* (London: HMSO, 1995), British Documents on the End of Empire Project, Series B, Volume 3. The part of Malaya is composed of three parts: Part I, The Malayan Union Experiment (1942–48); Part II, The Communist Insurrection (1948–53); and Part III, The Alliance Route to Independence (1953–57).

15. "The Situation in Malaya", cabinet memorandum by Lyttleton, the Secretary of State for the Colonies, 20 November 1951, see Stockwell (1995), *Malaya,* Part II, pp. 310–15.

16. A note by H. Gurney, the High Commissioner of the Federation of Malaya, expressing his concerns on the Chinese community, see Stockwell (1995, *Malaya,* Part II, pp. 300–1).

17. For a more detailed analysis on the 1955 election, see Francis G. Carnell, "The Malayan Elections", *Pacific Affairs* 28, no. 4 (1955): 315–30. For details of the 1964 election, see R.K. Vasil, "The 1964 General Elections in Malaya", *International Studies* 7, no. 1 (1965): 39–56; and K.J. Ratnam and R.S. Milne, *The Malaysian Parliamentary Election of 1964* (Singapore: University of Malaya Press, 1967).

18. Nordlinger (1972, p. 46).

19. R.S. Milne and K.J. Ratnam, "Politics and Finance in Malaya", *Journal of Commonwealth Political Studies* 1, no. 3 (1965): 196.

20. Heng Pek Koon, *Chinese Politics in Malaysia: A History of the Malaysian Chinese Association* (Singapore: Oxford University Press, 1988), p. 164.

21. For more details on citizenship regulations, see Federation of Malaya, *The Federation of Malaya Agreement, 1948 as Amended* (Kuala Lumpur: Government Press, 1956), pp. 40–43.

22. Lehmbruch (1975, p. 381).

23. Lijphart (1977, pp. 99–103).

24. For more detailed explanations on the Kapitan China System and the secret societies, see Victor Purcell, *The Chinese in Malaya* (London: Oxford University Press, 1948), pp. 155–73; C.S. Wong, *A Gallery of Chinese Kapitans* (Singapore: Dewan Bahasa dan Kebudayaan Kebangsaan, Ministry of Culture, 1963); and R.N. Jackson, *Pickering, Protector of Chinese* (Kuala Lumpur: Oxford University Press, 1965).

25. For details of the Communities Liaison Committee, see Gordon P. Means, *Malaysian Politics* (London: Hodder and Stoughton, 1976), pp. 122–24.

26. Means (1976, p. 124).

27. For discussions on non-communalism versus communalism within UMNO and Malay opposition to Onn bin Jaafar's plan, see Means (1976, pp. 124–27). An explanation of the early elections in Malaya is provided in Means (1976, pp. 132–37).

28. The MIC joined with IMP during the Kuala Lumpur Municipal Election of 1952.

29. *Straits Times*, 28 February 1952, quoted in Means (1976, p. 135).

30. For the specific results of municipal elections during this period, see Karl von Vorys, *Democracy without Consensus: Communalism and Political Stability in Malaysia* (New Jersey: Princeton University Press, 1975), p. 109, table 5.1.

31. Lijphart (1977, p. 25).

32. Lijphart (1977, pp. 25–52).

33. Jurg Steiner, "The Principles of Majority and Proportionality", *British Journal of Political Science* 1, no. 1 (1971): 63.

34. Nordlinger (1972, p. 23).

35. For exact listings of Alliance Action Committee and activities, see Cynthia H. Enloe, *Multi-Ethnic Politics: The Case of Malaysia*, Research Monograph No. 2 (California: Center for South and Southeast Asia Studies, University of California Berkeley, 1970), pp. 113–16.

36. N.J. Funston, *Malay Politics in Malaysia: A Study of the United Malays National Organisation and Party Islam* (Kuala Lumpur: Heinemann Educational Books, 1980), p. 13.

37. Funston (1980, pp. 13 and 22 footnote 30).

38. Nordlinger (1972, p. 26).

39. For examples of avoidance measures for conflict management, see Esman (1972, pp. 258–61).

40. For aspects of the process of constitutional bargaining, see Gordon P. Means, "Special Rights as a Strategy for Development: The Case of Malaysia", *Comparative Politics* 5, no. 1 (1972, pp. 29–61); Vorys (1975, pp. 124–39); and Means (1976, pp. 173–81).

41. Federation of Malaya Constitutional Commission, *Report of the Federation of Malaya Constitutional Commission 1957* (Rome: Food and Agriculture Organization of the United Nations, 1957), p. 72.

42. For the differences between the Constitutional Commission's Report and the 1957 Federal Constitution on the issue of the Malay special position, see *Report of the Federation of Malaya Constitutional Commission 1957*, pp. 71–73; Federation of Malaya, *Malayan Constitutional Documents* (Kuala Lumpur: Government Press,

1958), pp. 102–3 (Article 153).

43. For a full description of citizenship regulations, see *Malayan Constitutional Documents*, 1958, pp. 32–41 and L. A. Sheridan, *The Federation of Malaya Constitution* (Singapore: University of Malaya Law Review, 1961), pp. 22–38.

44. *Malayan Constitutional Documents*, 1958, p. 34.

45. Means (1976, pp. 175–77); Vasil (1980, pp. 34–38).

46. *Malayan Constitutional Documents*, 1958, p. 101.

47. For particulars of preferential policies and ethnic quotas, see Boo Cheng Hau, *Quotas versus Affirmative Action: A Malaysian Perspective* (Kuala Lumpur: Oriengroup, 1998).

48. For discussion on the issue of language and education, see K.J. Ratnam, *Communalism and the Political Process in Malaya* (Singapore: University of Malaya Press, 1965), pp. 126–41; Margaret Roff, "The Politics of Language in Malaya", *Asian Survey* 7, no. 5 (1967): 316–28; and Vorys (1975, pp. 199–218).

49. Funston (1980, p. 64).

50. Roff (1967, p. 323).

51. Roff (1967, p. 326).

52. Esman (1972, p. 25).

53. The background to the political unity between Malaysia and Singapore can be found in Means (1976, pp. 292–99) and Vasil (1980, pp. 145–48).

54. The figures are calculated from Federation of Malaysia, *Malaysia Population Statistics, Estimated Population by Races and Sex as at 31st December 1964* (Kuala Lumpur: Department of Statistics, 1965).

55. Vasil (1980, p. 148).

56. On the result of the 1963 election, see Means (1976, p. 334).

57. Though only nine PAP candidates contested parliamentary seats, the impact on the Malayan scene was far greater. Because PAP selected several strategic areas (urban and predominantly Chinese) to test its electoral strength, it was perceived as a challenge to the electoral strength of the MCA in the Federation. For further details, see Vasil (1980, pp. 148–52) and Means (1976, pp. 335–41).

58. Willard A. Hanna, "The Separation of Singapore from Malaysia", *American Universities Field Staff* 13, no. 21 (1965): 12–14; Michael Leifer, "Singapore in Malaysia: The Politics of Federation", *Journal of Southeast Asian History* 6, no. 2 (1965): 63–65.

59. On the 1964 racial riots in Singapore, see Richard Clutterbuck, *Conflict and Violence in Singapore and Malaysia, 1945–1983* (Boulder: Westview Press, 1985), pp. 319–22.

60. Means (1976, p. 343).

61. Vasil (1980, p. 156). The idea of Malaysian Malaysia was formulated by Lee Kuan Yew, the Singapore Prime Minister, during February–March 1965. See also Lee Kuan Yew, *Towards a Malaysian Malaysia* (Singapore: Ministry of Culture, 1965).

62. Vasil (1980, p. 158).

63. Roff (1967, p. 327).

64. For particulars of the National Language Bill, see Roff (1967, pp. 326–28); Esman (1972, pp. 32–34); and Funston (1980, pp. 66–67).

65. For more details on the 1969 racial riots, see National Operations Council, *The May 13 Tragedy: A Report of the National Operations Council* (Kuala Lumpur: Government Press, 1969); Tunku Abdul Rahman Putra 1969; John Slimming, *Malaysia: Death of a Democracy* (London: John Murray, 1969); Goh Cheng Teik, *The May Thirteenth Incident and Democracy in Malaysia* (Kuala Lumpur: Oxford University Press, 1971), chapter 3; J. Bass, "Malaysian Politics, 1968–1970: Crisis and Response", unpublished Ph.D. dissertation, University of California, 1973; and Leon Comber, *13 May 1969: A Historical Survey of Sino-Malay Relations* (Kuala Lumpur: Heinemann Asia, 1983), chapter 7.

66. For more specific casualty numbers of the May 13 racial riots, see National Operations Council, 1969, pp. 88–90 and *Straits Times*, 21 June 1969.

67. Bass claimed that the actual number of fatalities was perhaps ten times as great as the official toll. See Bass (1973, p. 249).

68. *Sunday Times*, 18 May 1969.

69. Tunku Abdul Rahman Putra (1969, pp. 8–21 and pp. 197–207).

70. *Straits Times*, 21 June 1969. Though it was not the government's intention, the earlier misperception of the government, police, and the army in considering the racial violence as the work of communists, mainly Chinese, resulted in more violent suppression of the racial riots and consequently led to the massive loss of life, mostly Chinese. On the perception and suppression of the racial riots by the Federal Reserve Unit (FRU, riot squad) and the Royal Malay Regiment, see Anthony Reid, "The Kuala Lumpur Riots and the Malaysian Political System", *Australian Outlook* 23, no. 3 (1969): 268–70.

71. *Straits Times*, 19 May 1969.

72. See the NOC report for more on the root causes of the May 13 riots, National Operations Council, 1969, especially pp. 23–24; and Government of Malaysia, *Towards National Harmony* (Kuala Lumpur: Government Press, 1971), pp. 1–2.

73. Vorys (1975, p. 249) and R.K. Vasil, *The Malaysian General Election of 1969* (Singapore: Oxford University Press, 1972), p. 1.

74. For the full content of the election manifesto by Gerakan, see Vasil (1972, pp. 61–65).

75. DAP directly attacked pro-Malay policies during the election campaign. It campaigned for multi-lingualism, whereby Chinese, Tamil, and English should be given official status along with the Malay language. It also encouraged the use of those languages as a medium for secondary and higher education. Particularly, the DAP gave firm support to a privately mooted scheme for a Chinese-medium university. For more details of the election manifesto of the DAP, see Vasil (1972, pp. 59–61, Appendix I).

76. On the situation in Perak, see Goh Cheng Teik (1971, pp. 25–26).

77. Reid (1969, p. 266).

78. *Straits Times*, 13 May 1969).

79. *Utusan Malaysia*, 13 May 1969.

80. Reid (1969, p. 266).

81. Tunku Abdul Rahman Putra (1969, p. 203).

82. National Operations Council (1969, p. 23).

83. Further analysis on group comparison/entitlement as sources of ethnic conflict can be found in Donald L. Horowitz, *Ethnic Groups in Conflict* (Berkeley: University of California Press, 1985), pp. 141–228.

84. Horowitz (1985, p. 147).

85. Horowitz (1985, p. 215).

86. Horowitz (1985, p. 213).

87. FELDA is engaged in land development and settlement projects, with the objectives of improving the standard of living and increasing the income of the rural population, which has been mainly made up of Malay peasants. Its primary objective was to undertake land reclamation and jungle clearing projects to open up new land for the cultivation of high-yield rubber and cash crops, primarily for Malay peasants. See Means (1976, p. 16).

88. RIDA's primary objectives were economic development and improved social services for rural areas. Its five divisions were concerned with transport, commerce and industry, training, technical services, and credit finance. For more details on RIDA and MARA, see J.H. Beaglehole, "Malay Participation in Commerce and Industry: the Role of RIDA and MARA", *Journal of Commonwealth Political Studies* 7, no. 3 (1969, pp. 216–45). During the period 1966–70, MARA provided about 4,800 loans totalling RM31 million for various projects. It established a number of companies in manufacturing and commerce, producing such products as batik garments, leather goods, handicrafts, timber products, tapioca starch, and pellets and processed rubber. It built shophouses for Malay businesses, and entered into wholesale supply and contracting for construction materials. It also initiated bus services. See Federation of Malaysia, *Second Malaysia Plan 1971–1975* (Kuala

Lumpur: Government Press, 1971), p. 15.

89. FAMA was established to improve the marketing system and to ensure that farmers obtained a fair price for their products. The Bank Bumiputera was established as a commercial bank providing credit, banking services, and technical assistance to Malays and other indigenous people in commerce, industry, and other economic activities. Up to 1970, the Bank Bumiputera had made loans and advances totalling RM134 million, a substantial proportion of which was granted to Malay individuals and businesses for housing development, construction, oil palm cultivation, logging and saw-milling, import and export businesses, manufacturing and small-scale commercial and industrial enterprises. See *Second Malaysia Plan 1971–1975*, pp. 17–18.

90. Treasury Malaysia, *Economic Report 1975–76* (Kuala Lumpur: Treasury's Economics Division, 1975), pp. lxxvi–lxxvii.

91. Federation of Malaysia, *Third Malaysia Plan 1976–1980* (Kuala Lumpur: Government Press, 1976), p. 192.

92. *Second Malaysia Plan 1971–1975*, p. 18, italics in original.

93. Diane K. Mauzy, "Malay Political Hegemony and Coercive Consociationalism", in *The Politics of Ethnic Conflict Regulation*, edited by John McGarry and Brendan O'Leary (London: Routledge, 1993), p. 108.

94. For a more in-depth explanation on the low rate of Malay participation in the field of tin and timber industry, see M.H. Lim, "Affirmative Action, Ethnicity and Integration: The Case of Malaysia", *Ethnic and Racial Studies,* 8, no. 2 (1985): 259.

95. Means (1972, p. 45).

96. For the breakdown of first-year students in the Humanities and the Sciences, see *Towards National Harmony* (Government of Malaysia, 1971), p. 14, table 3.

97. Means (1976, p. 20).

98. Rabushka and Shepsle (1972, p. 207).

Regime Change towards UMNO Dominance

In deeply divided societies where consociational techniques have not been, or cannot be, successfully employed, control may represent a model for the organization of intergroup relations that is substantially preferable to other conceivable solutions ... (Ian Lustick 1979).[1]

This government is based on UMNO and I surrender its responsibility to UMNO in order that UMNO shall determine its form — the government must follow the wishes and desires of UMNO — and it must implement policies which are determined by UMNO. (Tun Abdul Razak 1970)[2]

During the period 1957–69, the newly established Malaysian state opted for political compromise which meant by implication that Malays retained political prominence while the non-Malays, especially the Chinese, kept their strong economic position, even though the modern economy continued to be dominated by foreign capital. As described in the previous chapter, the component parties of the Alliance government had both incentive and capacity to engage in mutual compromise in order to avoid internal collapse and to maintain their legitimate influence over their segmental ethnic groups. It also appeared that the intensity and volume of communal demands were relatively moderate and negotiable to a large extent in such a mutual deterrence situation.

However, the relatively amicable ethnic relations were not built on strong foundations. As Mahathir Mohamad noted, racial harmony in the first decade of independence was "neither real nor deep-rooted" but was rather the "absence of open inter-racial strife". Moreover, the absence of overt struggle was not necessarily "due to lack of desire or reasons for strife" but mostly "due to a lack of capacity to bring about open conflict."[3] The changed political environment in the second decade of independence, however, demonstrated that such mutual compromise (or avoidance) was no longer effective. Towards the end of the 1960s, the non-Malay communities became more vocal in their demands for greater political equality. To a greater extent, the Malays, especially a group of young Malay leaders, were worried that the Alliance regime's compromising approach would ultimately cause them to be marginalized in the political and economic sphere. Consequently, growing ethnic anxieties led to the breakdown of political order which took the form of the bloody racial riots in May 1969.

It would be wrong to view the post-1969 situation exclusively in terms of the absence of inter-ethnic bargaining. The previous consociational compromises, however, were no longer perceived as workable means for maintaining the UMNO-led government's political hegemony. One of the most obvious features of post-1969 developments was the shift in the UMNO leaders' attitude from moderate consociational bargaining to one of more repressive hegemonic control. It was the May 13 racial riots which provided crucial impetus for the younger and more radical UMNO leaders to take the initiative in Malaysian politics and create "an alternative behavioural code". Although the political system was restored soon after the relatively short period of emergency rule and the existing constitutional contract (or compromise) continued to be implemented, the style of Malaysian politics changed significantly after the May 13 riots. Since then, "the threat of a racial riot" has been used by UMNO leaders as an enduring means of regime maintenance.

Consensual bargaining was not entirely absent in post-1969 ethnic politics. However, as Milne has argued, "the *existence* of hegemony sets stricter limits on the consensual element" and Malaysia became "closer to the control end" from "near the consensus end" on a control-consensus spectrum.[4] Lijphart also notes that post-1969 Malaysian politics violated the essential elements of consociationalism because of the emergence of the new rules of the game which prohibited Malay supremacy ever being seriously challenged.[5] In fact, even before 1969, non-Malays recognized the privileged position of Malays. It was nonetheless after 1969 that the Malays' advantage was further institutionalized at almost every level of Malaysian politics.

What then made the UMNO-led government transform its conflict management tactics into strategies of more repressive control in the aftermath of the 1969 racial riots? In other words, what were the motives for the Malay ruling élites changing the consensual way of regime maintenance? And, what were the essential elements of the new conflict management strategies? What new political developments occurred in the post-1969 phase of Malaysian politics? These questions are the main concerns of this chapter.

Chapter 4 is divided into three parts. The first part analyses UMNO's motives for shifting to hegemonic methods of control over consociational bargaining for resolving political conflict. The second part focuses on the key elements of the UMNO-led government's anti-crisis strategies after the May 13 racial riots. The third part describes the growth of intra-ethnic conflict, especially among the dominant UMNO leaders, in the 1980s.

Motives Behind UMNO's Hegemonic Control

Consociationalism, as a method of achieving political stability in deeply divided societies, focuses on the subnational élites' capacity for mutual compromise, bargaining, and accommodation. The likelihood of a consociational system increases when a number of favourable conditions are present.[6] The previous chapter noted that at the point of independence the Malaysian political configuration conformed to some favourable consociational conditions. Towards the end of the 1960s, however, the favourable conditions (or motives) for successful consociational arrangements were absent or had been replaced by negative elements. These changes seemed to help, or at least did not present obstacles to, the UMNO leaders' shift in conflict management strategies.

The Absence of the Existing Favourable Consociational Conditions and the Changed Role of the Masses

Lijphart claims that stable communal accommodation succeeds by disregarding pressure from the masses. This implies that successful adaptation of accommodative manœuvres by segmental group leaders requires restriction on the communication of sensitive public issues to the masses.[7] In a similar vein, it is believed that an "indirect and positive" attitude of the masses contributes to enhancing the degree of political autonomy among communal leaders. It appears that in the earlier period of Malaysian ethnic politics the UMNO and MCA leadership enjoyed a relatively high degree of autonomy, which enabled successful consociational bargaining.

However, as the Malaysian society moved into its second decade of independence, the role of the segmental masses became more "direct and negative". After the expulsion of Singapore in particular, the acquiescent attitude of the masses towards their traditional leaders were replaced by open criticism. The non-Malay communities, especially the Chinese, were upset because they believed Singapore was forced out of the Federation because it had raised the issues of non-Malays' political rights and the position of their cultures and languages.[8] For Malays, growing communal demands posed a serious threat to their special position and political supremacy. Although political élites continued to manage their respective communities when faced with the demands of the communal extremists, the principle of depoliticization seemed to operate no longer as both the Malay and the non-Malay communities became more and more politically aware.

Unlike the earlier period of independence in Malaysia, this time there were no external pressures or threats, which had provided the most effective incentive to consociational power-sharing arrangements. After the Indonesian "Confrontation", the Alliance leadership tried to drum up an external threat by exaggerating the dispute with the Philippines over the ownership of Sabah. The Alliance, however, did not successfully mobilize mass support at this time.[9] Instead, as the country approached the second decade of independence, the Alliance regime faced stronger internal pressure from both Malay and non-Malay opposition parties. In particular, the DAP functioned as a channel for raising sensitive ethnic problems and in so doing gained communal support. Unlike the PAP, which was removed from the Malaysian political scene, the DAP became an institutionalized challenger to the stability of the Alliance regime. In these circumstances, the principle of mutual benefit between Alliance component parties, one of the key inducements for inter-ethnic compromise, subsided or was even replaced by a principle of mutual costs, as shown in the 1969 election results.

Moreover, since the mid-1960s, the successful experience of inter-ethnic co-operation had gradually been overshadowed by worsening racial violence, as evidenced by the 1964 Singapore racial riots, the 1967 Penang racial crisis, and the 1969 severe racial riots. In these circumstances, mutually hostile and politicized attitudes became more common among the segmental masses who no longer played an indirect and positive role. When the masses began to engage in racial violence, the existing consociational practices failed either directly because of the masses' violence or because of the political leaders' inability to implement the necessary regulatory practices.[10] Crouch describes the changed situations after the 1969 racial riots:

> In circumstances where politicians from all communities feel compelled to adopt rigid policies on ethnic issues, compromise becomes almost impossible to achieve with the result that multi-ethnic coalitions either break apart or cannot be formed in the first place. Ethnic antagonisms continue to grow; and, in the end, multi-ethnic democratic government is likely to be replaced by a regime dominated by a single ethnic group that resorts to authoritarian means to consolidate its power.[11]

Undermining the Credibility of the Alliance Model

Lijphart argues that the successful operation of a consociational model necessitates not only a willingness on the part of the élites to co-operate and compromise with each other but also the ability to maintain the allegiance and support of their respective communities.[12] As mentioned in the previous chapter, the successful experience of UMNO and the MCA in the 1952 Kuala Lumpur Municipal Council elections motivated the beginning of the consociational Alliance regime. Since then, it has been assumed by some that the consociational power-sharing arrangements worked successfully to win elections in the first decade of independence in Malaysian politics as demonstrated by the uninterrupted election victories of the Alliance.

However, this assumption may not be correct in all cases. Detailed records of the general elections from 1955 to 1969 reveal that the Alliance-style of inter-ethnic co-operation was vulnerable to campaigns dominated by sensitive ethnic issues (for example, language, education, culture, political position of the non-Malays, and economic backwardness of the Malays). With the exception of the 1964 election, when the country was preoccupied with an immediate external threat, the performance of the Alliance deteriorated markedly in successive elections after 1955. In particular, the election results of 1969 revealed "the lack of confidence" that the respective ethnic communities had in the Alliance's component parties, especially the MCA and MIC.

Although Malay voters also showed an increasing preference for the Malay opposition PAS, UMNO's election results from 1955 to 1969 remained relatively stable and strong, as shown in Table 4.1. The biggest loser was the Chinese component party of the Alliance. Especially in 1969, the MCA lost twenty contested parliamentary seats, winning only thirteen seats out of the total thirty-three contested seats. Compared with an 81.8 per cent success in 1964, it had dropped sharply to 39.4 per cent in 1969. What was even worse, among the thirteen winning constituencies, three were in Malay-dominated constituencies and the remainder included relatively large numbers of Malay voters (average 30 per cent). Conversely, all of the lost constituencies were Chinese-

TABLE 4.1
The Alliance Federal Election Results, 1955–69:
Seats Won, Contested, and Percentage of Seats Won

	1955	1959	1964	1969*
UMNO	34/35 (97.1%)	52/70 (74.3%)	59/68 (86.8%)	51/67 (76.1%)
MCA	15/15 (100%)	19/31 (61.3%)	27/33 (81.8%)	13/33 (39.4%)
MIC	2/2 (100%)	3/3 (100%)	3/3 (100%)	2/3 (66.6%)
Alliance total	51/52 (98.1%)	74/104 (71.2%)	89/104 (85.6%)	66/103 (64.1%)

* The election in one constituency in 1969 was postponed.

Source: Compiled from Goh Cheng Teik, *The May Thirteenth Incident and Democracy in Malaysia* (Kuala Lumpur: Oxford University Press, 1971), p. 12.

TABLE 4.2
The 1964 and 1969 Parliamentary Elections: Seats Won, Contested,
and Percentage of Votes for the MCA, DAP, and Gerakan

	MCA (1964)	MCA (1969)	DAP (1969)	Gerakan (1969)
Johor	5/5 (23.8%)	5/5 (25.4%)	0/6 (21.5%)	0/2 (4.2%)
Kedah	2/2 (12.1%)	2/2 (8.3%)	—	0/2 (5.5%)
Kelantan	—	—	—	—
Melaka	2/2 (31.5%)	1/2 (25.9%)	1/1 (22.8%)	—
Negri Sembilan	2/2 (17.2%)	0/2 (15.4%)	3/3 (35.5%)	—
Pahang	1/1 (12.3%)	1/1 (—)	—	—
Penang	2/4 (19.3%)	1/4 (12.5%)	1/1 (11.2%)	5/5 (44.6%)
Perak	8/10 (28.8%)	1/10 (18.4%)	5/6 (16.1%)	1/1 (3.7%)
Perlis	—	—	—	—
Selangor	5/7 (25.4%)	2/7 (21.9%)	3/7 (31.4%)	2/4 (17.5%)
Terengganu	—	—	—	—
Total	27/33 (18.7%)	13/33 (13.5%)	13/24 (13.7%)	8/14 (8.6%)

— = Data not available.

Source: Compiled from Vasil (1972, pp. 85–96).

TABLE 4.3
The 1964 and 1969 State Elections: Seats Won, Contested, and
Percentage of Votes for the MCA, DAP, and Gerakan

	MCA (1964)	MCA (1969)	DAP (1969)	Gerakan (1969)
Johor	11/11 (21.9%)	9/10 (19.3%)	1/12 (18.0%)	0/3 (2.0%)
Kedah	5/5 (14.4%)	2/5 (10.1%)	—	2/3 (5.0%)
Kelantan	1/1 (2.2%)	1/1 (2.0%)	—	—
Melaka	4/6 (17.8%)	4/7 (13.0%)	4/5 (12.8%)	1/1 (4.5%)
Negri Sembilan	9/9 (22.2%)	4/9 (15.1%)	8/16 (36.4%)	—
Pahang	7/7 (15.8%)	4/7 (15.7%)	0/1 (1.7%)	1/1 (2.0%)
Penang	6/12 (19.7%)	0/12 (14.0%)	3/3 (8.4%)	16/19 (46.8%)
Perak	12/16 (21.6%)	1/17 (15.5%)	6/8 (9.5%)	2/2 (3.8%)
Perlis	2/2 (12.2%)	—	—	—
Selangor	9/12 (24.2%)	1/12 (17.5%)	9/12 (31.1%)	4/8 (16.5%)
Terengganu	1/1 (2.5%)	—	—	—
Total	67/82 (17.4%)	26/80 (12.7%)	31/57 (11.8%)	26/37 (8.8%)

— = Data not available.

Source: Compiled from Vasil (1972, pp. 73–84).

dominated and were won mainly by the Chinese opposition parties, the DAP and the Gerakan.[13] The MCA did even worse in the state assembly elections, recording miserable defeats in most state seats where the Chinese were predominant in Selangor, Penang, and Perak. As shown in Table 4.3, the MCA won only one out of the twelve contested seats in Selangor; it failed to obtain any seat out of twelve contested seats in Penang; and the party secured only one out of the seventeen seats it contested in Perak. Meanwhile, another Alliance party, the MIC, also lost seven out of the ten state seats it contested in 1969, whereas it obtained ten out of eleven contested seats in the 1964 state elections.[14]

These figures suggest that the non-Malay Alliance parties, especially the Chinese-based MCA, could not retain the support and confidence of their own rank and file. The results, therefore, triggered UMNO leaders to doubt the adequacy of Alliance-style co-operation as a winning formula and thus created severe strains within the Alliance regime after the 1969 elections.[15] Even before the outbreak of the May 13 racial riots, the MCA leadership faced increased pressure from UMNO leaders who blamed the MCA for Alliance losses. For example, shortly after the 1969 election, a group of young UMNO leaders proposed a new cabinet list which deprived the MCA of the two key portfolios of Finance, and Commerce and Industry.[16] This was followed by a sharp reaction from the MCA announcing its withdrawal from participation in the new government.[17] The MCA's move was widely viewed as a gesture to regain its support by focusing the Chinese community's attention on the inter-ethnic bargaining mechanisms of the Alliance government. Nonetheless, within MCA circles, there were growing fears of Malay dominance of the Alliance regime. Addressing a party seminar at Ipoh on 16 March, Tan Siew Sin, the leader of the MCA, expressed his concerns as follows:

> If the opposition manages to wrest key seats from the MCA, it will mean that the country will be ruled by an Alliance Government without Chinese participation. It would mean in effect a confrontation between a Government without Chinese participation and a practically all-Chinese opposition.[18]

In short, after the 1969 election and subsequent racial riots, the disastrous election outcome and the growing lack of confidence on the part of the non-Malays in their respective communal parties in the

Alliance provided a political reason for UMNO leaders to seek an alternative mode of regime maintenance.

National Tragedy as a Circumstantial Advantage

The May 13 racial riots, perceived as a national tragedy, provided a "circumstantial advantage" for UMNO leaders to adopt a new regime maintenance strategy strongly based on hegemonic control. In other words, the violent uprising of May 13 ensured that the political configuration inclined to unambiguous Malay dominance led by a more communally oriented younger UMNO leadership.

Within UMNO, the riots affected the power balance of party leadership and led to a change from a moderate and accommodative group, led by Tunku Abdul Rahman, to a more Malay-oriented group, led by then Deputy Prime Minister Tun Abdul Razak. Tun Razak was able to initiate pro-Malay policies as the racial crisis contributed to heightened communal consciousness among UMNO members as well as to Malays in general. They were able to force the conservative party leadership to implement government policies which the former had earlier avoided. Meanwhile, the national tragedy provided the immediate motives for a group of young and communally oriented UMNO leaders to return to mainstream Malaysian politics. After the unrest, Ismail Rahman, an UMNO stalwart who had retired in 1967, was recalled to a top government position as the Minister of Home Affairs. Further, as soon as Tun Razak replaced Tunku Abdul Rahman as Prime Minister in September 1970, Mahathir Mohamad and Musa Hitam, who had been the most overtly critical of Tunku Abdul Rahman's concessions to the non-Malays — and had, in Mahathir's case, been expelled from UMNO — were quickly brought back to mainstream UMNO politics.[19]

The brutal race riots also enabled UMNO's political leaders to adopt more rigid preferential policies which affected the non-Malay communities, in part because it was the only workable option for them. The Alliance's Chinese political leaders also acknowledged the necessity of changes to restore inter-racial harmony after the crisis. Although Chinese leaders did not necessarily agree with the detailed remedies proposed by the UMNO-led government, they acknowledged that a new course was required to restore political order in the post-racial crisis situation.[20] In short, the terrifying experience of open racial strife provided the UMNO-led government with a legitimate reason for the adoption of authoritarian government control.

To some extent, the rule of bargaining continued to be utilized. The political system, however, was much simpler and clearer after the racial upheaval. Various sensitive issues would not be resolved by traditional compromise among the Alliance partners. As Vorys notes, the final decision would be made by "what the top UMNO leaders considered fair".[21] On this point, Horowitz argues that the May 13 racial riots could be considered by the younger group of UMNO leaders as a "blessing in disguise" because they enabled "a realization of the need for drastic action". He commented that:

> As disasters are often used by advocates of a policy to put it on the policymakers' agenda and to neutralize opposition, the violence of 1969 performed these functions in Malaysia, making possible the adoption of policies previously shunned because they appeared ethnically biased and loaded against merit criteria.[22]

In sum, the 1969 general election results and the May 13 racial riots threatened the continued operation of consociational conflict resolution. These crises also provided an opportunity for the UMNO leadership to take definite measures, both to strengthen its political hegemony in the Alliance and to implement firmer government control over imminent and potential political opposition.

Renegotiating the Consociational Contract

Following the violent events of 1969, changes took place in almost every field of Malaysian society — political, legal, economic, social, and even ideological. The various changes or alternative strategies adopted by the UMNO-led government contained two main features. Firstly, most Malays rejected the existing consociational approach exemplified by Tunku Abdul Rahman's compromised political leadership. Secondly, alternative strategies necessarily led to the strengthening of UMNO as the dominant group in the government, in terms of its economic position as well as its political hegemony. These dramatic changes were initiated by the emergency government called the National Operations Council (NOC).

Immediately after the May 13 riots, a state of emergency was declared over Selangor and Kuala Lumpur by the Yang di-Pertuan Agong (the King) under Article 150 of the Constitution. As a result, both Parliament and state legislative assemblies were suspended and the elections scheduled for Sabah and Sarawak later in May and June were postponed indefinitely. More importantly, all government authority was assumed by an emergency government, the NOC, headed by Deputy Prime Minister Tun Razak. The NOC consisted of several Alliance leaders and top representatives of the police, armed forces, and public service. The nine council members were composed of seven Malays and two non-Malays, one Chinese from the MCA, and one Indian from the MIC, whereas the Cabinet was composed of ten Malays and four non-Malays. Therefore, the proportionality of the Alliance's consociational formula was completely abandoned.

The immediate aim of the NOC was to co-ordinate government, armed forces, and police activities in an effort to re-establish and maintain security and order. However, the NOC extended its role beyond the immediate attainment of social order and continued to exercise full power for twenty-one months until February 1971. During the NOC's rule, several thousand people were detained under emergency orders. According to the government, these included communists, hard-core terrorists, subversive elements, saboteurs, and secret society members. But they also included a number of prominent opposition leaders, such as the Gerakan's V. David and the DAP's Lim Kit Siang. Furthermore, several local newspapers, such as *China Press*, one of the country's largest Chinese-language dailies, were suspended and all party publications, pamphlets, and posters were banned, including those of the Alliance.[23] While the Cabinet continued to meet under the leadership of Prime Minister Tunku Abdul Rahman, its role had been reduced to a symbolic, or routine, role and substantial administrative power was in fact transferred to the NOC under the leadership of Tun Razak. Although the NOC made preliminary moves to restore representative institutions and inter-communal dialogue through the creation of new mechanisms, such as the National Consultative Council (NCC) and the Department of National Unity (DNU), ultimate power over policy and administration remained with the NOC. Commenting on the NOC's administration, Means argues:

> ... the emergency [government] represented *a termination of the intercommunal "élite accommodation system"* and it also may have effectively disguised *a quasi-coup* whereby the political leadership of the Prime Minister and Cabinet had been partly supplanted by the Deputy Prime Minister, Abdul Razak, backed by the combined powers of the army, police, and bureaucracy.[24]

Under the rule of the NOC, three main elements — the ideology, the bans, and the plan — were introduced as anti-crisis strategies. These three anti-crisis strategies would be seen as complementary elements in a tricky situation brought to the surface by the racial riots of 13 May 1969.

The Ideology: The "Rukunegara" as the Nation's Guiding Principle

Drafted by the DNU, debated in the NCC, and approved by the NOC, the national ideology or set of guiding principles was proclaimed on 31 August 1970 by the Yang di-Pertuan Agong. Officially, this was referred to as the *Rukunegara*.[25] It outlined five beliefs — achieving a united nation, maintaining a democratic society, creating a just society, ensuring a liberal society, and building a progressive society.[26] In order to materialize these beliefs, the *Rukunegara* presented five principles by which the Malaysian peoples were to be guided. The five principles were:[27]

Belief in God (*Keperchayaan kepada Tuhan*)
Loyalty to King and Country (*Kesetiaan kepada Raja dan Negara*)
Upholding the Constitution (*Keluhoran Perlembagaan*)
Rule of Law (*Kedaulatan Undang Undang*)
Good Behaviour and Morality (*Kesopanan dan Kesusilaan*)

In terms of beliefs and principles, the *Rukunegara* was a general statement. Most beliefs and principles of the *Rukunegara* had already appeared in the existing Malaysian Federal Constitution. As a major product of the NCC, an inter-communal body set up to provide a forum for discussion of important issues in the absence of Parliament, the *Rukunegara* tended to provide reassurance of fundamental agreements, the package deals of the Constitution, that had been the prime product of inter-élite communal bargaining.[28] In particular, the third principle of the *Rukunegara* emphasized the duty of Malaysian people to respect the letter, the spirit, and the historical background of the Constitution, including such provisions as those regarding: the position of the Yang di-Pertuan Agong and the rulers, the position of Islam as the official religion, the position of Malay as the national and official language, the special position of the Malays and other natives, the legitimate interests of the other communities, and the conferment of citizenship.[29] The fourth and fifth principles described rather general, or impartial, rights of citizens, as follows: "Fundamental liberties are guaranteed to all citizens. These include liberty of the person, equal protection of the law, freedom of religion, rights of property and protection against banishment ..."[30] and "No citizen should question the loyalty of another citizen on the ground that he belongs to a particular community".[31] It seemed that the *Rukunegara*, as a set of basic national principles, was neither favourable to the Malays nor unfavourable to the non-Malays. The *Rukunegara* seemed to be an appropriate preamble to the Malaysian Constitution.

However, the significance of the national ideology declaration would depend less on "the frequency with which people memorized it or invoked it", than on "the method and the persistence with which the government could implement it".[32] From this perspective, it is necessary to focus on how the rhetoric of the national ideology could be implemented practically. The key questions are: to what extent would the UMNO-led government substantially practise the tenets of the *Rukunegara* and succeed in influencing the people in that direction? How could the government utilize the *Rukunegara* as a behaviour code for daily life?

In response to these questions, it is worth noting that the UMNO-led government introduced or strengthened legal restrictions in nearly every field of political life. Such provisions, which related to the "sensitive" or "controversial" matters in Malaysian society, were included among new or revised laws, such as the Constitution (Amendment) Act, the Internal Security Act, the Official Secrets Act, the Sedition Act, the Printing Presses Act, and the Universities and University College Act. Practically, restrictions operated as a compelling force for political parties as well as for individuals to follow the national ideology as a behaviour code. Consequently, most sensitive and controversial issues of Malaysian society were removed from the realm of public discussion and the acceptance of the national ideology was to be "a prerequisite for participation in the political life of the country" after the May 13 racial riots.[33]

The Bans: Amendments to the Constitution
and Enactment (or Revision) of Repressive Laws

A clear trend towards authoritarian control was demonstrated in the amendments to the Constitution. After Parliament was reconvened in February 1971, its first decision was to pass the Constitution (Amendment) Bill. The new constitutional amendments were proposed in a White Paper (entitled *Towards National Harmony*) issued by the government. The proposed amendments to the Federal Constitution were designed to achieve two objectives: "to remove sensitive issues from the realm of public discussion so as to allow the smooth functioning of parliamentary democracy; and to redress the racial imbalance in certain sectors of the nation's life and thereby promote national unity".[34]

The overt purpose of the Constitution (Amendment) Act 1971 was the removal of certain topics identified as "sensitive issues" from the realm of public discussion or political debate. To achieve this aim, Article 10 (Freedom of speech, assembly, and association) of the Federal Constitution was amended so that Parliament was empowered to pass laws prohibiting the questioning of certain sensitive matters. The new Article 10(4) of the Constitution, aimed at restricting public discussion of four sensitive issues, made it an offence to question "any matter, right, status, position, privilege, sovereignty or prerogative established or protected by the provisions of Part [citizenship], Article 152 [the national language], 153 [the special position and privileges of the Malays and the natives of Sabah and Sarawak], or 181 [the sovereignty of the rulers]" of the Federal Constitution. Furthermore, the Constitution (Amendment) Act 1971, by amending Article 63 (Privileges of Parliament) and 72 (Privileges of Legislative Assembly), applied the same restrictions on freedom of speech to the members of Parliament and state assemblies, removing their parliamentary immunity when speaking on topics identified as sensitive issues.[35]

However, even before Parliament was restored and Article 10 of the Federal Constitution had been amended, these changes had already been largely in force through the amendment of the Sedition Act 1948. The Sedition Act 1948 was amended by Emergency Ordinance No. 45 of 1970 promulgated by the Yang di-Pertuan Agong. What was newly proposed in the Constitution (Amendment) Bill was the extension of these restrictions on the freedom of speech on certain sensitive issues to Parliament itself as well as to state assemblies. The opposition argued that to deprive the member of Parliament of the privilege of free speech in discussing certain topics was incompatible with the principle of the sovereignty of Parliament. Also, it was not clear whether the ban (on discussing the sensitive issues) could be applied to the discussion of the ban itself in Parliament. Given the difficulties of the ban's application and legal interpretation, the Constitution (Amendment) Bill was constitutionally complex.[36]

As well as the amendment to the provisions on the freedom of speech, assembly, and association, the Constitution (Amendment) Act 1971 also applied to Article 152. Article 152(1) originally declared that the Malay language shall be the national language, but this clause was subject to the proviso that "no person shall be prohibited or prevented from using (otherwise than for official purposes) ... any other languages".[37] There was no express definition of "official purposes".[38] However, this time, the Constitution (Amendment) Act 1971 added a new clause which defined the term "official purposes" as "any purpose of the Government, whether federal or state, and includes any purpose of a public authority". "Public authority" means the Yang di-Pertuan Agong, the ruler or Yang di-Pertuan Negeri of a state, the federal government, the government of a state, a local authority, a statutory authority exercising powers vested in it by federal or state law, any court or tribunal other than the Federal Court, the Court of Appeal and High Courts, or any officer or authority appointed by or acting on behalf of any of those persons, courts, tribunals, or authorities.[39]

Article 153, the provision which empowers the Yang di-Pertuan Agong to safeguard the special position of the Malays, was also amended. The Constitution (Amendment) Act 1971 added the words "and natives of any of the States of Sabah and Sarawak" immediately after the word "Malays" in Clause 6 of Article 153. By virtue of Clause 6 of Article 153, the natives of Sabah and Sarawak were given the same special status as the Malays. The elevation of the status of the natives of the Borneo states can be interpreted as part of the effort to restore Malay dominance in the political arena by including the indigenous peoples in East Malaysia. In this very context, as part of the NEP, the UMNO-led government introduced the concept of the *bumiputera* (incorporating both the Malays and other natives but excluding "immigrant races"). Prior to the Constitution (Amendment) Act 1971, the natives of the Borneo states were not entitled to reservation of special positions, such as fixed proportions in relation to scholarship, exhibitions, and other educational or training privileges and facilities for the natives. In addition to elevating the status of the natives of these states, Article 153(8A) empowers the Yang di-Pertuan Agong to direct any university, college, or other educational institutions at post-secondary level to reserve a certain proportion of places for Malays and natives of Sabah and Sarawak. The intention of such an amendment was "to reserve places in those *selected courses of study where the numbers of Malays are disproportionately small*".[40]

Finally, changes were made in Article 159 which provides for the amendment of the Constitution. The major impact of this amendment was to enhance the power and role of the Conference of Rulers in the amendment process itself. Certain provisions were already entrenched by Clause 5 of Article 159, which provides that the consent of the Conference of Rulers was required to amend them — Article 38, 70, 71(1), and 153. As a result of the amendment of Clause 5 of Article 159, however, various other constitutional provisions were included. Article 159(5) as amended now reads:

> A law making an amendment to Clause (4) of Article 10, any law passed thereunder, the provisions of Part III, Article 38, 63(4), 70, 71(1), 72(4), 152 or 153 or *to this Clause* shall not be passed without the consent of the Conference of Rulers. (Italics added)

All these Articles concern what have been categorized as "sensitive issues", and more importantly, Article 159(5) itself was entrenched. Consequently, as a result of these legal changes, discussion of so-called "sensitive" issues was banned.

In addition to the amendments to the Federal Constitution, the UMNO-led government also utilized its formidable instruments of new (or revised) coercive legislation for consolidating and extending its authoritarian control.

One of the first, and most notorious, bills presented to the new Parliament in 1971 was an amendment to the Internal Security Act (1960). The ISA was introduced immediately after the lifting of the first emergency in 1960 for the continuing fight against communist insurgency. Since the amendment to the ISA in 1971, however, the Act stressed "the preservation of intercommunal harmony" and it was actually utilized "to block political challenges and intimidate critics".[41] In practice, the ISA was, and still is, the most powerful law preventing any individual from questioning sensitive matters. The amendment to the ISA allowed the UMNO-led government to detain without trial anyone who may incite violence, cause public disorder, or promote hostility among races. Even after a detainee is released, "he may be served with a restriction order imposing conditions upon his movements and participation in political or social activities".[42] Consequently, the selective use of the ISA against political leaders, academics, trade unionists, NGO activists, and any critical individuals has effectively muted immediate and/or potential political dissent. One of the most frequently used instruments of control by the government to detain these political opponents without trial for any length of time is provided under Section 8(1) of the ISA (Revised 1972), as follows:

> If the Minister is satisfied that the detention of any person is necessary with a view to preventing him from acting in a manner prejudicial to the security of Malaysia or any part thereof or to the maintenance of essential services therein or to the economic life thereof, he may make an order ... directing that person be detained.[43]

Several other laws were also amended (or promulgated) to strengthen the government's control after the violence of 1969. For example, the Sedition Act 1948 (Amendment 1970), the Official Secrets Act 1972, the Printing Presses Act 1948 (Amendment 1971), and the University Act 1971 (later amended to the Universities and University College Act in 1975) were, and still are, utilized to inhibit discussion of some of the country's most controversial political issues. The Sedition Act 1948, especially as amended, restricted the political opposition's scope for public criticism. Following the May 13 racial riots, the original Sedition Act was amended and widely applied to cover "any matter, right, status, position, privilege, sovereignty or prerogative established or protected by the provisions of Part III of the Federal Constitution or Article 152, 153, or 181 of the Federal Constitution".[44] As mentioned earlier, the amended Sedition Act applied to Parliament itself and, as a result, removed parliamentary immunity after the passage of the Constitution (Amendment) Act 1971.[45]

The Official Secrets Act (OSA) 1972 placed another legal restriction on public criticism of the government. The OSA 1972 was very broad in its coverage. It prohibited the taking or making of copies of any unauthorized documents, measurements, sounding or surveys, no matter how insignificant the matters therein or even where they were considered common knowledge. The broad application of the OSA 1972 made it difficult for the opposition to reveal irregularities or malpractices within the government because such information had to be obtained through unauthorized channels, such as leaks. The first case under the amended OSA involved Lim Kit Siang, the DAP secretary-general, and P. Patto, the DAP member of Parliament in 1978. Lim disclosed the possibility of corruption in the procedure for purchasing four patrol vessels by the Royal Malaysian Navy. His allegations were reported in the DAP's periodical, *The Rocket*, in 1978. Lim and P. Patto, the editor of *The Rocket*, were charged under the OSA shortly before the general election of 1978.[46]

The 1969 riots were also the catalyst for solidifying mass media policy in Malaysia. The mass media, either as a source of information or a platform for public criticism of the government, was severely restricted by government in various ways. First of all, the original Printing Presses Act, promulgated at the beginning of the first emergency in 1948, was significantly amended in 1971 to provide for the right to withdraw newspaper licences. The criterion for issuing printing permits was broad enough to cover any political reason. Since 1971, all printing permits have been issued subject to the following conditions:

> no material or photograph or matter which is or is likely to be prejudicial to public order or national security shall be printed or published. … Presentation of facts related to public order incidents in Malaysia should not be in such a way as is likely to inflame or stir communal hostility.[47]

Students and universities were not exempt from increasing government control. As a result of intensifying student demonstrations against Tunku Abdul Rahman's compromised leadership post-1969, the government passed the University Act in 1971 outlawing student participation in off-campus political activities. Later in 1975, the University Act 1971 was amended and renamed as the Universities and University Colleges Act, to expand its controls on student activities in the political as well as the non-political arena.

The Plan: The New Socio-Economic Development Strategies

In addition to the proclamation of national ideology and the restrictive legislation on sensitive issues, the UMNO-led government introduced a new development plan. This was called the Second Malaysia Plan, which covered the period up to the end of 1974, but this plan, unlike the previous ones, was not a regular five-year plan. The Second Malaysia Plan was presented to Parliament on 11 July 1971 and it included the implementation of the New Economic Policy (NEP), a long-term national development strategy that ended in 1990. While the government acknowledged the "ideology" and the "ban" as one aspect of a long-term political strategy, the NEP was another long-term strategy stemming from its interpretation of the socio-economic background to the racial riots. Therefore, the detailed contents of the NEP had to cover the key issues or problems which were revealed in the first stage of Malaysian ethnic politics.

Given these problems, the new development strategy had to meet at least two interrelated challenges. Firstly, it aimed to overcome the deep-rooted psychological feeling of relative deprivation, alienation, and inferiority among Malays because of their relative economic and social backwardness which the UMNO-led government recognized as the root cause of the May 13 racial riots. Secondly, but no less important, the new development strategy should contain a remedy for the precarious position of the UMNO-led government. The most vulnerable feature of the UMNO-led government during the first twelve years of independence was that UMNO, as a ruling political group, had dominated state power without a strong economic base. In these circumstances, as Jomo notes, the Malaysian political system itself was "fragile and untenable in the long run".[48] Thus, the NEP had to map out in detail how ethnic political power could be converted into ethnic economic power, but without spoiling the economically dominant minority or disrupting the overall economy.

The NEP's primary objectives and targets made clear the UMNO-led government's strategies to resolve these two immediate but profound problems. The UMNO-led government declared that the NEP's ultimate goal was "national unity". In order to achieve this goal, the NEP specified two strategies. Firstly, it aimed "to reduce and eventually *eradicate poverty*, by raising income levels and increasing employment opportunities for all Malaysians, *irrespective of race*".[49] Secondly, the NEP sought to accelerate "the process of *restructuring Malaysian society* to correct economic imbalance, so as to reduce and eventually *eliminate the identification of race with economic function*".[50] In addition, it was assumed that the implementation of the policy will be "in such a manner that no one will be deprived of his rights, privileges, income, job or opportunity".[51]

In the aftermath of the severe inter-racial riots, the new plan appeared to be relatively well-balanced, at least at the level of rhetoric regarding its basic objectives and goals. Furthermore, of the three ways identified by Esman of redressing economic imbalance by a government representing the economically disadvantaged ethnic minority, the UMNO-led government seemed to adopt a "positive-sum strategy of ethnic redistribution" rather than "a strategy of no action" or "an expropriation strategy". In other words, the UMNO-led government believed that the task of economic redistribution should be carried out by expanding the economic pie without the expropriation of any group. To lessen non-Malays' concerns over the second task of the new plan on restructuring Malaysian society, Prime Minister Tun Razak added that "the rights, properties and privileges now belonging to whichever groups or individuals will not be taken and be given to others. What is envisaged by the government is that the newly created opportunities will be distributed in a just and equitable manner".[52]

Yet no matter how it was explained, it was apparent that the UMNO-led government viewed the primary goals of the NEP, especially "restructuring Malaysian society", almost exclusively from a Malay perspective. Though the primary objectives of the NEP were supposed to be implemented in the context of an expanding economic pie providing increased opportunities for a better life for all Malaysians regardless of race, the overriding emphasis was on the second task, restructuring society, with Malays and other indigenous peoples as beneficiaries.[53] In fact, there were no special remedial programmes for the poor, regardless of race, although concern for poverty alleviation was an important component of the overall strategy for economic growth. On the contrary, the task of restructuring Malaysian society was furthered by formulating a new system of quotas and Malay special rights in the field of education, jobs (professional and management positions), and commercial and industrial enterprises. Furthermore, the programme for restructuring Malaysian society gave Malays greater access to economic power while preventing similar access to political power to non-Malays.

There were several significant measures in "restructuring Malaysian society" under the NEP. First of all, the most uncompromising determination was reserved for the goal of achieving economic and social balance. Here, "balance" means that "those members of the Malaysian society who have benefited relatively little from past development must now be assured ample opportunities to gain a fairer share of the increased goods and services that development brings".[54] It also refers to "[equitable] racial shares in management and ownership and in employment in the various sectors of the economy".[55] For the purpose of rectifying disparities between the "haves" and the "have-nots", in reality between Malays and non-Malays, the government set a long-term target that "within two decades at least 30 per cent of total commercial and industrial activities in all categories and scales of operation should have participation by Malays and other indigenous people in terms of ownership and management".[56] At the end of 1969, of the total RM4,678 million share capital, Malays and Malay interests owned only 1.5 per cent, while the Chinese owned 22.8 per cent and foreigners owned 62.5 per cent of capital respectively.[57]

The objective of inter-ethnic balance was pursued through various programmes and policies to increase the participation of Malays and other indigenous people in the more dynamic and modern sectors of the economy. Included are programmes that provide business premises, finance, technical, and marketing advice, training and business contacts to aid such persons in starting their own commercial ventures. The programmes also included bringing about increased *bumiputera* management and ownership of modern urban industries. One crucial element was to establish "ethnic employment quotas" in the private sector of the economy as well, namely, Malay special rights, continued and extended by employment requirements that commercial and industrial enterprises should observe quotas for the participation of the *bumiputera*, and establish plans for training and promotion of the *bumiputera* to the more skilled and higher paid managerial positions. Such specific *bumiputera* employment quotas and plans were explicitly tied to the approval and renewal of government licences and the tax and tariff concessions available to the new industries.[58] Furthermore, to implement the objective of inter-ethnic balance, institutions such as MARA (Majlis Amanah Ra'ayat — Council of Trust for Indigenous People), PERNAS (Perbadanan Nasional Berhad — The National Trading Corporation), FIDA (Federal Industrial Development Authority), MIDF (Malaysian Industrial Development Finance), UDA (Urban Development Authority), and SEDCs (State Economic Development Corporations) would provide the necessary technical and financial assistance for Malay commercial and industrial enterprises, either wholly owned or in joint-ventures with non-Malays.[59]

The second implementation measures, rectifying inter-ethnic social imbalance and enlarging the bases for long-term Malay participation in modern economic activities, was the expansion of educational opportunities for the Malays. Accordingly, greater attention was given to ensuring that Malays as well as other indigenous people had better access to tertiary education in the sciences and other professional fields. For instance, more scholarships were made available to them to pursue tertiary education domestically and abroad; quotas and special remedial programmes were initiated to induce them to enter the sciences, technical, and other disciplines; educational opportunities for rural Malays in science and professional fields were expanded; and tertiary education facilities increased dramatically.[60]

A crucial feature of the education policy was the systematic implementation of the Malay language (*Bahasa Melayu*) as the main medium of instruction in the national education system. The new education policy was announced immediately after the 1969 racial riots. Beginning in 1970, in Standard One, all subjects formerly taught in English-medium schools (including mathematics and science but excepting English and the pupil's mother tongue) were to be taught in Malay. The next year conversion to Malay would apply to Standard Two, and so on, a year at a time, up to Form Six, which would come into effect by 1982. In so doing, Malay gradually replaced English as the medium of instruction in primary, secondary, and university education. Chinese primary schools continued to use Mandarin and some private Chinese secondary schools survived. However, for non-Malays this was the most discriminatory policy adopted by the government.[61] The rationale for the implementation of the new policies was to provide wider educational opportunities for Malays, especially those whose primary and secondary education was in Malay schools and who had difficulty in coping with tertiary education in English. At the same time it was believed that a common language would provide a stronger foundation for inter-communal harmony. Indirectly, of course, it also underlined the Malay nature of the state. In addition to the push for the Malay language, the task of creating a Malay-centric national and common culture for purposes of national unity was given greater priority during the NEP period (1970–90).

Finally, but most importantly, the NEP expanded the role of the state qualitatively as well as quantitatively. The Second Malaysia Plan stressed that, with the implementation of the NEP, "the government will participate more directly in the establishment and operation of a wide range of productive enterprises. This will be done through *wholly owned* enterprises and *joint ventures* with the private sector".[62] The main aims of direct government participation were to establish "new industrial activities in selected new growth areas" and to help "create a Malay commercial and industrial community".[63]

Before the launching of the NEP, as Jomo notes, the government had largely played "administrative, supportive, and regulatory" roles for the private sector but did not necessarily "represent direct and active efforts in promoting the interests of the governing group".[64] With the NEP, however, the role of the government expanded and moved to more direct participation in commercial and industrial undertakings, serving the particular interests of the governing group itself. UMNO, as the dominant party in the government, became a major beneficiary of the expanded role of the state. To be precise, with the NEP, the UMNO-led government functioned as a medium for the accumulation of capital. This was the most significant departure from past relations between political and economic power. With the growth of public enterprises, a partnership, or patron-client relationship, was formed between the UMNO-led government and businesses. Consequently, a combination of political and economic patronage enabled UMNO to convert its political power into significant economic power.[65]

In sum, the major anti-crisis strategies adopted by the emergency government — the ideology, the ban, and the plan — seemed to have been introduced as complementary elements to redress socio-economic racial imbalance and to consolidate political power of the governing group. Firstly, the national ideology asserted that the essential agreements of inter-élite communal bargaining were not to be rescinded in spite of ongoing racial discord, while it gave Malays psychological confidence that their special rights were inviolable. Secondly, the legal ban on the discussion of sensitive issues, including Malay special rights, embodied the rhetoric of the ideology in a substantial behaviour code in nearly every aspect of Malaysian daily life. Finally, the new development plan demonstrated how racial imbalance in terms of social and economic outlook could be at least partially rectified. More importantly, the new plan paved the way for the governing Malay group to convert its precarious political power into a more secure political hegemony with long-term economic foundations.

Realignment of Political Configuration and Authoritarian Control

The Formation of a New Ruling Scheme and Its Consolidation

Another post-riot political strategy was the Tun Razak–led UMNO reconstitution of the Alliance system by incorporating almost all previous opposition parties within the ruling coalition. The new ruling formula was designed to provide multiple representation within the government for each ethnic group, rather than each being represented by only one political party. The main reason for realigning the political framework was to build a stronger and wider base of support for the UMNO-dominated governing coalition.

The first step towards the new ruling formula was taken in July 1970 when the Sarawak United People's Party (SUPP) was invited to join the ruling coalition in Sarawak. There were many motives for the coalition to build links with opposition parties. In the case of the SUPP-Sarawak Alliance coalition, the purpose was to get a two-thirds majority in Parliament in order to pass the Constitution (Amendment) Bill 1971.[66] In February 1972, Gerakan joined the ruling coalition. One aim of the Gerakan-Alliance coalition was to increase Chinese support to compensate for the weakness of the MCA. As Mauzy notes, this coalition further reduced politicking in the nation and enabled the Alliance's participation in the Penang state government.[67] Further co-option of the Chinese opposition occurred three months later in May 1972 when the Alliance brought the PPP into the Perak state government. The last political party to join the ruling coalition was the Pan-Malaysia Islamic Party (PAS) in January 1973. By forming this coalition, the Alliance was represented in the PAS-controlled Kelantan state government. More importantly, the co-option of PAS into the new ruling formula "neutralized the only significant party capable of outbidding UMNO for Malay support and thus stopped the drift of Malay votes away from the government".[68] As the mid-1974 election approached, UMNO's overall coalition had transformed into a new ruling coalition, the Barisan Nasional or National Front (BN).

This realignment of the political landscape further undermined open political competition by restricting parliamentary opposition only to the predominantly Chinese DAP and the Sarawak National Party (SNAP). The effectiveness and influence of the new ruling scheme was demonstrated in the 1974 general election when the BN won an overwhelming majority both in Parliament and in each state legislative assembly. In parliamentary elections, the BN obtained 60.7 per cent of popular votes and won 135 of the 154 seats (87.7 per cent of the total parliamentary seats). Compared with the 1969 elections, the result showed a 14.4 per cent increase in the popular vote and a 25.9 per cent increase in parliamentary seats. Also, in the state assembly elections, the BN received solid support in every state. In Penang and Perak, where the Alliance had obtained only four of the twenty-four seats and nineteen of the forty seats respectively in 1969, the BN won twenty-three of the twenty-seven seats and thirty-one of the forty-two seats respectively. Moreover, Malay voters gave overwhelming support to both UMNO and PAS, winning all the seats they contested in sixty-one and fourteen parliamentary constituencies respectively. Meanwhile, the opposition DAP and SNAP won nine parliamentary seats each. Another minor opposition party Malaysian Social Justice Party (Pekemas) won only one parliamentary seat.[69] The SNAP, however, was persuaded to join the BN in 1976 leaving the DAP and the sole Pekemas representative as the only parliamentary opposition.[70]

The replacement of the Alliance by a considerably expanded coalition enabled UMNO to gain a decisive governing role in the post-1969 period. In particular, the admission of Gerakan and the PPP to the ruling coalition greatly undermined the MCA as the only representative of the Chinese in government. A former senior official of the MCA argues that:

> Although MCA faced the dominant game played by UMNO, we still had a balance of power within the Alliance system. Theoretically, the Chinese had a bigger voice as the MCA played as the sole spokesman in the ruling coalition. By having Gerakan side by side, however, UMNO could use a kind of check-and-balance to divide and rule. ... Although UMNO was not necessarily using this, the BN's Chinese parties were being prepared to be divided and ruled. We had put ourselves in this position. So, the UMNO leaders were very happy to make use of this condition whenever they wanted to do something.[71]

In fact, as Mauzy notes, the principle of proportionality, in qualitative terms, became less significant as the MCA lost key economic portfolios.[72] Following the loss of the Commerce and Industry portfolio in 1971, the MCA lost the Finance ministership in 1974. UMNO thus held all key portfolios in the Cabinet. After the mid-1970s, the political position of Chinese parties was weakened further within the BN when increasing dissension between the MCA and Gerakan, and intense factional struggles within the MCA itself, took place. The admission of Gerakan to the ruling coalition and the MCA top leadership's irresolute attitude in dealing with UMNO created internal conflict between the "old guards" and the "new blood" in the MCA. This led to the expulsion of a group of "new blood" in 1973 and their subsequent defection to Gerakan. At this time, the internal conflict resulted in further diminishing the MCA's bargaining power within the ruling coalition whereas Gerakan's bargaining position seemed to strengthen.[73]

After the 1969 racial riots, UMNO also experienced internal conflict between the old generation led by Tunku Abdul Rahman and his allies and the younger generation led by Tun Razak. Tun Razak's sudden death in January 1976, Hussein Onn's weak political base as new party president and the controversy over the appointment of a new deputy president accelerated factional rivalries in UMNO during the mid-1970s. UMNO factional conflict, however, eventually settled down in 1977 following the imprisonment of then UMNO Youth president Harun Idris, one of the most outspoken critics of Hussein Onn and the new UMNO leadership.[74]

Towards the end of 1977, UMNO's domination of the ruling coalition became stronger when PAS was expelled from the BN following their continued internal leadership crises and squabbling with UMNO in the Kelantan state government.[75] The departure of PAS from the BN allowed UMNO to regain its previous position as the sole representative of the Malay community in government. On the surface, PAS's return to the opposition meant that UMNO faced the challenge of a strong Malay communal party for the Malay vote. The leadership split in PAS and subsequent political instability in Kelantan, however, provided a golden opportunity for UMNO to manipulate the political situation and undermine PAS's influence. During the period of state emergency in particular, UMNO encouraged the Kelantan Menteri Besar Mohamad Nasir to form a PAS splinter party, Berjasa, and closely co-operated with the party in the Kelantan state elections of March 1978, held a month after the emergency laws were repealed. The state elections were mostly three-corner fights between UMNO, PAS, and Berjasa. UMNO's strategy then was to split the PAS vote between PAS and Berjasa, and this was why Berjasa did not immediately join the BN.[76] UMNO won twenty-three and Berjasa eleven seats, PAS was reduced to only two seats with

33.5 per cent of the total votes (declining from its total of 52 per cent in winning nineteen seats in 1969).[77] Berjasa later joined the BN. The ensuing leadership crises and subsequent electoral defeat made PAS's position extremely insecure after nineteen years of rule in Kelantan.

The decade after 1978 saw the consolidation of the BN's rule. In particular, UMNO's hegemony over the ruling coalition was reinforced during this period. First, the results of the 1978 general election, held soon after UMNO's success in the Kelantan state elections, showed that the electoral effectiveness of the BN was not seriously undermined despite the departure of PAS. Even compared with 1974 when the government enjoyed extraordinarily favourable electoral conditions, the BN recorded a remarkable victory, winning 131 of 154 parliamentary seats with only a minor decline of popular votes. At the state level, the election results gave the BN more than 85 per cent of winning seats, giving it control of all state governments. Similar performances by the BN continued in a series of general elections of 1982 and 1986, as shown in Table 4.4. The unusually high number of seats won by the BN was largely a result of unfair electoral boundaries advantaging the ruling coalition. Nonetheless, the BN's expanded-membership formula seemed to retain multi-ethnic support during this period, whereas opposition supporters were polarized between PAS on the Malay side and the DAP on the non-Malay side.

In particular, the election results of 1978–86 demonstrate that the BN's victories were spearheaded by UMNO. The MIC, as a minor component party of the BN representing the Indian community, also

TABLE 4.4
Votes and Seats Won by Barisan Nasional, 1974–86

	1974		1978		1982		1986	
	P	S	P	S	P	S	P	S
Popular votes (%)	60.7	60.7*	57.2	57.4	60.5	62.8	57.6	59.7
Seats won (%)	87.7	86.9*	85.1	86.9	85.7	90.3	83.6	85.2

* Included Sarawak in 1974. Sabah and Sarawak were excluded in 1978, 1982, and 1986.
P = Parliamentary elections.
S = State assembly election.

Source: NSTP Research and Information Services (1994).

performed creditably. However, the Chinese parties, the MCA and Gerakan, showed unstable electoral support from the Chinese community. Though the MCA and Gerakan recorded their best performance in the Chinese-majority constituencies in 1982, their combined twenty-three seats was less than the DAP's twenty-four in 1986. In terms of votes obtained in 1986, the DAP polled more votes (968,009 or 20.4 per cent of the total votes) than the MCA and Gerakan combined (738,933 or 15.6 per cent of the total votes).[78] Even in 1982 when the DAP recorded its worst results in the 1978–86 period, it was assumed that the DAP's popular vote was greater than the MCA's.[79] On the Malay side, the opposition PAS remained a strong competitor to UMNO. Especially in the heavily Malay-populated northern states of Kelantan, Terengganu, Kedah, and Perlis, PAS proved that it could still win the support of almost 40 per cent of Malay votes.[80] But PAS fared badly in terms of seats. As shown in Table 4.5, only five PAS candidates won out of over eighty who contested parliamentary seats in 1978 and 1982. In spite of its substantial support in terms of votes, PAS recorded its most dismal performance in 1986, winning only one seat out of the ninety-nine parliamentary constituencies it contested, compared with

TABLE 4.5
Seats Won and Contested by Major Political Parties,
1978–86 (Parliament)

	1978	1982	1986
UMNO	69 (74)	70 (73)	83 (84)
MCA	17 (27)	24 (28)	17 (32)
MIC	3 (4)	4 (4)	6 (6)
Gerakan	4 (6)	5 (7)	5 (9)
PAS	5 (89)	5 (82)	1 (99)
DAP	16 (53)	9 (63)	24 (64)

Source: Harold Crouch, Lee Kam Hing, and Michael Ong, eds., *Malaysian Politics and the 1978 Election* (Kuala Lumpur: Oxford University Press, 1980), p. 297; Harold Crouch, *Malaysia's 1982 General Election* (Singapore: Institute of Southeast Asian Studies, 1982), p. 58; and Sankaran Ramanathan and Mohd. Hamdan Adnan, *Malaysia's 1986 General Election: The Urban-Rural Dichotomy* (Singapore: Institute of Southeast Asian Studies, 1988), p. 51.

UMNO's overwhelming victories in all but one constituency contested. In short, UMNO's continuing support in the Malay community and the Chinese BN parties' unstable electoral performances in their respective constituencies enabled UMNO leadership to obtain an even more dominant position within and outside the ruling coalition in the 1970s and 1980s.

UMNO's Growing Economic and Political Hegemony

The consolidation of UMNO's dominance in the 1970s and 1980s was not limited to the political sphere. After 1971, one of the most significant features was a notable enhancement of UMNO's economic position. UMNO started to involve itself directly in major business ventures in the early 1970s. Its corporate investments were initially motivated by a need to reduce its financial dependence on non-Malay supporters, especially Chinese businessmen within the ruling coalition.[81] However, UMNO's direct involvement in business was closely associated with increasing authoritarian control over political processes, especially in the media sector, in the 1970s and 1980s.

The first UMNO-linked business venture was Fleet Holdings, incorporated in 1972 by then UMNO treasurer Razaleigh Hamzah, following a request from Tun Razak. UMNO's involvement in business can be traced back as far as the late 1940s. And in the early 1960s, UMNO took control of the Utusan Melayu Press, which published a widely circulated Malay daily *Utusan Melayu*. However, the control of the Utusan Melayu Press was not exercised by the party itself but by some UMNO leaders. It was in the 1970s that UMNO as a party first involved itself directly in major business ventures. Apart from the financial independence motive, one of the crucial reasons for establishing Fleet Holdings was to obtain control of the Singapore-controlled publishing company, the Straits Times Press. In so doing, Fleet Holdings took over the Straits Times Press shares for the Kuala Lumpur operations with a loan from Bank Bumiputera which was then headed by Razaleigh. The company was then renamed as the New Straits Times Press (NSTP) after completion of the acquisition. Later in 1976, Fleet Holdings formed a wholly owned subsidiary, Fleet Group Sendirian Berhad, to act as

UMNO's main investment holding company.[82] During Razaleigh's stewardship as UMNO treasurer (1977–82), UMNO's involvement in business operated primarily through Fleet Group's various subsidiaries, especially its main publicly listed company, NSTP.[83]

However, UMNO's corporate involvement grew markedly and there was a distinct change in management style when Mahathir assumed the UMNO presidency. As Gomez notes, the style of UMNO's corporate involvement became more and more that of a conglomerate. By the mid-1980s, Fleet Group used its control of publicly listed companies, NSTP, Bank of Commerce, American Malaysian Insurance, Sistem Televisyen (TV3), and Faber Group, to mount its corporate forays.[84] It was also in 1984 that another UMNO-owned investment arm, Hatibudi Sendirian Berhad, was formed to increase the ruling party's political patronage. Hatibudi, under the direct trusteeship of UMNO's top leadership, acquired a substantial stake in United Engineers Malaysia Berhad (UEM) in 1985.[85] Shortly after Hatibudi gained control of UEM, the Mahathir administration awarded UEM a series of lucrative government contracts, including the North-South Highway Project. The North-South Highway Project was the largest privatization project implemented in the 1980s and enabled UMNO to secure recurrent financial resources for thirty years by managing and collecting billions of ringgit in tolls and other fees along the North-South Highway. Apart from the North-South Highway contract, UEM was awarded several other government projects after the mid-1980s.[86] Separate from the Fleet Group and Hatibudi, another corporate group, Koperasi Usaha Bersatu Berhad (KUB), was deeply involved in UMNO's direct investment in business during the 1980s.[87] In early 1990, all UMNO's main business arms, Fleet Group, Hatibudi, and KUB, were consolidated under one company, Renong Berhad. The restructuring of UMNO's corporate assets under Renong enabled the emergence of one of the largest conglomerates in Southeast Asia and was "a testament to the economic clout commanded by UMNO in Malaysia's corporate economy".[88]

In sum, UMNO became involved directly in business with the implementation of the NEP. It is evident that the growth of UMNO's main investment arms, Fleet Group, Hatibudi, and KUB, were primarily attributable to government patronage. And, it was under Mahathir's leadership that each of UMNO's main business ventures became large conglomerates. What is more important, the conglomerate style of management in UMNO's corporate involvement under Mahathir led to unique forms of monopoly, especially in the media sector, and this resulted in further consolidation of UMNO's control over political processes.

In Malaysia, most mainstream vernacular newspapers are closely related to political parties in power. The existing control of the mainstream media by the ruling coalition became even stronger under Mahathir's leadership. By the end of the 1980s, UMNO and its coalition partners were able to control all the mainstream media, both in publishing and broadcasting, through ownership. The UMNO-owned NSTP publishes and markets newspapers, magazines, periodicals, and books. Its publications include: *New Straits Times, New Sunday Times, Malay Mail, Sunday Mail, Berita Harian, Berita Minggu, Business Times, Shin Min Daily News, Malaysian Business*. UMNO, through the Fleet Group and later Renong, also has a substantial share (43 per cent) in the commercial television network Sistem Televisyen Malaysia (TV3).[89] In addition, one of the most popular English daily newspapers, *The Star*, is published by Star Publications, which is controlled by Huaren Holdings, an MCA holding company. A Chinese daily, *Tong Bao*, is also controlled by the MCA. Also, the three Tamil dailies — *Tamil Nesan, Thinamurasu*, and *Malaysia Nanban* — are controlled by leaders of MIC, another senior member of the ruling coalition. Meanwhile, Radio Televisyen Malaysia (RTM) is government-owned and run by the Information Ministry headed by a senior UMNO minister.

Further to direct ownership of the media, the Mahathir administration increased control by tightening its regulations affecting the freedom of the press. First, incoming foreign news was restricted in a subtle move of censorship. In so doing, the government strengthened the role of Bernama (the government-controlled national news agency) by making it "sole distributor" of foreign news as of 1 May 1984.[90] Second, the Mahathir government passed restrictive amendments to the Printing Presses and Publications Act (PPPA) 1984, replacing the Printing Presses Act 1948 (revised 1971) and the Control of Imported Publications Act 1958 (revised 1972). The new PPPA empowered the Home Minister

— until recently, a portfolio held by Mahathir — "absolute discretion" to grant, revoke or suspend publishing and printing permits, both foreign and local, in Malaysia. Penalties for offences relating to printing, importing and publishing of a newspaper or magazine were also increased to a maximum of three years imprisonment and/or RM20,000 fine from a maximum prison term of one year and/or RM438 fine.[91] The PPPA was further amended in 1987 to enhance the executive's discretionary powers by removing the right of judicial review over the Home Minister's decision to revoke or suspend a printing permit.[92]

Further authoritarian methods were demonstrated by a series of amendments to the Official Secrets Act (OSA) in 1984 and 1986. The amended OSA 1984 requires that public officials must report immediately to the police anyone seeking official secret information. If an official fails to do so, and is convicted, he faces a possible five-year prison term. The new Act defines "secret" as any information entrusted to an official in confidence by another official, or obtained by virtue of a position in the public service. Both the leakage and the receipt of an official secret is a criminal offence and the broad definition of "secret" effectively covers all government activities. In addition, under the new OSA, anyone associating with a "foreign agent" is liable to prosecution, whether or not information is passed on.[93] The OSA was amended again in 1986 to enhance its intimidating effect by adding provisions for mandatory prison terms of a minimum one year to a maximum of fourteen years for anyone convicted. Moreover, the amendments confer upon the executive the power to classify any document, information, or material as an "official secret" and the classification "shall not be questioned in any court on any ground whatsoever".[94]

The enhanced restriction of press laws was, and still is, more than just cautionary. Since Mahathir came to power, many opposition-oriented publications lost their printing permits and journalists were occasionally punished for their contributions. Foreign newspapers and journals were also occasionally banned. *Nadi Insan*, a monthly magazine often carrying critical articles about poverty and injustices suffered by the peasants, was the first to be banned under the Mahathir regime. The suspension effectively showed how limited was the Mahathir administration's commitment to a free press.[95] For a few years after *Nadi Insan*'s ban until

1986, at least three other periodicals lost their publishing permits and several journalists were charged and pleaded guilty. For example, Sabry Sharif of *New Straits Times* was arrested under the OSA for using an Air Force document in an article and paid a fine of RM7,000. Two *Asian Wall Street Journal* (*AWSJ*) foreign reporters lost their work permits (one of them was expelled from Malaysia after being fined) because of their articles on cronyism in banking and economic mismanagement in government. The distribution of *AWSJ* was also suspended for three months. A *Far Eastern Economic Review* foreign correspondent was also charged under the OSA for citing an allegedly confidential government document and was fined the maximum RM10,000. Furthermore, in 1987 alone, two popular daily newspapers — *The Star* and *Sin Chew Jit Poh* — and a weekly *Watan* had their licences revoked for several months in the wake of UMNO's leadership crisis.

Consequently, media partisanship in favour of the ruling coalition and incremental authoritarian controls hardly made the Malaysian media neutral, apolitical, and impartial in their news reporting. During the election period in particular, unlike the BN component parties, the opposition as a whole suffered from the lack of equal access to the mainstream media in its attempts to convey its political messages to voters at the local level as well as at the national level.

TABLE 4.6
Length of Campaigning Periods for General Elections, Peninsular Malaysia

Year	Nomination	Polling	Campaigning Period[a]
1955	15 June	27 July	40 days
1959[b]	15 July	19 August	33 days
1964	21 March	25 April	34 days
1969[c]	5 April	10 May	35 days
1974	8 August	24 August	15 days
1978	21 June	8 July	16 days
1982	7 April	22 April	14 days
1986	24 July	3 August	9 days
1990	11 October	21 October	9 days

[a] The nomination day is not counted as part of official campaigning period.
[b] Nomination for state elections in 1959 was held on separate dates.
[c] Nomination in Kelantan was held on 12 April 1969.

Sources: NSTP Research and Information Services (1994, p. 146).

Moreover, political parties' opportunities for communication with the electorates were regularly undermined. The campaigning period had been shortened to fifteen days in 1974, compared with more than thirty days until the 1969 general election. And it was under Mahathir's leadership that the campaigning period was reduced to less than ten days, as shown in Table 4.6. Considering public rallies had been banned since the 1978 general election, opposition parties regarded the shortening of the election campaign period as a serious restriction on their potential to communicate with voters.[96] Especially at the local level, it appeared to be physically impossible for opposition parties to contact the 50,000 or so voters in a particular constituency without allowing public election rallies. Consequently, opposition parties could not properly take their issues to the voters and failed to respond to the ruling coalition's aggressive election campaign conducted mainly through the one-sided mainstream media.

Some claim that the Mahathir administration appeared to practise a relatively liberal policy towards critics of government, especially in the early 1980s. Indeed, many political prisoners were released and the numbers detained under the ISA remained relatively small after Mahathir came to power.[97] However, the growing authoritarianism of Mahathir's leadership was evident even in the earlier period. As well as a series of amendments to the press laws, Mahathir produced an even wider range of controls to reduce the scope of political societies which may have emerged as a potential threat to the government.

In particular, the amendment to the Societies Act in 1981 brought about one of the most intense concerns among political and non-political groups. The Societies Act (1966), which consolidated various colonial-era ordinances, required all societies, of whatever nature or objectives, to be registered with the Registrar of Societies. The new amendments, however, introduced a distinction between "political" and other societies. A political society was defined very broadly, covering organizations which seek to "influence in any manner the policies or activities ... or the functioning, management, or operation of the Government of Malaysia", including any state government and the administration of any local authority.[98] Under the amended Act, any organization had to register as a "political society" to make public comment on any matter related to the policies or activities of the government. The Registrar of Societies, a civil servant under the Home Ministry, was then empowered to interpret virtually any comment of societies as "political" and deregister that society accordingly. An appeal on the Registrar's decision could be made to the Home Ministry, but a court challenge was not allowed. The Act also stipulated that no society would be permitted to challenge any matter provided for under the federal and state constitutions, especially provisions on the monarchy, Islam, national language, and the special rights of Malays. As Barraclough stresses, the amendments clearly "targeted almost every single source of political challenge; and it has been especially focussed on any activities falling outside the readily identifiable party system".[99] New amendments were made in 1982 and 1983 to accommodate the growing opposition to the Societies Act 1981. However, most of the repressive provisions of the 1981 amendments remained intact. Barraclough argues that the powers of the Registrar of Societies broadened under the new amendments. As a result, the Registrar's decision still could not be challenged in court and searches of societies' premises could be done without warrants.[100]

The executive's dominance, especially the Prime Minister's, was also consolidated after Mahathir assumed office. First, the 1981 constitutional amendments empowered the Yang di-Pertuan Agong to issue a proclamation of emergency even "before the actual occurrence of the event which threatens the security, or the economic life, or public order" in the country simply if he "is satisfied that there is imminent danger of the occurrence of such event".[101] Given the fact that the Yang di-Pertuan Agong "shall act in accordance with the advice of the Cabinet or of a Minister acting under the general authority of the Cabinet", the amendments in practice gave the executive a kind of absolute discretion.[102] Moreover, the formidable scope of the emergency powers in Article 150(2) was further entrenched by another Article 150(8), which effectively ousts the jurisdiction of the courts in relation to the invocation of those powers. Article 150(8) stipulates that the satisfaction of the Yang di-Pertuan Agong in relation to proclamation of emergency "shall be final and conclusive and shall not be challenged or called in question in any court on any ground". According to the 1957 Constitution, it was Parliament that should decide that an emergency exists. If Parliament is not in sitting, the executive could issue an emergency ordinance. An emergency ordinance issued by the executive would cease to have force fifteen days after the date both Houses of Parliament were sitting. Article 150 of the Constitution was amended again in 1983 to substitute "Prime Minister" for "Yang di-Pertuan Agong" to make executive discretion more explicit and absolute. All the above-mentioned provisions existed, except that it was the Prime Minister's satisfaction — not the Yang di-Pertuan Agong's — whether an emergency exists or is likely to exist.[103] After much controversy, the change effected to Article 150 by the 1983 amendments was retracted in 1984, substituting "Yang di-Pertuan Agong" for "Prime Minister". However, the Cabinet's overarching power remained intact, and the possibility of a Prime Minister bypassing Cabinet on fundamental matters still existed under the 1984 amendments. And it must be noted that towards the end of the 1980s, Mahathir further expanded and centralized executive power in his personal domain at the expense of the legislature, the monarchy, and the judiciary, as will be discussed in the following chapters.

Towards a New Conflict Configuration

Factionalism had been common in UMNO for decades. UMNO's factional conflicts, however, never developed to the point where the essential unity of the party itself was at stake. It was only after Mahathir assumed power that UMNO's internal politics underwent serious factional conflicts which occasionally spilled into the open, as evidenced in 1981, 1984, and 1987. What were the conditions that led to the deepening of factional conflict within UMNO? How will increasing factional rivalries affect Malaysian politics, especially the dominant ruling élite's attempts to maintain its political hegemony?

Mahathir came third behind Ghafar Baba and Razaleigh Hamzah in the 1975 vice-presidential UMNO election, and he was an "outside" candidate when he was picked by Hussein Onn as Deputy Prime Minister in 1976. At that time, Mahathir's support within UMNO was relatively weak because he was cast as a political renegade for years by Tunku Abdul Rahman after the 1969 general election. Hussein Onn pointed out that he chose Mahathir as his deputy not because Mahathir had enjoyed popular grass-roots support but simply because he "had to pick a man with a solid education (eliminating Ghafar, who had no tertiary education) and a mature man (eliminating Razaleigh, who was still under 40)".[104] Similarly, Razaleigh argued that Mahathir's appointment as Deputy Prime Minister did not reflect his strong position within UMNO circles. According to Razaleigh, he personally recommended Mahathir as Hussein Onn's deputy when he was consulted by Hussein Onn because Mahathir was older than him, although he was the most senior vice-president at that time.[105] Hence, it was widely believed that Mahathir was not strong enough to dominate the ruling party when he took over power in 1981; he was not even in a position to select his own deputy. Mahathir thus needed to rely on moderate, but subtle, tactics of checks and balances to effectively manage strong and popular political figures who were competing for influence in the ruling party.

On taking over the prime ministership, Mahathir faced a critical choice in selecting his deputy. Mahathir may have given the impression initially that he was ready to accept Razaleigh, the most senior vice-president at that time, as his deputy when he succeeded Hussein Onn as the party president. Razaleigh himself said that "we had an agreement among us about the number two position" and stressed that this was why his total support was given to the Mahathir presidency in 1981.[106] Neither his seniority nor this agreement, however, proved sufficient for Razaleigh to secure the number two position. On the contrary, Mahathir needed to offset Razaleigh's strong base and thus check his influence within UMNO circles. Mahathir, therefore, allowed the choice to be made by open competition rather than appointment. But he tacitly supported Musa by encouraging him to compete for the deputy presidency, which he won in 1981. It has been argued that Musa would not have challenged Razaleigh without Mahathir's tacit support in the 1981 party election. According to Razaleigh, he was not prepared for the election and was even surprised by the choice to be made by the delegates.[107] In fact, holding open electoral contest for top party positions was unheard of in UMNO's thirty-five-year history.[108]

During his first term of office, Mahathir steadily and systematically strengthened his control over UMNO. To begin, Mahathir started to change the balance of power between "old guards" and "young turks" within UMNO by recruiting a new generation of Malay leaders who were either selected or co-opted by himself. In so doing, Mahathir utilized candidate nomination for the 1982 general election to absorb a new generation of Malay politicians and thus provided himself with a new form of leverage to check the balance of power within UMNO. For instance, almost half of the existing members of Parliament (45 per cent) and state assemblymen (46 per cent) were dropped from re-nomination for the 1982 general election. One of most influential young figures was Anwar Ibrahim, then president of the Malaysian Islamic Youth Movement (ABIM). Within a year of joining the party, Anwar was elected as UMNO's Youth chief (one of the five vice-presidents of the party) and appointed as a full minister.[109] Mahathir went further by publicly endorsing Musa as his running mate at the second contest for the deputy leadership in 1984 that gave an enhanced victory to Musa. Mahathir's grip on power within UMNO seemed to be stronger after the subsequent cabinet reshuffle of 1984.[110] Nevertheless, it has been argued that Mahathir's dominance of the ruling party was still relatively fragile at this time. Means argues that Mahathir commanded only a slim majority of support within UMNO at the beginning of his second term in 1984, based on the numbers of "loyal" and "disloyal" over the conflict between Mahathir and the Malay rulers in 1983.[111]

Meanwhile, Musa's consecutive victories for the deputy presidency increased his influence and popularity within the party. Musa's rise was seen as firmly establishing him as Mahathir's likely successor, although there was no sign of Mahathir's early retirement as he had only just begun his second term in office. Musa's supporters seemed to enjoy the term "2Ms leadership (Mahathir-Musa)" rather than "second-ranking leader" as Musa's influence grew within and outside UMNO circles. Perhaps more unpleasantly for Mahathir, Musa expressed strong concern about the retention of his arch-rival Razaleigh in the Cabinet, as he wanted to prevent another Razaleigh challenge and thereby strengthen his own position as Malaysia's prime-minister-in-waiting. Again, it was alleged that there was an "unwritten agreement" between the 2Ms leadership that Razaleigh would be purged from the Cabinet and denied any nominated post in UMNO if he contested again in 1984 and lost.[112]

Mahathir's dilemma, then, was how to offset Musa's influence. This time Mahathir used the Razaleigh card. He kept Razaleigh as Trade and

Industry Minister, a lesser but still influential post, despite the alleged unwritten agreement and Musa's efforts to remove Razaleigh from the political mainstream. Musa and his supporters argue that Mahathir kept only half of his promise by depriving Razaleigh of the party's treasurer post but keeping him as a cabinet minister, although Razaleigh initially offered his resignation from the Cabinet.[113] Apart from checking Musa's influence, it is believed that Razaleigh's widespread popular support especially in Kelantan, opposition PAS's stronghold, was one of Mahathir's major reasons for retaining Razaleigh as a cabinet minister.[114] Whatever the motive, Musa believes that Mahathir strategically kept the Razaleigh card alive at this time in order to leave the door open for a third competition in 1987 and thus check his growing influence within the party.[115] For years after this, rumours of a rift between Mahathir and Musa were reported. In the mean time, at the outset of his second term, Mahathir depended more and more on the hand-picked third-echelon party leaders, such as Daim Zainuddin, Anwar Ibrahim, and Sanusi Junid, to offset Musa's influence within UMNO.[116]

Given these circumstances, it was Musa's sudden resignation from his ministerial posts that gave rise to the long-simmering distrust between Mahathir and Musa bursting into the open and forcing party leaders and members to take sides. Musa submitted his resignation as Mahathir's deputy in party and government on 27 February 1986. In his seven-page letter to Mahathir, Musa revealed his lack of trust in Mahathir. Later, however, Musa decided to remain as party deputy president, resigning only his two cabinet portfolios — Deputy Prime Minister and Home Minister.[117] Towards the end of 1986, rumours were spreading that Razaleigh and Musa would join together in the 1987 party election with the common aim of ousting Mahathir. Indeed, by the mid-1980s, Razaleigh and Musa's resentment over Mahathir's leadership style had reached boiling point and both shared animosity towards Mahathir. It was, therefore, not a total surprise that the Razaleigh-Musa combination saw its formal beginnings in early December 1986, when Musa's aide and representative of Razaleigh joined to discuss a possible alliance between the two camps. At this meeting, it was alleged, an electoral pact was made between the two camps: Razaleigh contesting for the party presidency against Mahathir; and Musa defending his deputy presidency against Ghafar.[118] Although Razaleigh and Musa refused to acknowledge such a pact had been sealed, their alliance was confirmed symbolically by their invitations to each other's divisional meeting in Segamat, Johor, on 27 February 1987, and in Gua Musang, Kelantan, on 20 March 1987 respectively, about a month before the 1987 party election, scheduled on 24 April.[119]

As the contest intensified, factional alignment became more evident at almost all levels of UMNO along Mahathir-Ghafar and Razaleigh-Musa lines. Although forming electoral pacts had been outlawed by the newly introduced Code of Ethics, the two factions were publicly identified as "Team A" and "Team B" respectively by the media. The battle lines were finally drawn when Razaleigh officially announced his candidacy for the party presidency at a gathering on 11 April 1987, with the group of Team B supporters. The Team B supporters included almost half of the thirteen UMNO cabinet ministers, a number of former cabinet ministers and chief ministers. Two former Prime Ministers, Tunku Abdul Rahman and Hussein Onn, were also closely associated with Team B. Team A also made an extraordinary effort to increase its support. The core supporters of Team A mostly came from the incumbent party leaders, such as divisional leaders, chief ministers, elected MPs, and state assemblymen, who were hand-picked by Mahathir. As the campaign reached its final stages, it appeared that no aspirants for party posts were allowed to remain neutral; they had to openly declare their allegiance in order to secure the vote from either one or the other team. As a result, as shown in Table 4.7, the six candidates for three vice-presidents and the sixty-nine contenders for twenty-five supreme council seats fell evenly into one team or the other at the time of the party election. It was also alleged that about 85–90 per cent of the total 1,479 party delegates were evenly grouped into the two teams while only 10–15 per cent were considered fence-sitters before the voting day. Out of the sixty-nine contenders for the supreme council seats, thirty-four publicly declared their support for Mahathir-Ghafar team, and the remaining thirty-five for the Razaleigh-Musa team.

The results of the battle turned out in Mahathir-Ghafar's favour. Both Mahathir and Ghafar won, but by very slim margins of forty-three and forty votes — only 51.45 and 49.96 per cent of the total 1,479

TABLE 4.7
The 1987 UMNO Elections: Contenders and Winners

	"Team A"	"Team B"
President	Mahathir Mohamad*	Razaleigh Hamzah
Deputy President	Ghafar Baba*	Musa Hitam
Vice-President	Wan Mokhtar Ahmad*	Abdullah Ahmad Badawi*
	Anwar Ibrahim*	Rais Yatim
	Ramli Ngah Talib	Harun Idris
Supreme Council Member†	Yusof Noor*	Rithauddeen*
	Muhyiddin Yassin*	Mohammad Yacob*
	Khalil Yaakob*	Kadir Sheikh Fadzir*
	Sabaruddin Chik*	Rahman Othman*
	Muhammad Taib*	Shahrir Samad*
	Tajol Rosli*	Zainal Abidin Zin*
	Abu Hassan Omar*	Radzi Sheikh Ahmad*
	Siti Zaharah*	Marina Yusof*
	Mohamed Isa Samad*	Abdul Rahim Bakar*
	Osman Aroff*	Ajib Ahmad
	Hamid Pawanteh*	Adib Adam
	Rahim Tamby Chik*	Syed Hamid Jaafar
	Khalid Yunos*	Suhaimi Kamaruddin
	Megat Junid*	Kamaruddin Mat Isa
	Wan Abu Bakar*	Ibrahim Ali
	Napsiah Omar	Aziz Shamsuddin
	Kassim Ahmed	Malik Ahmad
	Mohamed Rahmat	Ibrahim Hassan
	Mustaffa Mohammad	Daud Taha
	Syed Nahar	Othman Saat
	Sharifah Dorah	Zakaria Rahman
	Dusuki Ahmad	Zainol Abidin Johari
	Abdullah Ahmad	Tajuddin Rahman
	Awang Jabar	Nik Hussein Rhaman
	Alias Ali	Muhsein Kader
	Nawawi Mat Awin	Ahmad Shahibuddin
	Abu Bakar Daud	Yahya Shafie
	Zain Ibrahim	Hisan Ibrahim
	Syed Hassan Al-Attas	Sulaiman Palastine
	Nordin Selat	Abu Bakar Rautin
	Razak Abu Samah	Tawfik Ismail
	Kamarulzaman Bahadon	Abu Bakar Shaari
	Ahmad Mustapha	Shariff Omar
	Idris Rauf	Hang Tuah Arshad
		Ahmad Manaf

† The number was originally seventy-three, but four withdrew from the contest.
* Elected.

Source: Shamsul A.B., "The Battle Royal: The UMNO Elections of 1987", *Southeast Asian Affairs* (Singapore: Institute of Southeast Asian Studies, 1988), pp. 182–83.

votes cast — respectively. Beyond the top two posts, the rest weighted 2:1 in Team A's favour. Two of the three vice-presidencies and sixteen of the twenty-five supreme council seats went to Team A, while Team B retained one vice-president and nine supreme council seats (see Table 4.7).[120]

Given the number of divisional nominations before the election, the Mahathir team's victory was widely expected, but the result was much closer than anticipated.[121] Wild rumours even speculated that Razaleigh was the "official winner" after the first ballot count, but Mahathir was declared the "official winner" after a recount.[122] A close associate of Razaleigh's claimed that Razaleigh was informed of the "unofficial result" a few years later by a senior official of Team A who had been deeply involved in the 1987 UMNO election processes.[123] Accusations were also made that the election itself was null and void, for there were illegal branches which participated in the assembly without adhering to the party's constitution and affected the election outcome. A legal challenge to the validity of the elections finally led to UMNO being banned in 1988 and the party split into two with the Mahathir-led UMNO (*Baru*) and Razaleigh-led Semangat 46.[124] The steps towards the ban of UMNO will be discussed in the following chapter.

Summary

UMNO's political dominance within and outside the ruling coalition became more and more definite in the 1970s and 1980s. A group of younger communally oriented UMNO leaders under the patronage of Tun Razak adopted a new regime-maintenance strategy based on hegemonic control rather than consociationalism in the aftermath of the May 1969 riots. Also, UMNO's economic position was enormously enhanced by dispensing patronage in the form of government contracts, privatization awards, and other business benefits through government and semi-government institutions. Consequently, critical features of consociationalism became increasingly irrelevant, though not entirely absent, in post-1969 Malaysian politics. Instead, elements of authoritarianism became more common, as in the single-party-dominant political configuration, the highly disproportional electoral system, and a dominant executive increasing control over the rest of government.

However, post-1969 Malaysian politics has also seen an increase in intra-ethnic conflict especially within the ruling coalition's component parties. The character of factionalism also changed. In particular, factional conflict within UMNO circles frequently spilt into the open in the 1980s and even developed to the point where the essential unity of the party itself was at stake. Some claim that the deepening of the leadership conflict during this period should not be viewed as simply a reaction to the challenge of political rivals. They stress that the growing factional conflict and subsequent UMNO leadership split should be understood in terms of social, economic, cultural, and even ideological differences between the Mahathir-led Team A and Razaleigh-led Team B. Indeed, the more substantive issues of economic policy and different socio-cultural visions among UMNO leaders had seemed to drive UMNO's factional rivalries especially when the country experienced a prolonged economic recession in the mid-1980s. However, UMNO's severe factional conflict was exacerbated by Mahathir's relatively vulnerable political position within UMNO and his consequent political manœuvrings for power. Given Mahathir's weak base in UMNO, the question of succession rose to such prominence as Mahathir manipulated strong and popular political figures in the ruling party in highly irregular ways.

During the years after independence when inter-ethnic conflict was perceived as the main threat to regime stability, inter-ethnic co-operation was the most crucial element in the maintenance of the dominant Malay ruling élites' power. In the first decade of independence (1957–69), therefore, UMNO leaders used consociational power-sharing to maintain regime stability. The 1969 general election and subsequent May 13 racial riots, however, demonstrated that inter-ethnic consociational bargaining was less relevant for the Malay ruling élite to maintain political power. This was one of the main reasons the Malay ruling élite adopted a more hegemonic strategy leading to the emphatic UMNO-led Malay dominance during the 1970s and 1980s. The nature of conflict undermining the power and position of the dominant ruling élites, however, changed again as factional conflicts within UMNO deepened in the mid-1980s. Especially towards the end of the 1980s, UMNO factional rivalries took an increasingly life-or-death quality and, thus, appeared to be a more crucial threat to the Mahathir-led ruling élite's power. Rivalries intensified after the 1987 UMNO leadership crisis, necessitating Mahathir's regime to engage in a greater degree of conflict resolution to maintain power. The maintenance and consolidation of Mahathir's power is the subject of the next chapter.

NOTES

1. Ian Lustick, "Stability in Deeply Divided Societies: Consociationalism versus Control", *World Politics* 31, no. 3 (1979): 336.

2. Remarks by Tun Abdul Razak, the second Prime Minister of Malaysia, *Straits Times*, 23 September 1970. Quoted in N.J. Funston, *Malay Politics in Malaysia: A Study of the United Malays National Organisation and Party Islam* (Kuala Lumpur: Heinemann Educational Books, 1980), p. 225.

3. Mahathir Mohamad, *The Malay Dilemma* (Kuala Lumpur: Times Books International, 1970), p. 5.

4. R.S. Milne, "Bicommunal Systems: Guyana, Malaysia, Fiji", *Publius* 18, no. 2 (1988): 112, italics in original.

5. Arend Lijphart, *Democracy in Plural Societies: A Comparative Exploration* (New Haven and London: Yale University Press, 1977), pp. 150–53.

6. For the list of favourable conditions for consociationalism, see Lijphart (1977, pp. 53–103).

7. Arend Lijphart, "Consociational Democracy", *World Politics* 21, no. 2 (1969): 221–22).

8. R.K. Vasil, *Ethnic Politics in Malaysia* (New Delhi: Radiant Publishers, 1980), p. 158.

9. R.K. Vasil, *The Malaysian General Election of 1969* (Singapore: Oxford University Press, 1972), pp. 23–24.

10. Eric A. Nordlinger, *Conflict Regulation in Divided Societies* (Cambridge, Mass.: Center for International Affairs, Harvard University, 1972), p. 41.

11. Harold Crouch, *Government and Society in Malaysia* (Ithaca and London: Cornell University Press, 1996), p. 152.

12. Lijphart (1969, p. 221).

13. For more detail on seats won and lost by the MCA and the racial composition of those electorates in the parliamentary seats, see Vasil (1972, pp. 103–5).

14. For details of MIC results in the 1969 elections, see Vasil (1972, pp. 73, 85).

15. The growing strains within the ruling Alliance after the 1969 elections are well described by Gordon P. Means, *Malaysian Politics: The Second Generation*

(Singapore: Oxford University Press, 1991), pp. 6–8; J. Bass, "Malaysian Politics, 1968–1970: Crisis and Response", unpublished Ph.D. thesis, University of California, 1973, pp. 502–22; and Anthony Reid, "The Kuala Lumpur Riots and the Malaysian Political System", *Australian Outlook* 23 (1969, pp. 262–63).

16. *Straits Times*, 13 May 1969.

17. *Straits Times*, 14 May 1969.

18. *Straits Times*, 17 March 1969.

19. On the activities of a group of younger leaders taking initiative after the May 13 racial riots and the conflicts within UMNO, see Karl von Vorys, *Democracy Without Consensus: Communalism and Political Stability in Malaysia* (New Jersey: Princeton University Press, 1975), pp. 370–85.

20. Donald L. Horowitz, *Ethnic Groups in Conflict* (Berkeley: University of California Press, 1985), p. 659.

21. Vorys (1975, p. 344).

22. Horowitz (1985, p. 659).

23. For details on the activities of the NOC, see Vorys (1975, pp. 345–69); R.S. Milne and D.K. Mauzy, *Politics and Government in Malaysia* (Singapore: Times Books International, 1978), chapter 5.

24. Means (1991, p. 8), italics added.

25. *Rukunegara* is a compound word of *rukun* and *negara*. The Malay word *rukun* means harmony but it also refers to the five basic principles of Islam (confession of faith, prayer, fasting, charity, the Haj). *Negara* refers country or nation. Therefore the word suggests fundamental national principles or national guiding rules, but with a rather strong religious Islamic connotation. It was often referred to as the national ideology. It appears to have been partly inspired by the Indonesian national ideology of Pancasila (Five Principles).

26. For the full text of five beliefs, see Government of Malaysia, *Rukunegara* (Kuala Lumpur: Jabatan Chetak Kerajaan, 1970), pp. 16–17.

27. *Rukunegara* (1970, p. 15).

28. Means (1991, p. 13).

29. Commentary on the third principle in *Rukunegara* (1970, p. 18).

30. Commentary of the fourth principle in *Rukunegara* (1970, p. 19).

31. Commentary on the fifth principle in *Rukunegara* (1970, p. 19).

32. Vorys (1975, p. 396).

33. Means (1991, p. 13).

34. Government of Malaysia, *Towards National Harmony* (Kuala Lumpur: Government Press, 1971), p. 2.

35. See Article 10(4), 63(4), and 72(4) of Constitution (Amendment) Act 1971. Fan Yew Teng, an MP from the DAP, was the first convicted of this offence in 1971. For more details of Fan Yew Teng's case, see F.A. Trindade and H.P. Lee, eds., *The Constitution of Malaysia: Further Perspectives and Developments* (Petaling Jaya: Penerbit Fajar Bakti, 1986), p. 17, footnote 61.

36. *FEER*, 27 August 1970 (James Morgan, "A Ban on the Ban?"). For more on the legislative procedures, see Tun Mohamed Suffian, H.P. Lee, and F.A. Trindade, eds., *The Constitution of Malaysia, Its Development: 1957–1977* (Kuala Lumpur: Oxford University Press, 1978), pp. 382–83.

37. Article 152(1)(a) of Constitution (Amendment) Act 1969.

38. Article 160 of Constitution (Amendment) Act 1969.

39. Article 160(2) of Constitution (Amendment) (No. 2) Act 1971.

40. *Towards National Harmony*, 1971, p. 6, italics in original. For ethnic distribution between the Malay and non-Malay students in certain courses of study, see *Towards National Harmony*, 1971, tables I, II, and III in the appendix, pp. 11–14.

41. Crouch (1996, p. 81).

42. Simon Barraclough, "The Dynamics of Coercion in the Malaysian Political Process", *Modern Asian Studies* 19, no. 4 (1985): 808.

43. Internal Security Act 1972, as cited by Barraclough (1985, p. 807).

44. Section 3(f) of the Sedition Act 1948 (as amended in 1970).

45. For several cases under the amended Sedition Act, see Crouch (1996, pp. 83–84).

46. *New Straits Times*, 8 November 1978. For the other cases of the OSA and its application, see Anne Munro-Kua, *Authoritarian Populism in Malaysia* (London: Macmillan Press, 1996), pp. 123–24.

47. Howard Coats and Frances Dyer, *The Print and Broadcasting Media in Malaysia* (Kuala Lumpur: South East Asia Press Center, 1972), p. 3.

48. Jomo K.S., *A Question of Class: Capital, the State, and Uneven Development in Malaya* (New York: Monthly Review Press, 1988), p. 247.

49. *Second Malaysia Plan*, p. 1, italics added.

50. *Second Malaysia Plan*, p. 1, italics added.

51. *Second Malaysia Plan*, p. 6.

52. See *Malaysian Digest*, 15 July 1971.

53. Means (1991, pp. 23–27).

54. *Second Malaysia Plan*, p. 41.

55. *Second Malaysia Plan*, p. 41.

56. *Second Malaysia Plan*, p. 158.

57. *Second Malaysia Plan*, p. 40, table 3.1.

58. The strategy for achieving economic balance is explained in *Second Malaysia Plan*, pp. 43–48. For a critical review of Malaysia's quota system, see Boo Cheng Hau, *Quotas versus Affirmative Action: A Malaysian Perspective* (Kuala Lumpur: Oriengroup, 1998).

59. For details on public sector programme and financing, see *Second Malaysia Plan*, pp. 66–82; 112–19; 155–62; and 177–80.

60. Until the end of the 1960s, there was only one university, the University of Malaya (UM), in Malaysia. During the period 1969–71, however, four more institutions of university status were established: the National University of Malaysia (UKM), University of Science Malaysia (USM), University of Agriculture (UPM), and Mara Institute of Technology (ITM).

61. For a broad debate on the development of the national language policy in Malaysia, see Richard Mead, *Malaysia's National Language Policy and the Legal System* (New Haven: Yale University Southeast Asia Studies, 1988), pp. 22–40. The reactions from Malays and non-Malays to the implementation of the new educational policies can be found in Vorys (1975, pp. 397–98) and Milne and Mauzy (1978, p. 88).

62. *Second Malaysia Plan*, p. 7, italics added.

63. *Second Malaysia Plan*, p. 7.

64. Jomo (1988, p. 266).

65. An excellent analysis of the ruling political parties' direct involvement in business in Malaysia is provided by Edmund Terence Gomez, *Political Business: Corporate Involvement of Malaysian Political Parties* (Townsville: Centre for Southeast Asian Studies, 1994). Also see Peter Searle, James Cook University of North Queensland, *The Riddle of Malaysian Capitalism: Rent-Seekers or Real Capitalists?* (St. Leonards, NSW: Allen & Unwin, 1999).

66. SUPP won five parliamentary seats in the 1969 general election. SUPP was the first party formed in Sarawak in 1959 and since its formation had enjoyed stable grassroots support. Although SUPP was formed with a mildly socialist and multi-ethnic platform, in the 1960s it increasingly acquired the image of a Chinese party. And, it was commonly believed that SUPP had uneasy relations with the federal government until the party joined the Sarawak Alliance coalition in 1970. For the background to SUPP's entry to the ruling coalition, see Diane K. Mauzy, *Barisan Nasional: Coalition Government in Malaysia* (Kuala Lumpur: Marican & Sons Sdn. Bhd., 1983), pp. 48–55.

67. For the background to the coalition with Gerakan, see Mauzy (1983), pp. 55–62.

68. Harold Crouch, "From Alliance to Barisan Nasional", in *Malaysian Politics and the 1978 Elections*, edited by Harold Crouch, Lee Kam Hing, and Michael Ong (Kuala Lumpur: Oxford University Press, 1980), p. 7. For more details of the

PAS-Alliance coalition, see Alias Mohamed, *PAS's Platform: Development and Change 1951–1986* (Petaling Jaya: Gateway Publishing House, 1994), pp. 107–29; Mauzy (1983, pp. 66–74); and Funston (1980, pp. 244–47).

69. For an analysis of the 1974 general elections, see Chandrasekaran Pillay, *The 1974 General Elections in Malaysia: A Post Mortem* (Singapore: Institute of Southeast Asian Studies, 1974).

70. SNAP is an Iban-based party with some Chinese support. The party was formed in 1961 and was in the Sarawak Alliance between 1963 and 1966. It moved to opposition in the aftermath of the 1966 internal leadership crisis. For the background to SNAP's entry to the BN, see Mauzy (1983, pp. 105–7).

71. Interview with Lee Kim Sai, Kajang, 25 February 1998.

72. Diane K. Mauzy, "Malay Political Hegemony and Coercive Consociationalism", in *The Politics of Ethnic Conflict Regulation*, edited by John McGarry and Brendan O'Leary (London: Routledge, 1993), p. 111.

73. For details of Chinese politics just after the 1969 racial riots, see Francis Loh Kok Wah, *The Politics of Chinese Unity in Malaysia* (Singapore: Maruzen Asia, 1982); Lee Kam Hing, *Politics in Perak, 1969–1974: Some Preliminary Observations with Reference to the Non-Malay Political Parties* (Kuala Lumpur: Department of History, University of Malaya, 1977); and Means (1991, pp. 57–61).

74. At the 1975 UMNO vice-presidential election, Harun Idris received 427 votes, coming after Tun Razak's prominent supporters, that is, Ghafar Baba (838), Razaleigh Hamzah (642), and Mahathir Mohamad (474). Harun's growing popularity and outspoken criticism of Tun Razak and Hussein Onn made him a substantial threat to the younger leadership in UMNO. In these circumstances, Harun was charged on sixteen counts of corruption just two months before Tun Razak's death. Soon after Hussein Onn assumed the office of prime minister, he was convicted of corruption and was sentenced to two years' imprisonment. His prison sentence was later increased to four years on appeal. Despite the imprisonment, Harun was re-elected as a supreme council member in the 1978 UMNO general assembly. However, no pardon was arranged for him and Harun served his prison sentence until mid-1981.

75. More details on the leadership crises in PAS in the early 1970s can be found in Alias Mohamed (1994, pp. 138–46). Also see Crouch (1996, pp. 104–6).

76. Crouch (1996, p. 106).

77. For details of the 1978 Kelantan state elections, see Alias Mohamed (1994, pp. 168–76).

78. Sankaran Ramanathan and Mohd. Hamdan Adnan, *Malaysia's 1986 General Election: The Urban-Rural Dichotomy* (Singapore: Institute of Southeast Asian Studies, 1988), p. 54, table 4.

79. Harold Crouch, *Malaysia's 1982 General Election* (Singapore: Institute of Southeast Asian Studies, 1982), p. 52.

80. Crouch (1982, p. 61, table 7).

81. The MCA was the first political party involved directly in business, setting up the Koperatif Serbarguna (M) Bhd. (KSM) in 1968. For a detailed study of MCA's business involvement and the growth of its various investment arms, see Gomez (1994, pp. 175–239).

82. For details on the formation of Fleet Holdings and its activities, see Edmund Terence Gomez, *Politics in Business: UMNO's Corporate Investments* (Kuala Lumpur: FORUM, 1990), pp. 51–58; Peter Searle (1999, pp. 104–7).

83. As well as NSTP, over twenty other major investments were made by the Fleet Group during Razaleigh's stewardship as treasurer of UMNO. These included Bank of Commerce, American Malaysian Insurance, BCB Nominees, Fleet Communications and Distribution. It was, however, believed that the performance of these subsidiaries, except NSTP, was rather unsatisfactory. For the full list of companies controlled by Fleet Group by the end of the Razaleigh era, see Gomez (1990, p. 57).

84. Gomez (1990, pp. 61–90).

85. The direct trusteeship of Hatibudi by the UMNO top leader was confirmed in July 1987 by then Public Works Minister Samy Vellu. According to him, UMNO president Mahathir Mohamad, deputy president Ghafar Baba, secretary-general Sanusi Junid, and treasurer Daim Zainuddin were trustees of Hatibudi by virtue of their positions in the party. See *The Star*, 10 July 1987, cited in Gomez (1990, p. 110).

86. For more details of the privatization of the North-South Highway Project and other government projects won by UEM, see Lim Kit Siang, *The $62 Billion North-South Highway Scandal* (Petaling Jaya: Democratic Action Party, 1987); Gomez (1990, pp. 127–30). For details of Hatibudi's corporate structure as of mid-1989, see Gomez (1990, p. 135).

87. KUB was launched in 1977 by then UMNO president Hussein Onn. Unlike Fleet Group and Hatibudi, KUB has been openly acknowledged as one of UMNO's business ventures. The growth of KUB is described by Gomez (1990, pp. 140–65).

88. Peter Searle (1999, p. 116). For the background to and processes of amalgamation of UMNO's corporate assets under Renong, see Gomez (1994, pp. 116–55).

89. *FEER*, 17 May 1990 (Doug Tsuruoka, "The UMNO Shuffle") and Gomez (1994, pp. 74–76, 80–83).

90. *The Star*, 4 July 1983.

91. For more details of the amendments to the PPPA, see *FEER*, 5 April 1984 (James Clad, "Press under Pressure").

92. *FEER*, 10 December 1987 (Suhaini Aznam, "Taming the Tame").

93. *FEER*, 20 September 1984 (Tan Boon Kean, "Orwell's Year in the Malaysian Press").

94. Official Secrets Act 1972 (ACT 88), Section 2 and 16A. For more details on the amendments to the OSA in 1986, see *FEER*, 18 December 1986 (Suhaini Aznam, "An Act of Approval").

95. *FEER*, 17 November 1983 (Mohideen Abdul Kader, "The Press in a Climate of Fear").

96. Public rallies were banned after 1978 because of the armed communist insurrection. Although the forty-one-year armed struggle of the Malayan Communist Party ended with a peace agreement in December 1989, public rallies, even during general election, are still banned.

97. The total number of ISA arrests per annum notably decreased as follows: 1979 (800); 1980 (668); 1981 (470); 1982 (377); 1983 (196); 1984 (168). See Munro-Kua (1996, p. 146, table 9.1).

98. See Societies (Amendment) Act 1981, Section 2.

99. Simon Barraclough, "Political Participation and Its Regulation in Malaysia: Opposition to the Societies (Amendment) Act 1981", *Pacific Affairs* 57 (1984, p. 454).

100. An overview of the series of amendments to the Societies Act can be found in Barraclough's article (1984). Also see *FEER*, 26 November 1982 (K. Das, "Societies in Shock"); *FEER*, 31 March 1983 (Jeffrey Segal, "The Third Time Around").

101. See Constitutional (Amendment) Act 1981, Article 150 clause 2.

102. The requirement for the Yang di-Pertuan Agong to act on advice is contained in Constitutional (Amendment) Act 1981, Article 40 clause 1.

103. For more background, context, and implications of the 1983 constitutional amendments, see Azmi Khalid, "Emergency Powers & Constitutional Changes", *Aliran Quarterly* 3, no. 3 (1983, pp. 5–8). Also see H.P. Lee, *Constitutional Conflicts in Contemporary Malaysia* (Kuala Lumpur: Oxford University Press, 1995), pp. 22–42.

104. *FEER*, 8 May 1981 (K. Das, "After Hussein, What?").

105. Interview with Razaleigh Hamzah, Kuala Lumpur, 17 February 1998.

106. Interview with Razaleigh Hamzah, Kuala Lumpur, 23 February 1998.

107. See Ranjit Gill, *The UMNO Crisis* (Singapore: Sterling Corporate Services, 1988), p. 20. For more on the 1981 party election, see *FEER*, 3 July 1981 (K. Das, "The Old Guard Changes").

108. UMNO's incumbent president was once challenged during the UMNO general election in 1978. Hussein Onn, the then acting UMNO president, was challenged

by Sulaiman Palestin, a candidate put up by the Harun Idris faction, in order to register their disapproval over the way Hussein Onn treated Harun Idris. By then, Harun Idris, one of the most outspoken critics of Hussein Onn, had been expelled from UMNO on corruption charges. But Sulaiman was easily defeated. For more detail, see Means (1991, pp. 56–57).

109. *FEER*, 24 July 1981 (K. Das, "Mahathir Picks His Men").

110. *FEER*, 7 June 1984 (K. Das, "All the President's Men"); and *FEER*, 26 July 1984 (K. Das, "New Faces of 1984").

111. See Means (1991, pp. 113–20). The conflict between Mahathir and the rulers was related to the 1983 constitutional amendments aimed at removing certain powers of the rulers, especially the royal assent to a Bill. And this created much controversy among the UMNO leaders and members. See H.P. Lee (1995, pp. 22–42).

112. Interview with Musa Hitam, Kuala Lumpur, 13 February 1998.

113. It was alleged that Mahathir persuaded Razaleigh, in a ninety-minute discussion, to remain in the Cabinet. See Ranjit Gill (1988, p. 21).

114. *FEER*, 5 July 1984 (K. Das, "The Mahathir Dilemma").

115. Interview with Musa Hitam, Kuala Lumpur, 13 February 1998.

116. *FEER*, 26 July 1984 (K. Das, "New Faces of 1984").

117. On the culminating leadership conflict between Mahathir and Musa, see *Asiaweek*, 16 March 1986 ("Rift at the Top").

118. Means (1991, pp. 200–1).

119. *FEER*, 12 March 1987 (Suhaini Aznam, "In Everything but Name").

120. For the full election results, see *NST*, 24 April 1987; 25 April 1987; and *FEER*, 7 May 1987 ("The Vital Forty-Three").

121. During the nomination process, Mahathir, as the incumbent leader, was able to secure a public pledge of support from all Malay chief ministers. Also, he had been nominated as party president by more than 70 per cent of the total party divisions. Larger support from the incumbent officials was expected since their appointments were the result of Mahathir's patronage.

122. Ranjit Gill (1988, p. 37) and Means (1991, p. 204).

123. Confidential interview in February 1998.

124. For details of the controversy after the 24 April election, see Ranjit Gill (1988, pp. 41–44).

Towards Mahathir's Personal Dominance

5

[T]he first critical threshold in the transition to democracy is precisely the move by some group within the ruling bloc to obtain support from forces external to it. (Adam Przeworski 1986)[1]

I am sad and disappointed that UMNO which my colleagues and I had built and supported until it became a huge and powerful party, a party which for 42 years the Malays depended upon to protect their well-being has suddenly been demolished and destroyed. ... It is those with power that have destroyed UMNO. It is because they have become intoxicated with their power that they forgot to save UMNO. (Tunku Abdul Rahman Putra 1987)[2]

Until recently, many scholars have given primary attention in their analysis of conflict management in multi-racial societies to the role of national élites and sub-élites. And it has been assumed that in a severely divided society the national élites and sub-élites tend towards a consociational framework in preserving regime stability as well as democratic procedures. In a recent study of Malaysia, Case argues that the behaviour of the ruling élites and the extent of consensual unity between them is crucial in managing socio-political and ethnic conflicts.[3]

But, what if the ruling élites are not unified? What if they are divided, being from different ethnic communities and from different factions within the ruling bloc? In other words, how do rivalries within the dominant ruling élites affect their behaviour and the extent of consensual unity in a multi-racial society? In Malaysia, would the unambiguous Malay dominance after the 1969 racial riots be renegotiated towards the recovery of consociational frameworks or would the Malay dominance be strengthened and consolidated, if the national leadership were severely fragmented? Or would it eventually be replaced by another, possibly more severe, form of authoritarian rule?

For our purpose, the few years after the 1987 UMNO general assembly, which led to a bitter split in the ruling bloc, provide an invaluable and unprecedented situation to examine not only the relations between élite disunity and ethnic politics but also the very nature of the Malay ruling élites' political adaptability and responsiveness to the changing structure of conflict in an ethnically divided society. While the 1969 inter-racial riots marked a new epoch in renegotiating the post-independent consociational contract in Malaysian society, the 1987 intra-Malay leadership crisis was another turning point. The dominant Malay political party, UMNO, had never experienced such a divisive and bitter fight over the question of leadership. And the country was able to witness political events which had never been seen, heard nor even read of before.

The period 1987–90 was very controversial. On the one hand, this period has been perceived as a more responsive and competitive one than any other in the history of Malaysian politics.[4] There might have been a transition from "semi" to "full" democracy due to the factional rivalries and the growing electoral competitiveness within ruling-élite circles during this period.[5] Indeed, as Przeworski observes in his chapter in *Transitions from Authoritarian Rule: Comparative Perspectives*, regime change in authoritarian or semi-authoritarian states has often been attributed to conflicts and/or disintegration within the ruling group, especially in countries with a strong tradition of single dominance power.[6] In Malaysia, therefore, a more responsive political system would be expected to emerge from the severe factional split in the country's dominant political party, UMNO. Gomez and Jomo speculated that the breakdown of an authoritarian regime, if it is to emerge, may come from severe factionalism within UMNO circles.[7]

However, there is another side to this argument. While conflicts within the ruling bloc seem to have contributed to more competitiveness and more favourable consociational conditions in the political sphere than ever before, such a desperate situation also encouraged the ruling élites to adopt more repressive and intransigent strategies to defend their political positions. Musa Hitam, former Deputy Prime Minister, stressed in a recent interview that "the national leaders tend to look for a scapegoat when faced with a desperate crisis situation". In a multi-ethnic society like Malaysia, they are inclined to racial tactics to justify repressive controls and to fill their own "empty stomach".[8] Similarly, a senior government official argued that the period 1987–90 can be viewed as a "systematic process to consolidate Mahathir's personal dominance within UMNO circles as well as nationwide".[9] If there were any accommodative gestures by Mahathir in managing political and ethnic conflicts at this time, they could be attributed to tactical calculations to avoid greater risks to his control, rather than his growing commitment towards political democracy. As Lustick has stressed, a consociational or responsive approach can be deployed effectively only if an alternative form of control or domination is available to the ruling élite.[10]

This chapter explores Mahathir's strategies towards regime maintenance during the controversial period 1987–90. The main focus will be on an analysis of how Mahathir successfully restored political power and national leadership from the challenges of a bitter leadership struggle and an unusually strong opposition led by dissident UMNO factions.

Motives behind Mahathir's Personal Dominance

Immediately after the battle over the party leadership in 1987, Mahathir seemed to face two contradictory political options, both of which would pose difficulties. One was to eradicate all remnants of leadership rivalry within UMNO. This option would have secured his own hegemony in UMNO, but possibly have created a permanent split within the Malay community as a whole. The other was to accommodate the losers according to his own advice to the MCA leaders during their leadership crisis a few years earlier. Commenting on the 1985 MCA party election which was accompanied by a severe factional dispute within MCA,

Mahathir mentioned that "winners should not take all, while those defeated should not lose all. After all, even losers have their supporters and they have the right to their views".[11] While this may be seen as preserving the accommodative tradition of Malaysian politics, for Mahathir it may also have led to the existence of continuous factional rivalry within UMNO and have left the door open for his political rivals in the next party election in 1990.

Of these two alternatives, Mahathir signalled clearly that he would choose the first option. Immediately after the election he stated that he had no intention of *menang sorak kampung tergadai* (win cheers but lose the land). In his closing speech at the 1987 party assembly, Mahathir stressed that "[w]e must be aware that if we win, we get something and that if we lose, we will not get it. I myself realized that fairly early and I accepted the fact that in the event that I lost, it was impossible for me to continue living in *Seri Perdana* and remain as Prime Minister."[12] In line with Machiavelli's suggestion in *The Prince*, Mahathir, this time as a dominator, set about ruthlessly driving out all of his political rivals rather than acting as a manipulator and forming a viable coalition to overcome his leadership crisis.[13] If there were any room for the accommodative tradition after 1987, it would not appear until 1990 when Mahathir had completely consolidated his dominance within the ruling party.

In contrast to his relatively moderate attitude during the earlier period, why did Mahathir show such ruthless determination towards his political opponents within UMNO after the 1987 leadership crisis? Also, what enabled Mahathir to take total control of and tighten his own grip on UMNO after the 1987 leadership crisis?

Factionalism is a common feature of party organization although political parties are often perceived as unitary actors in political theories. Likewise, factional conflicts, especially within dominant political parties, are a significant means of restraining the oligarchic tendencies of party leaders, though internal strife is deemed sometimes negative. Given that factionalism had been common in the party since its formation in 1946, UMNO's experience was, and still is, not all that distinctive. Although UMNO factional conflicts had not often occurred within the public purview, the internal life of UMNO had undergone a series of quiet, but constant, struggles for the strengthening of factional alliances during the 1960s and 1970s, which frequently spilt into the open in the 1980s.[14] To some extent the incumbent party leaders' influence was effectively checked, at least until the mid-1980s, by the strength of well-defined factional alliances within UMNO circles. This was one key feature that kept the Malaysian political system dynamic and relatively responsive, despite the long occupancy of government by dominant parties in the ruling coalition, specifically UMNO.

As described in the previous chapter, Mahathir, as the new leader, adopted a checks-and-balances strategy to manage strong and popular political figures within the ruling party. Many believe that Mahathir's subtle tactics were quite successful in dealing with party stalwarts in the period 1981–87, given the vulnerability of his political dominance in UMNO. However, such a strategy was only half successful in the end. A more critical view claimed that it was Mahathir's complete failure as he deliberately allowed further development of identifiable factions within the party. Ironically, the unprecedented level of electoral competitiveness provided Razaleigh Hamzah and Musa Hitam with the opportunity to mobilize grassroots support.[15] Perhaps more unpleasantly for Mahathir, the dynamics of political competition contributed to the emergence of more clearly defined and better organized factional alignments around his political rival's personality within the ruling party, and eventually caused the leadership crisis in 1987. For Mahathir, this was a totally unexpected result.

Several other post-election phenomena may have motivated Mahathir to switch to other means of maintaining his leadership. Most of all, the behaviour of the election losers was largely unexpected and even unprecedented in Malay tradition. The unusual open declaration of support for the defeated challengers and the resistance to the elected incumbent were enough to indicate that the traditional UMNO shadow-play (*wayang kulit*) would be replaced by direct confrontation. Neutrality would no longer be possible. The vigorous and open factional antagonism was enough to convince Mahathir that there would be continuous reactions and responses to his leadership, despite his electoral victory. A clear example was the series of nationwide tours after the 1987 UMNO elections, organized by Razaleigh and Musa, expressing resentment of Mahathir's leadership and demonstrating their factional strength.

Furthermore, there were indications from dissident leaders, especially from the Razaleigh faction, that they would not accept Mahathir's leadership style and would provide an alternative to it.[16] Although dissident leaders occasionally pledged their support to Mahathir, they stipulated conditions such as "no witch-hunting", "no intimidation", and/or "change of leadership style".[17]

Even worse, there was open speculation that another attempt to overthrow Mahathir's leadership might be launched at the next UMNO election in 1990 and that, given his narrow margin of victory in 1987, Mahathir would not survive such a battle. Tunku Abdul Rahman, the first Prime Minister of Malaysia, argued that Team B could claim a moral victory and there would be fighting until the next party election in 1990.[18] The battle lines between Team A and Team B were already being drawn after the 1987 party election. As a clear example, on 9 May 1987, one day before Team B started its nationwide tour to promote "Malay unity", Razaleigh made it clear that his team's strategy for the next UMNO supreme council elections of 1990 would be launched at the UMNO Youth and *Wanita* elections in 1988. Razaleigh also instructed his followers in Kelantan to boycott *Berita Harian* and *New Straits Times* for allegedly publishing "wild and biased" reports in the run-up and the aftermath of the 1987 UMNO general assembly. Then he urged his business associates to withhold advertising in the two newspapers.[19] He also called on his supporters "to choose only branch and division leaders who could see eye-to-eye with him if they wanted him to continue his involvement in politics".[20]

In short, although the results of the "battle royal" favoured Mahathir, the aftermath of the party elections showed that Malay politics in particular, and Malaysian politics as a whole, would never be the same again. Everything was openly discussed as factional antagonism became more intense. For Mahathir, there were enough signs that the checks-and-balances strategy was no longer enough to maintain his leadership. It can therefore be assumed that Mahathir felt the necessity of shifting from a moderate checks-and-balances strategy to one of more direct domination in order to consolidate his position within the ruling party.

Prelude to Mahathir's Loyalist Party

In the midst of his own leadership crisis, Mahathir needed to overcome an internal party problem and tighten his political grip on UMNO. However, Mahathir must have been aware that it would not go down well among the already-split Malay community, even among the Malays who supported him, if he were seen to be suppressing dissident factions in UMNO at this time. Mahathir therefore used the racial card to legitimize drastic action and thus to move towards the tightening of his grip on power in the ruling party.

Indeed, relations between the Malays and the Chinese were tense in the early 1980s. The severe economic recession in the mid-1980s, in particular, caused the non-Malay communities to voice their anxieties about the affirmative-action economic policy and its probable continuation. Furthermore, opposition parties and various social activists increased their criticisms of the Mahathir government — over such issues as corruption, scandals, government wrong-doing, and draconian laws. Given the relatively liberal situation of the early 1980s, sensitive racial issues were openly debated. Examples involved the issues of Bukit China, Chinese signboards, the Lion Dance, elective subjects at the University of Malaysia, and the new primary school curriculum.

Nonetheless, ethnic tensions did not evolve into overt political antagonism until the UMNO leadership crisis in 1987. The event which stirred ethnic tension between the Malays and the Chinese was the collapse of many deposit-taking co-operatives (DTCs), some of which had been associated with MCA. By April 1987, the DTCs had experienced massive financial losses mainly due to the economic downturn and financial mismanagement. In May 1987 the MCA leadership proposed bailing out the DTCs in a dollar-for-dollar rescue scheme to save Chinese investors. The requested bailout by the MCA was similar to a previous bailout, when the Mahathir government propped up some troubled *bumiputera* financial institutions such as Bank Bumiputera and Bumiputera Malaysia Finance when they lost over RM2.5 billion in Hong Kong. Another *bumiputera* firm, Perwira Habib, had also been rescued by the Mahathir government in early 1987.

The Mahathir government, however, appeared reluctant to accommodate MCA's proposal, especially after the 1987 UMNO elections. Consequently, relations between the Malays and the Chinese, UMNO and MCA in particular, worsened. In particular, then MCA deputy president Lee Kim Sai warned that the party might withdraw from the BN coalition if their refund scheme for the DTCs was not approved by the government.[21] In responding to this, Najib Tun Razak, then acting UMNO Youth chief, mentioned in an open statement that UMNO would review MCA's position within the BN coalition before the party decided to pull out.[22] Ethnic tension increased again in mid-September 1987 when the government posted non-Mandarin-educated headmasters and senior assistants to national-type Chinese primary schools.[23] Racial tension subsequently rose to a new high as a result of strained interactions between UMNO and the Chinese community. Eventually, escalating ethnic conflict provided a rationale for a series of mass arrests under the Internal Security Act (ISA), commonly known as *Operasi Lalang*, in October 1987.

Why did Mahathir's government adopt such an uncompromising attitude towards the Chinese community in the wake of the 1987 UMNO leadership crisis? Whatever the motives behind its stance, the issue of non-Mandarin school teachers was so sensitive within the Chinese community that even the ruling Chinese parties, MCA and Gerakan, felt compelled to involve themselves in public protests along with many other Chinese associations, including the DAP. A former minister and senior MCA leader said that the MCA had no option but to fight hard on this issue to retain any credibility among the Chinese community. The party had recently lost enormous credibility over the DTCs issue.[24]

Even though the MCA, UMNO's main partner in the ruling coalition, was in a dilemma dealing with its Chinese supporters at the time, the Mahathir government's response to MCA's request appeared to be intransigent. For example, on 4 October, Anwar Ibrahim, then Education Minister, made it clear that the government would stand by its decision on the non-Mandarin school teacher issue and would not bend to political pressure from the Chinese community. Thereafter, the Mahathir government's stand over the issue was reiterated without change, even though various Chinese associations suggested that they were willing to accept even non-Chinese teachers as long as they were qualified in Mandarin.[25]

In these circumstances, on 11 October, the agitation in the Chinese community came to a head at a public rally at Thean Hou Temple in Kuala Lumpur organized by the MCA, Gerakan, the DAP and fifteen other Chinese organizations. At the rally, they decided to boycott classes in Chinese primary schools on 16 and 17 October.[26] In the mean time, UMNO Youth also organized a mammoth rally at the Jalan Raja Muda Stadium in Kuala Lumpur on 17 October.[27] The Ministry of Home Affairs, of which Mahathir was Minister, announced that the government would allow UMNO Youth to carry on with the rally even though it was aware of increasing racial tension.[28] At the rally, which was attended by about 15,000 people, some UMNO politicians deliberately stirred up Malay racial sentiment and various provocative banners were also displayed. They claimed that the Chinese component parties in the BN were threatening Malay special rights by secretly working with the DAP in the wake of the intra-Malay leadership crisis.[29]

UMNO then announced that it would hold a mammoth rally on 1 November to celebrate its forty-first anniversary in the Merdeka Stadium in Kuala Lumpur. About 500,000 UMNO members and sympathizers were expected to participate in the planned UMNO unity rally and UMNO national leaders made a considerable effort to mobilize Malay support. UMNO had originally planned to hold its forty-first anniversary in Johor but later changed the place to Merdeka Stadium in Kuala Lumpur for the purpose of asserting Malay political dominance and maximizing mobilization of the people. The sheer size of the UMNO unity rally, and the gathering place reminiscent of the May 13 riots, added to the atmosphere of uncertainty and fear. Adding fuel to an already explosive situation, in an unrelated shooting incident on 18 October 1987, a Malay soldier ran amok in a predominantly Chinese area and killed a Malay and wounded a Chinese and another Malay. While the incident turned out to be an isolated criminal act, tension mounted as wild rumours circulated about the nature of the shooting.

It was in these circumstances that the police launched a series of arrests under the ISA on 27 October. By the end of the day, fifty-five people had been detained and the figure increased to at least 106 by mid-January 1988. The detainees included the parliamentary opposition leader, MPs, state assemblymen, academics, social activists, Chinese educationists, environmentalists, and even humble workers. Among the arrested were three UMNO members, eight MCA members, five Gerakan members, fifteen PAS members, sixteen DAP members, and two PSRM members. The inclusion of these BN politicians was viewed as a token gesture that *Operasi Lalang* was a multi-racial exercise. The ISA had to appear even-handed, otherwise, the arrests would have increased resentment among the non-Malay. In fact, all detainees from UMNO, MCA, and Gerakan were released within two months, while many others from opposition parties and NGOs were detained much longer. The three UMNO members arrested were all closely associated with Team B, although the UMNO rallies were strongly supported and initiated by Mahathir's allies.[30] Their arrests, therefore, were widely viewed as a stern warning to dissident factions in UMNO.

Furthermore, the Mahathir government immediately banned two popular daily newspapers — the English-language *The Star*, and the Chinese-language *Sin Chew Jit Poh* — as well as the Malay-language biweekly *Watan*. A senior journalist from *The Star*, who asked not to be named, said that the newspapers were carefully targeted to include ones in different languages. This was intended to warn the media as a whole. *The Star*, in particular, was banned because the paper had provided some avenues for the expression of alternative views from non-established groups, specifically some dissident Team B leaders.[31] Finally, the UMNO rally scheduled for 1 November was cancelled.

Government officials later announced that the ISA arrests were for security, not political, reasons. Mahathir claimed that he had to take immediate action to prevent racial riots and save the country from eventual danger and disaster, as the ISA detainees had been creating unnecessary tensions for years.[32] The Ministry of Education also insisted that the number of Mandarin-educated teachers applying to teach in Chinese primary schools was insufficient.[33] It was also claimed that some Chinese educationists and politicians, including the MCA and Gerakan leaders, were strident in voicing their views and played on racial sentiment to prove their commitment to the Chinese community. Clearly the nation was rushing towards a headlong collision in September and October 1987, particularly in Kuala Lumpur. According to government officials, the ISA arrests were simply a means of defusing escalating ethnic tension.

This interpretation, however, overlooked some obvious questions. Who had been responsible for heightening racial tension, especially during the few weeks before the 1 November UMNO unity rally? Why did the Mahathir government make the highly contentious move of transferring the non-Mandarin-educated teachers to national-type Chinese primary schools at a time when racial relations were fraught and, despite widespread protests, maintained such an uncompromising stance? Indeed, the shortage of non-Mandarin-educated teachers had been a decade-long issue in Malaysian society. Moreover, it was widely acknowledged among the Chinese community that the UMNO-led government would not send non-Mandarin-educated teachers to national-type Chinese primary schools, except teachers of Malay or English. In addition, for this issue at least, the Mahathir government had the capacity to keep it out of the public arena, if it were merely an administrative matter. For this reason, a senior MCA official believes that there was a "hidden agenda" pursued by certain UMNO factions to divert public attention away from their own desperate leadership crisis by using "a deviation in implementation of the Chinese education policy".[34] Interestingly, whether it is a coincidence or not, racial tension reached a climax when the "UMNO eleven case" finally went to the High Court for judgement after the UMNO unity council failed to reach an out-of-court settlement, on 14 October, over the question of the legality of the 1987 UMNO general assembly. After that, the issue of the internal UMNO crisis was suddenly removed from media coverage as well as public attention. Instead, fanning racial tension became a real issue.[35] Tunku Abdul Rahman, the first Prime Minister of Malaysia, argued that Mahathir desperately needed to create a national crisis to mobilize the Malays "as a united force to a common enemy — and the imaginary enemy in this case was the Chinese community".[36]

It is difficult to prove whether Mahathir deliberately allowed, or even encouraged, the rise of ethnic tension at this time to foster an atmosphere of fear, thereby providing conditions for strengthening his own political position within UMNO circles. However, it cannot be denied that escalating racial tension gave Mahathir a circumstantial advantage for reinstating emergency rule, just as the 1969 racial riots had given a similar advantage to the ruling Malay élite almost two decades ago. While the background and causes of rising racial tension in both cases appear to be different, the outcome was similar. In short, Mahathir was the main beneficiary of the heightened racial tension and the subsequent security situation after the ISA arrests.

Operasi Lalang in October 1987 created considerable fear outside and inside UMNO circles. As one ISA detainee argued, "it was not the matter of the number of the detainees but the fears that Mahathir created … anybody can be detained. Mahathir created the fears and paralyzed the whole Malaysian society by the invention of *Operasi Lalang*".[37] A senior Team B leader also stressed that *Operasi Lalang* was quite successful in creating a culture of fear within dissident UMNO circles and thus served its purpose very effectively in the midst of Mahathir's own leadership crisis. He argues that it was not until Mahathir obtained maximum effect that the planned UMNO unity rally was called off. According to him, if Mahathir had not achieved his expected objective with the ISA arrests, the UMNO mass rally on 1 November would not have been cancelled.[38] Lim Kit Siang, then parliamentary opposition leader who was also detained under the ISA, summed up the situation:

> Mahathir used the racial sentiment and even allowed the escalation of the situation so that he could crack down to consolidate his position against his internal challenge. So I would say the ISA arrest was more UMNO directed and motivated rather than the racial crisis during that time. This was in fact in order to fight for real challenges from inside [UMNO].[39]

Creation of a New Ruling Party around Mahathir's Personality

While *Operasi Lalang* created a culture of fear which favoured Mahathir, the formation of a new party provided another situational advantage for the consolidation of Mahathir's power in the ruling party. In fact, what Mahathir did for the first year after the 1987 UMNO general assembly was to destroy the existing party and rebuild the ruling party around his dominant personality. In doing so, his actions closely resemble Machiavelli's advice in *The Discourses*: the best thing a leader can do in order to retain his influence, if the foundations of his power are weak, is to reorganize everything in the state from scratch.[40]

First Step: An Immediate Political Purge and Intransigence

Mahathir's intransigence over those in UMNO who were critical of his leadership was clear even before the end of the 1987 UMNO general assembly. The very first hint that those in cabinet posts were likely to be replaced by a choir of pro-Mahathir yes-men came in his adjournment speech at the assembly: "If I had chosen those who were loyal to me, then there would not have been any contest for the presidency this time."[41] This was an oblique, but clear, message to the dissident UMNO leaders to step down voluntarily. Mahathir openly attacked dissident UMNO factions as treacherous by claiming that they disclosed a series of classified government documents during the party election campaigns.[42]

Less than a week after the UMNO election and one day after they had submitted their resignation letters, Mahathir accepted the resignations of Razaleigh as Trade and Industry Minister, and Rais Yatim as Foreign Minister. A day later, Mahathir also sent dismissal letters — stating that their services were no longer required after 7 May — to three other ministers and four deputy ministers who had mounted a campaign against him during the last UMNO election. The political purges were announced just a few hours before Mahathir went overseas on a personal visit to the United States and Japan. The ministers dropped from the Cabinet were: Defence Minister Abdullah Ahmad Badawi; Welfare Minister Shahrir; and Minister in the Prime Minister's Department Ajib Ahmad. The deputy ministers were Kadir Sheikh Fadzir (Foreign Affairs Ministry); Rahman Osman (Transport Ministry); Zainal Abidin Zin (Energy, Telecommunication and Posts Ministry); and Radzi Sheikh Ahmad (Primary Industries Ministry).[43]

The timing and extent of Mahathir's political purge surprised many people, even though such a move had been widely expected after the party election. According to Rais Yatim, Mahathir's drastic action on the very first day of *Ramadan* — the fasting month to seek forgiveness and to forgive fellow Muslims for any trespass they may have committed during the past year — sacking the three ministers and four deputy ministers shocked the Malay community. Moreover, it was claimed that these seven ministers and deputy ministers "had no intention" of resigning from their positions because they had won at the 1987 UMNO election.[44] The dismissal of Abdullah Badawi even surprised Mahathir's supporters. Abdullah Badawi had won a vice-president's post with the second highest number of votes, and both Ajib Ahmad and Shahrir had retained their supreme council seats in the party election. All four deputy ministers had also been elected as supreme council members. In light of these surprising dismissals, Mahathir's immediate political purge was regarded as a clear indication that there would be no spirit of consensus nor accommodation after the tightly contested leadership struggle. Even Mahathir's allies saw that he was "taking revenge" against his political opponents during this period.[45]

As expected, all of Mahathir's allies, including Daim Zainuddin, Anwar Ibrahim, Megat Junid, and Rafidah Aziz, retained their ministerships and the vacancies were filled by Mahathir's loyal supporters on 19 May. In a further move to consolidate his position, the Federal Territory Ministry was abolished and its functions transferred to the Prime Minister's Department. In addition to the Home Affairs Ministry, Mahathir also held the Justice Ministry, left vacant since 1986. According to Means, Mahathir's takeover of the justice portfolio was a significant step as "legal issues were assuming more political importance for the future of his government".[46]

In the same way, Mahathir made changes in the line-up of the state liaison chairmen of UMNO. According to Clause 13.5 of the UMNO constitution, the party president need only consult division heads in the respective states on the appointment of state chairmen and deputies but is not bound by their opinion. In addition, their services could be terminated by the president at any time. Consequently, the reshuffle of the state liaison chairmen affected Abdullah Badawi (replaced by Anwar) and Ajib Ahmad in their respective states, Penang and Johor.

Shortly after the reshuffle at the higher level, political purges continued at the lower levels not only within the party but also in both federal and state governments. Within a week of the dismissal of the dissident cabinet ministers, several Johor state executive council members were "forced to resign".[47] Political purges were carried out extensively in other states as well and were a clear warning to dissident factions.

An example of Mahathir's intransigence was his refusal to participate in round-table talks with Team B leaders. As the internal leadership struggle deepened, Tunku Abdul Rahman urged Mahathir, as the incumbent, to invite Razaleigh and Musa for talks to strengthen party unity.[48] However, Mahathir made it clear that there was no need for such talks because there had never been such a practice in UMNO or the Barisan Nasional.[49] Rather, Mahathir blamed his political opponents and branded them "traitors" during his state unity tours a few days later.[50] Instead of unity talks, Mahathir attempted to separate Razaleigh from the other dissident leaders in Team B, that is Musa and Abdullah Badawi. A prominent political commentator said that, based on a "very reliable source", there was a secret meeting between Mahathir and Musa as well as Abdullah Badawi during this early period.[51] It was not until 3 October, almost six months later, that Mahathir and Razaleigh finally met for the first time since the UMNO election.

Second Step: Towards the Dissolution of UMNO

Another illustration of Mahathir's inflexibility was shown in the political developments that led to the dissolution of UMNO itself. It was even speculated that Mahathir and his supporters deliberately allowed the dissolution of UMNO. Two months after the acrimonious "battle royal", twelve UMNO members, from seven party divisions, filed a suit in the High Court on 25 June 1987 asking for the April 24 UMNO election to be declared "null and void".[52] In the suit, the twelve UMNO members argued that about seventy-eight of the 1,479 delegates were "deliberately" or "recklessly" involved in illegalities, in spite of their verbal and written complaints to the incumbent party leaders, including party secretary-general Sanusi Junid before the general assembly.[53] They claimed that fifty-three unregistered branches from seven party divisions had sent delegates to the divisional elections which then elected the delegates to the UMNO general assembly. Consequently, the results of the election were substantially affected by the seventy-eight illegal delegates, from the seven party divisions, since the margins of victory for the two top posts (president and deputy president) — forty-three and forty votes — were very narrow. The twelve UMNO members thus alleged that the UMNO assembly was "unconstitutional and illegal" and sought a court order for a fresh general assembly and election of all posts. Later in

August, one of the twelve UMNO members withdrew his appeal.[54]
Finally, Justice Harun Hashim of the Kuala Lumpur High Court, in
dismissing the UMNO eleven case on 4 February, ruled that under
Section 12 (3) of the Societies Act, UMNO was an unlawful society "at
that material time" because of the existence of unapproved branches.
Section 12 (3) of the Societies Act says: "Where a registered society
established a branch without the prior approval of the registrar, such
registered society and the branch so established shall be deemed to be
unlawful societies." Justice Harun said if the facts showed that UMNO
had established branches without the approval of the Registrar of
Societies, it seemed to him that UMNO itself was an unlawful society.[55]

What are the indications of Mahathir's intransigence, and why did
he deliberately allow the dissolution of the party itself during this period?
To begin with, it was widely viewed that the eleven UMNO members'
suit was filed on behalf of anti-Mahathir factions since three of the seven
divisions were in Kelantan, the stronghold of Razaleigh, and three more
came from Penang, home of Abdullah Badawi. Furthermore, there was
speculation that Razaleigh was funding the suit as well as providing legal
assistance.[56] Razaleigh, however, said that some of the eleven members
were "pro-Mahathir people" and "they were in Team A". At that time,
he was unable to explain properly because "these people [pro-Mahathir]
said they are all Team B members, but actually they are not."[57] If this is
true, what does it imply? Whether or not this is true, the UMNO eleven
case did not come as a surprise to Mahathir's faction as they had been
aware of it for several weeks. Sanusi, then UMNO secretary-general and
close confidant of Mahathir, said that the party headquarters, in fact,
expected legal action and were quite well prepared for it.[58]

In fact, it was largely due to the uncompromising attitude of the
incumbent party leaders that the early settlement within the party failed
and the case eventually went to the legal judgment, which led to the
dissolution of the party. After UMNO had set up a five-member UMNO
unity committee on 26 September 1987, the High Court granted a
postponement of the hearing for two weeks to enable the committee to
solve its legal problem in an out-of-court settlement.[59] Nevertheless,
during the committee's negotiations from 1 October to 14 October, the
incumbent UMNO leaders showed no intention of granting concessions

to appease Team B leaders and members regarding the guarantee of their political future and/or the issues relating to the validity of the recent UMNO election.[60] Although Mahathir claimed that the five-member UMNO unity committee was given "the necessary powers" to solve UMNO eleven's legal action in an out-of-court settlement, the UMNO unity committee's essential role seemed not to accommodate differences between Team A and Team B, but to prevent any immediate and possible challenges to the party leadership.[61] The failure of the negotiated settlement meant that the final decision was eventually forwarded to the High Court.

After the High Court decision, Mahathir did not take any steps to prevent the judiciary's death sentence to UMNO, nor to save the party from de-registration by the Registrar of Societies. Furthermore, the very person who first brought the legal status of UMNO into question, by drawing the attention of the High Court to Section 12 (3) of the Societies Act, was none other than Sri Ram, the leading counsel for UMNO. In contrast to this, the leading counsel for the eleven UMNO members, Raja Aziz Addruse, made it very clear that he wanted the High Court to concentrate on the illegal branches only, rather than to link their case to the question of UMNO's legality as a whole. By raising that line of questioning by Sri Ram, however, the party leadership gave the High Court no option but to declare the party null and void. On this decision, Tunku Abdul Rahman argued that "UMNO was deliberately allowed to be declared unlawful through the action of the UMNO lawyer himself".[62]

In addition, Mahathir's government intensified its pressure on the judiciary before the High Court judgment over the UMNO eleven case. This was largely due to strained relations between Mahathir's government and the judiciary over the period before the judgment. Specifically in the preceding two years, there had been several cases where the judiciary decided in favour of the plaintiff against the Mahathir government, as shown in the series of cases of the *Asian Wall Street Journal* (*AWSJ*) in November 1986, *Aliran* in 1987, and United Engineers (Malaysia) just a few months before the crucial UMNO eleven case in February 1988.[63] To make matters worse, several prominent judges increasingly emphasized the essential role of judicial independence during this period.[64] Put simply, the several court judgments in favour of plaintiffs and the emphasis on judicial independence were enough to worry the Mahathir government as the UMNO eleven judgment was approaching.

In this context, Mahathir criticized the independent judges in an interview with *Malaysian Business* just one month before the hearing of the UMNO eleven case. Mahathir likened the independent judges to "black sheep" and blamed these "fiercely independent" judges who "hammer the government" just to prove their independence and courage.[65] This criticism was followed by the government's reshuffle of the judiciary just a few weeks before the decision of the UMNO eleven case. Nine judges, including Justice Harun Hashim who was due to preside over the UMNO eleven case, were transferred between state capitals or between different departments of the Kuala Lumpur High Court. Justice Harun, well known for his independent judgments, was transferred from appellate and special powers to commercial crimes. This was widely viewed as a warning to the judiciary, even though Harun was still in charge of the UMNO eleven case.[66] In these circumstances, the High Court decided in favour of the incumbent party leadership against the plaintiff, which led to UMNO being declared an unlawful organization.

Even after UMNO was declared unlawful, there was still a chance to save the party from de-registration. The incumbent UMNO leadership, however, was unwilling to take the necessary steps to revive the party. Rather, they took a tougher stand and did not offer a compromise to the dissident UMNO leaders. Salleh Abas, then Lord President, made it clear that Mahathir showed no interest in reviving UMNO.[67]

Firstly, it is claimed that UMNO would not have been de-registered if then UMNO secretary-general, Sanusi, had submitted a stronger appeal to the show-cause letter sent by the Registrar of Societies asking why UMNO should not be declared illegal. But he submitted only a one-page reply to the show-cause letter. In the same way, the party leaders, including supreme council members, division heads, secretaries, information chiefs, Youth and *Wanita* leaders, could have been asked to make a strong appeal to the Registrar of Societies not to de-register the party. Such steps necessary to save the party, however, were not taken by the party leadership at that time.

Secondly, it is believed that Mahathir as Home Minister could also have invoked Section 70 of the Societies Act to exempt the party from Section 12 (3) and even from the entire Societies Act, if he had really wanted to save UMNO from de-registration.[68] In this case, Mahathir could have re-registered the illegal branches and called for a fresh UMNO general election. Mahathir, however, refused to use his power as Home Minister because the incumbent UMNO headquarters would be required to conduct a fresh party election after the illegal branches had been re-registered. Mahathir claimed that he did not use his powers as Home Minister because he had to take into account the fact that the court had ruled the party as unlawful. He said that even if he had the powers to cancel the Registrar of Societies' de-registration order, "it did not mean that he could do as he liked".[69] Instead of reviving the de-registered UMNO, the ruling UMNO faction (Team A) believed that the creation of a new party was the most desirable solution to internal leadership problems. This is supported by the remark of Ghafar Baba, then party deputy president, as follows:

> To me, the formation of UMNO (*Baru*) is the best way out of the crisis of the [old] UMNO. What can be lost and what is wrong in forming UMNO (*Baru*) to continue the struggle of UMNO 1946.[70]

Third Step: Creation of a New Loyalist Party

After the High Court judgment, the setting up of the new party by Mahathir was done in cloak-and-dagger style. To begin with, Mahathir submitted an application to register a new party called UMNO 88 on 9 February, a day after UMNO Malaysia's application was made by Tunku Abdul Rahman and Team B of the old UMNO.[71] The Registrar of Societies, however, rejected both applications because the old UMNO had not been de-registered yet. A few days later, Mahathir gave a speech in front of about 600 Barisan Nasional supporters at the Banquet Hall of the Parliament House in which he said that "the laws of man could be changed" whereas the laws of God could not be. The impression was that the Societies Act might be amended to allow the revival of the de-registered UMNO.[72] This was on 14 February, one day after Mahathir resubmitted a fresh application for setting up a new party and apparently intended to disguise Mahathir's real intentions. Finally, the application was approved by the Registrar of Societies on 15 February and Mahathir announced that a new political party — Pertubuhan Kebangsaan Melayu Bersatu (*Baru*) or United Malays National Organization (New) — had been officially registered. The new party, hereafter UMNO (*Baru*), was accepted as a member of the Barisan Nasional on the same day. It was widely believed that the Registrar of Societies, who was under the authority of the Home Minister, informed Mahathir of the status of the old UMNO before Mahathir submitted a new application in the name of UMNO (*Baru*). In this context, Team B leaders argued that the registration of UMNO (*Baru*) was made unduly in favour of the ruling Mahathir faction to the detriment of the dissident factions in old UMNO.[73]

The formation of a new party provided Mahathir with another opportunity for strengthening his power since replacing all dissident cabinet members with the newly appointed Mahathir loyalists after the April 24 party election. Again, Mahathir was quite exclusive when forming the pro-tem committee for the new party. As expected, most elected supreme council members allied to Team B were not included in the UMNO (*Baru*) pro-tem committee.[74] A senior UMNO (*Baru*) official said the members of the UMNO (*Baru*) pro-tem committee were strictly limited to Mahathir loyalists and were all hand-picked. With this hand-picked pro-tem committee, Mahathir could ensure that all the divisions and branches of UMNO (*Baru*) were filled by his own people from the very beginning.[75] It was believed that at least thirty-three former UMNO divisional heads were excluded from the new party's *pro-tem* divisions. As shown in Table 5.1, many former UMNO leaders were dropped as divisional heads in UMNO (*Baru*) because either they were associated with Team B leaders during the last UMNO elections or they failed to show their loyalty to Mahathir after the elections. Some of them were not even accepted as members of the new party.

Along with the exclusion of the dissident leaders from the pro-tem committee at national, state, and divisional level, the ordinary member-ship to UMNO (*Baru*) was also limited only to those who supported Mahathir's leadership. Mahathir made it clear that the new party would

TABLE 5.1

**The Thirty-Three Divisions Whose Heads Were Replaced in UMNO (*Baru*)
and Their Divisional Nominations during the 1987 UMNO Elections**

Division	President	Deputy President	Vice-Presidents		
Balik Pulau	Mahathir	Ghafar	Badawi	Mokhtar	Sanusi
Baling	Mahathir	Ghafar	Sanusi	Anwar	Mokhtar
Jelebu*a*	Mahathir	Ghafar	Badawi	Rais Yatim	Mokhtar
Kangar*b*	Mahathir	Ghafar	Badawi	Anwar	Mokhtar
Padang Terap	Mahathir	Ghafar	Badawi	Anwar	Mokhtar
Sepang	Mahathir	Ghafar	Badawi	Mokhtar	Kamaruddin
Sik	Mahathir	Ghafar	Badawi	Anwar	Sanusi
Sungai Siput	Mahathir	Ghafar	Talib	Anwar	Sanusi
Taiping	Mahathir	Ghafar	Badawi	Talib	Sanusi
Tanjung Karang	Mahathir	Ghafar	Sanusi	Kamaruddin	Talib
Bagan Serai*c*	Mahathir	Musa	Badawi	Talib	Anwar
Jelutong	Mahathir	Musa	Badawi	Sanusi	Mokhtar
Kulim-Bandar Batu	Mahathir	Musa	Badawi	Ghafar	Sanusi
Rasah	Mahathir	Musa	Badawi	Rais Yatim	Mokhtar
Bakri	Razaleigh	Musa	Badawi	Mokhtar	Yusoff
Batu Gajah	Razaleigh	Musa	Badawi	Rais Yatim	Talib
Besut	Razaleigh	Musa	Badawi	Rais Yatim	Mokhtar
Bruas	Razaleigh	Musa	Ghafar	Talib	Sanusi
Gua Musang*	Razaleigh	Musa	none	none	none
Kuala Krai	Razaleigh	Musa	Badawi	Ghafar	Rithauddeen
Kuala Nerus	Razaleigh	Musa	Badawi	Rais Yatim	Mokhtar
Ledang	Razaleigh	Musa	Badawi	Anwar	Ghafar
Mersing	Razaleigh	Musa	Badawi	Ghafar	Mokhtar
Muar	Razaleigh	Musa	Badawi	Mokhtar	Yusoff
Puchong	Razaleigh	Musa	Harun Idris	Sanusi	Anwar
Raub	Razaleigh	Musa	Badawi	Yaakub	Anwar
Seremban	Razaleigh	Musa	Badawi	Rais Yatim	Anwar
Tanjung	Razaleigh	Musa	Badawi	Anwar	Sanusi
Tasek Chenderoh	Razaleigh	Musa	Badawi	Anwar	Mokhtar
Tasik Gelugor	Razaleigh	Musa	Badawi	Anwar	Mokhtar
Johor Baru	Musa	Razaleigh	Badawi	Harun Idris	Mokhtar
Kuantan*	n.a.	n.a.	n.a.	n.a.	n.a.
Pengkalan Chepa*	none	none	none	none	none

a Former Foreign Minister Rais Yatim (Team B) was the head of the division.

b Former Deputy Primary Industries Minister Radzi Sheikh Ahmad (Team B) was the head of the division.

c Former Deputy Energy, Telecommunication and Post Minister Zainal Abidin Zin (Team B) was the head of the division.

* Gua Musang: no nominations for the vice-president post; Kuantan: null and void; Pengkalan Chepa: no nominations for all posts.

n.a. = Not available.

Sources: Compiled from *Malaysian Business*, 1 April 1987, pp. 10–12 and daily newspapers from March 1988 to June 1988.

not accept those who had rejected the election results of the old UMNO held on 24 April 1987.[76] He also clarified that the pro-tem committee members and the supporters of UMNO Malaysia would not be qualified as members of UMNO (*Baru*).[77] In sum, UMNO (*Baru*) was entirely formed around Mahathir's personality. Indeed, the formation of a new party provided a long-awaited opportunity for Mahathir to eliminate all his political rivals from the ruling party's mainstream. In this context, the dissident leaders in the old UMNO argued that they were "forced to become opposition" in the midst of Mahathir's leadership crisis.[78] Likewise, Tunku Abdul Rahman criticized Mahathir's political behaviour as follows:

> Dismissing or sacking people from any organization is a normal practice. It happens in every organization, but what Dr. Mahathir has done is to form a new party to do this.[79]

Final Step: The End of the Legal Battle

Although Mahathir had formed a new political party, the legal battle for the revival of the old UMNO continued. The eleven UMNO members filed their notice of appeal to the Supreme Court soon after the formation of UMNO (*Baru*).[80] The main focus of their appeal to the Supreme Court was that the High Court should not have gone to the extent of deeming UMNO unlawful, but should have judged only the illegal branches to be unlawful and allowed their claim for fresh party elections.

This appeal had enormous political significance, especially for the future of the UMNO (*Baru*) leadership. If the Supreme Court ruled in favour of the appellant, the legal status of the de-registered UMNO would be restored and Mahathir would have to contend with all his political enemies again for the party leadership at a fresh party election. The outcome might not be in the interests of the incumbent Mahathir faction.[81] Further, the odds seemed to be unfavourable for the incumbent UMNO (*Baru*) leadership due to rising tensions between the Mahathir government and the judiciary at that time.

In the middle of the conflict between Mahathir and several independent judges, the Lord President Salleh Abas suddenly set 13 June 1988 as the date to hear the UMNO eleven case and stipulated that all nine judges of the Supreme Court would preside — the first case heard by a full panel in Malaysian history. Four days later, however, the Lord President Salleh Abas was unexpectedly summoned by Mahathir and was suspended. Almost immediately after the suspension of Salleh Abas, the new Acting Lord President Abdul Hamid Omar postponed the case until August 1988. A few weeks later, five other Supreme Court judges were also suspended. Many Malaysians believed that these five Supreme Court judges were critical of the suspension of the Lord President during the process of Salleh Abas's impeachment tribunal. Finally, on 8 August 1988, the UMNO eleven case was heard not by a full panel but by the three remaining Supreme Court judges and two judges of the High Court nominated by the Acting Lord President. On the following day, 9 August, the Supreme Court dismissed the UMNO eleven case and the legal battle ended.

According to the official announcement from the Attorney General, Salleh Abas was dismissed from his post due to misbehaviour as Lord President.[82] However, Salleh Abas insisted that the crisis was precipitated by his decision to fix two particular cases — the UMNO eleven case and Karpal Singh's case — and that he had been victimized by Mahathir due to his alleged bias in the UMNO eleven case.[83] His allegation about victimization by Mahathir was largely based on the contents of a private meeting with Mahathir on 27 May 1988. According to Salleh Abas, in a private meeting together with Ghafar, the Deputy Prime Minister, and Sallehuddin Mohamed, the Chief Secretary, Mahathir accused him of "bias" and therefore he was "not qualified to sit in UMNO [eleven] cases". Meanwhile, Sallehuddin Mohamed "was writing in a note book".[84] Mahathir strongly denied that he had made such a remark. In an interview, Mahathir claimed that he was never "prepared to discuss politics with a judge in those circumstances".[85]

Who lied about this matter? There is no way of clarifying conflicting allegations relating to the UMNO eleven case and the assault on the judiciary except their own verbal allegations. Therefore, background factors and circumstantial evidence are essential to any attempt to understand this matter. As mentioned earlier, the judgment of the Supreme Court would have affected the political future of the incumbent UMNO (*Baru*) leadership enormously if the decision had been made in favour of the appellants. More importantly, this would have seriously affected Mahathir's prime ministership according to the constitution of the old UMNO. The constitution prescribed that "any of its members joining another political party would automatically cease to be its member". Hence, according to the legalistic argument, it can be assumed that Mahathir, as the then pro-tem president of a new party, would lose his membership if the old UMNO recovered its legality. Mahathir's eligibility to be Prime Minister would then have been in question because it was an established convention for the UMNO president to become the Prime Minister of Malaysia.[86] In this connection, the results of the eleven UMNO members' appeal would have affected the political survival of not only the party but also of Mahathir himself. This is a very legalistic argument and politically it is quite implausible. Nevertheless, such a legal provision seemed to be significant at the time UMNO dissidents fought strongly for the revival of the old UMNO. In fact, Mahathir asserted that it was "absolutely sure" that the old UMNO would "never be revived unless the law is disregarded".[87] This was just a few days before the suspension of the Lord President.

Bearing in mind the crucial significance of the UMNO eleven case, Mahathir seemed uncertain as to whether the impending legal battle in the Supreme Court would bring him a favourable result. It can be assumed that Mahathir was genuinely concerned that the Supreme Court might overturn the High Court's decision in the midst of growing tension between him and members of the judiciary.[88] In fact, it was none other than Salleh Abas who had paved the way for the uneasiness between Mahathir and the judiciary. In November 1986, Salleh Abas overturned the High Court's decision over two correspondents of the *Asian Wall Street Journal* against the Mahathir government's withdrawal of their work permits.[89] This was the starting point for growing tension between Mahathir and members of the judiciary, which continued for the next two or three years.

To make matters worse, the tension between them deepened just before and after the High Court's judgment, and Salleh Abas as Lord President was supposed to preside over the UMNO eleven case in the Supreme Court. Sharpening tension between Mahathir and Salleh Abas was revealed in a critical response of Salleh Abas to Mahathir's attack on the "fiercely independent" judges in January 1988. At a book launching ceremony on 12 January 1988, Salleh Abas criticized Mahathir as follows:

> ... some of the comments made recently [by Mahathir] ... not only question our neutrality and independence but the very nature of it as an institution. It is very much to be regretted if a court decision is to be understood as an act of hostility against the government if it loses the case and as a proper decision if it wins it. Our responsibility of deciding the case "without fear or favour" ... does not mean ... that the court decision should, whatever happens, be in favour of the Government all the time.[90]

Later, on 26 March 1988, Salleh Abas wrote a letter to the King, on behalf of all the judges of the country, which was circulated among the Malay rulers. In this letter, Salleh Abas claimed that Mahathir made "the various comments and accusations" against the judiciary "not only outside but within the Parliament".[91]

Given these circumstances, it was not surprising that the Mahathir government increased its assault on the judiciary. All the events which led to the suspension of the Lord President, however, happened "at a frenzied pace".[92] As mentioned above, Mahathir summoned Salleh Abas to his office on 27 May 1988, just four days after he had fixed the hearing date of the UMNO eleven case. Immediately after the private meeting with Mahathir, Salleh Abas received a letter from Mahathir informing him of the King's order that he be suspended from the Lord Presidency with effect from 26 May 1988, a day before the meeting with Mahathir. And it was the very first task of the Acting Lord President to postpone the UMNO eleven case on the same day Salleh Abas received the letter.

To sum up, the suspension of the Lord President and the challenge to judicial independence seemed to be largely a by-product of the legal battle over the UMNO crisis, although the events were in part linked to the mutually uneasy relationship between Mahathir and the judiciary. As a consequence, Mahathir's new loyalist party became the only registered party which could claim the old UMNO's legacies.

UMNO Legacies: Old and New

Mahathir made two main efforts to strengthen his political position after he formed the new party. One was to recover the strong psychological and physical attachments of the Malays to his new party. The other was to create new legacies within the different political configuration.

The Recovery of the Old UMNO's Legacies

In order to recover the old UMNO's legacies, a series of necessary and systematic measures was taken to identify UMNO (*Baru*), as the patron party of the Malays, with the old UMNO.

Along with the pre-emption of the term "UMNO", the first move to identify, or rather confuse, the new party with the old UMNO came with UMNO (*Baru*)'s flag and symbol. Minimum alterations had been made to the old UMNO flag design so that UMNO (*Baru*)'s flag and symbol were almost identical to those of the old UMNO, as shown below:

Old Flag   New Flag   Old Symbol   New Symbol

Source: *New Straits Times*, 22 February 1988

Secondly, the new party gradually removed the term *Baru* and called itself UMNO, like the de-registered old UMNO. During a membership drive in July 1988, the UMNO (*Baru*) Information Chief, Senator Hussein, officially directed party members to drop the word *Baru* on banners and other documents. He argued that the term *Baru* was not used when the new party was registered with the Registrar of Societies. Although the Malay version was Pertubuhan Kebangsaan Melayu Bersatu (*Baru*), the English name remained as United Malays National Organization. Accordingly, he claimed that it was wrong to use the word *Baru*.[93] One week later, Mahathir admitted that he registered the party as UMNO (*Baru*) but "there is no need to call it by that name, just refer to it as UMNO".[94] Considering that most Malays had, and still have, a strong emotional attachment to the magic name of UMNO, it was important to use the same name in order to attract old UMNO members not only physically but also psychologically.

UMNO (*Baru*) leaders' steps to drop the word *Baru* provoked a strong reaction from the dissident factions in the old UMNO. Initially, as a result of a legal complaint by two former UMNO members, the High Court, on 5 August 1988, placed an interim injunction on two newspapers — *Utusan Melayu* and *New Straits Times* — requiring them to refer to the party as UMNO (*Baru*), not UMNO. The Supreme Court, however, eventually lifted the interim injunction upon *Utusan Melayu* on 19 October 1988 and set aside the High Court's order requiring *New Straits Times* to use the word *Baru* on 31 October 1988.[95] Immediately after this, the word *Baru* was dropped from all newspapers when they referred to the new party.

Thirdly, during its first general assembly on 31 October 1988, Mahathir decided to celebrate the anniversary of UMNO (*Baru*) on 11 May, the foundation date of the old UMNO, not on 4 February, the actual registration date of the new party. In the same way, the UMNO (*Baru*) general assembly agreed that the term of the supreme council members would be continued only until 31 December 1990, the same expiration date as the old UMNO supreme council members.[96] As Means mentions, gradually but systematically, "the political transmigration" of symbolic legacies from the old UMNO to Mahathir's new party was completed, as if the new party was merely a continuation of the old party.[97]

Finally, the real transfer of old UMNO's legitimacy as the patron of the Malays appeared in its aggressive membership drive during the first year of UMNO (*Baru*). Unlike various symbolic features — name, flag and symbol — the membership drive was directly related to the recovery of the assets of the de-registered UMNO.[98] To begin with, soon after the creation of the new party, the Mahathir government tabled an amendment to the Societies Act on 15 March 1988. Although several other amendments were proposed to the Societies Act, the primary concern seemed to be to allow a favourable and smooth transfer of various properties and share-holdings from the de-registered UMNO to the UMNO (*Baru*). According to the amendment, without accepting all the former members as new members, the new party could still claim all the assets and liabilities, as long as it had the backing of the majority of members, at least 50 per cent, from the old party. After the amendment of the Societies Act, it was a natural step that UMNO (*Baru*) leaders repeatedly claimed that the membership of the old UMNO had been highly overestimated. It was in this light that Mahathir claimed that the total membership of the old UMNO had not reach the claimed 1.4 million but was less than 1 million.[99] Similarly, Mohamed Rahmat, then secretary-general of UMNO (*Baru*), announced that the old UMNO merely had between 800,000 and 900,000 members before it was deregistered in February 1988. He insisted that the total membership of the old UMNO was overestimated mainly due to double membership.[100] Nevertheless, it was believed that the reduction of the estimated membership of the old UMNO was directly linked to the smooth transfer of assets to UMNO (*Baru*). Ironically, Mohamed Rahmat announced again that the total membership of the old UMNO was 1,326,627 after UMNO (*Baru*) successfully recovered almost 80 per cent of the old UMNO members.[101]

Various methods were used to attract the maximum number of the old UMNO members. The Mahathir government organized a year-long series of public rallies, the so-called "*Semarak* Movement', throughout the country. Of course, most public rallies were sponsored by federal and state funds. The public rallies were closely co-ordinated with the UMNO (*Baru*) membership drive to obtain the majority of the old UMNO members.[102] The various advantages of incumbency were openly utilized for the same purpose. For example, the reappointment of village chiefs and other influential officials was used by state governments to woo, and/or threaten, the current village chiefs or leaders into supporting UMNO (*Baru*). In a clear case, Johor *Menteri Besar* Muhyiddin Yassin, who was also the Johor UMNO (*Baru*) state chief, announced that village chiefs who refused to join the new party would not be reappointed when their terms came to an end. In the same way, he promised that positions on the *kampung* development and security committees would be granted only to UMNO (*Baru*) members or sympathizers.[103]

Meanwhile, the UMNO (*Baru*) leadership made a more direct threat to the former UMNO members who were reluctant to join UMNO (*Baru*). The UMNO (*Baru*) secretary-general Mohamed Rahmat, who was also Information Minister, openly warned Team B UMNO members that they would be obliged to bear all debts incurred by the old UMNO if they failed to join the new party within a limited time, whereas UMNO (*Baru*) members need not worry as they had signed forms handing over assets or liabilities to the Official Assignee. Without revealing the exact amount of assets or liabilities, he claimed that the debts of the de-registered UMNO had been estimated to exceed its assets.[104]

By 12 January 1989, due to the various incentives and warnings used to maximize membership of UMNO (*Baru*), it was estimated that 1,055,348 people (about 82 per cent of the membership of the old UMNO) applied to join UMNO (*Baru*) whereas only 231,097 of the old UMNO members had not applied. The membership in two states — Terengganu and Kedah — had even exceeded the original numbers in the old UMNO. At divisional level, four divisions — Baling, Kuala Nerus, Marang, and Dungun — had doubled their original membership while another five divisions — Sik, Setiu, Kuala Terengganu, Puchong, and Jasin — increased about 150 per cent in membership compared with the old UMNO. As a whole, eighty-two divisions had increased membership by more than 50 per cent while seventeen — thirteen in Johor and four in Kelantan — increased less than 50 per cent.[105] It appeared that UMNO (*Baru*) had achieved more than its original target during the first year of its membership drive as shown in Table 5.2, even though there were some "double applications".

A year later (by January 1990), membership of UMNO (*Baru*) had increased by about 10 per cent compared with the old UMNO. Details of membership comparison between the old UMNO and UMNO (*Baru*) up to January 1990 are as follows: Perlis (105 per cent), Kedah (130 per cent), Kelantan (113 per cent), Terengganu (190 per cent), Pahang (113 per cent), Selangor (106 per cent), Federal Territory (103 per cent), Malacca (108 per cent). Among twelve states, only four — Johor (83 per cent), Penang (97 per cent), Perak (92 per cent), and Negeri Sembilan (81 per cent) — could not reach the level of the old UMNO.[106] With the recruitment of a majority of former members, UMNO (*Baru*) was able to claim all the assets registered in the name of the de-registered UMNO from the Official Assignee. Along with the political transmigration of symbolic legacies of the old UMNO to UMNO (*Baru*), the successful membership drives enabled Mahathir to recover the financial resources needed to provide patronage to UMNO (*Baru*)'s clients.

TABLE 5.2
Differences in Membership between UMNO and UMNO (*Baru*), January 1989

	Old UMNO	New UMNO	Variation (%)
Terengganu	59,349	99,505	167.7
Kedah	131,566	135,639	103.1
Pahang	102,243	97,230	95.1
Selangor	152,922	136,871	89.5
Penang	68,699	60,504	88.1
Malacca	52,688	46,285	87.8
Federal Territory	48,122	40,521	84.2
Negeri Sembilan	92,821	75,522	81.4
Perak	139,350	137,795	98.9
Kelantan	136,559	93,586	68.5
Perlis	30,676	19,225	62.7
Johor	271,450	112,665	41.5
Total	1,286,445	1,055,348	82.0

Source: Modified from *Berita Harian*, 18 January 1989.

Making UMNO (Baru)'s New Legacies

Open competition for the top posts of the party, as occurred in 1981, 1984, and 1987, had become a new "tradition" in UMNO politics and the role of the political party therefore had been enhanced since Mahathir took over. Electoral competitiveness in UMNO during the early Mahathir years was a key democratic feature of the Malaysian political system. However, as mentioned earlier, such electoral competitiveness resulted less from the party leadership's strong commitment to democracy than from the relative weakness of Mahathir's position within the party. As a result, Mahathir suffered a challenge from well-organized dissident factions within the party.

It can be assumed that Mahathir had felt the necessity of limiting electoral competitiveness and factionalism in the new political framework. He stressed, in a speech just a few months before the first of the divisional elections of UMNO (*Baru*), the importance of the "no-contest tradition" for the leadership of the old UMNO.[107] This was followed by strong advice to the party members to "avoid contests" at the first branch and divisional elections in 1989 to prevent a possible split in the party. Mahathir's advice appears to have been heeded as almost 70 per cent of the total UMNO (*Baru*) division heads — ninety-three out of 133 —

retained their posts without contest in the divisional elections in 1989. Compared with the bitterly fought 1986 divisional elections (held prior the general election), 70 per cent was unusually high especially at a time when an early general election was widely expected.[108] Further, eighty-six out of ninety-three who were returned unopposed were incumbents. Besides, more than half of the contested divisions were retained by the existing division heads. To sum up, 110 out of 133 divisions were retained by the incumbent division heads who had been appointed by Mahathir when he formed the new party in February 1988. Furthermore, most of the new division heads were also regarded as pro-Mahathir people. This marked a practical turning point towards a new development — reducing politicking or de-politicization, in the Malaysian political system which continued into the 1990s.

The initial steps to reduce politicking, however, were taken much earlier. During the first special supreme council meeting of UMNO (*Baru*) on 14 April 1988, three key proposals were approved in an effort to cut down rampant internal politicking.[109] These were finally added to the newly amended UMNO (*Baru*) constitution in October 1988 during the first UMNO (*Baru*) general assembly.

Firstly, the elections for the top two positions of the Youth and *Wanita* wings were abolished. Hence, for the first time in UMNO politics, the heads and deputy heads of the Youth and *Wanita* wings were to be appointed by the party president among division heads, with the concurrence of the supreme council.[110]

Secondly, the branch and divisional elections were to be carried out triennially not biennially as in the old UMNO. There was a proposal that the branch and divisional leaders be appointed by the party president. This proposal, however, was rejected by the UMNO (*Baru*) special assembly.

Thirdly, a new voting system was introduced for the election of the party president and deputy president. This was called the "ten-bonus-votes system". Under the new voting system, any person nominated by a division for the party presidency and deputy presidency would automatically receive ten extra votes. These ten extra votes from each divisional nomination were to be added to the actual number of votes secretly cast by the delegates at the triennial party election. As a result, an extra 1,330 votes were created from the total of 133 UMNO (*Baru*) divisions in addition to the original 1,479 votes case by the eleven delegates from each divisions. Considering the total number of extra votes (47.3 per cent of the total 2,809 votes), it was a decisive factor in the contest for the party president and deputy. This was a by-product of Mahathir's frustration over the 1987 UMNO election when individual delegates voted against candidates nominated by their division in secret ballots. Many viewed the introduction of the automatic ten bonus-votes system as a step to consolidate Mahathir's political grip as incumbent because it was anticipated that anti-Mahathir divisions would not want to openly oppose him at the nomination stage.

Finally, UMNO (*Baru*) also amended the party constitution to stop party members from going to court to resolve internal party issues. While the party members could directly appeal to the judiciary in the old UMNO, in the UMNO (*Baru*) taking internal party matters to court would lead to expulsion. In addition, anyone opposing the supreme council's decision would be taken to the disciplinary committee of the party.

A Return to "Normalcy"

As UMNO (*Baru*) was successfully built around the dominating personality of Mahathir, he needed to do something to soften his intransigent image to a more accommodative one as the battle with the UMNO dissidents was moving towards the political level. For Mahathir, this change was necessary because one of the key criticisms of the UMNO dissidents focused on his uncompromising leadership style. Moreover, their attack on Mahathir's leadership style was appealing to voters and the political battle seemed more fierce than the legal battle as dissident UMNO factions were forced into open opposition. They planned a series of by-elections to gauge the legitimacy of Mahathir's new party in terms of political influence at the grass-roots level.

The turning point in Mahathir's strategy was the Johor Baru parliament by-election on 25 August 1988, the first electoral battle between UMNO (*Baru*) and the dissident groups in the old UMNO.[111] The Johor Baru by-election was held because Shahrir, who refused to join UMNO (*Baru*), vacated his parliamentary seat and forced the by-election to test Mahathir's new party.[112] The Johor Baru by-election had enormous political significance because of its racially mixed urban voters (48.2 per cent Malay, 40.7 per cent Chinese, 8 per cent Indians, and 3.1 per cent others). In this crucial battle, Shahrir, as an independent candidate from Team B in the old UMNO, gained 23,581 (64.6 per cent of the total votes) while the UMNO (*Baru*) candidate received only 10,968 (29.8 per cent). In the 1986 general election, Shahrir, as an UMNO candidate, had obtained 19,346 (51.8 per cent of the total votes) while a PSRM candidate had taken 17,114 (45.8 per cent). It was widely believed that Shahrir had won a substantial share of the Malay vote although his Chinese support was also impressive, especially from DAP. The DAP did not contest the by-election and asked its supporters to vote for Shahrir. This was possibly the first time the DAP had campaigned for someone linked to UMNO. Due to UMNO (*Baru*)'s crushing defeat in this first political battle, Mahathir seemed to experience a loss in standing as a national leader. This was mainly because one of the key issues during the Johor Baru by-election was Mahathir's leadership style. While the BN component parties focused election issues on development and unity and tried to downplay the by-election itself as just another by-election to fill only one vacancy in a 177-member Parliament, it was Mahathir himself who brought the key issue back to his intransigent leadership style.[113]

Consequently, Mahathir's uncompromising attitude started to change before another crucial by-election in Parit Raja, Johor, on 20 October 1988. The Parit Raja state assembly by-election was the second battle for support between the old and new configurations of UMNO.[114] Like the Johor Baru by-election, the main issue was Mahathir's leadership style. But, unlike Johor Baru, Parit Raja was overwhelmingly Malay in composition. For Mahathir, if UMNO (*Baru*) were to lose the Parit Raja by-election, it would not be just a second loss but a fatal blow to his claim for majority support among the Malay constituencies. In this connection, on 15 October 1988, Mahathir announced the three decisions of the UMNO (*Baru*) supreme council regarding the dissident UMNO members. This was just four days before the Parit Raja by-election took place. Firstly, Mahathir lifted the ban on the former UMNO leaders and members who had earlier been blacklisted and barred from joining UMNO (*Baru*). They included the eleven UMNO members who had taken the party to court in February 1988. Secondly, the three leaders of Team B in the old UMNO were given back their supreme council seats which they had won in the 1987 UMNO elections.[115] Finally, Mahathir invited Razaleigh and Musa to join him and Ghafar for Malay unity talks.[116]

It is doubtful whether Mahathir was sincere in wanting to accommodate all his political foes at this time; rather his accommodative approach may have been no more than an election tactic before the crucial by-election. Mahathir's reconciliation move, however, at least softened his image as an intransigent national leader in contrast to the over-cautious response from Razaleigh and Musa. With respect to the proposed unity talks with Mahathir, Musa immediately said that Mahathir's action could be a political ploy.[117] Razaleigh was also doubtful about the sincerity of Mahathir's offer of reconciliation talks. Finally, a few days later, Razaleigh decided to reject the invitation after meeting with the UMNO dissidents, including Musa.[118] As a rationale for the rejection, Razaleigh claimed that Mahathir's invitation was nothing but a political ploy to lure former members of the old UMNO into joining UMNO (*Baru*). Mahathir's action, however, seemed to appeal to many Malays who were unhappy with the continued acrimonious quarrel which could weaken the long-term political interest of the Malays. In the Parit Raja by-election, the independent candidate from Team B was beaten by the UMNO (*Baru*) candidate by a very narrow majority of 413 votes, although it was widely believed that he was comfortably in the lead during the election campaign.[119]

Mahathir repeated this accommodative move on the final day of the first UMNO (*Baru*) general assembly on 30 October 1988. In striking contrast to the aggressive and hostile attitudes towards the dissident groups shown by most division leaders and delegates, Mahathir offered an unexpected invitation to Razaleigh and Musa to join his cabinet as ministers without portfolio for the sake of Malay unity. The first UMNO (*Baru*) general assembly seemed to be a deliberately designed drama. Just one day before Mahathir's adjournment speech to the general assembly, one delegate after another took the rostrum to denounce the dissident UMNO leaders and members. It was evident to any observer that "non-compromising with the dissident UMNO factions" was the main theme in most delegates' speeches representing various party organization. Some delegates even urged Mahathir to arrest the splinters of the old UMNO in order to ensure the security of the nation.[120] Again, on 2 December 1988, in the wake of the rejection and/or hesitation by Razaleigh and Musa, Mahathir offered supreme council seats to five prominent critics of his leadership. These people were regarded as die-hard members of the old UMNO. All five were elected supreme council members of the de-registered UMNO and were rejected as members of the new UMNO supreme council.[121]

Razaleigh's and Musa's options seemed to be very limited at this time. Refusal of Mahathir's reconciliation offer might have been interpreted as proof of their unwillingness to support Malay unity. On the other hand, if they accepted the offer, they might have been accused of abandoning their struggle and the principles they had upheld for the past two years. Even if they decided to join the new party to continue their struggle, they would have to run the risk of being marginalized in the new configuration of UMNO (*Baru*). This was mainly because the new party was already built around Mahathir's preferences and it was not until all the key posts were occupied by his choices that his conciliatory gesture was offered.[122] Razaleigh and Musa faced a dilemma as Mahathir eventually consolidated his position and authority within the new party and the government. Due to their shared antipathy towards Mahathir's leadership, Musa joined what was popularly known as Team B, but the movement was overwhelmingly dominated by Razaleigh. In fact, it would be a misnomer to describe their relations as a Razaleigh-Musa "alliance" due to the mutual distrust and disagreement between them as well as their supporters.

Musa's continued role as a junior partner had been under question since the April 24 UMNO election. While Razaleigh turned his back irreversibly on UMNO (*Baru*) and risked his political fortunes by attempting to revive the old UMNO, Musa remained in UMNO (*Baru*) and was rewarded with appointment as UMNO (*Baru*)'s divisional chairman in Segamat. He resigned later and left UMNO (*Baru*) to seek his political future as an independent. He then supported his protégé Shahrir in the Johor Baru by-election and was able to enhance his political image as a leader who brought victory to the independent candidate. A few weeks after the Johor Baru by-election, Musa proposed reconciliation talks to Mahathir but Razaleigh's faction was unhappy with the way the call for unity had been made by Musa. Various reasons are given for their discordance, depending on the source. Razaleigh's supporters argued that Musa had not been consistent in his opposition to Mahathir's new party; as a team player, he had often been fickle and even "dubious".[123] On the other hand, those aligned with Musa said that the two groups had always differed in their approach to the problem. In this context, Musa himself insists that he "was associated [with them] for convenience".[124]

Mahathir's gesture of appeasement in October 1988, therefore, seriously tested the fragile Razaleigh-Musa alliance. Mahathir also started to separate Musa's faction from the dissident group at this time. Mahathir announced in public that he had received written replies from Razaleigh and Musa about his offer to appoint them as cabinet ministers. Mahathir said that Razaleigh had rejected his offer whereas Musa had indicated several possible bases for reconciliation and the restoration of Malay unity in the new party.[125]

Given the circumstances of mutual distrust, it was at the Johor Malay unity forum, held on 18 December 1988, that relations between the two dissident groups worsened and eventually led to the termination of their ill-matched teamwork. Ostensibly, the Johor Malay unity forum was initiated by fifty-one Malay organizations in Johor Baru to re-unite the UMNO dissidents and UMNO (*Baru*). However, it was widely believed that the unity forum was initiated by the Johor faction of UMNO dissidents led by Musa. At the unity forum, 170 delegates unanimously passed a six-point resolution for Malay unity. The six-point resolution called for: restoration of the former UMNO constitution; the automatic acceptance of former UMNO members; reinstatement of former branch and divisional leaders; acceptance of the UMNO national leadership elected on 24 April 1987; legal steps to ensure there was only one UMNO for the Malays; and the creation of a political environment conducive to Malay unity and solidarity.[126] As expected, the six-point resolution echoed Musa's approach.

Razaleigh's supporters argued that the unity forum's purpose was to undermine the position of Razaleigh and his supporters. They maintained it was a deliberate step initiated by the Johor faction of the UMNO dissidents to prepare a face-saving excuse for them to join the new party. A former deputy minister from the Razaleigh group even claimed that the unity forum itself was planned and sponsored by UMNO (*Baru*).[127]

The UMNO (*Baru*) supreme council decided to accept the six-point resolution. According to Mahathir's statement, however, the acceptance of the six-point resolution would be implemented within the framework of the existing provisions of the UMNO (*Baru*) constitution. More importantly, the procedure for joining the new party, like automatic acceptance, applied only to the former UMNO members in Johor. Mahathir made it clear that UMNO (*Baru*) would not extend the same procedure to the other states.[128] On 31 January 1989, Musa announced his decision to join UMNO (*Baru*). Therefore, the Razaleigh-Musa coalition, so-called Team B, was formally dissolved after a marriage of convenience lasting only twenty-two months. Later, automatic admission into UMNO (*Baru*) was extended to other states.[129] This decision, however, was not made until Razaleigh announced in public that there would be "no more negotiations" and he would "fight the existing leadership to the end".[130]

By accepting the six-point resolution, Mahathir and his new party were able to obtain several advantages. Firstly, Mahathir further softened his obstinate image and reduced the general anti-Mahathir mood. Secondly, UMNO (*Baru*) doubled its membership in Johor (from 41.5 per cent of the old UMNO membership in January 1988 to 83 per cent in January 1989) due to the acceptance of the Johor dissidents. Thirdly, UMNO (*Baru*) successfully delivered Malay votes to defeat the independent candidate, Harun Idris, at the Ampang Jaya parliamentary by-election, which was held just two weeks after the acceptance of the six-point resolution. Unlike the two previous by-elections, the Musa faction did not make any serious move to jeopardize the BN candidate during the Ampang Jaya by-election campaign. Finally, by separating Musa from Razaleigh, the political situation eventually took a favourable turn for Mahathir. Musa's defection from the anti-Mahathir front left very little room for Razaleigh to manoeuvre and put him in danger of being isolated and pushed to the periphery. More seriously, Musa's political influence would be eventually neutralized as he was absorbed into the new party.

Efforts to marginalize the Musa faction started immediately after he joined UMNO (*Baru*). First of all, Ghafar proposed to the supreme council a time limit for the automatic admission of former members into the new party. There was, of course, no time limit when the UMNO (*Baru*) supreme council accepted the Johor Malay unity forum's resolution. Besides, he made it clear that the applications "have to be studied first" although they would not be rejected automatically.[131] Finally, the supreme council set 31 March 1989 as the deadline for the automatic admission of former UMNO members.[132] Thus, all applications for the entry to UMNO (*Baru*) were subjected to screening from 1 April 1989.

It seems that "delaying tactics" were practised to prevent the return of certain former UMNO leaders and members into UMNO (*Baru*). The shortage of membership forms was a typical ploy to delay and/or prevent the admission of former UMNO members. For example, Shahrir insisted that he received less than 2,000 membership forms while there were 3,717 former UMNO members in Johor Baru who wanted to join with him.[133] Also, it was alleged that about 4,000 former UMNO members in Perak were prevented from rejoining UMNO (*Baru*) because of the shortage of membership forms.[134] Regarding the reasons for the shortage of membership forms during this period, Muhyiddin Yassin, then Johor UMNO (*Baru*) chief, explained that it could be a result of some branch and division leaders keeping the forms for the purpose of future registration.[135] The real background, however, was revealed in the warning of Mohamad Rahmat, the then UMNO (*Baru*) secretary-general. He warned that certain groups were persuading as many former UMNO members as possible to return to UMNO (*Baru*) in order to undermine the party from the inside.[136]

In addition, the reinstatement of former branch and divisional leaders, one of the six-point resolutions, was not properly implemented because of the unwillingness of existing branch and divisional leaders. Rather, the UMNO (*Baru*) leaders made it clear that the old UMNO leaders could not be re-appointed to their former posts at the expense of the existing people.[137] In these difficult circumstances, Shahrir's application to join UMNO (*Baru*) took almost five months after he submitted an application on 1 March 1989. Even before the application, forty-two of the forty-five branches in the Johor Baru UMNO (*Baru*) division sent a memorandum to the state liaison committee rejecting Shahrir's return to the division.[138] Shahrir's application was finally accepted on 29 July 1989. This was just one week before the Tambatan state by-election in Johor on 5 August 1989, the first election in which Razaleigh's supporters participated with a registered political party.[139] However, it took another seven months for Shahrir to be reinstated as a Johor Baru division leader on 3 March 1990. Meanwhile, Musa had been sent abroad as Malaysia's special envoy to the United Nations in August 1989 before UMNO (*Baru*) held its general assembly in November 1989. At first glance, this appointment was regarded as a "conciliatory step" by Mahathir or even as a sign of Musa's "rehabilitation".[140] However, as Case noted, it turned out to be "a customary way of removing influential, but disloyal UMNO élites with minimal disruption".[141] Finally, restoration of the old UMNO constitution, one of the six points in the Johor Malay unity forum resolution, was also rejected by Mahathir. Mahathir made it clear that UMNO (*Baru*)'s constitution would be amended from time to time rather than have the old UMNO constitution restored.[142]

In the mean time, Mahathir made a gesture of appeasement towards Razaleigh and the remainder of the old UMNO. On 3 June 1989, Mahathir announced the acceptance of several dissidents, including Hamdan Yahya, the defeated independent candidate in the Parit Raja by-election. In a similar conciliatory gesture, on 11 November 1989, Mahathir invited Tunku Abdul Rahman to attend the UMNO (*Baru*) general assembly where he publicly kissed his hand. Mahathir's invitation was viewed as a dramatic move mainly because this gesture was made just a few weeks after Tunku Abdul Rahman's scathing statement about Mahathir and UMNO (*Baru*).[143] Again, during the UMNO (*Baru*) general assembly in November 1989, Mahathir reiterated his willingness to meet Razaleigh with a view to strengthen Malay unity. However, it was commonly believed that neither Mahathir nor Razaleigh were seriously considering Malay unity at that time. As to why Mahathir should reach out to the dissident group in a situation where he had secured most of the old UMNO members, perhaps he needed to avoid blame for the failure of talks aimed at Malay unity, as the next general election was approaching soon. Whatever his motives, a series of conspicuous conciliatory gestures by Mahathir helped him to be perceived as a magnanimous leader seeking to end his differences with his opponents.

The End of the Mahathir Controversy

If the past three years were characterized by escalating intra-ethnic militancy within UMNO circles, the year 1990 was of broader significance for the Malaysian political system as another general election was approaching.[144] The October 1990 general election was the first time Mahathir's new party tested its popularity and political legitimacy at the national level. Mahathir himself needed a mandate not only from the Malay community but also from the non-Malay electorate to put an end to the dispute over his national leadership style. Also, for the first time in Malaysian electoral history, the ruling coalition faced a challenge by opposition coalitions led by the UMNO dissidents with long experience in government. Indeed, many political observers saw the 1990 general election as a golden opportunity for Malaysia's single-party-dominant political landscape to realign to a new two-coalition party system.

Unprecedented Political Realignment among the Disparate Opposition Parties

Having failed in the legal battle to revive the old UMNO, Razaleigh's faction moved to form a new political party known as Semangat 46. Semangat 46 means "Spirit of 1946" referring to the year of the establishment of the old UMNO. The Razaleigh-led Semangat 46 was allowed to register as a political party on 3 June 1989, even though its registration certificate was given on 5 May 1989 by the Registrar of Societies. The Razaleigh group had to wait about a month until the Election Commission finally approved its symbol, the numbers 46. The first application by the Razaleigh group to register Semangat 46 as a political party was rejected by the Registrar of Societies because the symbol of Semangat 46 bore too close a resemblance to that of UMNO (*Baru*).[145] The difficulties faced by the Razaleigh group to register

Semangat 46 contrasted sharply with the ease with which the Mahathir-led UMNO (*Baru*) obtained permits to hold its forty-third anniversary celebrations at the Istana Besar in Johor Baru on 10 and 11 May 1989, the same place and date on which the old UMNO was formed in 1946.

Soon after the formation of the new party, Razaleigh initiated a political alignment with other disparate Malaysian opposition parties, including the Chinese-based DAP and the Islamic fundamentalist PAS. The very first assessment of the political alignment came during the Teluk Pasu state by-election in Terengganu held on 24 June 1989.[146] In this by-election, three Malay opposition parties, namely Semangat 46, PAS, and Berjasa, offered themselves as an alternative opposition coalition to the ruling BN coalition through their Angkatan Perpaduan Ummah (Muslim Community Unity Movement, APU).[147] At the Teluk Pasu by-election, PAS, backed by Semangat 46, won with 3,671 votes to the BN's 3,530. Despite a slim 141-vote majority, PAS's victory was very significant because electoral co-operation during the Teluk Pasu by-election showed that both former political rivals could work together as a team to challenge the UMNO (*Baru*)-led ruling coalition. For PAS, which had never before defeated the BN candidate in a by-election, it seemed that the alignment of Razaleigh's Semangat 46 was crucial for the victory of the PAS candidate. In mid-1990 APU was officially registered as a Muslim-based electoral alliance, comprising Semangat 46, PAS, Berjasa and Hamim, to unseat the ruling coalition during the 1990 general election.

As well as the electoral alliance with several Muslim opposition parties, Semangat 46 also tried to co-operate with the non-Malay opposition parties. The Tambatan by-election in Johor on 5 August 1989 was the first election in which Semangat 46 had nominated its own candidate and provided another assessment of the electoral alliance among the opposition parties, especially Semangat 46, DAP, and PRM. In view of PAS's win in the recent Teluk Pasu by-election, Semangat 46 had met separately with DAP and PRM leaders to field a candidate who could represent the opposition parties.[148] As a result, DAP and PRM decided not to contest the Tambatan by-election so that non-Malay votes could flow to Semangat 46.[149] Although Semangat 46 lost this by-election, such co-operation developed into the first joint rally between Semangat

46 and DAP in Penang in February 1990, and eventually resulted in the formation of another electoral alliance just before the 1990 general election. This multi-racial electoral alliance was called Gagasan Rakyat Malaysia (Malaysian People's Front), comprised of Semangat 46, DAP, PRM, and a newly formed All-Malaysia Indian Progressive Front (IPF).

In spite of disparate ideologies, serious organizational weaknesses and image problems, Gagasan Rakyat was considered an unprecedented *de facto* multi-ethnic and multi-religious opposition coalition" in Peninsular Malaysia.[150] One frequently asked question, therefore, was whether the nation could move towards a two-coalition party system, that is, the Barisan Nasional coalition led by Mahathir's UMNO (*Baru*) versus an alternative opposition coalition led by Razaleigh's Semangat 46. It was estimated that the ruling BN coalition would lose its traditional two-thirds parliamentary majority with only a 10 per cent swing of the vote to the opposition coalition. If the swing was 20 per cent, then the opposition coalition would be in power.[151] Unlike Chinese educationists who had supported the non-Malay BN component parties in the previous elections, this time some twenty leaders of the Chinese teachers' guilds and schools associations, known collectively as the *dongjiaozong*, announced, in August, their support and direct participation in the 1990 elections with an opposition DAP ticket. Furthermore, it was the first time ever that the Malaysian Trade Unions Congress (MTUC), the largest trade union in Malaysia, openly endorsed the opposition.

Even the leaders within the ruling coalition were somewhat cautious in their assessments of the election results. It was alleged that the main Chinese component party in the ruling coalition, MCA, openly debated "the option of attempting to realign Malaysian politics" by affiliating with the Razaleigh-led opposition coalition in the 1990 election, due to its "nearly powerless" position in the Mahathir government.[152] Gerakan, the junior Chinese party in the ruling coalition, was also "quietly contemplating a switch".[153] Although the major component parties decided on remaining within the ruling coalition, a number of leaders in non-Malay parties, especially MCA, privately wished that the factional split within the ruling Malay political élite would become "a permanent feature of the Malaysian political landscape".[154] For them, at least, there would be every probability of returning to the previous consociational system of rule because each coalition was made up of different ethnic and religious groups.

Indeed, the anti-establishment mood appeared to be spreading to the masses as the polling date approached. The anti-Barisan atmosphere in peninsular Malaysia at this time even brought about the crossover of the Kadazan-based Parti Bersatu Sabah (PBS), which had controlled the state of Sabah as a partner of the ruling coalition since 1986, to the opposition coalition just five days before the election day.[155] The withdrawal of PBS from the BN in the midst of the election campaign boosted the anti-establishment mood before the 1990 general election. This was the first time in its electoral history that the ruling coalition started unfavourably compared with opposition parties, in contrast to the high number of uncontested victories in the previous elections. The withdrawal of PBS from BN after the closure of nominations deprived the BN of the opportunity to field its own candidates in the fourteen BN seats allocated to PBS in Sabah. Besides, BN won only two parliamentary seats in East Malaysia unopposed in the 1990 general election, whereas it had enjoyed a relatively high number of unopposed victories in the previous elections.[156] In previous elections, the ruling coalition faced fragmented opposition parties but this time there was a strict division between the ruling coalition led by Mahathir's UMNO (*Baru*) and the opposition coalition led by Razaleigh's Semangat 46 in almost 90 per cent of the parliamentary constituencies in peninsular Malaysia.[157] In these circumstances, Mahathir was deeply concerned whether his new party would be able to obtain significant electoral support, especially from the Malay voters in the 1990 general election. Mahathir's uncertainty about the 1990 elections was shown in his personal phone call to his former political rival Musa Hitam, who was living in New York at that time. It was alleged that, in an almost twenty-minute telephone discussion, Mahathir expressed his deep anxiety about the materialization of an unprecedented opposition coalition and asked Musa Hitam to be a parliamentary candidate in order to mobilize the Malay voters. According to Musa Hitam, Mahathir was deeply disappointed to hear that he euphemistically refused Mahathir's offer.[158]

Frustrated *"Now or Never Opportunity"* for a Two-Coalition Party System

The results of the 1990 general election did not confirm expectations of an anti-establishment swing. The ruling BN coalition was returned to power with more than its traditional two-thirds parliamentary majority, although it lost ground compared with previous elections. In brief, as shown in the Tables 5.3 and 5.4 below, Mahathir's ruling coalition secured a convincing majority of 127 seats in a 180-seat Parliament, whereas the combined opposition clearly performed below expectations with only forty-nine out of 180 parliamentary seats and ninety-eight of 351 state assembly seats.

Although initial reports carried mixed assessments, the detailed results of the 1990 general election demonstrate at least two distinct features:

TABLE 5.3
Comparison of the 1986 and 1990 General Elections (Parliamentary)

	Barisan Nasional			Opposition and Independents		
	1986	1990			1986	1990
UMNO	83 (84)	71 (86)	Semangat 46		—	8 (61)
MCA	17 (32)	18 (32)	DAP		24 (64)	20 (57)
MIC	6 (6)	6 (6)	PAS		1 (98)	7 (30)
Gerakan	5 (9)	5 (9)	PRM		0 (4)	0 (3)
Hamim[a]	1 (2)	—	Hamim		—	—
PBS[a]	10 (14)	—	PBS		—	14 (14)
USNO	5 (6)	6 (6)	AMIPF[b]		—	0 (5)
PBB	8 (8)	10 (10)	Permas		—	0 (9)
SNAP	5 (5)	3 (5)	Plus		—	0 (1)
SUPP	4 (7)	4 (8)	Akar		—	0 (4)
Berjaya	0 (8)	—	Independent[c]		4 (52)	4 (64)
PBDS	4 (4)	4 (4)				
Total	148 (185)	127 (166)	Total		29 (218)	53 (248)

Note: Figures within parentheses are the numbers of seats contested.
[a] Groups which quit the BN to join the opposition bloc in the 1990 general election.
[b] Newly formed by dissidents from the MIC.
[c] The large majority were in Sabah and Sarawak — twenty-four and twenty-five respectively.

Sources: *NST*, 23 October 1990; *FEER*, 1 November 1990; and Khong Kim Hoong (1991).

TABLE 5.4
Comparison of the 1986 and 1990 General Elections
in Peninsular Malaysia (State)[a]

Barisan Nasional			Opposition Parties		
	1986	1990		1986	1990
UMNO	228 (240)	196 (246)	Semangat 46	—	19 (152)
MCA	43 (62)	34 (64)	DAP	37 (118)	45 (87)
MIC	12 (13)	12 (13)	PAS	15 (266)	33 (114)
Gerakan	13 (22)	11 (21)	Berjasa[b]	—	1 (1)
Total (won)	299	253	Total (won)	52	98

Note: Figures within parentheses are numbers of seats contested.
[a] State elections in Sabah and Sarawak were held separately.
[b] Berjasa was a component party of the BN and did not take part in the 1986 elections.

Sources: *Utusan Malaysia*, 5 August 1986; *NST*, 23 October 1990; NSTP Research and Information Services (1994), pp. 69–92; and Khong Kim Hoong (1991).

Mahathir's UMNO (*Baru*)'s overall success and a considerable decline in support for the Chinese political parties, MCA and Gerakan, in the ruling coalition; and a miserable defeat of Razaleigh's Semangat 46 and the relative success of the other opposition parties, DAP, PAS, and PBS, in the opposition coalition.[159]

In Kelantan, the Muslim-based opposition alliance APU swept all fifty-two parliamentary and state seats it contested and added a few more seats in Terengganu, compared with the 1986 elections. In particular, PAS made substantial gains in this election. As shown in Tables 5.3 and 5.4 above, PAS obtained seven parliamentary seats and thirty-three state seats in 1990, an increase from the one parliamentary and fifteen state seats it won in 1986. More importantly, PAS could control the Kelantan state government with its twenty-four seats won in the thirty-nine-seat legislative assembly regardless of its coalition partner Semangat 46.

In Sabah, the opposition PBS, after its recent defection, secured all the fourteen parliamentary seats it contested with the endorsement of DAP. As a result, in the aftermath of the 1990 general election, the Mahathir government was faced with two state governments, in Kelantan and Sabah, run by the opposition parties.

Furthermore, the election results in Penang showed that the Chinese voters tended to swing in favour of the opposition. Although MCA added one parliamentary seat in 1990, the party could not recover its disappointing parliamentary election results in 1986, when it won only seventeen of the thirty-two seats it contested (compared with twenty-four out of the twenty-eight seats in 1982). Gerakan, another Chinese component party of the ruling coalition, suffered a further setback in the 1990 elections. On the other hand, DAP repeated its good performance of the 1986 elections. Though the number of its parliamentary seats dropped from twenty-four to twenty and its percentage of total parliamentary votes declined marginally from 20.4 to 16.9, the party cleaned up most Chinese urban seats. It has to be noted also that the party contested fewer seats as part of its electoral understanding with the other opposition parties. DAP's most significant improvement was in the Penang state elections where it added four more seats, bringing the total to fourteen compared with BN's nineteen.[160]

Overall, the opposition parties whittled down the electoral superiority of the ruling coalition, reducing its share of the total votes for parliamentary seats from 57 per cent in 1986 to 52 per cent.[161] Nevertheless, the relatively good performance of DAP, PAS, and PBS was viewed as a limited success. The voting patterns did not indicate a country-wide political change from single-party dominance to a two-coalition party system mainly because of the localized nature of opposition parties' electoral success.

Perhaps the most significant result of this election was the overwhelming success of Mahathir's UMNO (*Baru*) and the miserable defeat of Razaleigh's Semangat 46. Despite strong anti-establishment votes in several states, Malay voters clearly favoured Mahathir's UMNO (*Baru*). UMNO (*Baru*) won all the sixty-five parliamentary constituencies it contested except in Kelantan and Terengganu. In Terengganu, the party secured six out of eight contested seats. It was only in Kelantan that UMNO (*Baru*) totally lost ground.[162] Overall, the party won seventy-one out of the eighty-six parliamentary seats it contested (82.6 per cent), less than eighty-three of the eighty-four constituencies in 1986. UMNO (*Baru*)'s electoral strength was also shown in the state elections. Although there was a marginal decline from 1986, UMNO (*Baru*) won in 196 of the 246 (79.7 per cent) state constituencies in 1990. In short, despite the severe setback in the northeastern states, Mahathir's UMNO (*Baru*) had successfully drawn the traditional support of the Malay community.

However, the results demonstrated a tremendous blow to UMNO dissidents in general. The old UMNO breakaway party Semangat 46 won in only eight of the sixy-one parliamentary constituencies (13.1 per cent) it contested. Semangat 46, which had twelve MPs before Parliament was dissolved, lost eight of these seats. The party's performance in the state elections was even worse. The party won in only nineteen seats of the total 152 contested constituencies (12.5 per cent). It was only in Kelantan, Razaleigh's home state, that the party did very well, winning all fourteen state seats it contested. This meant that Semangat 46 gained only five of the 138 contested seats (3.6 per cent) in the other states. Indeed, the poor electoral performance of UMNO dissidents raised serious questions regarding their long-term viability in the aftermath of the 1990 general election.

In sum, the 1990 general election demonstrated that the Razaleigh-led Semangat 46, as the adhesive of the multi-racial opposition coalition, had not made much headway in this nation-wide showdown for who or which party represented the Malay community. Also, the Chinese component parties in the ruling coalition were completely unsuccessful in seizing the chance to restore the former Alliance type of consociational rule, in spite of the increasing electoral significance of the non-Malay, especially Chinese, voters. Ironically, UMNO (*Baru*)'s dominant position in the ruling BN coalition was further strengthened after the 1990 general election. It seems that the long-lasting leadership split within the old UMNO circles intensified communal demand for the assertion of Malay supremacy in politics, instead of evolving towards a new political landscape based on a more equitable multi-ethnic power sharing.

Inherent Unfairness of Malaysian Electoral Procedures and Racial Politics

Several reasons can be suggested to explain the overall success of the ruling coalition and UMNO (*Baru*) in circumstances where the anti-establishment mood was widespread amongst Malays as well as non-Malays. Most of all, under Mahathir's leadership, the power of incumbents had increased greatly. Although this built-in incumbent advantage was not new in Malaysian electoral history and was common in many other countries, it reached a new level of sophistication in the 1990 general election.

By law, no campaigning was to occur until elections were announced. But in fact Mahathir's UMNO (*Baru*) had already been on the campaign trail far more than six months before the 1990 general election. An example was the nationwide "mock general election exercise" by UMNO (*Baru*) from 16 February to 30 February. During this period, all 114 UMNO (*Baru*) divisions were conducting various *de facto* pre-election campaigns, including house-to-house campaigning, *ceramah*, and helping voters locate their voting centres.[163] For example, the UMNO (*Baru*) divisions in Kelantan distributed the first batch of 150,000 Barisan Nasional posters to its thirteen divisions in February.[164] It was the first time in Malaysian electoral history that the ruling party had simulated a general election exercise, although on other occasions the regular party machinery had moved into high gear before the dissolution of Parliament.

Another feature of inherent unfairness for the opposition was BN's ability to offer patronage to voters. Though similar things had happened in all previous elections, it was believed that Mahathir's government spent more than ever before in the run-up to the 1990 general election. Even official figures show that the Mahathir government increased the government budget sharply in running the 1990 elections compared with the 1986 elections, from RM11 million to RM20 million.[165] However, it was alleged that the actual expenses incurred by BN candidates in 1990 were at least ten times more than the legally allowed RM50,000 per parliamentary candidate. Especially in some constituencies where there was a close contest, the BN candidates were given nearly RM2 to RM3 million. A BN candidate was even reported to have spent almost RM12 million in one constituency.[166]

In addition, a newly introduced vote-counting system made voters reluctant to vote for the opposition parties in 1990. On 15 March 1990, the Mahathir government altered vote-counting procedures to allow ballot counting at the individual polling stations whereas in the previous elections the votes were all mixed and then counted in one common centre for each constituency. One reason given for the new vote-counting system was that it would reduce the chance of ballot boxes being tampered with in transit to common counting centres.[167] With this new vote-counting system, however, it could be easily seen whether voters in a particular town, village, or even several blocks of streets in a constituency had voted for the ruling party or the opposition. This new system was considered threatening to voters since there were only about 700 voters per polling station.[168] Given the fact that so-called development funds had been granted or withheld in proportion to the level of support for the government, it was widely believed that voters were frightened and/ or reluctant to vote for the opposition coalition in the 1990 elections for fear of being labelled as an anti-government area, especially in rural Malay areas and Chinese-dominated new villages. Also, elected representatives from the opposition were not entitled to the funds for minor development projects, such as the construction or repairs of roads, bridges, community halls, and mosques; the improvement of water supplies; and the supply of materials for schools.

Furthermore, various electoral malpractices and discrepancies seemed to favour Mahathir's ruling coalition. For example, postal votes from the police and armed forces were not scrutinized by any official of the Election Commission.[169] According to the report by the twelve-member Commonwealth observer team, there was a total of 196,522 postal votes in 1990, including 120,000 from military personnel and 72,000 from the police.[170] That means about 3.4 per cent of the total 5,786,920 ballots cast in parliamentary elections in 1990 were postal ballots. Considering the small margin of 4 per cent between 52 per cent and 48 per cent of the total votes obtained by the ruling coalition and opposition coalition respectively, the total 3.4 per cent of postal ballots, which went mostly to the ruling coalition, were more crucial in the 1990 general election than ever before. In addition, according to the Election Commission, it was estimated that discrepancies in the numbers of voters amounted to about 300,000 of the total 7.96 million registered voters (3.8 per cent) during the 1990 elections.[171] It even reached up to 5.2 per cent of the total vote cast in the parliamentary elections. These electoral discrepancies could have affected the outcomes in closely contested constituencies since most of the phantom voters were in these areas.[172]

Finally, once again but far more seriously, the unequal access to the

media and unbalanced reporting were crucial factors in the victory of
the ruling coalition and specifically UMNO (*Baru*) in the 1990 general
election. In particular, Mahathir's massive racial onslaught through the
mainstream media, especially in the three to four days before the polling
day, turned the anti-establishment mood among the Malay community
to one of a siege mentality. Of course, arguments about the media's
effect on public opinion are always controversial. Nonetheless, the 1990
general election demonstrated how far a party-tied and controlled media,
as ideological state apparatus, was able to divert the public's attention
away from the serious issues by reporting pseudo-events and exaggerating
trivial issues in the interests of the ruling party.[173]

In fact, the run-up to the 1990 general election was not particularly
marked by communal emotion though a racial theme has been a constant
factor in Malaysian election campaigns. This was mainly because of the
multi-racial character of both ruling and opposition coalitions. Mahathir's
electoral slogans, however, changed dramatically just before polling day.
The turning point was the PBS's withdrawal from the ruling BN coalition
to the opposition coalition Gagasan Rakyat on 15 October. From the
very moment of PBS's withdrawal, UMNO (*Baru*) and Mahathir
campaigned ferociously, exploiting both religious and racial sentiments
to create fear among Malay and non-Malay communities. Within a day,
Mahathir turned the PBS's withdrawal into a major racial issue and
managed to create a siege mentality amongst a substantial segment of
the Malay community. Swiftly, news came through the ruling party–
tied mainstream mass media of the "Christian" PBS teaming up with
the "Chinese" DAP and other non-Malay groups to destroy *"Ketuanan
Melayu* (Malay Supremacy)" in politics. Semangat 46 and PAS were
alleged to be traitors to the Malays and their leaders were reported as
being guilty of destroying Malay supremacy because of their co-operation
with other non-Malay and non-Muslim political groups. It was at this
point that the ruling coalition's multi-racial slogans were overwhelmed
by the fear in the Malay communities of losing their political leverage.

How then did Mahathir generate such fear in the Malay
communities? Mahathir portrayed the Kadazan-based PBS as a Christian
party that had the ulterior motive of proselytizing Malay-Muslims. He
claimed in several TV interviews and in the major Malay newspapers

that the PBS wanted a television station in Sabah as a vehicle for "Christian propaganda".[174] Also, he accused PBS of receiving financial aid from foreign non-Muslim sources and extended the accusations to the Muslim-based opposition coalition APU.[175] It was at this time that a letter, allegedly written by Pope John Paul II to the PBS president Pairin Kitingan urging him to demolish mosques and to continue Christianizing Sabah, was widely distributed in mosques throughout the country.[176]

In addition to Mahathir's propaganda was his unrelenting onslaught on the Semangat 46 president Razaleigh, alleging he had given in to the so-called Christian PBS by sacrificing Malay political supremacy. The malicious and deliberate allegations reached a peak when Razaleigh visited Sabah on 18 October. From the time of his visit to Sabah until polling day, Razaleigh was slandered in most major newspapers for wearing traditional Kadazan headgear (*sigah*), which allegedly had a Christian cross on it. Mainstream media coverage, including TV3, was slanted in such a way as to make the ethnic Kadazan headgear appear to have a Christian cross on it, thus leading the Malay-Muslims to a general belief that Razaleigh's Semangat 46 was selling out Malay interests as well as the Islamic faith in order to win the 1990 general election. Although the Archbishop Emeritus of the Catholic Church issued a press statement denying any connection between the ethnic Kadazan headgear and Christianity, and the statement was carried only in the Chinese press, no Malay daily reported it.[177] With the UMNO (*Baru*)-tied mass media providing such coverage, the damage was done and the suspicion surrounding Razaleigh was enough to create insecurity among the Malays.

In addition, the Mahathir government stirred up more racially based fear by resorting to the "May 13 syndrome", a psychological after-shock of the racial riots which had occurred over twenty-one years ago in 1969. The opposition leader, Lim Kit Siang, claimed that Mahathir's exploitation of the politics of racial fear was the most inflammatory ever in Malaysia's electoral history, in its imagery and visual impact.[178] Indeed, the very day after PBS's withdrawal from the ruling coalition, Mahathir publicly announced that the May 13 racial riots would be repeated if the ruling coalition failed to retain its two-thirds majority in Parliament.[179] A few days later there was a full-page advertisement in *Utusan Malaysia* and the same full-page advertisement, but in colour this time, in *Nanyang Siang Pao* to maximize racial fears among Malaysian voters. The advertisement was the painting of a blood-splattered battle for the defence of the Melaka (Malacca) sultanate by the Malays against the Portuguese, under the headings of *"Sokong Membawa Rebah* (Support Brings to Collapse)" and "Recollection of History" respectively.[180] Without doubt, the advertisement was intended to strike terror into the hearts of both Malays and non-Malays by warning of the repetition of May 13 bloodshed, violence, arson, and carnage.[181] In describing UMNO (*Baru*) and Mahathir's sudden exploitation of the racial card, a senior opposition leader observes that:

> In any country, the party in power that controls all the instruments, in particular the mass media, decide the direction of the politics. In Malaysia, *as long as* UMNO *is mono ethnic, therefore, no matter what opposition parties or coalition do, it will be coined in terms of the strait-jacket of racialism.* Because it is not UMNO's advantage to portray opposition parties as multi-racial.[182]

On the effects of the exploitation of the politics of race, a senior UMNO (*Baru*) official believes that the culmination of racial fear amongst voters was crucial for regaining lost ground especially among the Malays. The deliberate promotion of a Malay siege mentality through the mass media, especially in the two or three days before polling day, prompted a substantial proportion of Malay voters to unite behind the Mahathir leadership.[183] Musa Hitam summarizes it thus:

> I simply say that, whatever Razaleigh-led opposition's strategies were, they were confined to a marginal force as long as they did not have access to the masses. It was really amazing how the Mahathir government had been using the incumbent power [for the distortion of the facts or bad image making over the opposition] especially during the 1990 general election. That is what I mean by *the awesome power of incumbency.*[184]

Summary

By the end of 1990, the political framework was firmly set. A new ruling party, UMNO (*Baru*), had been built around Mahathir's personality through the creation of new political legacies as well as the recovery of the symbolic and physical legacies of the old UMNO. Mahathir's intransigent image had also been softened to a considerable degree through a series of appeasement gestures towards UMNO dissidents.

Moreover, Mahathir's new ruling party confirmed its nationwide popularity and political legitimacy through the general election of 1990. Indeed, the 1990 general election was a turning point for Mahathir's leadership, which up to that point had been disputed. In short, the new electoral mandate and the decisive defeat of his long-time political rivals in the 1990 elections enabled Mahathir to further consolidate his political grip over the political process without having to seriously consider opposition.

Since Mahathir took power, open competition for the party's top posts, as happened in 1981, 1984, and 1987, became a new tradition in UMNO, and the role of factionalism has grown. Thus, some might claim that it was under Mahathir's early leadership that UMNO politics added another key element to the lists of so-called democratic features found in the Malaysian political system. It cannot be denied that the Malaysian political system became more competitive and more responsive in the period 1987–90. At least on the surface, political observers viewed this period as holding out the prospect of a more competitive and accommodative political system in Malaysia. There was indeed a series of intermittent concessions to the non-Malay communities in an attempt to attract their votes during the by-election campaigns.

However, such openness and competitiveness did not appear to stem from the ruling Malay élites' growing commitment to political liberalization. Rather, the leaders were taking a calculated risk in order to maintain power. Considering Mahathir's vulnerable leadership and the strong criticism he endured from his political rivals in the wake of the UMNO leadership crisis, it would have been more risky for Mahathir to refuse a greater degree of competition towards the end of the 1980s. One should note that the electoral competitiveness has been limited or completely suspended after Mahathir eventually restored his dominance. That is, in the middle of 1989, UMNO (*Baru*) submitted a proposal to amend the Election Act which stated that unless elected representatives resigned for valid reasons (such as sickness), they were prevented from recontesting for five years.[185] In March 1990, this became law after the Mahathir government tabled a Constitution (Amendment) Bill in the Dewan Rakyat. Although the Mahathir government claimed the new law was necessary to spare Malaysian taxpayers, it was commonly believed that the reason was to obstruct the opposition's by-election tactics of checking its political influence among the Malay community. After describing these motivations, the competitiveness and responsiveness in the political sphere during the period 1987–90 should be understood as *an aberrant phenomenon* in the political process of Malaysia. Mahathir had manoeuvred to consolidate his position within and outside the ruling party. This had been done at the expense of democratic constraints and practices. Examples included political scapegoating of opponents, the widespread ISA arrests and the subsequent marginalization of the judiciary. In short, this controversial period, 1987–90, illustrates that the necessary conditions for the practice of democracy, or even the granting of basic civil rights, can be allowed only if the ruling élite's political ground, especially that of the top leader, is not seriously threatened.

NOTES

1. Adam Przeworski, "Some Problems in the Study of the Transition to Democracy", in *Transition from Authoritarian Rule: Comparative Perspectives*, edited by Guillermo O'Donnell, Philippe C. Schmitter, and Laurence Whitehead (Baltimore and London: Johns Hopkins University Press, 1986), p. 56.

2. Tunku Abdul Rahman's speech on the situation in UMNO after the party was declared unlawful. Quoted in *Aliran Monthly* 7, no. 12 (1987): 1–2.

3. William Case, *Elites and Regimes in Malaysia: Revisiting a Consociational Democracy* (Clayton: Monash Asia Institute, 1996).

4. Harold Crouch, *Government and Society in Malaysia* (Ithaca and London: Cornell University Press, 1996), especially pp. 114–29.

5. William Case, "Semi-Democracy in Malaysia: Pressures and Prospects for Change", in *Regime Change and Regime Maintenance in Asia and the Pacific*, Discussion Paper Series Number 8 (Canberra: Research School of Pacific and Asian Studies, Australian National University, 1992).

6. Przeworski reviews several other factors which lead to the breakdown of authoritarian regimes and, thus, the possibility of political liberalization. They include functional needs for regime changes, loss of legitimacy, conflicts within the ruling élite, and foreign pressures. See Przeworski (1986, pp. 47–63).

7. Edmund Terence Gomez and Jomo K.S., "Authoritarianism, Elections and Political Change in Malaysia", *Public Policy* 2, no. 3 (1998): 113–44.

8. Interview with Musa Hitam, former Deputy Prime Minister, Kuala Lumpur, 13 February 1998.

9. Interview with Rais Yatim, former Foreign Minister and deputy president of Semangat 46, Kuala Lumpur, 4 February 1998.

10. Ian Lustick, "Stability in Deeply Divided Societies: Consociationalism versus Control", *World Politics* 31, no. 3 (1979): 325–44.

11. *The Star*, 26 November 1985.

12. *The Star*, 27 April 1987.

13. Harvey C. Mansfield, trans., *Niccolo Machiavelli, The Prince* (Chicago and London: University of Chicago Press, 1998), pp. 68–71.

14. An excellent overview of the UMNO leadership crisis in the 1970s is provided by Harold Crouch, "The UMNO Crisis: 1975–77", in *Malaysian Politics and the 1978 Election*, edited by Harold Crouch, Lee Kam Hing, and Michael Ong (Kuala Lumpur: Oxford University Press, 1980), pp. 11–36.

15. Although Razaleigh lost to Musa, he consistently captured more than 40 per cent of the total vote and enjoyed widespread grassroots support within the ruling party, not only in his home state of Kelantan but also in the other states. See Ranjit Gill, *The UMNO Crisis* (Singapore: Sterling Corporate Services, 1988), pp. 6–7.

16. Razaleigh's resistance to Mahathir's leadership was closely related to the fairness of the 1987 UMNO election. He alleged that there was unfairness in the vote counting because it was run by the headquarters of the party which was controlled by Mahathir. Razaleigh heard of corruption in vote counting from a former minister and senior UMNO leader who was allied to Mahathir, although he decided not to protest about it. Interview with Razaleigh Hamzah, Kuala Lumpur, 23 February 1998.

17. For examples of strong statements by dissident leaders, see *The Star*, 27 April 1987 (Rais Yatim); *The Star*, 28 April 1987 (Tunku Abdul Rahman); and *The Star*, 1 May 1987 (Razaleigh).

18. For more details, see *FEER*, 7 May 1987; *The Star*, 28 April 1987; and *The Star*, 1 May 1987.

19. *NST*, 9 May 1987.

20. *NST*, 10 May 1987.

21. *NST*, 24 May 1987.

22. *NST*, 19 June 1987. For detail of political developments on the controversy over the DTCs issue, see *FEER*, 29 January 1987 (Nick Seaward, "New Year's Resolution"); 5 March 1987 ("Picking up the Pieces"); 2 April 1987 (Nick Seaward,

"The Tangled Web of Deposit Cooperatives"); 9 July 1987 (Suhaini Aznam, "Staying on the Inside"); and 16 July 1989 (Nick Seaward, "Cooperative Venture").

23. Headmasters and teachers of national-type Chinese primary schools, and fourteen non-Chinese educated teachers were similarly promoted in Malacca, five in the federal territory and two in Selangor. See *NST*, 11 October 1987.

24. Interview with Lee Kim Sai, then deputy president of MCA, Kajang, 25 February 1998.

25. Kua Kia Soong, *A Protean Saga: The Chinese Schools of Malaysia* (Kuala Lumpur: Resource and Research Center, 1990), p. 169.

26. The boycott of classes was called off later, except in Penang.

27. Before the massive Malay rally on 17 October 1987, more than 500 UMNO members held a protest rally on 12 October 1987, organized by the Bagan UMNO division, against MCA for objecting to the appointment of non-Chinese-educated teachers as administrators of Chinese primary schools.

28. Kua Kia Soong (1990, p. 172).

29. The main slogans were "Sack Lee Kim Sai" and "MCA Get Out". Among other banners were: "May 13 Has Begun"; and "Revoke the Citizenship of Those Who Opposed the Malay Rulers". *NST*, 18 October 1987.

30. For example, Anwar made a statement, just a day before the UMNO Youth rally on 17 October 1987, that UMNO should demonstrate to make no mistake about its strength (*NST*, 17 October 1987). Also, at the UMNO Youth rally, Najib Tun Razak summed up his speech thus: "Our elders should not compromise anymore. We are simply fed up." (*NST*, 18 October 1987). Even after the ISA arrests started, Ghafar strongly supported the 1 November UMNO unity rally, while assuring the safety of all Malaysians. He said that "what is there to be afraid of [the 1 November UMNO rally]? We guarantee the safety of everyone." (*The Star*, 28 October 1987).

31. Interview with a senior journalist from *The Star*, Petaling Jaya, February 1998.

32. *NST*, 29 October 1987. For the official explanation of the ISA arrest in October 1987, see Ministry of Home Affairs, *The Government White Paper: Towards Preserving National Security*, 14 March 1988. For a counter explanation of the basis of the ISA arrests, see Fan Yew Teng, "The Mahathir Concoction: An Alternative White Paper on the ISA Detentions", in *The White Paper on the October Affair and The Why? Papers*, edited by SUARAM and K. Das (Kelana Jaya: SUARAM Kommunikasi, 1989), pp. 32–53.

33. It is alleged that it takes at least seven to ten years of experience to apply for posts in national-type Chinese primary schools, although different states have different rules on this. A senior Chinese educationist suggested that the government should have relaxed its ruling on the minimum number of years of service rather than

opening the position to teachers who were not qualified in Mandarin. Interview with Lee Ban Chen, deputy director of Planning and Development Bureau in United Chinese School Committees' Association of Malaysia (*Dong Zong*), Kajang, 20 January 1998.

34. Confidential interview in February 1998.

35. The "UMNO eleven Case" will be discussed in the following part of this chapter.

36. Quoted in K. Das and SUARAM (1989, p. 10).

37. Interview with Nasir Hashim, pro-tem president of Socialist Party, Kuala Lumpur, 15 January 1998.

38. Interview with Rais Yatim, Kuala Lumpur, 4 February 1998.

39. Interview with Lim Kit Siang, Petaling Jaya, 19 February 1998. In the same way, a DAP national leader argues that the ISA detainees were not the cause but the scapegoat in the middle of the intra-UMNO leadership struggle. See Chen Man Hin, "DAP Made Scapegoat for UMNO's Civil War", *The Rocket* 20, no. 6 (November 1987).

40. Leslie J. Walker, trans., *The Discourses of Niccolo Machiavelli*, vol. I (London: Routledge, 1991), pp. 273–74.

41. *NST*, 27 April 1987.

42. *NST*, 27 April 1987.

43. For details of the dismissal of several ministers, see *FEER*, 14 May 1987 (Suhaini Aznam, "Dr. Mahathir's Surgery").

44. Interview with Rais Yatim, Kuala Lumpur, 4 February 1998.

45. *NST*, 2 May 1987 and *The Star*, 6 May 1987.

46. Gordon P. Means, *Malaysian Politics: The Second Generation* (New York: Oxford University Press, 1991), p. 205.

47. For more details on the resignation of state executive council members, see *The Star*, 6 May 1987; *FEER*, 14 May 1987 (Suhaini Aznam, "Dr. Mahathir's Surgery"); and *Malaysian Business*, 16 May 1987 (Jayasankaran, "Clean-Up Time").

48. *NST*, 14 September 1987.

49. *NST*, 16 September 1987. In response to Mahathir's rejection of round-table talks, Tunku Abdul Rahman commented that there had been no previous occasion to call for such talks because there had never been such trouble in UMNO. See *The Star*, 21 September 1987

50. *The Star*, 21 September 1987.

51. *The Star*, 27 September 1987 (Mohamed Sopiee, "Will UMNO Split Like the Congress Party?").

52. For the lists of twelve UMNO members and their divisions, see *The Star*, 26 June 1987 and *FEER*, 9 July 1987 (Suhaini Aznam, "See You in Court").

53. *The Star*, 26 June 1987.

54. Hereafter, I will refer to the number as eleven.

55. *NST*, 21 February 1988.

56. Means (1991, p. 206).

57. Interview with Razaleigh Hamzah, Kuala Lumpur, 17 February 1998. A senior journalist suggested that six of eleven were Mahathir's men and that Mahathir set up the legal case to destroy UMNO. Interview with M.G.G. Pillai on 24 February 1998.

58. *FEER*, 9 July 1987.

59. The committee comprised a mix of Team A and Team B supporters. It included vice-president Abdullah Badawi and supreme council member Kadir Sheikh Fadzir of Team B; party secretary-general Sanusi Junid, UMNO information chief Senator Hussein Ahmad and supreme council member Napsiah Omar of Team A.

60. It should be noted that racial tension between UMNO and the Chinese community had reached a climax at this time.

61. For Mahathir's remarks, see *The Star*, 30 September 1987.

62. Quoted in *Aliran Monthly* 7, no. 2 (1987): 2 ("Stop Press: UMNO's Misfortune").

63. On 3 November 1986, the Supreme Court, presided over by then Lord President Mohamed Salleh Abas, reinstated the work permit of two *AWSJ* Malaysia-based correspondents after the Immigration Department's cancellation of them on 26 September 1986. For more details, see *FEER*, 9 October 1986 (Nick Seaward, "Silenced Voices") and *FEER*, 13 November 1986 (Suhaini Aznam, "Journalist Reprieved"). In 1987, the court also ruled in favour of *Aliran*, which was permitted to publish a Bahasa version of its English-language monthly journal after the Home Minister had refused it a licence. Moreover, just a few weeks before the first ISA arrest on 27 October 1987, the High Court decided against the Mahathir government and United Engineers Malaysia (UEM)'s bid to remove an injunction preventing them from signing a proposed contract for the privatization of the North-South Highway. The suit against Mahathir, including several cabinet ministers, had been lodged by opposition leader, Lim Kit Siang. In the suit, he alleged corruption for approving the award of a letter of intent to UEM to build and operate the 900-kilometre North-South Highway. See *FEER*, 15 October 1987 (Nick Seaward, "Their Day in Court").

64. For example, in response to Mahathir's resentment over the case of *AWSJ*, Mohamed Suffian Hashim, former Lord President, asserted that "judges are neither pro nor anti-government. Judges are neutral servants of the law" (*NST*, 5 February 1987).

65. *Malaysian Business*, 1 January 1988. For more details on Mahathir's criticism of the judiciary during this period, see *The Star*, 7 September 1987; *NST*, 8 September 1987; *NST*, 3 October 1987; *NST*, 4 December 1987; *FEER*, 14 January 1988; and *NST*, 18 March 1988.

66. For more details of the judiciary reshuffle, see *FEER*, 14 January 1998 (Suhaini Aznam, "A Judicial Shake-up").

67. Salleh Abas and K. Das, *May Day for Justice: The Lord President's Version* (Kuala Lumpur: Magnus Books, 1989), p. 57.

68. For details of the UMNO eleven case, see Rais Yatim, *Freedom under Executive Power in Malaysia* (Kuala Lumpur: Endowment Sdn. Bhd., 1995), chapter 7; and Salleh Abas and K. Das, 1989, chapter 6.

69. *NST*, 7 December 1988.

70. *Utusan Malaysia*, 8 May 1988.

71. Hereafter I refer to UMNO as old UMNO to distinguish it from UMNO (*Baru*).

72. *Aliran Monthly* 7, no. 12 (1987): 3–7 ("Commentary on the UMNO Saga") and *NST*, 7 December 1988.

73. Interview with Rais Yatim, Kuala Lumpur, 4 February 1998.

74. Those who were not in the UMNO (*Baru*) supreme council members from Team B were: former Welfare Minister Shahrir, former Minister in the Prime Minister's Department Ajib Ahmad, former Deputy Foreign Minister Abdul Kadir Sheikh Fadzir, former Deputy Energy, Posts and Telecommunication Minister Zainal Abidin Zin, former Deputy Home Affairs Minister Radzi Sheikh Ahmad, former Deputy Transport Minister Hajjah Rahman Osman, and lawyer Marina Yusoff. See *NST*, 22 February 1988.

75. Interview with Ibrahim Saad, former Deputy Chief Minister of Penang and UMNO (*Baru*) supreme council member, Petaling Jaya, 19 February 1998.

76. *NST*, 8 March 1988.

77. *NST*, 12 March 1988.

78. Interview with Razaleigh Hamzah, Kuala Lumpur, 23 February 1998. There was an allegation at this time that members of the new UMNO would be required to swear allegiance to Mahathir. See *Aliran Monthly* 8, no. 4 (1988): 40.

79. *The Star*, 16 May 1988.

80. *NST*, 20 February 1988.

81. Interview with Rais Yatim, Kuala Lumpur, 4 February 1998.

82. There were five charges against Salleh Abas: a critical speech at the University of Malaysia on 1 August 1987; a critical book-launching speech on 12 January 1988;

adjourned *sine die* a case which involved the issue of a minor's choice of religion; the letter to the King and the Malay rulers on 26 March 1988, criticizing Mahathir's interference with the Malaysian judiciary; and various public statements after his suspension. For the full contents of the written charges by the Attorney-General, see *Aliran Monthly* 8, no. 4 (1988): 3–5.

83. For more details on the relations between the suspension of the Lord President and the UMNO eleven case, see Salleh Abas, *The Role of the Independent Judiciary* (Kuala Lumpur: Percetakan A-Z Sdn. Bhd., 1989), pp. 1–51; Raja Aziz Addruse, *Conduct Unbecoming* (Kuala Lumpur: Walrus Books, 1990), pp. 83–88; Peter Alderidge Williams, *Judicial Misconduct* (Petaling Jaya: Pelanduk Publications, 1990), pp. 26–50; and Rais Yatim (1995, chapter 7).

84. Private notes made by Salleh Abas. For their full content, see *Aliran Monthly* 8, no. 4 (1988): 7.

85. For the full transcript of Mahathir's interview, see Williams (1990, pp. 229–33).

86. Raja Aziz Addruse (1990, p. 87).

87. *NST*, 22 May 1988.

88. Rais Yatim (1995, p. 331).

89. For more details, see *FEER*, 13 November 1986 (Suhaini Aznam, "Journalist Reprieved"). Salleh Abas's judgment against the government was the reason why the Mahathir government amended the Printing Press Act soon after his judgment. According to the amendment, any decision by the Home Minister, Mahathir himself, to refuse to issue, revoke, or suspend a licence would be final and would not be reviewed by any court on any grounds whatsoever. See *FEER*, 14 January 1988 and *Aliran Monthly* 8, no. 3 (1988): 10–11.

90. Cited in Salleh Abas (1989, p. 145).

91. Salleh Abas (1989, p. 152).

92. Rais Yatim (1995, p. 330).

93. *The Star*, 11 July 1988.

94. *The Star*, 17 July 1988.

95. *NST*, 1 November 1988.

96. *NST*, 31 October 1988.

97. Means (1991, p. 230).

98. The estimated RM1 billion assets of the old UMNO had been placed under the custody of the Official Assignee since de-registration by the High Court in February 1988. For details, see *FEER*, 10 March 1988 (Nick Seaward, "UMNO's Who Owns What").

99. *Berita Harian*, 25 June 1988.

100. *The Star*, 3 August 1988.

101. *NST*, 14 February 1989.

102. For more details on the *Semarak* Movement, see Means (1991, pp. 229–30).

103. *The Star*, 14 February 1989.

104. *NST*, 16 January 1989.

105. *Berita Harian*, 18 January 1989.

106. Compiled from *Berita Harian*, 24 January 1990.

107. *The Star*, 12 May 1989.

108. For specific results of the divisional elections in 1989, see *The Star*, 10 September 1989.

109. Among the other rejected proposals were: reclassification of the status of the Youth and *Wanita* as a bureau not as a national movement; appointment of the branch and divisional leaders by the party president; and automatic ten-bonus-votes system for the posts of divisional head and its deputy.

110. Many division leaders and delegates, however, believed that the appointment of the Youth and *Wanita* national leadership was a temporary expedient until the internal situation calmed down, while they claimed the appointment for the posts of division level was unnecessary. After all, later in November 1991, the party constitution was amended to allow the heads and deputy heads of the Youth and *Wanita* wings to be elected. See *NST*, 7 November 1991.

111. In fact, the first electoral test for UMNO (*Baru*) was the Tanjung Puteri state assembly by-election in Johor Baru, where Malays formed the majority of voters, on 5 March 1988 (*NST*, 20 February 1988). The UMNO (*Baru*) candidate, Yunos, was returned to the state assembly seat in one of the closest electoral battles in Malaysian electoral history. He won by a thirty-one vote majority against a PSRM candidate, compared with 506 in the 1986 general election. UMNO dissidents did not contest this Tanjung Puteri by-election.

112. Three UMNO MPs — Shahrir Abdul Samad (Johor Baru), Tawfik Tun Ismael (Sungai Benut), and Radzi Sheikh Ahmad (Kangar) — announced their decisions to become independent MPs on 18 April, 8 May, and 14 May, respectively. The UMNO (*Baru*) supreme council then decided to recommend to the BN supreme council that all MPs and state assembly members from the old UMNO who refused to join UMNO (*Baru*) should be expelled from the BN. They included 100 old UMNO members, including MPs and state assemblymen. By the middle of 1988, at least sixteen MPs and ten state assembly members had been expelled from the BN. For details on the independent MPs, see *The Star*, 15 May 1988; *The Star*, 20 May 1988; *NST*, 22 May 1988; *NST*, 23 May 1988; *The Star*, 10 June 1988; and *The Star*, 11 June 1988.

113. *FEER*, 8 September 1988.

114. The Parit Raja state assembly seat in Johor fell vacant following the death of its assemblyman, Syed Zain Idrul Al-Shahab.

115. These three were former Minister in the Prime Minister's Department Ajib Ahmad, former Deputy Foreign Minister Kadir Sheikh Fadzir, and former Pahang *Menteri Besar* Rahim Bakar.

116. *The Star*, 16 October 1988.

117. *The Star*, 18 October 1988.

118. *NST*, 23 October 1988.

119. See NSTP Research and Information Services, *Elections in Malaysia: Facts and Figures* (Kuala Lumpur: NSTP Research and Information Services, 1990), p. 168. After the Parit Raja by-election, there were thirteen by-elections prior to the 1990 general election. The UMNO (*Baru*)-led BN was successful in twelve by-elections. For more details, see NSTP Research and Information Services (1990, pp. 168–70) and NSTP Research and Information Services, *Elections in Malaysia: A Handbook of Facts and Figures on the Elections 1955–1990* (Kuala Lumpur: NSTP, 1994), pp. 61–62.

120. For details, see *The Star*, 30 October 1988.

121. The five members were former Welfare Minister Shahrir, former Deputy Primary Industries Minister Radzi Sheikh Ahmad, former Deputy Transport Minister Rahmah Osman, former Deputy Energy, Telecommunications and Posts Minister Zainal Abidin Zin, and lawyer Marina Yusoff.

122. Interview with Ibrahim Saad, Petaling Jaya, 19 February 1998.

123. Interview with Rais Yatim, Kuala Lumpur, 4 February 1998.

124. Interview with Musa Hitam, Kuala Lumpur, 13 February 1998.

125. *The Star*, 3 December 1988.

126. *NST*, 19 December 1988.

127. *The Star*, 25 December 1988.

128. *The Star*, 14 January 1989.

129. *NST*, 21 February 1989.

130. *The Star*, 18 February 1989.

131. *The Star*, 9 February 1989.

132. *NST*, 5 March 1989.

133. *Utusan Melayu*, 2 March 1989.

134. *The Star*, 20 March 1989.

135. *NST*, 3 April 1989.

136. *NST*, 18 March 1989; *The Star*, 14 April 1989.

137. For examples of statements, see *The Star*, 13 February 1989 (Najib Tun Razak, UMNO [*Baru*] Youth chief); *The Star*, 15 February 1989 (Mohamed Khalil Yaakob, Pahang *Menteri Besar*); and *The Star*, 17 February 1989 (Muhyiddin Yassin, Johor *Menteri Besar*).

138. *The Star*, 28 February 1989.

139. For the relations between the acceptance of Shahrir and the Tambatan by-election in Johor, see *The Star*, 13 August 1989 (Mohamed Sopiee, "UMNO Move Helped to Win Tambatan").

140. *FEER*, 14 September 1989.

141. Case (1996, p. 224).

142. *The Star*, 8 October 1989.

143. On 12 October 1989, in his address at the inaugural general assembly of Semangat 46, a new political party formed by the dissident group in the old UMNO, Tunku Abdul Rahman had called on the Malays to destroy Mahathir's new party by throwing their support behind Semangat 46. Immediately after his speech, many UMNO (*Baru*) leaders called for the withdrawal of the title of *Bapa Kemerdekaan* (Father of Independence) accorded to Tunku Abdul Rahman and the removal of his statue from Parliament House.

144. The Election Commission scheduled federal and state elections in Peninsular Malaysia for 21 October 1990 and the federal election in East Malaysia for 20–21 October 1990.

145. *The Star*, 2 May 1989.

146. Teluk Pasu is a rural Malay constituency comprising all Malays, except for two Chinese and one Indian. In the 1986 general election, the BN candidate defeated the PAS candidate by a 776 majority.

147. Berjasa was founded by the former PAS Kelantan Chief Minister, Mohammad Nasir and other PAS dissidents in September 1977. It initially joined the BN in December 1977 to fight against PAS in the 1978 state election. Following the election, Berjasa formed the state government with UMNO in Kelantan in 1982. Berjasa, however, decided not to take part in the 1986 general election due to its dissatisfaction over the acceptance of Hamim, another breakaway group from PAS, into the BN. Finally, Berjasa left the BN in May 1989 to join forces with PAS and Semangat 46 in a new Muslim-based opposition coalition.

148. *The Star*, 11 July 1989.

149. Tambatan is a semi-urban constituency, comprising Malay 58.4 per cent, Chinese 35.1 per cent, and Indians 6.3 per cent. In the 1986 general election, UMNO

gained 8,726 votes while PRM obtained 5,586 votes. In the by-election on 5 August 1989, PRM decided not to field a candidate.

150. Jomo K.S., "Election's Janus Face: Limitations and Potential in Malaysia", in *The Politics of Elections in Southeast Asia*, edited by R.H. Taylor (Cambridge: Woodrow Wilson Center Press and Cambridge University Press, 1996*a*), p. 101.

151. *Asiaweek*, 19 October 1990.

152. Means (1991, p. 249).

153. Diane K. Mauzy, "Malay Political Hegemony and Coercive Consociationalism", in *The Politics of Ethnic Conflict Regulation*, edited by John McGarry and Brendan O'Leary (London: Routledge, 1993), p. 124.

154. Means (1991, p. 250). For details of internal politics in the ruling BN coalition during the period 1987–89, see Means (1991, pp. 248–50).

155. For further details on the relationship between the UMNO-led federal government and PBS-led state government, see Francis Loh Kok Wah, "Modernization, Cultural Revival and Counter-Hegemony: The Kadazans of Sabah in the 1980s", in *Fragmented Vision: Culture and Politics in Contemporary Malaysia*, edited by Joel S. Kahn and Francis Loh Kok Wah (Sydney: Allen & Unwin, 1992), pp. 225–53; Audrey Kahin, "Crisis on the Periphery: The Rift between Kuala Lumpur and Sabah", *Pacific Affairs* 65, no. 1 (1992): 30–49; and *Aliran Monthly* 12, no. 11 (1992): 2–12.

156. The numbers of unopposed BN victories are as follows: 1955 (one); 1959 (three); 1964 (two); 1969 (twenty); 1974 (forty-seven); 1978 (eight); 1982 (twelve); and 1986 (six). For greater detail on uncontested constituencies in parliamentary elections, see NSTP Research and Information Services (1990, pp. 177–79).

157. NSTP Research and Information Services (1994, pp. 109–18).

158. Interview with Musa Hitam, Kuala Lumpur, 13 February 1998.

159. For figures of the 1990 general election, see Khong Kim Hoong, *Malaysia's General Election 1990: Continuity, Change, and Ethnic Politics* (Singapore: Institute of Southeast Asian Studies, 1991); NSTP Research and Information Services, 1994, pp. 69–122; *FEER*, 1 November 1990, Suhaini Aznam, "Price of Victory", pp. 10–13; and *Asiaweek*, 2 November, "In Victory, New Tests", pp. 20–21.

160. *FEER*, 1 November 1990.

161. *Asiaweek*, 2 November 1990.

162. NSTP Research and Information Services (1994, pp. 110–12).

163. *NST*, 13 February 1990.

164. *The Star*, 20 February 1990.

165. Government budget for each general election: 1955 (RM1.125 million); 1959

(RM1.047 million); 1964 (RM1.9 million); 1969 (RM2.42 million); 1974 (RM2.426 million); 1978 (RM4.3 million); 1982 (RM8.25 million); 1986 (RM11 million), and 1990 (RM20 million). See NSTP Research and Information Services, 1994, p. 138.

166. For these allegations, see *Aliran Monthly* 10, no. 12 (1990): 11 (Tan Chee Khoon, "Opposition Has to Prove Itself First"). The opposition alleged that UMNO (*Baru*) spent RM300 million during nine days of campaigning. It was reported that voters in different constituencies were paid different rates ranging from RM50 up to RM1,000 to vote for UMNO (*Baru*). For example, in Gua Musang voters were given RM1,000 in an attempt to topple the Semangat 46 president Razaleigh Hamzah. See Lim Kit Siang, *The Dirtiest General Elections in the History of Malaysia* (Petaling Jaya: Oriengroup Sdn. Bhd., 1991).

167. *NST*, 16 March 1990.

168. *Asiaweek*, 20 April 1990.

169. Lim Kit Siang (1991, p. 5).

170. Commonwealth Secretariat *General Elections in Malaysia 20–21 Octorbor 1990: The Report of the Commonwealth Observer Group*, 1990, p. 18.

171. *FEER*, 27 December 1990.

172. A Malay businessman, who asked not to be named, said some UMNO (*Baru*) members who lived near the state boundaries voted twice in the morning and afternoon at two different states respectively in 1990. Interviewed in March 1996, Petaling Jaya.

173. For details of the role of the media and the 1990 general election, see Mustafa K. Anuar, "The Malaysian 1990 General Election: The Role of the BN Mass Media", in *Kajian Malaysia* 8, no. 2 (1990): 82–102.

174. *Berita Harian*, 18 October 1990 and *Utusan Malaysia*, 19 October 1990.

175. *NST*, 19 October 1990.

176. *Aliran Monthly* 10, no. 10 (1990): 8.

177. Any Sabahan knows that the so-called cross on the Kadazan headgear has nothing to do with Christianity. The headgear is usually made by the Bajau community, the majority of whom are in fact Muslims, and is usually given to guests as a gesture of welcome. In fact, during his previous visits to Sabah, Mahathir himself was also given similar headgear with exactly the same motif on it. For the picture of Mahathir with the Kadazan headgear bearing the so-called "Christian cross", see *Aliran Monthly* 10, no. 11 (1990): 12.

178. Parliamentary speech by Lim Kit Siang, then DAP secretary-general, on 5 December 1990.

179. *NST*, 17 October 1990.

180. *Utusan Malaysia*, 19 October 1990; and *Nanyang Siang Pao*, 20 October 1990.

181. It was even alleged that some voters were given money a day before voting with very specific message that "they should use them to buy rice and provisions in case there was trouble or May 13 on polling day". See Lim Kit Siang (1991, p. 8).

182. Interview with Tan Seng Giaw, vice-chairman of DAP, Petaling Jaya, 4 February 1998.

183. Interview with Ibrahim Saad, Petaling Jaya, 19 February 1998.

184. Interview with Musa Hitam, Kuala Lumpur, 13 February 1998.

185. *The Star*, 22 June 1989.

6

Politics in the 1990s: Regime Change or Regime Consolidation

Why not say bravely that the people of Malaysia are too immature for a workable democracy? Why not say that we need some form of authoritarian rule? We are doing that anyway and it looks as if we are going to do that for a very long time to come. The racial composition of our country is such that real democratic process can promote as much ill-will as authoritarian rule. The disadvantage of the democratic process is that it satisfies no one. Authoritarian rule can at least produce a stable strong government. ... we must accept that there is not going to be a democracy in Malaysia; there never was and there never will be. (Mahathir Mohamad 1969)[1]

DAP's defeat in the last 1995 general election was not because DAP did not make reform ... BN's great victory was because Mahathir was more liberal. Several issues, like language, culture and education, which DAP fought for before was adopted and practised by the BN government. (Lim Kit Siang 1997)[2]

As shown in the period 1987–90, the presence of substantial opposition within the dominant Malay community did not necessarily bring about greater political openness or democratic accountability in Malaysia. On the contrary, since the mid-1980s, deepening UMNO factionalism seemed to encourage the dominant Malay political élite to adopt a more assertive approach. The élite curtailed the political and civil liberties of its opponents, while provoking racial sentiment when politically expedient. As a result of the political challenge from UMNO dissidents, regaining Malay support became a priority for the Mahathir government. Under these circumstances the government could hardly exhibit greater sensitivity to the demands of non-Malay supporters, despite their growing political importance. A series of tactical appeasement gestures, before and during the 1990 general election, was also implemented in ways that avoided alienating Malay support. The situation during 1987–90 was such that the Mahathir government could not afford to appear to be making concessions to non-Malays which might incite Malay emotions.

However, in the 1990s, there was greater tolerance for traditional non-Malay concerns, despite the expected erosion of the consociational elements in Malaysian politics, resulting from the vulnerability of the Chinese component parties within the ruling coalition. Soon after UMNO secured its political dominance in the 1990 general election, the Mahathir government introduced a series of accommodative policies aimed at the non-Malay communities through the so-called "cultural liberalization". It was therefore in the years after 1990 that political sensitivity towards the non-Malays, involving minority cultural heritage, language, and education, was noticeably tolerated. Moreover, some issues that were central to Malay demands, such as the position of the Malay rulers, Malay language, and Islam, were treated in a more relaxed way, or at least redefined, on the initiative of the UMNO leaders, and Mahathir in particular. Since the non-Malay communities have long been sensitive to preserving cultural expression as a political right, the Mahathir government's initiative in liberalizing these controversial issues was politically attractive. Even the Chinese-dominated DAP regarded the years after 1990 as a period of "minor liberalization" in Malaysian politics.[3]

Nevertheless, as implied in the term "minor liberalization", growing cultural tolerance was not necessarily accompanied by greater political liberalization. Instead, the tolerance level for political expression in the Malaysian political system became increasingly limited, despite the cultural liberalization of the 1990s. Continuing political detention, using selective and politically motivated discriminatory laws, highlight the vulnerability of Malaysian civil society at this time. In the 1990s the political dominance of the ruling coalition, especially its dominant partner UMNO, was further consolidated. By the mid-1990s, loose alliances among the opposition parties were considerably undermined by internal weaknesses, as well as by external pressures from the Barisan government. Eventually, the multi-ethnic opposition coalition Gagasan Rakyat was dissolved before the 1995 general election, and its component parties became even more marginal in Malaysian politics after their miserable defeat in the 1995 elections. Similarly, inherent ideological differences between the secular Semangat 46 and the Islamic PAS began to widen soon after they took over the Kelantan state government in 1990 and the fragile relationship eventually broke down soon after the 1995 general election. In 1996, the Razaleigh-led Semangat 46 finally returned to the fold of Mahathir's UMNO following defections of party leaders and members.

Furthermore, Mahathir appeared to be much less tolerant towards potential challengers to his political dominance, both within and outside the ruling party. It was obvious that Mahathir's main concern in the 1990s was to systematically increase the centralization of power under his personal control. He frequently invoked the fear of intra-Malay strife to modify the UMNO constitution in a more authoritarian direction and, in addition, the underlying reasons behind the constitutional amendments of this period increasingly reflect the obvious motives of aggrandizing executive power in the hands of Mahathir as Prime Minister. As Jomo stressed, the key features of political democracy in Malaysia were further eroded in the 1990s due to the growing concentration of power in Mahathir's personal grip.[4] In fact, the notion of a strong executive authority had been enshrined in Malaysian politics in the decades after independence, but what Mahathir did in the years after 1990 illustrate how the power of one man came to be seen in a more centripetal way. In short, the years after 1990 saw an intermittent replay of the key authoritarian features of the previous period 1987–90, especially in the political sphere.

How can these ambivalent features of Malaysian politics in the 1990s be understood? What were the motives behind such contradictory degrees of tolerance for political and cultural expression? Malaysia's political system has been variously characterized by scholars, both foreign and domestic, as "semi-democracy", "limited democracy", and "illiberal democracy". These concepts tend to categorize "mixed" features of the Malaysian political system along a continuum between liberal democracy and authoritarianism. In this regard, Crouch characterizes the admixture of the Malaysian political system as a "repressive-responsive regime".[5] Although the notion of "repressive-responsive" is not directly related to the contradictory tendency of the Mahathir government towards political and cultural expression, such an admixture helps us to understand "ambiguous" features of the Malaysian political system in the 1990s. This chapter analyses the background, context, and outcome of the "repressive-responsive" Malaysian political system after the general election of 1990 and towards the mid-1990s.

Mahathir's Supremacy within UMNO Consolidated

To maintain his influence in the 1990s, Mahathir appeared to mix two tactics: indirect checks-and-balances, and tighter domination. Mahathir adopted these two strategies, not alternately, but as mutually supportive strategies for his power maintenance within the ruling party. To a certain extent factional rivalries among the second-echelon leaders were allowed, or even encouraged, to counter the growing pressure of a generational shift in the party leadership. However, Mahathir did not forget to reiterate the "rhetoric of de-politicization": that excessive internal politicking would lead to a repetition of the same disastrous schism of 1987. At the same time, it was necessary for Mahathir to appear to have the toughness of the dominator, as he had shown in the process of rebuilding UMNO around his personality after the 1987 leadership crisis. By doing this, throughout the 1990s, whenever new factional forces attempted to increase their influence and thus undermine Mahathir's supremacy in the ruling party, tighter authoritarian rules were applied to further consolidate Mahathir's grip on political power.

A Process of Grooming, Filtering, and Tighter Ground Rules

As expected, the process of UMNO (*Baru*)'s first party election of 1990, scheduled for 29 November to 2 December, appeared to be a quiet affair. Of the total 133 party divisions, Mahathir and his deputy Ghafar Baba received 128 nominations each. Kubang Pasu, chaired by Mahathir, and Jasin, led by Ghafar, were the only divisions that did not nominate candidates for all party posts by the direct request of Mahathir, whereas the other three divisions had technical difficulties in nominating candidates. In this context, in effect 100 per cent of the party divisions nominated Mahathir and Ghafar as the party president and deputy president respectively in this very first party election. Under the new voting system of the party, they automatically received 1,280 bonus votes each. Considering the total number of 1,519 delegates in the 1990 party elections, they were virtually certain of being returned as party president and deputy president. However, there was no necessity for the new ten bonus-vote system to be applied this time as both posts were filled without contest.

By contrast, the competition for the three vice-presidential posts was intense and costly. This was mainly because, given that both Mahathir and Ghafar were in their mid-sixties, one of the three vice-presidents would be the most likely successor to the party presidency in the not-too-distant-future. This was a preview of the growing factional competition among the possible successors to the Mahathir presidency as the party election approached. Mahathir appeared neutral during the intense campaigning for the vice-presidencies. Mahathir's most common warning to party leaders before party election was to prevent vice-presidential candidates from forming electoral factions to consolidate their support.[6]

Nevertheless, it became clear that Mahathir was grooming Anwar Ibrahim as his possible successor after the 1990 general election. Given a clear, though indirect, sign of being Mahathir's favourite, Anwar amassed the highest number of votes among the field of six vice-presidential candidates.[7] In a cabinet reshuffle in February 1991 following the resignation of Daim Zainuddin, Anwar, then Education Minister, was appointed Finance Minister.[8] At this time, the Finance portfolio was regarded as a necessary step to the Malaysian prime ministership due to the rise of the entrepreneurial and business classes among the Malays. The move, therefore, was regarded as a clear sign of Mahathir promoting Anwar as his favourite successor.

Mahathir, however, did not neglect to check the new balance of power among the second-echelon leaders within the party. In particular, Anwar's political rise within UMNO was effectively counter-checked by the influence of the other two elected vice-presidents, Abdullah Ahmad Badawi and Sanusi Junid. Both were viewed as Anwar's long-time political rivals and possible candidates to succeed Mahathir. Abdullah Badawi's victory in the party election was unexpected because Mahathir made clear his intention of prolonging the former Team B leader Abdullah Badawi's stay in the political wilderness by leaving him outside the government in the post–general election cabinet reshuffle in 1990.[9] However, Abdullah Badawi's political comeback ironically provided Mahathir with a chance to check Anwar's growing popularity within UMNO. Eventually, Abdullah Badawi returned as Foreign Minister in February 1991 after nearly four years in the political wilderness.

At this time, any talk of leadership succession seemed premature and a number of developments in the early 1990s were viewed as grooming and filtering processes for the second-echelon leaders of UMNO. Mahathir himself rarely discussed the succession issue. Nevertheless, political rivalries among possible successors to the Mahathir presidency were heating up ahead of the UMNO divisional elections scheduled for 1992. For possible successors, these elections were regarded as crucial battles, due to the important role of delegates who would be sent to vote at the second party elections scheduled in 1993. Therefore, internal politicking had already reached such an extent that it spilled into the open, even a year before the 1992 divisional elections. There were regular reports that possible successors to Mahathir ceaselessly manoeuvred to expand their national and divisional political networks in the early 1990s.[10]

Given the vigorous second-echelon jockeying for power, Mahathir postponed the scheduled 1992 divisional elections, except for Sabah, until just a few months before the party general assembly of 1993.[11] Speculation also arose that the 1993 party election would be postponed until 1994 to reduce the level of mutual recrimination and internal politicking among the second-echelon leaders of UMNO. Mahathir said that the one-year delay of the divisional elections was a necessary move "to pre-empt politicking in the run-up to UMNO Supreme Council elections in 1993".[12] The decision, however, had been projected as a measure to prevent possible successors from enhancing their nation-wide grassroots influence too early. Mahathir effectively turned the intensifying power struggle among the second echelon leaders to his advantage by removing or constraining opportunities for possible successors to exercise their powers of patronage among the rank and file.

Soon after the delay of divisional elections, Mahathir also amended the party constitution to consolidate the incumbent's built-in advantages.[13] The authority of the supreme council was enhanced not only to determine the election date but also to postpone divisional elections for a maximum of eighteen months. The new amendment gave the incumbent leaders a free hand in party affairs for up to eighteen months in the name of reducing internal party politicking among the ranks. While the power of the supreme council was extended, Mahathir's control in it was further consolidated by another amendment to the party constitution, which allowed the party president to increase the number of appointed members of the supreme council from seven to ten.

Furthermore, tighter ground rules were imposed on the party leaders and members by the supreme council a few months before delegate meetings at the branch and divisional levels of 1993. The supreme council, in the name of curbing "over-politicking", banned divisions from inviting national leaders to open delegates' meetings, as was previously the practice in the party. It only allowed such meetings to be opened by the respective divisional heads. In addition, a shorter time-frame for delegates' meetings at branch and divisional levels was also set in order to reduce politicking. Consequently, all divisional meetings had to be held within a twenty-two-day period from 9 September 1993. In an unprecedented move, the supreme council also decided to hammer out "guidelines on campaign styles and convening of division and branch meetings".[14] Although most party leaders and members dutifully welcomed a set of tighter regulations, some sections of the party were worried that the party leadership was "over-doing things" to avoid "over-politicking" at this time.[15]

Mahathir's Choice in 1993:
Intentional Shift or Reluctant Endorsement?

Mahathir's deft way of handling the growing pressure for the generational leadership change was vividly revealed in the process of the 1993 party election. Despite tighter ground rules and Mahathir's repeated calls for party unity throughout the year, it became clear that the factional conflicts crystallized around his possible successors. The battle line became more distinct as the 1993 party election approached. The two incumbent vice-presidents, Abdullah Badawi and Sanusi, were moving closer to Ghafar, while the other younger leaders, Najib Razak, Muhyiddin Yassin, and Muhammad Muhammad Taib, were viewed as Anwar's men. Even Mahathir could not simply deny the growing demands for a succession race between the old and new factional forces in the party.

Perhaps one of the most heated controversies during this period was Mahathir's shift in attitude from one where he emphasized the tradition of the party and then that of neutrality to more direct intervention. At an early stage of the leadership competition in 1993, Mahathir's main concern was keeping the growing politicking between old and new guard from running out of control. At one point, Mahathir showed his apparent support for the party's incumbents and advised a "no-contest" for the two top posts. Mahathir, however, also appeared reluctant to close the competition for the post of his deputy. It was indeed Mahathir himself who stirred up public debate on the competition in the early phase of the nomination process, by emphasizing both "party tradition" and "democratic values". For example, on the final day of the 1992 party assembly Mahathir said: "the man who holds the No. 2 post or deputy succeeds the president and that is still the way I feel it should be".[16] However, a day before, Mahathir also emphasized that for him naming his successor would be "undemocratic" and "merely naming a successor will not reduce politicking and ensure party unity".[17] Mahathir's two-pronged attitude was demonstrated throughout the succession race in 1993.

When Anwar first openly denied his intention to challenge the incumbent deputy president Ghafar on 24 April 1993, Mahathir pointed out that it was the delegates' democratic right to nominate Anwar for the deputy president's post, though he welcomed Anwar's decision.[18] A few weeks after Anwar's second denial of challenging Ghafar, Mahathir again qualified his support for a "no-contest" for the party's top two posts as something which should be decided by the divisions and members themselves.[19] After that, in reiterating the rhetoric of "no-contest" as a party tradition, Mahathir emphasized that "the tradition is that there is usually no contest but the party constitution allows a contest".[20] Party members thus believed that Mahathir had indirectly thrown the game open at this time.[21]

As nomination day drew closer, Mahathir finally announced that he would remain neutral if there was a contest for the deputy's post.[22] Mahathir's shift to such a neutral stand was a tactical but *de facto* endorsement of Anwar's challenge. Mahathir claimed in his opening address at the 1993 party assembly that he did not intentionally give the impression that he was not neutral during the election campaign for the party leadership.[23] In fact, there was frequent intervention by Mahathir to preserve the status quo at the top level. However, Mahathir made no serious intervention to check Anwar's influence in the process of the leadership elections. Anwar's political opponents believed that Mahathir, as a party president who had spoken out strongly against excessive politicking and its potential to split the party, should have wielded his influence in more unequivocal terms to stop the party leaders from backing Anwar.[24] Several senior UMNO officials and journalists stressed that it was highly unlikely that Anwar would be making his bid for the deputy presidency without his mentor Mahathir's tacit approval, given that Mahathir was in much greater control of the party than ever before. Anwar himself mentioned that he would not have challenged Ghafar if Mahathir had objected when he approached Mahathir about his intention to contest. He insisted that there were no objections from Mahathir.[25]

Consequently, Mahathir's promise of neutrality paved the way for Anwar to contest the deputy presidency. Soon after Mahathir made it clear he was neutral, several well-known Mahathir men openly expressed their opinion on the succession race. At first, the then Law Minister Syed Hamid announced that "[the party] tradition should never be allowed to overrule the party constitution".[26] Also, the party secretary-general Mohamad Rahmat pointed out that "the regeneration process in which the young takes over the leadership from old guardians must continue to preserve the strength of the party".[27] On 23 August 1993, Anwar finally announced his willingness to accept divisional nominations and this was followed by successive nominations for Anwar from one division after another, leaving Ghafar far behind in the race. Anwar's press conference on announcing his candidacy was more a show of strength than anything else with a high level of support from almost all senior leaders of UMNO. Anwar was accompanied by the party secretary-general, all eight *menteri besar* and a (Malacca) chief minister, nine UMNO cabinet ministers, eighteen deputy ministers, and five parliamentary secretaries. The gathering even included leaders from the Federal Territory and Sabah, which Ghafar was heading. Nineteen of the twenty UMNO divisions in Sabah decided to support Anwar. But most interesting of all was the presence of those who used to belong to the Ghafar camp, for instance, Information Minister Mohamad Rahmat, Terengganu Menteri Besar Wan Mokhtar Ahmad, Justice Minister Syed Hamid, and Negeri Sembilan Menteri Besar Mohd Isa Abdul Samad. Those who were absent at the press conference were Foreign Minister Abdullah Badawi, Agriculture Minister Sanusi Junid, and International Trade and Industry Minister Rafidah Aziz. It was inconceivable for all the UMNO state chief ministers and most cabinet ministers to show up at such a power-packed press conference without Mahathir's support for Anwar.[28] Ghafar received only seven nominations from the 153 UMNO divisions.[29] Even after Anwar's announcement to challenge Ghafar, Mahathir emphasized his neutral stand. However, there was no doubt that Mahathir strongly pressed for Ghafar to give way to Anwar. Some examples are as follows: (1) Immediately after Anwar's press conference, Mahathir openly expressed his hope that one of the two deputy presidential candidates would withdraw from the race; (2) Mahathir made it clear that the no-contest for the deputy presidency had become history; and (3) in his statement in Terengganu in September, Mahathir mentioned that "the person who felt to be the loser should withdraw".[30] Following Ghafar's resignation from all his official and party posts before the election, Anwar finally secured the deputy presidency without contest.

In a dramatic shift, Mahathir then changed his attitude from a "neutral" stance to that of "direct intervention" by showing his unequivocal disapproval of a "team approach" and "money politics" in the succession race.[31] His message obviously targeted Anwar's *Wawasan* team, a pack of aspiring young party leaders in their forties competing for the vice-presidency. Anwar's vision team included Muhyiddin Yassin, Najib Tun Razak, and Muhammad Muhammad Taib as vice-presidential candidates, as well as Rahim Tamby Chik as UMNO Youth chief candidate. His caustic remarks were repeated a day before the vice-presidential election and increased uncertainty among party members. Mahathir's intervention may have come too late to affect the results, as Anwar's *Wawasan* team swept all the top elected positions. However, the actual votes were more evenly distributed than had been earlier indicated by the number of nominations. In fact, the rival faction enjoyed much more support in the election than had been reflected in the nominations received. In the process of divisional nominations, Badawi and Sanusi received only sixteen and thirteen each, while Najib Tun Razak, Muhammad Muhammad Taib, and Muhyiddin Yassin secured 148, 138, and 133 respectively. The difference in the number of votes in the election, however, was unexpectedly narrow, especially between Badawi and the third vice-president. Badawi and Sanusi obtained 927 and 525 votes each, compared with Muhyiddin Yassin, Najib Tun Razak, and Muhammad Muhammad Taib who received 1,413, 1,202, and 1,189 votes respectively. More interestingly, Rahim Tamby Chik, the *Wawasan* team's UMNO Youth chief candidate, won by only forty-four votes out of a total of 484 votes, even though he had secured 106 divisional nominations against only ten for his opponent, Mohamed Isa Abdul Samad. Furthermore, although it was widely viewed that the supreme council was dominated by Anwar's followers at the expense of old party leaders, in fact only four were newly elected to the twenty-five elected seats in the supreme council.[32] Anwar's supporters believed that this was largely due to Mahathir's sudden shift in attitude to check the new balance of power especially after Anwar's landslide victory.[33]

Mahathir's moderate attitudes on party tradition and the neutral position on contesting party posts did not appear to change when internal politicking deepened even further among the second-echelon leaders. Then why did Mahathir shift his attitude to one of more direct intervention at the very moment when Anwar emerged victorious in a landslide?

Political observers expected Anwar to sweep most of the divisional nominations, but not by such a margin that it compelled the incumbent Ghafar to withdraw from the race even before the election was held. Mahathir was also dumbfounded at such an unprecedented wave of support for Anwar.[34] It was even claimed that Anwar's remarkable victory demonstrated that his grassroots support within the party was greater than that of Mahathir.[35] Although Mahathir's own political leadership remained intact, such considerable support for Anwar could impact on Mahathir's own political grip on the party much sooner than he thought. Mahathir desperately needed to create "as many buffers as possible", especially after the devastating downfall of the old guard in the party.[36] Therefore, it was a necessary step for Mahathir to promptly shift his key concern to checking Anwar's rise within the party, a change from neutrality to stern intervention. Too much delay might further increase the pressure from the new factional forces for a generational shift in the national leadership as a whole. As Zainuddin asserted:

> Mahathir knew what he was doing. He felt his role had ended when he laid down the path for his successor [Anwar]. He did not feel it was his job to deal with the nitty gritty of the succession right down to the composition of the political line-up for Anwar's team.[37]

Checking the New Balance of Power

After the 1993 party election, there were other examples of Mahathir's intention not only to check Anwar's growing popularity but also to further consolidate his own grip within the party. At first, Mahathir strategically delayed the time-frame of appointment for his deputy in order to assert his authority, as the balance of factional forces within the party had shifted clearly in Anwar's favour. Political observers believed that the too-early appointment of Anwar might have weakened Mahathir's own leadership position within the party at that time. In fact, Mahathir had already downplayed the significance of the 1993 party election by emphasizing that he would not be bound by the election results in determining the likely successors to the national leadership.[38] Mahathir finally appointed Anwar as Deputy Prime Minister sooner than expected on 1 December 1993. Observers, however, saw this as an attempt by Mahathir to check further demands for changes in the party and government hierarchy, to reflect the new balance of power after the party election of 1993. Again, Mahathir did not forget to appoint all electoral losers and several other loyalists as members to the supreme council, soon after the appointment of Anwar. Abdullah Badawi and Sanusi were also included. In addition, Ghafar later came back to the mainstream of party politics in March 1995, just a month before the 1995 general election. Although Ghafar's comeback was widely viewed as his possible role in the forthcoming general election, UMNO leaders also speculated that his return was meant somehow to check Anwar's power within the party.[39]

In his closing speech at the 1993 party general assembly, Mahathir proposed another amendment to the party constitution in order to check money politics in the party. The proposed amendment to the party constitution was approved at the UMNO extraordinary general assembly held in June 1994. The key element of the new amendment was the introduction of a "Code of Ethics" for party members, as follows: (1) observe party directives; (2) carry out party policies; (3) abide by and respect party decisions; (4) protect party secrets; (5) safeguard the good name of the party; and (6) at all times reflect good ethics. More importantly, the new amendments to the party constitution included provisions which further empowered the supreme council with punitive authority. Now, the supreme council could inflict the following punishments on any party member who violated the "Code of Ethics": (1) warning; (2) suspension; (3) barring from contesting party posts or standing as a candidate in state or general elections for a period of time determined by the supreme council; and (4) dismissal from the party.[40]

The wide-ranging coverage of the "Code of Ethics" led many party leaders and members to fear that the new amendments could lead to further control by the top party leadership in the name of checking unhealthy party trends. However, as a senior party official said, they had little choice but to accept, although they knew what the new amendments were all about.[41] This was largely because the extraordinary general assembly to amend the party constitution was held just a few weeks before the pro-tem committee appointments for the forthcoming general election, following the constituency delineation exercise of 1993.[42] Hence, the delegates for the extraordinary general assembly, mostly divisional leaders, were more worried about whether they would be retained in the pro-tem line-up. The pro-tem committee was supposed to continue to serve the party until the next general election which was scheduled before December 1995. It was generally believed that the members of the pro-tem committee would be the same set of state and parliamentary candidates in the forthcoming general election. Indeed, during the UMNO extraordinary general assembly of 1994 and the following annual general assembly in November 1994, there seemed to be "an unspoken understanding" among the party leaders and members that the party president was not to be offended or even questioned.[43]

At this juncture, it seemed that Mahathir had no plans for early retirement. Instead, whether it was intended or not, Mahathir's own political grip within UMNO had become practically unassailable as the 1995 general election approached. Until recently, it was, and occasionally still is, argued that factionalism within UMNO gave more room for democracy in Malaysian politics no matter how authoritarian the political system was perceived. However, towards the mid-1990s UMNO factionalism became more and more dependent upon Mahathir's personal tolerance rather than bringing checks and balances to his authoritarian form of governance.

Conciliation, Discrimination, and Victimization

While Mahathir consolidated his power in the 1990s, UMNO and the BN government's political dominance also appeared to be strengthened. Three distinct types of political strategies were used by Mahathir and UMNO leaders towards opposition parties after the 1990 general election: "conciliatory gestures", whereby the Mahathir government co-opted the irritant opposition members; "marginalization", a more indirect but discriminating approach to paralysing opposition forces; and "victimization", a more direct and coercive measure by the UMNO-led government. However, it must be stressed that the Mahathir government's political dominance in the years after 1990 escalated through a mixture of these distinct political manoeuvrings, from conciliation as a milder approach through marginalization to victimization as a more coercive one.

Pressure and Conciliatory Gestures towards Semangat 46

As analysed in Chapter 5, dissident UMNO members led by Razaleigh failed to emerge in 1990 as a new element capable of providing an alternative leadership with another multi-ethnic coalition in Malaysian politics. Furthermore, Semangat 46 itself was no longer viewed as a viable political force with a national presence. The UMNO-splinter party was much less represented than its counterpart DAP both at state and parliamentary levels and the party had been downgraded as a junior partner of the other Malay Muslim party, PAS.

Nevertheless, there is no doubt that Razaleigh's Semangat 46 was an annoying element in so far as UMNO politics was concerned. As Gomez notes, the presence of the UMNO-splinter group in Malaysian politics symbolizes the lack of consensus within the Malay community, and therefore suggests that the rhetoric of "Malay unity" by the UMNO leaders is "at best illusory".[44] Apart from this symbolic aspect, Semangat 46 was still capable of influencing Malay voters, as evidenced in Semangat 46's victories in two Kelantan state by-elections held in August 1991.[45] Moreover, the presence of Razaleigh's Semangat 46 seemed to play a key role in heightening anti-federal sentiments in Malaysian politics in the years after 1990. The 1990 general election at least proved that Razaleigh was a crucial factor in shifting a major portion of the UMNO supporters in Kelantan to the anti-UMNO side. Without Semangat 46's secular-Muslim votes based on regional sentiments, PAS could not recapture Kelantan on the basis of its traditional Islamic vote in the 1990 elections. As Chin observed, post-1990 general election circumstances in Kelantan suggested that PAS held winning electoral formulae, that is, a religious element (Islam) and an anti-federal sentiment (regionalism).[46] For Mahathir and UMNO leaders, there was fear that these winning formulae would become a continuing threat to UMNO's political supremacy in certain Malay-dominated states if necessary measures were not taken to stop, or at least impede, growing regional sentiment in Kelantan.

Great efforts, therefore, were made by the UMNO leadership to undermine Semangat 46's influence after the 1990 general election. Typically, UMNO leaders fostered the break-up of Semangat 46 by inducing its leaders and members to return to UMNO. Especially in early 1991, hardly a day passed without the BN-controlled media publicizing defections of Semangat 46 members to UMNO and the dissolution of Semangat 46 branches and divisions. It was even widely speculated that the party itself would be dissolved in the near future. Although reports of Semangat 46's imminent death were perceived as premature, UMNO's propaganda exercise had been very successful. The speculation became more intense when the UMNO leaders spread rumours about the possible defections of a number of elected representatives of Semangat 46, by either identifying their names or anonymously.

The first major sign of UMNO's recovery in Kelantan was the defection of Ibrahim Ali, Semangat 46 Youth chief and MP for Pasir Mas, in March 1991. Ibrahim Ali was the first elected representative to join UMNO and his defection prompted many other Semangat 46 leaders to follow suit. Within a few weeks after Ibrahim Ali's defection, two more Semangat 46 state assembly members quit the party and joined UMNO.[47] Then in August 1991, another Semangat 46 MP Ahmad Shukri Hassan returned to the UMNO fold together with about 3,000 supporters. As a result, less than a year after UMNO had lost all thirteen parliamentary and thirty-nine state assembly seats in Kelantan at the 1990 general election, the party had regained two parliamentary seats and two state assembly seats. Moreover, a number of top Semangat 46 leaders retired from active politics, either quitting their party posts or going on long study leave. For example, party deputy president Rais Yatim took study leave to London; vice-president Marina Yusoff resigned from all party posts; and *Wanita* chief Hajjah Rahmah Osman also took a two-year study leave.[48]

On the surface, despite the massive influx of Semangat 46 members into UMNO, Razaleigh did not appear defensive, claiming that it was indeed better to rid the party of traitors or those who strove for personal gains. Nevertheless, few other Semangat 46 leaders and PAS leaders regarded the increasing number of defections so lightly. In particular, PAS leaders appeared concerned over Razaleigh's ability to hold his influence both at the grassroots and top levels. Semangat 46 supporters at *ceramah* were dwindling even in Razaleigh's solid bases in Kelantan after a series of defections of the Semangat 46 elected representatives.[49]

Accordingly, the PAS-led Kelantan state government was keen to amend the state constitution requiring an elected state assembly member to vacate his or her seat in case of defection to another party. In a rather hasty manner, the Kelantan state government even proposed that the amendment would be retroactive to the date the opposition assumed power in Kelantan in October 1990.[50] The "anti–party hopping" law was finally passed with its retroactive provisions by the Kelantan state assembly in April 1991.

UMNO's approach towards Semangat 46, however, opened up after the Kelantan state government proposed to amend its constitution to adopt the anti–party hopping law. On the one hand, UMNO expanded its efforts to encourage the departure of Semangat 46 leaders by assuring re-nomination of Semangat 46 defectors as UMNO candidates in any by-election, if they were made to vacate the state assembly seat.[51] In this context, the two former Semangat 46 state assemblymen, who had returned to UMNO before the introduction of the anti–party hopping law, were re-nominated as UMNO candidates in the Kelantan state by-elections held in August 1991. Meanwhile, the Mahathir government brought a legal suit against the Kelantan anti–party hopping law to remove obstacles and facilitate the transfer of Semangat 46 leaders to UMNO. As expected, in November 1991, the High Court ruled against the Kelantan state assembly and asserted that the amendment to the state constitution was against the federal constitution. A few months later in April 1992, the Supreme Court finally confirmed the High Court's decision that the Kelantan anti–party hopping law as *ultra vires* of the federal constitution.

Another major appeasement gesture towards the Semangat 46 members occurred at the UMNO special assembly in November 1991, when the UMNO leadership approved the amendments to the party constitution to prevent the branch and divisional levels from delaying or rejecting membership application of Semangat 46 members to UMNO.[52] There were reservations among UMNO branch and division leaders who feared the increasing number of Semangat 46 defectors would threaten their political interests. Especially in Kelantan, the large numbers of defections of Semangat 46 members became an obsession with the existing UMNO branch and division leaders because they were worried that the increasing numbers of former Semangat 46 members would threaten the present UMNO branch and division leadership when the next divisional elections were held in mid-1993. So, as a typical way of obstructing the influx of Semangat 46 members, membership applications were often delayed or even rejected at the UMNO branch levels. Under the new amendment, however, any applicant who had not received a reply from a branch or divisional level three months after submitting an application form could appeal directly to the UMNO supreme council to seek automatic admission to the party. To demonstrate its conciliatory gesture, top UMNO leaders occasionally warned the branch and divisional leaders who were reluctant to re-admit former Semangat 46 members.[53] It was also around this time that a special "co-ordinating committee" was set up in Kelantan by forty-two former Semangat 46 leaders to facilitate the efficient re-entry of former Kelantan UMNO members.[54] However, it must also be noted that the UMNO leaders intermittently counter-warned of infiltration by Semangat 46 members who were out to sow discord after joining UMNO.[55]

The so-called "open-door policy" towards Semangat 46 was continued in the early 1990s by Mahathir and UMNO leaders. Consequently, another key figure of Semangat 46, Harun Idris, former Menteri Besar of Selangor, returned to UMNO in January 1992. In addition, ten out of the eleven former UMNO politicians who had challenged the validity of the 1987 UMNO election, were accepted as new members by early 1992.[56] Semangat 46 vice-president Marina Yusoff, who had retired from politics after the 1990 general election, also joined UMNO in May 1993. Immediately after Marina's defection, UMNO announced that all Semangat 46 leaders, except Razaleigh, were free to join the party and vie for divisional posts in the coming party elections scheduled for mid-1993.[57] This announcement came when the dispute between the existing UMNO members and Semangat 46 defectors was intensifying a few months before the scheduled branch and division elections. Despite feuding at branch and divisional levels, it is widely believed that these conciliatory gestures reflected the increasing confidence of Mahathir and top UMNO leaders over Malay hegemony.

On one level, the influx of Semangat 46 leaders and members into UMNO seemed to reflect their dissatisfaction with the way the PAS-led state government handled state matters. In particular, the marginalization of their role in the Kelantan state government was a major complaint among Semangat 46 officials in the early 1990s. One telling case is the failure of a 50:50 allocation of positions in the state administration and government-owned companies in Kelantan. The appointment of the second deputy *menteri besar* in Kelantan was another issue between Semangat 46 and PAS. After the 1990 elections, Semangat 46 wanted the position of deputy *menteri besar* to go the party. But the issue was resolved by creating two deputy *menteri besar* and this caused serious internal conflict in the Kelantan state government. UMNO leaders repeatedly instigated, through the BN-controlled mass media, the fragile partnership between Semangat 46 and PAS as a *kahwin mutaah* (temporary marriage of convenience) whereas all the key positions in the Kelantan state government were monopolized by the latter.

However, irrespective of increasing feuds between Semangat 46 and PAS, it seemed that there were already strong demands and internal discussions among Semangat 46 leaders to return *en bloc* to UMNO immediately after the 1990 general election. In particular, several top party leaders, including deputy president Rais Yatim, proposed to Razaleigh to join UMNO as one group and fight within UMNO circles for the purpose of Malay unity. It was alleged that Razaleigh was very agitated by such strong demands from the top Semangat 46 leaders to go back to the old UMNO circles.[58] Razaleigh, however, firmly denied that there were increasing demands from the top party leaders to return to the old UMNO circle.[59] Whether this is true or not, there was a growing fear within Semangat 46 circles that they would eventually be sent to the political wilderness if they remained any longer out of the establishment circles. This was, and still is, the psyche of the UMNO members who were habituated to the high absorptive capacity of the ruling party. For them, it was obviously hard to endure the political hardships expected of opposition forces, and "political survival" in all likelihood was the most practical reason to return to the UMNO mode.

Unlike Razaleigh, most other Semangat 46 leaders and members were not financially independent. Given the vulnerable circumstances of being heavily dependent on government patronage networks such as business licences, bank loans, and state contracts, they had no option but to creep back to the establishment circles when their patronage resources were called in by the UMNO-led government. Case argued that the retaliatory process by the Mahathir government after the 1990 general election covered not only business élites associated with Razaleigh but also relatives of opposition supporters.[60] For the remnants of Razaleigh's supporters, Semangat 46 was no longer viewed as an alternative or even potentially viable "guardian" for their political and financial survival. In fact, Razaleigh himself admitted that he could not afford to provide enough patronage resources to his supporters as he lost mainstream political platforms in Malaysia. He therefore believed that a number of Semangat 46 leaders left not because they had given up Semangat 46's cause or because of internal disputes in the Kelantan state government, but because they were financially rewarded or persecuted to leave the party by the Mahathir government.[61] However, as a Semangat 46 official correctly observed, most Semangat 46 defectors were gradually pushed into "oblivion", or at best "rehabilitation", after returning to the UMNO fold.[62]

Marginalization and Discrimination

The Mahathir government's undermining of opposition forces in the 1990s is also evident in the process of the paralysation of the opposition-run state governments in Kelantan and Sabah, by their exclusion from the political mainstream and patronage resources for development. Mahathir's intransigent attitude towards the opposition-run state governments can be seen in his speech on the UMNO general assembly of 1990:

> The Federal Government will not go out of its way to help the PAS government. We know that any form of [federal] assistance will be used by PAS to prove that there is nothing to lose in electing PAS as a government. ... For this reason, the Federal Government will not help the PAS government to succeed.[63]

From the very beginning after the 1990 general election, Mahathir left out the chief ministers of Kelantan and Sabah when he called federal meetings with state chief ministers to discuss economic activities in the states. Kelantan and Sabah were instead represented by the most senior ministers from these states in the ruling BN coalition. Mahathir then announced that the federal government would not give any financial assistance to Kelantan and Sabah, apart from their annual budgets in conformity with the minimum requirements provided under the federal constitution.[64] Given that the financial status of local authorities has long been dependent on the federal government's patronage resources, there seemed to be little the opposition-run Kelantan and Sabah state governments could do in carrying out economic activities without federal assistance. Also, the federal constitution restricts, to a large extent, the discretionary power of state governments to raise alternative financial resources for themselves.[65] Although Mahathir intermittently claimed that development should not be mixed with politics, it was commonly believed that the Mahathir government utilized federal assistance for development projects as an effective way of discriminating against the Kelantan and Sabah state governments. A senior member of the Kelantan Chinese Chamber of Commerce stressed that there was not a single new development project in Kelantan for at least the first six months after the 1990 general election and no new foreign investment came into the state during this period.[66]

The Mahathir government, however, could not sever development projects and federal funding altogether because it would result in the deepening of anti-federal sentiment among the people in the states of Kelantan and Sabah. The most effective scenario for the Mahathir government was, therefore, to paralyse those opposition-run state governments without giving the impression of victimization. Accordingly, the federal funds were directly channelled through a newly created federal agency, the Federal Development Department (FDD) directly under the Prime Minister's Department, to bypass the Kelantan and Sabah state governments. In the same way, especially in Kelantan, Mahathir empowered the UMNO division chiefs to approve development projects in their respective constituencies, even though they were no longer elected representatives.[67] Then, Mahathir openly promoted that sufficient federal funds would be allocated to finance various development projects approved by the UMNO division heads in Kelantan. It was also advised that all the Kelantan division heads set up "service centres" in their respective constituencies to facilitate development projects.[68] By doing this, UMNO was able to promote its traditional selling point, that is, patronage networks for development, to the people in the opposition-run states.

Even so, the Mahathir government did not neglect to apply sanctions against the people of Kelantan and Sabah who had brought the opposition into power at the 1990 general election. Although development projects were being carried out in both states, the numbers and size of the projects were not equal to those in other states and there were frequent delays in their implementation. There was therefore widespread speculation that the Mahathir government was seeking to strangle the opposition-run state governments of Kelantan and Sabah at the expense of economic development, mainly because of their political differences.

TABLE 6.1
Federal Government Development Allocation by the State, 1981–95

State	1981–85[b] RM (millions) %	1986–90[c] RM (millions) %	1991–95 RM (millions) %
Selangor	3,924 (8.0)	2,288 (6.1)	4,295 (7.8)
Federal Territory	5,264 (10.7)	2,228 (6.0)	4,608 (8.4)
Johor	3,357 (6.9)	2,658 (7.1)	3,794 (6.9)
Malacca	653 (1.3)	378 (1.0)	924 (1.7)
Negeri Sembilan	1,297 (2.7)	911 (2.4)	1,548 (2.8)
Pahang	3,091 (6.3)	2,496 (6.7)	2,837 (5.2)
Perak	3,676 (7.5)	2,054 (5.5)	2,563 (4.7)
Perlis	637 (1.3)	421 (1.1)	505 (0.9)
Penang	1,469 (3.0)	725 (1.9)	1,548 (2.8)
Sarawak	3,286 (6.7)	1,946 (5.2)	3,209 (5.8)
Terengganu	2,544 (5.2)	2,063 (5.5)	2,729 (5.0)
Kedah	2,621 (5.3)	2,363 (6.3)	2,826 (5.1)
Sabah	*2,585 (5.3)*	*2,253 (6.0)*	*2,307 (4.2)*
Kelantan	*2,618 (5.3)*	*1,933 (5.2)*	*2,063 (3.8)*
Multi-state[a]	12,015 (24.5)	12,566 (33.7)	19,243 (35.0)
Total	49,026 (100.0)	37,290 (100.0)	55,000 (100.0)

[a] "Multi-state" means those whose beneficiaries are nation-wide and whose locations cannot be determined by state.
[b] 1981–85 figures round off the fractions to decimal place from the original figures.
[c] 1986–90 figures are revised allocation.

Sources: *Fifth Malaysia Plan 1986–1990*, p. 231 (table 7.4); and *Sixth Malaysia Plan 1991–1995*, p. 64 (table 2.4).

A prime example of economic sanctions can be found in the case of the federal development allocation by states under the Sixth Malaysia Plan, covering the period 1991–95. As shown in Table 6.1, the percentage of the post-1990 general election development allocation by the federal government sharply decreased in both Kelantan and Sabah from 11.2 per cent (1986–90) to 8.0 per cent (1991–95), compared with the relative increase, or at most minimal decrease, in the other states. It is worth noting that when the BN controlled the states in the 1980s there was an increase in total federal development allocation in Kelantan and Sabah, from 10.6 per cent (1981–85) to 11.2 per cent (1986–90). It was alleged that the federal allocation for development in Kelantan was slashed by about a third after UMNO's defeat in the 1990 elections from the initially requested allocation by the previous UMNO-controlled Kelantan state government.[69] Furthermore, the actual federal development allocation in Kelantan was later cut to 2.6 per cent from the initial 3.8 per cent in the period 1991–95.[70] Also, some portion of the federal allocation had to be deducted as a payment for accumulated state debt of some RM753 million, most of it being owed to the federal government by the previous UMNO-controlled Kelantan state government. Moreover, out of the original development allocation (RM2.063 billion), only RM676 million (33 per cent) had been expended by the end of 1993 while the national average expenditure reached about 53 per cent.[71] According to a PAS leader, it was only after mid-1993 as another general election was approaching that some of the federal allocation was given to the PAS-led Kelantan state government.[72]

Meanwhile, there was only a marginal increase in approved manufacturing projects especially in Kelantan, from twenty-five in the period 1986–90 to twenty-six in the period 1991–95 (4 per cent), whereas other states recorded noticeably higher increases from 3,205 to 4,297 (34 per cent) in the same period. In addition, Kelantan received the lowest amount of capital investments, totalling RM1.1 billion out of RM116.2 billion (0.9 per cent) under the Sixth Malaysia Plan (1991–95), whereas capital investments mostly increased among the other states. Terengganu, for example, received the second highest amount of capital investments valued at RM16.4 billion (14.1 per cent), while Perlis, which had recorded the lowest number in the period 1986–90, increased from

RM36 million to RM2.2 billion (double Kelantan's total capital investments) along with increasing numbers of manufacturing projects from ten to thirty-nine for the same period.[73]

During the 1980s, the ratio of GDP per capita to the national average had gradually decreased from 0.46 to 0.39 in Kelantan and from 0.95 to 0.83 in Sabah. Compared with the other states, the ratio of per capita income in Kelantan and Sabah to the national average remained steady in the 1980s. But after the 1990 general election, their shares fell behind the other states and the national average, as evidenced in Table 6.2. Sabah's share of GDP per capita has sharply decreased from 0.83 per cent in 1990 to 0.61 per cent in 1995. Consequently, Sabah, one of the middle-income states in the 1980s, fell to the level of Kelantan as a low-income state by 1995. On the other hand, Kelantan's relative economic backwardness became even worse during this period, declining from 0.39 per cent in 1991 to 0.34 per cent in 1995. Furthermore, there is no significant sign that Kelantan and Sabah's economic status *vis-à-vis*

TABLE 6.2
Ratio of Per Capita GDP to Malaysian Average, by State, 1980–2000
(In 1978 prices)

State	1980	1985	1990	1995	2000[b]
Selangor	1.43	1.32	1.43	1.49	1.46
Federal Territory	1.98	2.07	1.92	2.00	2.02
Johor	0.91	0.88	0.92	0.97	1.03
Malacca	0.71	0.74	0.84	0.94	1.04
Negeri Sembilan	1.07	1.02	0.85	0.88	0.96
Pahang	0.99	0.93	0.82	0.79	0.80
Perak	0.89	0.85	0.80	0.83	0.91
Perlis	0.70	0.69	0.66	0.65	0.66
Penang	1.13	1.10	1.19	1.34	1.43
Sarawak	0.71	0.82	0.88	0.80	0.78
Terengganu	1.15	1.26	1.58	1.50	1.48
Kedah	0.65	0.63	0.59	0.65	0.71
Sabah[a]	*0.95*	*0.95*	*0.83*	*0.61*	*0.49*
Kelantan	*0.46*	*0.46*	*0.39*	*0.34*	*0.32*

[a] Includes the Federal Territory of Labuan.
[b] Estimated ratio of per capita GDP to Malaysian average.

Sources: *Fifth Malaysia Plan*, pp. 172–75 (tables 5.2 and 5.3); and *Seventh Malaysia Plan*, p. 142 (table 5.2).

the other states was rising during the five years from 1995, as shown in Table 6.2.

Victimization and Direct-Intervention

The Sabah opposition was in a weaker position to resist the political manoeuvring by the federal government than its counterpart in Kelantan as the entire machinery of UMNO and the federal authority were mobilized to enter directly in Sabah politics. Indeed, federal government harassment was widely expected even before the 1990 general election as Mahathir himself had laid the blame on PBS's defection to the opposition and described it as "a stab in the back" on the eve of the general election. Mahathir's anger towards the Sabah opposition was often revealed in his post-election speeches. As a clear example, he warned during the 1990 UMNO general assembly that

> I would like to emphasize that the Federal Government will not hesitate to act against anyone who goes against the law even if the Federal Government is accused of suppression by taking such action. Those guilty should be regarded as such, irrespective of the political implications.[74]

About a month after Mahathir's warning, Maximus Ongkili, a close aide and relative of Sabah Chief Minister Pairin Kitingan, was arrested under the ISA on charges of endangering national security.[75] Then, two days later, Pairin himself was charged and briefly detained under the Anti-Corruption Agency (ACA) on three charges of corruption, allegedly committed in 1985. A few months later, Pairin's younger brother Jeffery Kitingan, executive chairman of IDS and director of the Sabah Foundation, was also arrested under the ISA for alleged involvement in a plot to take Sabah out of the Malaysian federation. Since then, federal-state relations have been particularly tenuous in Sabah. While Mahathir and UMNO leaders denied any political malice, many political observers viewed a series of arrests of PBS leaders as politically motivated victimization by the Mahathir government.

It was also in early 1991 that UMNO, for the first time since the formation of Malaysia in 1963, set up branches in Sabah with the ultimate aim of directly controlling the state government. Until PBS's defection to the opposition, UMNO leaders reiterated that UMNO had no intention of expanding into Sabah unless national security was threatened. It was, however, just a couple of days after the 1990 general election that the UMNO supreme council decided to set up UMNO branches in Sabah.[76] Although it has generally been assumed that UMNO's membership was open only to the Malays in the peninsula, Sabah UMNO relaxed its boundaries by opening its membership to non-Malay indigenous groups in Sabah. Within a few months of UMNO's expansion into Sabah, the Muslim-based USNO president Mustapha Harun left the party and won a by-election held in Usukan as an UMNO candidate. Soon after the by-election, Mustapha became UMNO's Sabah liaison chief and was later appointed as Federal Minister for Sabah Affairs in May 1993. However, with the exception of its president Mustapha, the eleven other USNO state assemblymen had been prevented from joining UMNO by Sabah's anti–party hopping law which bars the assemblymen from switching parties on pain of losing their seats. It was in this context that, immediately after the Supreme Court ruling on 3 April 1992 declaring the Kelantan anti–party hopping law as *ultra vires* of the federal constitution, UMNO decided to challenge Sabah's anti–party hopping law to enable the eleven USNO assemblymen to join the party without having to vacate their seats. The Supreme Court finally ruled on 8 March 1993 that Sabah's anti–party hopping law was invalid and seven USNO assemblymen joined UMNO by early April 1993.[77] Shortly thereafter, USNO, the once-powerful Muslim-based party which had ruled Sabah between 1967 and 1975, was defunct as the party completed its duty as UMNO's vehicle for entry into Sabah.

UMNO's political manoeuvring to take control of the state leadership climaxed in the run-up to the 1994 Sabah elections and its aftermath. Shortly before the state elections in February 1994, PBS deputy president Yong Teck Lee withdrew PBS's Chinese portion to form a new party, the Sabah Progressive Party (SAPP). The new Chinese-based SAPP immediately allied itself with the UMNO-led BN and garnered PBS's traditional Chinese support for BN in the 1994 Sabah elections. Although money politics is nothing new in Malaysia's electoral history, UMNO's campaigning in Sabah at this time was characterized by "an unusually high level of financial inducement".[78] The electoral results, however, revealed that PBS retained the state leadership, but with a narrow majority of two seats (twenty-five of the forty-eight seats) and with a reduced popular vote (dropping from 53.9 to 48.7 per cent).[79] Given the slim majority, it was not altogether surprising when a series of crossovers by three PBS assemblymen enabled Sabah UMNO to topple the PBS state government within a few weeks of the PBS victory. It is widely speculated that the PBS defectors were offered RM3 million each to cross over to BN.[80] Shortly afterward, the post-election defections of PBS assemblymen were followed by the emergence of new political parties led by former PBS leaders, leaving PBS with just five seats.[81]

UMNO's expansion into Sabah exacerbated the politics of ethnicity there. Certainly, UMNO's resort to racial sentiment was a key element of its inroads into Sabah politics, as evidenced by the 1994 election results. UMNO took all the eighteen state seats it contested in Muslim-majority constituencies, while almost all Kadazan-Dusun majority areas continued to endorse PBS. Although PBS's support was clearly more multi-ethnic than that of the Sabah UMNO-led BN, PBS was forced to become a Kadazan-Dusun party. Meanwhile, the newly formed SAPP substantially divided the previously united Chinese vote, winning three of the seven Chinese-majority seats, whereas PBS had gained a majority of the Chinese vote in two previous elections. It was therefore not surprising that the redelineation of state constituencies in 1993, which would be applied from the next state elections, favoured Sabah UMNO in particular. Muslim-dominated constituencies were increased to twenty-six, more than half of the forty-eight state seats. The number of Kadazan-Dusun seats, however, was reduced markedly from eighteen to twelve in the 1994 elections. As Chin notes, the new electoral boundaries in Sabah ensured that Kadazan-Dusun would never be in a position to challenge Muslim dominance in the polls.[82]

Restricting "Limited Democracy"

In Malaysia, the political system has continually been modified to curtail any opposition challenge to the ruling coalition's dominant position, using a battery of discriminatory laws and precautionary measures. In this context, despite continuous electoral competition and political stability which have been features of Malaysian politics since independence, the political system cannot be described as fully democratic but rather as a "semi", "illiberal" or "limited" democracy. It was, then, in the 1990s that the ruling coalition increasingly used its two-thirds majority in Parliament to prevent the emergence of any significant political challenge to its dominance.

Probably the most notable restriction on Malaysia's limited democracy was the redelineation of parliamentary and state constituencies undertaken in the early 1990s. Under the federal constitution, the Election Commission is responsible for reviewing the delineation of electoral boundaries at "an interval of not less than eight years".[83] However, a much earlier move to redelineate the electoral boundaries was initiated soon after the 1990 general election, even though the minimum eight-year period only ended on 8 November 1992. Moreover, despite the UMNO leaders' claim that the ruling party was not involved in the redelineation exercise, it was evident that the manipulation of electoral boundaries had to do with the design and plan of the ruling coalition, UMNO in particular. As a clear example, even a few months before the Election Commission decided to create twelve new parliamentary constituencies, the UMNO supreme council had already decided on the establishment of twelve new divisions of UMNO.[84] Considering that UMNO divisions are based on the parliamentary constituencies, there was little doubt that the UMNO leadership was actively involved in dictating when and how the Election Commission should redelineate the electoral boundaries, thus violating the independence of the Election Commission.

As expected, the redelineation exercise again strengthened the dominance of the ruling coalition, especially UMNO. For example, in Sabah, as briefly mentioned in the earlier section, a considerable number of voters were carved out to the advantage of the newly launched Sabah UMNO, turning at least four Kadazan-Dusun majority areas into Muslim-dominated constituencies.[85] Unfair constituency delineation also occurred with the provision of state seats within parliamentary constituencies in peninsular Malaysia. In Selangor's case, the opposition-stronghold parliamentary constituencies of Klang, Petaling Jaya (Utara), and Petaling Jaya (Selatan), despite their relatively large numbers of voters, were allocated only two state seats each, whereas the other fourteen constituencies were all allocated three state seats each. The opposition-held parliamentary constituency of Puchong was divided into two —

one a Malay-majority seat and the other a mixed constituency — by taking part of Shah Alam (a BN stronghold). Similar gerrymandering benefiting the ruling coalition took place in Kuala Lumpur with the increase of three new parliamentary seats.[86]

Apart from this, the redelineation of electoral boundaries continued to defy the basic democratic principle of the one-person one-vote system. Penang, which has traditionally been DAP's stronghold, failed to add an additional parliamentary seat, though the state's 50,838 electorates had outnumbered the national average of 47,000 voters per constituency. By contrast, Kedah, Kelantan, Pahang, and Perlis added one more seat each, despite the numbers of voters per constituency in these states being less than the national average. Consequently, Perlis had an average of 34,732 voters per constituency after redelineation. Moreover, after the 1993 redelineation the disparity in numbers of voters between constituencies became even more marked at state level. For example, the post-delineation figures show that Penang has an average of 19,234 voters per state constituency compared with 6,946 in Perlis. Before the redelineation, the figures were 16,946 in Penang and 7,078 in Perlis respectively.[87]

The 1957 *Merdeka* Constitution originally stipulated that the disparity in voters' numbers between constituencies shall not exceed 15 per cent. A series of constitutional amendments, however, has increased the limit. In the 1995 elections for example, while Hulu Rajang parliamentary constituency in Sarawak had 15,849 voters, Ampang Jaya in Selangor recorded the largest numbers with 85,954 voters.[88] It must be noted that the numbers of voters in constituencies has always been disproportionally larger in opposition-supporting areas than in the relatively smaller electorates in the BN-supporting constituencies. Such unfair constituency delineation was revealed in the election results of 1990 (see Table 6.3).

It is indeed nothing new in Malaysian politics for the Constitution to be amended whenever it suits the government's need to maintain its hegemonic control over the political procedure, especially in dealing with the opposition. The unbroken two-thirds majority in Parliament has allowed the UMNO-led government to introduce amendments to the Constitution at an average of once a year since independence. The

TABLE 6.3
Disparity in Size of Constituencies Won by the BN
and Opposition (Parliamentary), 1990

	Penang	Terengganu	Perak	Selangor	Kuala Lumpur	Malacca
BN	40,151	38,071	42,481	58,604	74,171	48,363
Opposition	59,745	48,984	56,062	92,659	76,330	71,608

* All seats from Perlis, Kedah, Pahang, Negeri Sembilan, and Johor were won by the BN, whereas the opposition coalition took all seats from Kelantan.

Source: Compiling from NSTP Research and Information Services, *Elections in Malaysia: A Handbook of Facts and Figures on the Elections 1955–1990* (Kuala Lumpur: NSTP, 1994), pp. 109–18.

pace of constitutional amendments, however, accelerated in the aftermath of the 1987 UMNO leadership crisis, and the underlying reasons for constitutional amendments pertained to Mahathir's desire to concentrate power in the Executive, especially in his hands.

The most significant move to enhance Mahathir's dominance over the political process in the years after 1990 was his "unfinished" contest against the Agong and the state rulers. As Milne and Mauzy correctly note, in the process of Mahathir's assertion of executive power from 1981–90, the struggle to define "magic powers of monarchy" in a stricter and more predictable way "did not end in a complete victory for Mahathir".[89] The Malaysian Constitution stipulated that, by the time Mahathir took over power in 1981, all Bills passed by Parliament must receive the royal assent before they could be gazetted as laws. The royal assent, in other words, was necessary to complete the legislative process, providing the monarchy with certain powers beyond ceremonial duties and symbolic privileges. Mahathir therefore tried to redefine the role of the constitutional monarchy by proposing amendments to the Constitution which sought to make Bills passed by Parliament automatically law without receiving the royal assent. This sparked a constitutional crisis in 1983. The rulers and almost half of the UMNO leaders came out flatly against Mahathir's move to strip the monarchy of its powers. Eventually, after intense negotiations between UMNO and the rulers, a compromise was reached: the rulers accepted the amendment on the condition that the royal assent was retained, although a Bill, which is not a money Bill, presented to the Agong for his assent shall be assented by him for a period not exceeding thirty days. According to the Constitution (Amendment) Act 1984, even if the Agong refuses to give his consent, a Bill shall become law by the votes of not less than two-thirds majority in Parliament. In practice, the amendments simply empowered the Agong to delay the royal assent for a longer period with no actual power to veto a Bill. Nonetheless, the rulers still retained their power to participate directly in the drafting of laws and their role could be enhanced when the government failed to obtain a two-thirds majority in Parliament.[90] Since the constitutional crisis of 1983, a tense relationship existed between Mahathir and the rulers.

Towards the end of the 1980s, the Mahathir government and the rulers often came to loggerheads over the palace's alleged interference in administrative and political matters in the states. The situation was made worse by UMNO's disastrous electoral results in Kelantan during the 1990 elections. Some state UMNO leaders believed that UMNO's disastrous performance in Kelantan was partly due to the palace's involvement in a "silent campaign" against the Mahathir government in favour of the Razaleigh-led opposition coalition.[91] It is therefore not surprising that the years after 1990 saw unprecedented public outbursts by Mahathir and UMNO leaders over the palace's involvement in political affairs, and its role in a constitutional monarchy.

First, the cue to attack the rulers came from Mahathir soon after the 1990 general election. Mahathir emboldened UMNO leaders and members to such an extent that they were now prepared to question the Malay rulers, who had hitherto been regarded as beyond question. The Sedition Act expressly prohibits public discussion, even in the legislatures, on the "matter, right, status, position, privilege, sovereignty, or prerogatives" of the Malay rulers. However, Mahathir made it clear that "it is not seditious to criticize the behaviour of any Ruler who misbehaves". Further, he mentioned that "the Sedition Act only made it seditious if a person advocated the abolition of the monarchy" and he stressed that "UMNO would continue to speak out against any Ruler deemed to have overstepped his role as a constitutional monarchy".[92] Next, UMNO adopted a resolution in the 1990 general assembly advising the palace to adhere strictly to its role as a constitutional monarchy. The

1991 general assembly was to then scrutinize whether the resolution had been implemented or not. From late in the year 1992, Mahathir and UMNO leaders frequently used the media to expose the rulers' scandalous misbehaviour and extravagant life-styles to the Malaysian public.[93] Towards the end of 1992 in the midst of growing tension between UMNO and the rulers, the alleged assault of hockey coach Douglas Gomez by the Johor Sultan unleashed a flood of public opinion against Royal excesses. The unfair treatment of the *rakyat* at the hands of the state ruler even united the ruling coalition and the opposition MPs to amend the Constitution, withdrawing royal immunity. On 10 December 1992, then Deputy Prime Minister Ghafar Baba tabled a substantive motion in Parliament expressing the Dewan Rakyat's concern over the Gomez incident. The motion was unanimously passed by ninety-six BN and opposition MPs. This was immediately followed by the UMNO supreme council's resolution for a constitutional amendment to remove the ruler's immunity. The final blow to the Malay rulers came in 1993 when the federal constitution was amended to include the policy of removing certain powers and the royal immunity of the rulers.

As expected, the rulers initially rejected the proposed constitutional amendments that sought to remove their personal immunity from criminal and civil prosecution. However, they had to accept the slightly modified amendments in circumstances where their rejection would have quickly raised public outbursts and apprehensions. As a result, firstly, the personal immunity of the rulers was removed, except for the legal process relating to their performance of official duties. Secondly, a ruler was precluded from hearing an appeal on his own behalf and from pardoning himself, his wife and children. Thirdly, it was no longer seditious for Parliament to question matters relating to the rulers, although the freedom of elective representatives did not extend to the advocacy of the abolition of the constitutional monarchy.[94]

Another amendment to the Constitution in May 1994 had far-reaching consequences for the position of the rulers. While the Agong had been permitted to withhold his assent and return a Bill to Parliament for reconsideration, the constitutional amendment of 1994 did away with the Agong's assent to a Bill passed by Parliament. The Agong now had to assent to a Bill within thirty days of its being presented to him. If he did not do so, the Bill automatically became a law upon the expiration of that period whether he has assented to it or not.[95] With the passing of this amendment, the royal assent was no longer necessary to complete the legislative process. Knowing that the royal assent in the legislative process was the main issue of the 1983 constitutional crisis between Mahathir and the rulers, the constitutional amendment of 1994 can be perceived as the completion of "unfinished business" between them. Rais Yatim observes that the Constitution (Amendment) Act 1994 was nothing but "the final 'seal' of the Rulers' fate" by Mahathir's executive power.[96] Although it is a moot point whether the removal of the royal assent in the legislative process takes away an important check and balance on the executive, there is little doubt that the dominant executive in total control of all significant political institutions can be perceived as the essence of the authoritarian trend in Malaysian politics in the years after 1990.[97]

Further absorption of executive power in Mahathir's personal domain can also be found in the episode surrounding the 1994 constitutional amendment. In relation to the position of the judiciary, the Constitution was amended to provide broader grounds for removing a judge in a new provision, namely, "any breach of any provisions of the code of ethics" into Article 125 which stipulates tenure of office and remuneration of judges of the Federal Court.[98] Further, the newly inserted code of ethics would be prescribed by the government, especially the Prime Minister, rather than the judiciary.[99] This implies that the judges must abide by a government-drafted code of conduct and thus "remove any separation between the judiciary and the executive".[100] Commenting on the amendment, a senior judge called it "repugnant to the basic concept of democracy" and marked "the end of the independence of the Judiciary" in Malaysia.[101]

Other pieces of legislation have also significantly reinforced the coercive powers of the executive and curtailed democratic rights. Apart from direct ownership of the media, various measures were taken by the government to ensure its full control over the press through coercive legislation, discontinuance of critical publications, harassment of journalists, and even promotion of self-censorship among journalists. Following *Operasi Lalang* and the suspension of two daily newspapers and a Malay magazine in October 1987, the Printing Presses and Publication Act was amended in 1988 to disallow judicial review of the Home Minister's decision in revoking or suspending a publishing permit. Then in late 1991, the government imposed a new ruling on the publishing permit of the opposition parties' organs, especially the DAP's *The Rocket* and PAS's *The Harakah*, restricting their circulation to party members only. Just a few weeks later, the printing permit of *Mingguan Waktu*, a Malay political weekly, was revoked on the grounds that it had published in its inaugural issue a critical article describing Mahathir's first ten years as Prime Minister as a failure.[102]

The scope and frequency of politically motivated detentions were maintained at relatively low levels in the years after 1990. Nonetheless, it must be noted that the threat of using repressive laws continued and served well to constrain participation in political activities among social and political activists during this period. In particular, incremental amendments to the ISA extended the authoritarian executive powers of the Mahathir government by removing the power of judicial review in the ISA cases. For example, on 26 June 1989, the Mahathir government amended the ISA, stripping away the judicial safeguards designed to prohibit its abuse.[103] The rationale for the amendments was that they enabled the government to act swiftly for the protection of national security, whereas previously matters went through a time-consuming judicial review. The amended ISA, however, made executive decisions on "detentions without trial" final with no effective recourse to legal protection for the ISA detainee. With this amendment, the ISA gave the executive exceptional power, with almost no safeguard.

Among the politically motivated detentions of the 1990s were the ISA arrest of Sabah Chief Minister Pairin Kitingan's brother, Jeffrey Kitingan, and six other PBS members soon after the 1990 general election, for their alleged involvement in a plot to withdraw Sabah from the Malaysian Federation; the ISA arrest of the leaders and members of the Muslim Al-Arqam group in late 1994 for their alleged deviationist Islamic activities; and the arrest of Lim Guan Eng, a DAP parliamentary member, under the Sedition Act and Printing Presses and Publication Act in 1994, for "inciting public disaffection with the administrations of justice" and "maliciously publishing false information", in relation to the alleged statutory rape case of the former chief minister of Malacca, Rahim Tamby Chik.[104]

The banning of Al-Arqam and the subsequent ISA arrests provide a clear example of political manoeuvres by the UMNO-led government, not only in curtailing democratic rights in Malaysia's limited democracy, but also in pre-empting a possible challenge against its political dominance.[105] Various explanations were given for the banning of Al-Arqam, one of the long-standing *dakwah* (missionary) movements in Malaysia. According to Milne and Mauzy, the two most plausible explanations were that the Al-Arqam group increasingly emerged as a significant political threat to the hegemonic UMNO regime; and that Al-Arqam constituted a challenge to the government's rural development programmes with its own apparently successful approach to rural development.[106] Some political observers claim that Al-Arqam's "deviationist teachings" provided the rationale behind the banning of the group. However, none of these sufficiently explains the Mahathir government's motives, and especially timing, in taking such excessive and decisive action against Al-Arqam.

There is no doubt that over the years the Al-Arqam movement had grown among both the urban Muslim middle class and in rural areas.[107] Nonetheless, Al-Arqam was hardly a significant political threat to the UMNO-led government, although rumours of the emergence of a new political party led by Al-Arqam had been floated since the early 1990s. In relation to Al-Arqam's successful developmental approach and its threat to the ruling government, in fact, since the mid-1980s the movement had acted as an effective tool to reduce or check the influence of PAS in rural Malay areas. This led to mutual co-existence and patronage between the Mahathir government and the Al-Arqam group. There were many reports and photographs showing top UMNO leaders' support at Al-Arqam functions. Mahathir himself often applauded Al-Arqam as a genuine and successful Islamic movement.[108] Moreover, considering the country's rapid economic growth in the early 1990s, it is not satisfactory to assume that the Al-Arqam way posed a serious threat at this juncture. Why was Al-Arqam outlawed especially when the next general election was just around the corner?

It is worth noting that Mahathir's and UMNO's weakest platform in the early 1990s was always related to the issue of Islam, especially since PAS took over the Kelantan state in 1990. Furthermore, sensitive Islamic matters were perceived as the only threatening element left to bother UMNO's political dominance, since all other significant political forces had been considerably debilitated by the mid-1990s. And it was widely expected that PAS would incite Islamic sentiment in the forthcoming general election. It was at this juncture, with the general election on the horizon in late 1994, that Al-Arqam was outlawed as a "deviant" movement and its leaders and members arrested under the ISA. Certainly, the timing of Al-Arqam's banning was in the interests of the UMNO-led government. As Razaleigh stressed, the Al-Arqam case was quite useful for UMNO to overcome its apparent weakness on Islamic issues especially when another general election was widely anticipated.[109] The Al-Arqam warning was largely directed at the Islamic opposition PAS, but also penetrated the rest of Malaysia's political and civil societies. The successful and highly visible disbanding of one of the country's major Islamic forces highlighted Mahathir's hegemonic control over political processes.

In sum, after the leadership crisis of the late 1980s, Mahathir successfully dealt with political rivalries within UMNO circles. This was followed by clever manoeuvrings in dealing with other political opponents outside the ruling party, including Semangat 46, PAS, and other non-Malay opposition parties. All other significant political institutions, that is, the judiciary, the press, the rulers, and even Islam, were systematically enervated by the centralization of executive power. It therefore eventuated that, towards the mid-1990s, there was scarcely any element remaining to check the growing authoritarian rule of the Mahathir government.

Minor Liberalization Without Consociational Bargaining

For the two decades after the communal upheaval of 1969, the UMNO-led government was involved in a range of preferential approaches through the NEP, designed to improve or consolidate the economic and political position of Malays. At its broadest level, the NEP was directed to redistribute material imbalances between the Malay and non-Malay communities. However, as described in Chapter 4, the NEP was not only confined to economic reallotment, but also extended to renegotiate the social equilibrium of multi-ethnic Malaysian society, towards unambiguous Malay dominance in the sensitive spheres of language, education, religion, and national culture.

Indeed, prior to 1970, Malaysia had already adopted a system of positive discrimination for Malays. Also, non-Malay communities continued to live their lives in accustomed ways during the NEP period, despite the UMNO-led government's primary concern to create "one-language and one-culture" in Malaysian society. Communal tensions, however, were regularly exacerbated as the UMNO-led government systematically instituted a series of affirmative programmes in language, education, and national culture policy during the 1970s and 1980s. This did not mean that socio-political stability was severely undermined in these periods, but that inter-ethnic co-operation, even within the ruling coalition, often came under pressure from the strong communal demands of various ethnic groups. As Crouch notes:

> The roots of communal conflict in Malaysia do not lie in economic imbalances or political rivalries alone but also involve the struggle to preserve and project ethnic identity — the aspirations of Malays as the indigenous community to project their culture and values onto the state and the determination of non-Malays to preserve their distinctive cultural identities.[110]

A Shift in the Politics of Ethnicity

The years after 1990, however, illustrated that inter-ethnic tolerance had increased dramatically in Malaysian society. In particular, the Mahathir-led UMNO showed more flexibility towards the non-Malay communities, in respect of their language, education, religion, and cultural heritage. Mahathir underlined his government's more liberal approach to ethnic relations in his Vision 2020 speech, delivered at the inauguration of the Malaysian Business Council in February 1991. As one of the nine central strategic challenges for Malaysia's full development by 2020, Mahathir stressed that the nation had to confront:

> the challenge of establishing a matured, liberal and tolerant society in which Malaysians of all colors and creeds are free to practise and profess their customs, cultures and religious beliefs and yet feeling that they belong to one nation.[111]

The ideas of multi-ethnic nation-building were then articulated in Mahathir's Vision 2020 speech as "one *Bangsa Malaysia* with political loyalty and dedication to the nation".[112] And the multi-ethnic connotation of *Bangsa Malaysia* gradually evolved as a new national identity by the mid-1990s, in some degree superseding the concept of *Bangsa Melayu* that had connoted the potent symbol of mono-ethnic Malay communal solidarity for the past several decades. A few months after BN's victory in the 1995 general election, Mahathir explained:

> *Bangsa Malaysia* means people who are able to identify themselves with the country, speak Bahasa Malaysia and accept the Constitution. To realize the goal of *Bangsa Malaysia*, the people should start accepting each other as they are, regardless of race and religion.[113]

In similar vein, Mahathir stressed the spirit of multi-culturalism by discrediting the previous assimilative approach in Malaysia. He said in an interview with *Time* magazine that:

> The idea [of assimilation] before was that people should become 100 per cent Malay in order to be Malaysian. We now accept that this is a multi-racial country. We should build bridges instead of trying to remove completely the barriers separating us. We do not intend to convert all the Chinese to Islam, and we tell our people, the Muslims, "you will not try to force people to convert".[114]

Meanwhile, the Mahathir government announced its National Development Policy (NDP), with a ten-year Second Outline Perspective Plan (OPP2) for 1991–2000, to replace the NEP in mid-1991. The objectives of the NDP were not fundamentally different from those of the NEP. The NDP, however, showed the shift in emphasis from NEP's emphasis on inter-ethnic wealth redistribution, to economic growth and privatization with an envisaged decline in the role of the public sector. Some argue that Mahathir's Vision 2020 and the NDP reveal a mere "reformulation" and "reiteration" of the objectives already embodied in the *Rukunegara*, or National Ideology, and the NEP, both announced in 1970.[115] However, it must be noted that cultural and economic liberalization has been continually encouraged by the government throughout the 1990s, in line with the long-term objectives of Vision 2020 and the NDP. There is no doubt that non-Malay communities reacted favourably to the idea of *Bangsa Malaysia* as the concept was widely perceived as a "complete retraction" of the UMNO-led government's provocative assimilation policy in the 1970s and early 1980s.[116]

First of all, the government appears to have recognized the private sector as a co-provider of tertiary education in the 1990s. The early 1980s had already witnessed the significant changes in the role of private colleges as providers for tertiary education in pursuing a certificate, diploma, or professional course leading to foreign qualifications. It was, however, not until the early 1990s that private higher educational institutions gained considerable recognition as an alternative means of access to university education for those unable to gain entry into local universities, due to the quota system. In encouraging the private tertiary education system, by mid-1997, the government had approved approximately 335 private higher educational institutions throughout the country.[117] Meanwhile, the government allowed private colleges to adopt various types of inter-institutional arrangements with foreign universities, such as twinning programmes, credit transfers, and distance learning arrangements. This enabled local students to acquire a foreign degree with a substantial saving on living expenses and tuition fees. To a large extent, the increasing alternative opportunities for tertiary education and inter-institutional arrangements with foreign universities relieved one of the Chinese community's major grievances. A survey by the author of the ethnic distribution of the thirty-five major private colleges shows that non-Malay students, mostly Chinese, constitute about 80 to 95 per cent of the total enrolment with a few exceptions.[118]

In addition, one of the government approaches to promote the private sector's involvement in education was the introduction of new legislation aimed at liberalizing education policy. For example, the new Private Higher Educational Institution Act 1996 led to the establishment of private universities and branch campuses of foreign universities. Consequently, in 1997, Malaysia witnessed the birth of the first private university, Telekom University, followed by Tenaga Nasional University, and the Petronas University of Technology. After that, three more private universities, Multimedia University, International and Commonwealth University, and Malaysia University of Science and Technology, were approved by the government. Significantly, the ethnic quota system is not applied to the private higher educational institutions.

In relation to Chinese education, further liberalizing steps were taken by the government in the post-1990 period. In particular, UMNO leaders became more supportive of national-type Chinese primary schools, whereas in the 1970s and 1980s these institutions were regarded as counter-productive to the fostering of national unity.[119] The government even encouraged Malay and Indian families to send their children to Chinese language primary schools and the number of non-Chinese enrolments increased dramatically in the 1990s. Mid-1995 statistics show that there were over 35,000 non-Chinese students, including 25,000 Malays, enrolled in 1,281 national-type Chinese primary schools in the country. The figure represents an increase of more than 400 per cent over 1985 when there were fewer than 8,000 non-Chinese pupils nation-wide.[120] In addition, in the mid-1990s more state funds were allocated to promote Chinese educational institutions at primary, secondary and tertiary levels. The government's growing support for Chinese education is well reflected in the increased allocation for education under the Sixth Malaysia Plan 1991–95. In the case of the MCA-sponsored Tunku Abdul Rahman (TAR) College, the government allocation has increased tenfold from RM2 million under the Fifth Malaysia Plan to RM20 million under the Sixth Malaysia Plan. TAR College expanded its main campus in Kuala Lumpur and established new branch campuses in Johor and Penang in the mid-1990s.[121] Another MCA-sponsored Langkawi Project, launched in 1993 to help school children especially in the Chinese new villages, had also raised some RM25 million by mid-1994 supplemented by a RM5 million donation from the government.[122] In addition, the MCA's various fund-raising campaigns for independent Chinese secondary schools gained a good deal of support from the Chinese community. In the mid-1990s, the decade-long acrimonious relationship between the MCA and *Dongjiaozong*, a national grouping of Chinese educationists, eased for the first time since the 1950s.[123]

There was also less politicization of sensitive issues such as national culture and national language by UMNO leaders. In the early 1990s, despite reaffirming Malay as the national language, Mahathir and other UMNO leaders increasingly stressed the importance of English.[124] In the mid-1990s, the government finally allowed English to be the medium of instruction in local universities for subjects such as science, technology, mathematics, and medicine. In addition, Malay was not used as the sole medium of instruction in many other subjects. English, therefore, was gaining more popularity in local university education and more local lecturers used a mixture of English and Malay in their classes. This was a complete retraction of the UMNO-led government's one-language policy introduced in 1971.

In relation to cultural policy, non-Malay culture became quite liberally accepted as part of the national culture by most Malay intellectuals and cultural organizations. In particular, the increased flexibility towards Chinese cultural activities was a noticeable sign of greater communal tolerance than existed in the 1970s and 1980s. There are still criticisms from some Malay intellectuals as to the status of Malay language and national culture.[125] But such criticisms no longer receive the serious attention they did in the 1970s and early 1980s, when the non-Malay communities were often referred to as *pendatang asing* (foreign immigrants). Anwar Ibrahim, then the Deputy Prime Minister, with his own Mandarin calligraphy *Wo men dou shi yi jia ren* (We are one happy family) has often been portrayed as a well-known symbolic example of amicable Malay-Chinese relationships.[126] The decades-long restrictions on Chinese lion dances were not only lifted but they were often witnessed by Mahathir and other UMNO leaders. Furthermore, following the lifting of restrictions on travel to China, bilateral trade between Malaysia and China substantially increased in the years after 1990. And the number of high-level visits between Malaysia and China also markedly increased during this period. Mahathir visited China three times between 1993 and 1996, while Anwar also made one visit in 1994. In return, similar high-level visits were made from China to Malaysia. It was also during this period that the government emphasized inter-civilization dialogues between Islam and other Asian civilizations, including Confucianism, Buddhism, and Hinduism. In an effort to illustrate the modernization in the implementation of Islamization, a series of government-sponsored conferences on inter-civilizational dialogues were held at the University of Malaya in the mid-1990s. The first conference was about inter-civilizational dialogue between Islam and Confucianism in March 1995; this was followed by an inter-civilizational dialogue between Islam, Japan, and the West in September 1996. The two conferences eventually led to the establishment of the Centre for Civilizational Dialogue at the University of Malaya when the third inter-civilizational dialogue was held in September 1997.

The Rules of the Game: Change or Continuity?

To what extent, then, did this cultural and economic liberalization stem from the Mahathir government's growing commitment towards the necessity of multi-ethnic nation-building? Was UMNO's move towards minor liberalization attributable to consociational bargaining to reassess the socio-political power equilibrium in multi-ethnic Malaysian politics? In other words, what factors enabled or motivated the UMNO-led government to introduce the so-called minor liberalization in the years after 1990?

It is commonly believed that the political role of minority communities becomes pre-eminent when there is a severe breakdown in the dominant political group. It might be expected, therefore, that the non-Malay communities would gain a more significant political presence following the UMNO leadership split in mid-1987. A series of parliamentary or state by-elections in the years after 1987 had proven how decisive the non-Malay — especially Chinese — voters were for competing Malay political parties. In this regard, some argue that the Mahathir government had to make more accommodative gestures to non-Malay demands even before the 1990 general election. As an example, the government approved an application to set up a private Chinese college, Southern College, just before the Johor Baru by-election in August 1988.[127] Similarly, a new Education Act was proposed by Anwar Ibrahim, then Education Minister, as a way of abolishing the racially sensitive Section 21(2) of the Education Act 1961, which enabled the Education Minister to convert Chinese and Tamil language primary schools to Malay-medium schools.[128] It was also around this time that the government officially recognized the diplomas and degrees obtained through the MCA-sponsored TAR College, for employment in the public service. Indeed, the UMNO-led government's dilemma at this time was how to attract the non-Malay voters without alienating Malays in an increasingly insecure environment after the leadership splits.

As the 1990 general election results illustrated, UMNO appeared to fully recover its dominant political position in Malaysian politics. Nonetheless, the support given by Chinese voters to the opposition in the two general elections in 1986 and 1990 sustained pre-election conditions which pressured the Mahathir government to embark on a more accommodative approach to Chinese demands. A clear example is shown in the appointment of the Penang Chief Minister after the 1990 elections. In normal circumstances, UMNO would have taken over the Penang state leadership with its twelve state assembly seats compared with Gerakan's seven. UMNO, however, had to concede the chief minister position to Gerakan in an increasingly unpredictable post-election political atmosphere. With its poor performance in the 1990 elections, Gerakan announced that the party would not join the state executive council in Penang. Then, the opposition DAP, with its fourteen state assembly seats, offered its "unconditional co-operation" with the Gerakan to form an opposition-led state government in Penang to prevent UMNO's political dominance.[129] Although the co-operation between DAP and Gerakan was unlikely to happen, even some Chinese leaders in the Barisan government felt that the Gerakan should have worked with the DAP so that, by having one Chinese dominant party within the ruling coalition, the Chinese would have greater bargaining power.[130] At this time, any move on UMNO's part to further erode the Chinese leadership in Penang could entice Gerakan, which after all had once been an opposition party before the formation of BN, into the opposition camp again. This may have resulted in the emergence of the third opposition-led state government in Malaysia, following Sabah and Kelantan. Given these factors, some political observers claimed that the post-election atmosphere in the Chinese community appeared to put pressure on the Mahathir government, and this created the conditions for the liberalization in ethnic politics to "recoup a loss in Chinese votes" since 1990.[131]

There is no doubt that a series of concessions to the non-Malay communities in the 1990s reduced communal and cultural discontent in Malaysian society. However, as a senior MCA official stressed, this change in ethnic policies was not promoted by society-driven pressure to assert communal rights, but was largely initiated by state-driven motives. Although the political role of minority communities became more critical at this time, he believes that Malaysia's ethnic politics was, and still is, conditioned by the rules of what is politically permissible for inter-ethnic contestation imposed by the dominant UMNO.[132] It must also be noted that Malaysian politics since independence has long been guided by one main principle: that any political and/or communal contestation operates only within the framework of an unambiguous Malay — to be exact UMNO — supremacy in power. When this political dominance is under threat or perceived to be under threat, the rules of the political and communal contestation are easily modified with greater restrictions, if not totally removed, as occurred in the aftermath of the 1969 general election and the 1987 UMNO leadership crisis.

In this regard, Musa Hitam argues that the shift in ethnic politics in the 1990s was not a concession to the Chinese but a result of the "high level of tolerance" displayed by Mahathir and UMNO leaders. He believes that the willingness of the Mahathir government to adopt a more flexible approach in ethnic policies, even if these appeared to initially benefit the non-Malays, stems from a decisive power shift favouring Mahathir and his new loyalist party UMNO (*Baru*) after the 1990 general election.[133]

Even in the case of the Penang chief minister, there was little likelihood that the appointment of a chief minister from Gerakan was made at the expense of UMNO's political dominance in the state. Although greater pressure from the Chinese continued in the aftermath of the 1990 elections, the Chinese parties in the BN were by no means in a position to bargain for the Chinese state leadership after their miserable defeat in the elections.[134] It was therefore public knowledge that the state leadership would be dominated by UMNO with the real power being held by the re-introduced deputy chief minister, even though officially Koh Tsu Koon of the Gerakan took over the chief ministership.[135] As expected, in addition to the deputy chief ministership, UMNO occupied four state executive councillor seats in Penang; the other three were given to the Gerakan. In an interview, Ibrahim Saad of UMNO, who had been appointed as Penang's deputy chief minister, makes it clear that:

> The reason why UMNO gave the CM position to the Chinese was not because there was strong pressure from the Chinese, but because UMNO's position became much more solid by that time. There was a Chinese sentiment that somehow UMNO should know, but the bargaining power of the Chinese was not there after the 1990 elections. The Deputy Chief Minister position was newly introduced as a political consideration not only to control the Penang state leadership but also to satisfy the Malay community. At that time, Koh Tsu Koon was only a puppet and UMNO was the one who controlled the whole family with full confidence.[136]

It is clear that a more tolerant climate evolved in the 1990s in dealing with some of the traditional non-Malay concerns involving culture, language, and education. Nevertheless, the tolerant climate had only been allowed to evolve within certain boundaries set by the Malay ruling group. Although greater liberalization in ethnic politics was initiated by the UMNO leaders in the 1990s, the change in policy was hardly motivated by their growing commitment to address the grievances of minority communities in Malaysian society.

A better explanation for the shift of ethnic politics can be found in the increasing confidence of UMNO leaders in their dominant political and economic position. The country's persistently growing economy, averaging over 8 per cent annually since 1988, benefited both the Malay and non-Malay communities and, thus, the liberalization in ethnic policies at this time did not come at the expense of other races. In particular, the strategic shift in the NDP focusing on deregulation and privatization of the economy mostly benefited the Malay corporate élite and served as an essential tool for the consolidation of Mahathir and UMNO's political patronage networks in the 1990s.[137]

The government's recognition of the private sector as a co-provider of tertiary education, notably the proliferation of private educational institutions, provided an alternative for tertiary education, especially for Chinese students. Nonetheless, this did not necessarily show that the education policy in Malaysia had been liberalized. The country already faced a significant challenge for more educated and skilled personnel with the rapid economic growth of the late 1980s, and the existing public universities could no longer provide the necessary work-force. The promotion of the private sector as an alternative source of tertiary education was to meet rapidly growing student enrolment in public universities, hence the private higher educational institutions were not dominated by the non-Malay students. As shown in Seventh Malaysia Plan 1996–2000, the overall enrolment at the various levels of tertiary education, including certificate, diploma, and degree course, increased by 52.7 per cent from 100,590 in 1990 to 153,610 in 1995. However, it must also be noted that opportunities for *bumiputera* to pursue tertiary education were expanded in the same period. For instance, Institute Teknologi MARA (ITM) increased its enrolment from 27,000 to 32,480 in the period 1991–95. Furthermore, it was expected that the enrolment of ITM would further increase by 61.6 per cent from 32,480 in 1995 to 52,500 in 2000.[138] In this context, a senior government official emphasized that the primary reason for the government's liberal approach towards private education was based purely on administrative considerations to meet the imperative of economic competitiveness rather than a political decision to accommodate non-Malay communities' concerns from a multi-ethnic perspective. He thus believed that there could always be a retraction of the government's liberal educational policy towards private tertiary educational institutions if the country's economic pie shrank in a prolonged economic recession.[139] Nevertheless, whatever the motives for the new policy, the result in fact was an opening up of educational opportunities for non-Malay students.

Indeed, it is worth noting that newly introduced educational legislation of the mid-1990s was actually double-edged. On the one hand, the new legislation, in particular the Private Higher Educational Institutions (PHEI) Act 1996, promoted a more active involvement of the private sector in tertiary education. On the other hand, the new legislation allowed a further consolidation of the government's jurisdiction over educational activities in private education as well as in public education, whereas previously there were not as many restrictions on private higher education. In particular, the National Council on Higher Education Act 1996 reflects the government's intention to place a single administrative body in charge of both the public and private educational sectors. The PHEI Act 1996 also categorically outlines the government's regulatory control over educational activities of the private higher educational institutions by granting extensive discretionary power to the Education Minister. More importantly, the PHEI Act 1996 empowered the Education Minister to direct that the national language be used to conduct all courses at all times. In addition, the PHEI Act 1996 stipulates that all private higher educational institutions must teach Islamic religion for Muslim students and moral education for non-Muslim students.[140] In short, despite the seeming liberal approach to private education, the government effectively expand its control in terms of the legal framework.

In addition, the Education Act 1996 assigned the Education Minister inordinate powers, to the extent of denying judicial review. Under the Education Act 1996, the Minister's decision, such as deregistration of educational institutions and teachers, dissolution of boards of governors and intervention in links between educational institutions, cannot be appealed in court. Besides, while the Education Act 1961 merely stipulated fines in hundreds of ringgit for contravention of the regulations imposed by the Minister, the new Education Act makes offenders liable to fines of up to RM300,000 and jail sentences of up to five years. Many Chinese educationists aired their misgivings:

> Whereas previously, there were not as many prohibitions, in the new Bill [now the Education Act 1996] there is almost a blanket prohibition on the educational activities that we are involved in unless we apply for exemption from the Minister.[141]

In relation to mother tongue education, Chinese and Indian communities still feel strongly that their fundamental rights are not recognized, or are becoming even less respected, despite the more liberal educational policy in the 1990s. Although the controversial Section 21(2) of the Education Act 1961 no longer exists, Chinese and Tamil educationists believe that the same risks to the survival of mother tongue education in Malaysia remain in the new Education Act 1996, as the newly introduced Section 17(1) stipulates that:

> The national language shall be the main medium of instruction in all educational institutions in the National Education System *except a national-type school established under section 28 or any other educational institution exempted by the Minister from this subsection.*[142]

The legal implication of Section 17(1) is that all existing national-type Chinese and Tamil schools must use the Malay language as the main medium of instruction unless the Education Minister's exemption is obtained, as they were not established under Section 28 of the Education Act 1996. By qualifying autonomy of the national-type schools in this manner, it is claimed that the conversion of mother tongue education has already taken place with the introduction of the Education Act 1996, whereas the old Education Act 1961 did not make any provision for the use of Malay as the main medium of instruction in the Chinese and Tamil primary schools.[143] Although the forced conversion of existing national-type primary schools into Malay-medium schools is unlikely to happen due to its sensitivity, many Chinese educationists worry that the position of mother-tongue education is becoming more vulnerable as its future depends entirely on the "benevolence" of the Education Minister.[144] The several rejections and the extraordinary length of time taken for the approval of New Era College proposed by the Chinese education movement *Dongjiaozong* showed the government's reluctance to approve mother-tongue tertiary education and the arbitrary exercise of power of the Education Minister. The New Era College, aiming at eventual conversion into a Chinese university, finally received the official approval of the Ministry of Education in May 1997, almost three years after its first application and several revised applications. The approved main medium of instruction was Bahasa Malaysia.

Currently, there are 1,281 Chinese-medium primary schools and 534 Tamil-medium primary schools in the country. Some of these schools are fully subsidized by the government; the rest are partially subsidized or not subsidized at all. Compared with the other national schools, the allocation of development funds for these national-type schools are seriously disproportionate, as shown in Table 6.4.

Apart from the national-type primary schools, there are sixty Chinese-medium independent secondary schools, which are not recognized by the government. Indeed, it is a remarkable change that the government even provided funds for the independent Chinese secondary schools in the 1990s. However, such financial assistance was insufficient and, more importantly, such funds were concentrated in the mid-1990s as one-off cases, with another general election on the horizon. What is worse, the Education Act 1996 prohibits individuals from making any form of monetary contribution, including gifts or donations, for the purpose of

TABLE 6.4
Development Fund Allocation and
Student Numbers (Primary Schools), 1996

	Funds Allocation		Student Numbers	
	RM (million)	%	Number	%
National primary schools	1,027.167	96.6	2,128,227	75.3
National-type primary schools (Chinese)	25.970	2.4	595,451	21.1
National-type primary schools (Tamil)	10.902	1.0	102,679	3.6
Total	1,064.039	100.0	2,826,357	100.0

Source: Reply by the Education Minister to the question raised by the MP of Kota Melaka in Parliament, 5 November 1996, quoted in SUARAM, *Malaysian Human Rights Report* (Petaling Jaya: Suaram Komunikasi, 1998), p. 211.

establishing higher educational institutions.[145] Considering most mother-tongue private schools are largely sustained by the community's monetary contribution, the new Education Act will further undermine the status of mother-tongue education. Moreover, the prohibition on monetary contributions will affect any possible establishment of community-subsidized mother-tongue tertiary institutions in the country.

The series of liberal measures in cultural policy appeared to be a multi-ethnic move away from mono-ethnic Malay concerns. It is nonetheless doubtful whether this shift in ethnic politics was driven by a need to address the misgivings of the non-Malay communities. Some traditional non-Malay concerns seem to have been accepted as part of the country's national culture. However, it is also often found that there have been recurrent retractions by the UMNO leaders over the implementation of cultural activities held by the non-Malay communities.[146] Although a series of accommodative measures in ethnic politics occurred, not all of these changes were considered by the UMNO leaders as a concession to the non-Malay communities based on the principle of equality. They believed that such concessions did not constitute any threat to Malay political pre-eminence even in the process of an apparent concession to the Chinese. A good example of practising affirmative action for the assurance of Malay preference can be found in the public-funded tertiary educational institutions. The racial quota system, which provides 55 per cent for the *bumiputera* and 45 per cent for the non-*bumiputera* of which 35 per cent is for the Chinese, is one of many affirmative programmes. Interestingly it is reported that the quota of non-*bumiputera* even further favoured the dominant Malays. A survey showed that in the intakes in seven public universities in the academic year of 1994–95 and 1995–96, Chinese students comprised 28.78 per cent and 28.86 per cent respectively.[147] A former senior UMNO Youth official summarizes the ethnic liberalization in the 1990s:

> I don't think that UMNO is implementing greater liberalization as a way of giving away everything. The Barisan government's flexible move in Chinese culture, language and education only shows that we are enjoying the higher level of tolerance. And the tolerance level is purely based on the level of confidence in terms of political and economic position of the Malays. We share the political power with the Chinese. When the Chinese component parties need to increase their political support from their community it is very important for them to serve the main concerns of the Chinese. So, why shouldn't we allow that? We can show a very high level of tolerance in so far as we can achieve a win-win situation. This is a purely political move. ... Similarly, we [UMNO Youth] have to be often seen as a very racialist political group fighting for the Malay interests. In politics, we cannot be simply static but have to be flexible. However, those finished agendas that we have done, such as Islam, *Bahasa Melayu* and the special status of the Malays, should not be questioned in any circumstance because these are very sensitive issues. I hope I don't miss this fundamental rule of the game in Malaysia's ethnic politics.[148]

Indeed, the more conducive climate for greater tolerance in Malaysia's ethnic politics depends on the Malay community's sense of physical and psychological security and comfort in the political and economic domination of the Malay ruling élites. In other words, the shift in the politics of ethnicity in the 1990s was not driven by any consociational bargaining or a society-initiated struggle to assert minority communities' fundamental rights, but was initiated by Mahathir and UMNO leaders with full confidence in their own power. It is, therefore, presumed that a U-turn involving the retraction of the so-called minor liberalization would be quite likely if Mahathir and UMNO leaders were to face an increasingly insecure situation that threatened their political and economic hegemony.[149]

The 1995 General Election and Its Implications

As the mid-1990s general election approached, another victory for the BN seemed inevitable. Mahathir's supremacy had become unassailable and no possible rival for power could emerge. In short, all the pre-election conditions appeared to enable the UMNO-led ruling coalition to win with its traditional two-thirds majority in Parliament.

Firstly, the performance of the Malaysian economy favoured the ruling coalition. The country's 8 per cent-plus economic growth rates over the last seven years created a general public sentiment of satisfaction with the government, in particular within business and the middle class in urban areas. Secondly, it was unavoidable for the Chinese opposition to accept the UMNO-initiated liberalization in language, cultural, and educational policies in the years since 1990. Besides, the Malay opposition faced difficulties in mobilizing support as the country's rapid economic growth accommodated the material demands of the Malay community. In short, the remarkable economic growth and subsequent liberalization process were accompanied by the depoliticization of traditionally controversial issues in Malaysian society. Therefore, with the next general election on the horizon, the opposition parties seemed to lack issues on which to campaign while the Mahathir government effectively promoted the discourse of "developmentalism", including Vision 2020 and cultural liberalization.[150] Thirdly, apart from BN's ever-ready electoral assets, "3Ms" (money, media, and government machinery), Mahathir's increased popularity was another credible "M" factor for the ruling coalition.[151] Mahathir's popularity was even apparent among many ethnic Chinese who had traditionally voted for the opposition.

These external factors, however, were not the only impediments to the opposition parties. Another element foreshadowing the coming debacle could be found in internal factors for which the opposition themselves were largely responsible. Soon after the 1990 general election, there were efforts within the opposition circles to keep their electoral alliances alive by focusing on reformulating the loose election packages, Gagasan Rakyat and APU, as a more unified opposition coalition. For example in early 1991, the reorganization of Gagasan Rakyat was initiated by Razaleigh to include PAS, DAP, PBS, and Semangat 46 under a single opposition coalition with common symbol and manifesto. The effort to form a BN-type multi-ethnic coalition, however, did not succeed mainly due to conflicting ideologies and political interests among the opposition parties. In particular, PAS refused to join given that the party considered the other opposition parties, DAP and PBS, as anti-Islamic. Also, Semangat 46 increasingly adopted the agenda of "Malayness" to claim Malay supporters. DAP's relations with Semangat 46 thus deteriorated towards the mid-1990s, leading to the virtual breakup of the Gagasan Rakyat arrangement between Semangat 46 and DAP just before the 1995 general election.[152] In the end, the opposition parties could not present themselves as a viable alternative, despite the next general election being just around corner.

As expected, BN was returned to power in the general election in April 1995. The winning margin of the BN, however, was quite

TABLE 6.5
Comparison of the 1990 and 1995 General Elections (Parliamentary)

	Barisan Nasional			Opposition Parties and Independents	
	1990	1995		1990	1995
UMNO	71 (86)	89 (102)	DAP	20 (57)	9 (50)
MCA	18 (32)	30 (35)	PAS	7 (30)	7 (46)
MIC	6 (6)	7 (7)	Semangat 46	8 (61)	6 (66)
Gerakan	5 (9)	7 (10)	PBS	14 (14)	8 (28)
USNO[a]	6 (6)	—	PRM	0 (3)	0 (3)
PBB	10 (10)	10 (10)	AKIM	—	0 (2)
SNAP	3 (5)	3 (4)	AKAR[c]	0 (4)	—
SUPP	4 (8)	7 (7)	AMIPF[d]	0 (5)	—
PBDS	4 (4)	5 (5)	Independent	4 (64)	0 (43)
Others[b]	—	4 (12)			
Total[e]	127 (180)	162 (192)	Total	53 (180)	30 (192)

Note: Figures within parentheses are numbers of seats contested.
[a] USNO was deregistered in August 1993 after being expelled from the BN.
[b] SAPP won three seats and LDP one seat.
[c] AKAR joined the BN in 1991 but did not contest in 1995.
[d] AMIPF did not contest in 1995 after declaring its support for the BN.
[e] Figures within parentheses are total numbers of parliamentary seats.

Sources: *NST*, 23 October 1990; Khong Kim Hoong (1991); *NST*, 27 April 1995; and Gomez (1996).

remarkable, securing more than a five-sixths parliamentary majority. The BN captured 162 parliamentary seats (84.4 per cent of the total of 192 seats) and 338 state assembly seats (85.8 per cent of the total of 394 seats). In sharp contrast to the 1990 general election, these figures show an increase of 13.8 per cent in parliamentary seats and 13.7 per cent in state assembly seats respectively (see Tables 6.5 and 6.6). This was the largest victory for the ruling coalition over the last three decades. The BN also increased its popular vote from 53.4 per cent in 1990 to almost 65.1 per cent in 1995. In all states except Kelantan, the BN wrested almost total control of both parliamentary and state seats.

The most distinctive result of the 1995 elections was the considerable shift in Chinese votes in favour of the BN. The Chinese-dominated DAP retained only nine parliamentary seats, compared with twenty in 1990. In terms of total votes, the party suffered a serious setback, from 17.7 per cent in 1990 to 12.1 per cent this time. The DAP's losses were even more obvious at the state level. While the DAP had won forty-five of eighty-seven contested state seats (51.7 per cent) in 1990, this time it could only take eleven of ninety-three contested seats (11.8 per cent). The total votes at the state level also dropped to 11.7 per cent from 14.9 per cent. Especially in Penang where the DAP had made a great effort to take over the state government, the party could only win one of the

TABLE 6.6
Comparison of the 1990 and 1995 General Elections
(State, Peninsular Malaysia)

	Barisan Nasional			Opposition Parties	
	1990	1995		1990	1995
UMNO	196 (246)	230 (275)	DAP	45 (87)	11 (93)
MCA	34 (64)	71 (77)	PAS	33 (114)	33 (177)
MIC	12 (13)	15 (15)	Semangat 46	19 (152)	12 (131)
Gerakan	11 (21)	22 (26)	Berjasa	1 (1)	0 (1)
Total[a]	253 (351)	338 (394)	Total	98 (351)	56 (394)

Note: Figures within parentheses are numbers of seats contested.
[a] Figures within parentheses are total numbers of state seats.

Sources: *NST*, 23 October 1990; Khong Kim Hoong (1991); *NST*, 27 April 1995; and Gomez (1996).

thirty-three state seats, compared with fourteen seats in 1990.[153] The DAP's heavy losses led to a large increase for the Chinese BN parties. The MCA, in particular, won twelve new parliamentary seats, bringing its total to thirty in 1995. At the state level, the MCA more than doubled the number of its seats, from thirty-four in 1990 to seventy-one in 1995. Another Chinese party, Gerakan, also doubled its state seats from eleven to twenty-two. It is worth noting that Barisan Nasional secured average support of 64.5 per cent of the total vote in fifty-eight constituencies where the Chinese were more than one-third of the total electorate. The average increase of the majority votes in fifty-one of those fifty-eight constituencies was 12.2 per cent, compared with the 1990 elections.[154]

Nonetheless, this considerable swing in Chinese votes to the government did not seem to increase the bargaining power of the Chinese component parties within the ruling coalition. First of all, UMNO notably enhanced its grip on power in the election. Although the ruling coalition lost again in Kelantan, UMNO secured two parliamentary seats and seven state seats in that state at this time, compared with the complete defeat in 1990. In addition, UMNO recovered its traditional support in most Malay-dominant constituencies at the expense of the splinter party Semangat 46. Following incessant disputes with its counterpart PAS in the aftermath of the 1995 elections, Semangat 46 dissolved itself and returned to the UMNO fold in mid-1996 in the name of Malay unity. The former UMNO members' return increased UMNO's dominance in parliamentary seats to ninety-five, only one seat short of what would be needed to form an UMNO government without its BN partners. Adding on the ten *bumiputera* parliamentary seats won by the Sarawak-based PBB, it appeared that the political position of the Chinese BN parties had become more vulnerable at this juncture.

Moreover, as Francis Loh implies, a shift in the discourse of Malaysian politics from "ethnicism" to "developmentalism" in the 1990s also considerably undermined the MCA and Gerakan's political role within the ruling coalition. The UMNO-initiated cultural and economic liberalization removed a key issue for non-Malay politicians, regardless of whether they belonged to government or opposition parties, from controversial political debate and thus the decades-long issues of ethnicity were no longer perceived as the primary means to enhance the Chinese BN parties' bargaining position. In addition, the seemingly illiberal political processes of the 1990s were hardly questioned as the country's fast-growing economy was able to accommodate the material demands of the growing business and middle classes in urban areas. In this context, a former MCA leader, Lee Kim Sai, stresses that:

> MCA's bargaining power is very much dependent on what kind of issues MCA can bring up. On the one hand, we have to work together with UMNO. But, on the other, what is important is we need to provide the political issues. During my time [in the 1980s], MCA, as a political party representing Chinese interests, had faced a lot of controversial issues so we had to fight it out. But, now no more issues are left and MCA can live happily under UMNO's big umbrella. ... Even DAP is supporting the PM's approach. Now you can see the way DAP leaders talk is seen as if they are already a component part of the BN. Initially, MCA had been the only bargaining partner of UMNO. But, later on, UMNO had one more option — Gerakan within the BN. Now UMNO has another possible option — DAP since the 1995 general election. This is a totally new development.[155]

As implied in the above remarks, it is ironic that the diminishing role of the DAP as an opposition party was accompanied by a considerable setback in the bargaining position of Chinese parties within the ruling coalition. Nonetheless, the more important factor undermining the Chinese BN parties' political negotiation with their Malay counterpart UMNO was, and still is, their own confined style of leadership. In theory, the MCA and Gerakan's bargaining power had to be enhanced as the Chinese voters gave them a strong mandate in the elections. However, the increasing popularity of the MCA and Gerakan at this time had largely been dependent on UMNO's willingness to accommodate Chinese demands, and Mahathir's personal popularity in particular. In fact, there is little doubt that the MCA and Gerakan leaderships adopted a soft approach in dealing with their counterparts in the BN and became increasingly accustomed to the politics of marginalization after the 1995 general election. It was during this period that, in many cases, the so-called controversial issues have been avoided even in the Chinese parties' internal debates.[156] A clear example of self-restrained leadership style can be found in the MCA president Ling Liong Sik's comment as follows:

I often tell my party leaders if you are a minority, you have to learn to behave
like a minority race. Don't start behaving like a majority race or else you are
asking for trouble.[157]

Summary

The discussion on the sustainability of democratic systems has long been
influenced by modernization theories of a close relationship between
economic development and democratization. Several decades of evidence
from comparative political studies also confirms Lipset's classic hypothesis
that "democracy is related to the state of economic development".[158]
This evidence led Diamond to adapt Lipset's argument in the 1990s as:
"the more well-to-do the people of a country, on average, the more likely
they will favour, achieve, and maintain a democratic system for their
country".[159]

In Malaysia, however, increasing economic benefits of the 1990s
did not produce a momentum towards political democratization. In
other words, the country's economic growth and the emergence of a
large middle class did not engender a greater degree of democracy as
modernization theories would have predicted. Rather, it became clear
that the rhetoric of "developmentalism" was used as the principal
justification for authoritarianism and thus led the Mahathir regime to
impose greater state controls in the years after 1990. During this period,
the Mahathir-led UMNO exhibited an enhanced flexibility towards non-
Malay communities, pertaining to their language, education, religion,
and cultural heritage. Greater liberalization in ethnic politics, however,
was not motivated by a growing commitment to address the misgivings
of the minority communities in Malaysian society. Nor did the state-
driven cultural liberalization accompany greater political liberalization.

With UMNO's dominant control over the political process and
Mahathir's overwhelming popularity among both Malay and non-Malay
communities, it was unlikely that the Mahathir regime would be
challenged in the near future. Factional conflicts were still found in
UMNO politics in the early 1990s, but they were no longer seen as a
significant means of restraining the oligarchic tendencies of party leaders.
If factional alignments were allowed during this period, it was only when
Mahathir needed to check and balance the second-echelon leaders of

the party, without the risk of a direct leadership challenge against himself. Any attempt to restrain Mahathir's personal influence, by an individual or a faction, has always been followed by a tightening of authoritarian control inside and outside of the ruling party, and hence a further consolidation of his personal grip on power. In short, no one in UMNO could effectively check or balance Mahathir's power, but rather, towards the mid-1990s, everybody else was being checked and balanced by Mahathir.

Nonetheless, this did not mean that Mahathir, who was then seventy, would be free from the pressure of leadership succession. Although there was no sign of Mahathir's early retirement at this juncture, his age made it obvious that the leadership succession would not be far off. And, it was widely believed that political interest in succession would revive after the 1995 general election. Indeed, it was around this time that political commentators were openly discussing a rift between Mahathir and his deputy Anwar Ibrahim. Rumours of a possible challenge by Anwar to Mahathir's party presidency had also been speculated upon frequently in journalistic circles. Mahathir, much sooner than expected, encountered rapidly growing pressure from the new factional forces, led by Anwar, for a generational change of the national leadership. This was Mahathir's new political dilemma after the 1995 general election, and the following chapter revisits the nexus between growing factional conflicts in the ruling bloc and democratic transformation of authoritarian regime in this period.

NOTES

1. Mahathir Mohamad, "Democracy Is Dead", in *Opinion*, 25 August 1969, quoted in *Aliran Monthly* 10, no. 2 (1990, p. 39).

2. Interview with Lim Kit Siang, *Massa*, 12 July 1997 ("Wawancara: Dasar Liberal BN Bunuh DAP"); quoted in Francis Loh Kok Wah, "Pluralism and Democracy in Malaysia: Political, Cultural and Social Challenges", paper presented at the Islam, Culture and Democracy: A Regional Roundtable, 17–18 August 1998, Kuala Lumpur, p. 10.

3. Democratic Action Party, *DAP Policies For Malaysia: Full Liberalization*, released on 3 October 1994 as the basis of the 1995 general election campaign, available on <http://www.malaysia.net/dap/poll-1.htm>.

4. Jomo K.S., "Deepening Malaysian Democracy with More Checks and Balances", in *Malaysia Critical Perspectives*, edited by Muhammad Ikmal Said and Zahid Emby (Petaling Jaya: Persatuan Sains Sosial Malaysia, 1996*a*), p. 74.

5. Harold Crouch, *Government and Society in Malaysia* (Ithaca and London: Cornell University Press, 1996), p. 236.

6. For example, see *The Star*, 12 November 1990; *NST*, 13 November 1990; and *FEER*, 13 December 1990 (Suhaini Aznam, "Prune and Propagate").

7. Born in the Chinese-majority state of Penang, Anwar was a former student leader once detained under the ISA for two years when Mahathir was Education Minister. As a young Muslim leader, who also founded ABIM, Anwar had been strongly critical of UMNO. Ironically, it was Mahathir who brought Anwar into UMNO soon after he took over power in 1981. Since then, Anwar rose steadily within the party with Mahathir's help. In 1982, in the same year he joined UMNO, Anwar won a seat in Parliament and was appointed Deputy Minister in the Prime Minister's Department. In the same year, he was elected as UMNO Youth chief. Mahathir subsequently appointed him Minister of Culture, Youth, and Sports, then Agriculture, then Education. In 1987, Anwar was elected one of three vice-presidents of UMNO.

8. For details of the cabinet reshuffle in February 1991, see *FEER*, 21 February 1991 (Doug Tsuruoka and Suhaini Aznam, "Filling Daim's Shoes").

9. For details of the post-election cabinet line-up, see *FEER*, 8 November 1990 (Suhaini Aznam, "Cabinet-maker's Tools").

10. *Aliran Monthly* 13, no. 2 (1993): 2–6 (Edmund Terence Gomez, "Anwar's Men Gain Media Control?"); *Aliran Monthly* 13, no. 9 (1993): 35–39 (Edmund Terence Gomez, "Anwar's Friends: Factionalism and Money Politics in UMNO [*Baru*]").

11. *NST*, 13 October 1991.

12. *FEER*, 31 October 1991 (Michael Vatikiotis, "Contest on Hold").

13. *NST*, 7 November 1991.

14. For details of the list of regulations, see *The Star*, 28 March 1993 ("Rules for Smooth Polls").

15. *The Star*, 3 April 1993 ("UMNO Members Happy with Proposed Rules").

16. *The Star*, 9 November 1992.

17. *The Star*, 8 November 1992.

18. *NST*, 28 April 1993.

19. *The Star*, 23 July 1993. A week after Mahathir's advice, the majority of UMNO backbenchers, thirty-five out of thirty-eight, came out to support Anwar for the deputy president's post. See *The Star*, 30 July 1993.

20. *The Star*, 6 August 1993.

21. *The Star*, 10 November 1992 ("Ridding UMNO of Ghosts of 1986").

22. *The Star*, 8 August 1993.

23. *The Star*, 5 November 1993.

24. See *FEER*, 28 October 1993 (Michael Vatikiotis, "End Game"); *Aliran Monthly* 13, no. 8 (1993): 2–4 ("Battle for the UMNO Crown").

25. See *The Star*, 8 September 1993 ("Anwar: I Would Not Contest If PM Objected").

26. *NST*, 13 August 1993.

27. *The Star*, 20 August 1993.

28. For a specific list of who was at Anwar's press conference and the text of Anwar's announcement, see *The Star*, 24 August 1993.

29. For the full list of divisional nominations for the 1993 party elections, see *The Star*, 14 October 1993.

30. See *NST*, 24 August 1993; *The Star*, 7 September 1993; and Zainuddin Maidin, *The Other Side of Mahathir* (Kuala Lumpur: Utusan Publication & Distributors Sdn. Bhd., 1994), p. 245.

31. For Mahathir's open warning about the team approach and money politics at this time, see *The Star*, 3 November 1993.

32. *NST*, 14 October 1993; *Utusan Malaysia*, 4 November 1993 and 5 November 1993.

33. *The Star*, 3 November 1993 ("Veep Race Thrown Wide Open").

34. *Aliran Monthly* 13, no. 9 (1993): 2–6 ("Anwar Ibrahim: Prime Minister-To-Be").

35. Jomo K. S., "Election's Janus Face: Limitations and Potential in Malaysia", in *The Politics of Elections in Southeast Asia*, edited by R.H. Taylor (Cambridge: Woodrow Wilson Center Press and Cambridge University Press, 1996*b*), p. 108.

36. *FEER*, 18 November 1993 (Michael Vatikiotis, "A Matter of Time").

37. Zainuddin Maidin (1994, p. 246).

38. *The Star*, 1 June 1993 ("PM: It's No Big Deal").

39. For more detailed explanation, see *FEER*, 23 March 1995 (S. Jayasankaran, "Back to the Front").

40. For the full texts of the amendments to the party constitution, see *The Star*, 18 June 1994.

41. See comments by several senior party officials in *The Star*, 18 June 1994 ("Assembly to Focus on Appointments").

42. The number of state and parliamentary seats was increased in line with the re-

delineation exercise in 1993. And the appointment for the members of new pro-tem committee was scheduled in July 1994, while the extraordinary general assembly was held in June 1994.

43. For further explanation of the UMNO general assembly held in November 1994, see *Aliran Monthly* 14, no. 10 (1994): 2–5 ("The UMNO [*Baru*] General Assembly: Reading between the Lines").

44. Edmund Terence Gomez, *Political Business: Corporate Involvement of Malaysian Political Parties* (Townsville, Centre for East and Southeast Asian Studies: James Cook University of North Queensland, 1994), p. 64.

45. There were seven by-elections in 1991. BN won all but two by-elections to Semangat 46. See NSTP Research and Information Services, *Elections in Malaysia: A Handbook of Facts and Figures on the Elections 1955–1990* (Kuala Lumpur: NSTP, 1994), pp. 63–65.

46. James Chin, "Politics of Federal Intervention in Malaysia with Reference to Sarawak, Sabah and Kelantan", paper presented at the First International Malaysian Studies Conference, University of Malaya, 11–13 August 1997, p. 16.

47. *The Star*, 28 March 1991 and *NST*, 11 April 1991.

48. *The Star*, 21 January 1991 and *NST*, 8 January 1991.

49. For PAS's concern, see *The Star*, 8 September 1991 ("More Cracks in the Semangat House").

50. *The Star*, 27 March 1991.

51. *NST*, 11 April 1991.

52. *NST*, 9 November 1991.

53. For examples, see *The Star*, 4 April 1991 ("Kelantan UMNO Told to Curb Resentment"); *NST*, 23 September 1991 ("UMNO May Allow Appeals to Council").

54. *NST*, 9 November 1991.

55. A good example is shown in *NST*, 6 July 1992 ("Be Wary of Group out to Split UMNO").

56. *The Star*, 29 February 1992.

57. *The Star*, 10 May 1993.

58. Interview with Rais Yatim, Kuala Lumpur, 4 February 1998.

59. Interview with Razaleigh Hamzah, Kuala Lumpur, 23 February 1998.

60. William Case, "Pseudo-Democracy in Southeast Asia: Uncovering State Leaders and the Business Connection", paper presented at the Asia in Global Context Conference, University of New South Wales, 28 September to 1 October 1998, pp. 23 and 35.

61. Interview with Razaleigh Hamzah, Kuala Lumpur, 23 February 1998. In this interview, Razaleigh pointed out that Ibrahim Ali's defection was a typical example of Mahathir's pressure and financial reward for the Semangat 46 members. He believes that Ibrahim Ali was nearly bankrupt when he decided to leave the party and there was no doubt that the Mahathir government could have punished him financially if he did not return to UMNO.

62. Interview with Ahmad Shabery Chik, former Semangat 46 information chief, Kuala Lumpur, 13 January 1998.

63. *The Star*, 1 December 1990.

64. *FEER*, 22 November 1990 (Suhaini Aznam, "Out in the Cold").

65. For an analysis of how the federal government utilizes its financial resources to control the local authorities in Peninsular Malaysia, see Shafruddin B.H., *The Federal Factor in the Government and Politics of Peninsular Malaysia* (Singapore: Oxford University Press, 1987). Also, see Phang Siew Nooi, *Financing Local Government in Malaysia* (Kuala Lumpur: University of Malaya Press, 1997).

66. See *Malaysian Business*, 1–15 June 1991 (Jayasankaran, "The Siege Within").

67. It must be noted that only elected MPs and state assembly persons from the ruling BN coalition were authorized to identify development projects for implementation in their respective constituencies before the 1990 general election.

68. *The Star*, 7 April 1991.

69. *Malaysian Business*, 1–15 June 1991 (Jayasankaran, "The Siege Within"), p. 20.

70. *Seventh Malaysia Plan 1996–2000*, p. 181, table 6.4.

71. *Mid-Term Review of the Sixth Malaysia Plan 1991–1995*, p. 50, table 2.16.

72. Kelantan Menteri Besar Nik Aziz Nik Mat's interview in *Malaysian Business*, 1–15 February 1994 ("Growing with Islam"), p. 3.

73. Total investment in approved manufacturing projects doubled from RM58.6 billion in the period 1986–90 to RM116.2 billion in 1991–95. For more details of approved manufacturing projects by state, see *Seventh Malaysia Plan 1996–2000*, p. 147, table 5.4.

74. Mahathir's speech at the 1990 UMNO general assembly. See *NST*, 1 December 1990.

75. Maximus Ongkili was the deputy chief executive of the state government's "think tank" IDS (Institute of Development Studies) and was working as a press consultant for the PBS during the 1990 general election. Mahathir's government often accused IDS of inciting anti-federal sentiments. See *NST*, 10 November 1990.

76. *NST*, 24 October 1990.

77. *NST*, 6 April 1993.

78. James Chin, "The Sabah State Election of 1994", *Asian Survey* 34, no. 10 (1994): 911.

79. For a detailed breakdown of the 1994 Sabah elections, see James Chin (1994, pp. 911–12). See also *FEER*, 3 March 1994 (Michael Vatikiotis, "A Close Run Thing").

80. James Chin (1994, p. 912). Also, see *Aliran Monthly* 14, no. 10 (1994): 29–31 (K. George, "Beware! Money Politics Will Boomerang").

81. Initially three new parties were to formed: the Parti Bersatu Rakyat Sabah (PBRS); the Parti Democratik Sabah Bersatu (PDSB); and the Parti Demokratik Sabah (PDS). PDSB led by Jeffery Kitingan, however, was unable to register as a political party. See James Chin (1994, p. 913).

82. On the redelineation exercise in Sabah, see James Chin, "'Kataks', Kadazan-Dusun Nationalism and Development: The 1999 Sabah State Election", *Regime Change and Regime Maintenance in Asia and the Pacific*, Discussion Paper Series Number 24 (Canberra: Research School of Pacific and Asian Studies, Australian National University, 1999), pp. 13–14.

83. Legal Research Board, *Federal Constitution* (Kuala Lumpur, International Law Book Services, 1995), p. 135, Article 113 (2) (ii) and (iii).

84. *Utusan Malaysia*, 14 September 1992.

85. Edmund Terence Gomez, *The 1995 Malaysian General Elections: A Report and Commentary* (Singapore: Institute of Southeast Asian Studies, 1996), p. 11.

86. For a more detailed analysis of the 1993 redelineation exercise, see Gomez (1996, pp. 6–11).

87. For the average numbers of the state voters in 1990, see NSTP Research and Information Services, 1994, pp. 69–107. For the figures after the redelineation of 1993, see *The Star*, 26 April 1995.

88. *The Star*, 26 April 1995.

89. R.S. Milne and Diane K. Mauzy, *Malaysian Politics under Mahathir* (London and New York: Routledge, 1999), p. 29.

90. For more details, see H.P. Lee, *Constitutional Conflicts in Contemporary Malaysia* (Kuala Lumpur: Oxford University Press, 1995), pp. 22–42; Hari Singh, "UMNO Leaders and Malay Rulers: The Erosion of a Special Relationship", *Pacific Affairs* 68, no. 2 (Summer 1995): 187–205; and Rais Yatim, *Freedom under Executive Power in Malaysia* (Kuala Lumpur: Endowment Sdn. Bhd., 1995), pp. 97–100.

91. For example, see *NST*, 30 October 1990.

92. See *The Star*, 22 December 1990.

93. For examples of the media exposure of the rulers' involvement in commercial enterprise and personal affairs, see various issues of *NST*, *The Star*, *Berita Harian*,

Utusan Malaysia, Nanyang Siang Pau, Sin Chew Jit Poh, and *Tamil Nesan* on 14, 16, 19, 29 January 1993; 12, 14, 18, 19, 28 February 1993; and 2, 3, 5, 7, 8, 11, 15–21, 23 March 1993.

94. For details of political developments in the 1993 constitutional conflicts and the constitutional amendments in 1993, see *Aliran Monthly* 13, no. 1 (1993): 2–5 (Anil Netto, "No One Is Above the Law") and H.P. Lee (1995, pp. 89–93).

95. See Legal Research Board, *Federal Constitution*, 1995, pp. 81–82, Clause (4) and (4A) of Article 66.

96. Rais Yatim (1995, p. 113).

97. In his letter from Sungai Buloh prison on 3 November 1998, Anwar Ibrahim wrote that "We supported him [Mahathir] in the constitutional amendment issue, thinking rather naively that the powers taken from the Rulers would revert to the people and not go to him alone. How blind we were then not to see through his vile plan to eventually overthrow the traditional Malay Rulers and install himself as the supreme feudal lord of the Malays."

98. The existing provisions of Clause (3) of Article 125 of the Federal Constitution stipulated that a judge of the Supreme Court (now Federal Court) ought only to be removed on the grounds "of misbehaviour or of inability, from infirmity of body or mind or any other cause, properly to discharge the functions of his office". See Legal Research Board, *Federal Constitution*, 1995, p. 90.

99. Clause (3A) of the amended Article 125 states that: "The Yang di-Pertuan Agong on the recommendation of the Chief Justice, the President of the Court of Appeal and the Chief Judges of the High Court, may, *after consulting the Prime Minister*, prescribe in writing a code of ethics which shall be observed by every judge of the Federal Court." See Legal Research Board, *Federal Constitution*, 1995, p. 151, Italics added.

100. *FEER*, 19 May 1994 (Michael Vatikiotis, "King and Country: Government Further Clips Rulers' Wings").

101. *Aliran Monthly* 14, no. 5 (1994): 11 (Zainur Zakaria, "The 1994 Constitutional Amendment: End of Judicial Independence").

102. See *FEER*, 9 January 1992 (Michael Vatikiotis, "A Tabloid Tamed"); *Aliran Monthly* 12, no. 1 (1992): 2–3 (Mustafa K. Anuar and Francis Loh, "Color, Puzzles, Feng Shui and the Malaysian Press").

103. For more details of the ISA amendments, see *FEER*, 6 July 1989 (Suhaini Aznam, "ISA Amendments Abolish Judicial Review: Appeal No More").

104. Background information on Lim Guan Eng's case, see Amnesty International, *The Trial of Opposition Parliamentarian Lim Guan Eng: An Update*, 28 March 1997. For further details on the political arrests in the 1990s, see Amnesty International, *Malaysia: Human Rights Undermined — Restrictive Laws in a*

Parliamentary Democracy, 1 September 1999. Also see SUARAM, *Malaysian Human Rights Report* (Petaling Jaya: SUARAM Komunikasi, 1998), pp. 213–58.

105. By November 1994, at least twelve Al-Arqam leaders and several hundred members were arrested, including its leader Ashaari. On 26 October 1994, Ashaari and seven other followers made confessions of their deviation from the Islamic true teachings at the national *fatwa* committee which were telecast. On 31 October, the Al-Arqam supreme council announced that the movement no longer existed. Almost all Al-Arqam facilities in the country were closed down within a few months of the banning of Al-Arqam.

106. Milne and Mauzy (1999, pp. 87–88). Some useful background analysis on the motivations for banning of Al-Arqam can be found in D. Camroux, "State Responses to Islamic Resurgence in Malaysia: Accommodation, Co-option and Confrontation", *Asian Survey* 36, no. 9 (1996): 863–65; Ahmad Fauzi Abdul Hamid, "Political Dimensions of Religious Conflict in Malaysia: State Response to an Islamic Movement", *Indonesia and the Malay World* 28, no. 80 (2000): 32–65; and *Aliran Monthly* 17, no. 1 (1997): 38.

107. A study of Al-Arqam's origin, growth and its developmental approach can be found in Muhammad Syukri Salleh, *An Islamic Approach to Rural Development: The Arqam Way* (London: Asoib International, 1992).

108. See Jomo K.S. and Ahmad Shabery Chik, "Malaysia's Islamic Movements", in *Fragmented Vision: Culture and Politics in Contemporary Malaysia*, edited by J.S. Kahn and Francis Loh (Sydney: Allen and Unwin, 1992), p. 84.

109. Interview with Razaleigh Hamzah, Kuala Lumpur, 23 February 1998.

110. Crouch (1996, p. 156).

111. Mahathir Mohamad, "Malaysia: The Way Forward", in *Malaysia's Vision 2020: Understanding the Concept, Implications and Challenges,* edited by Ahmad Sarji Abdul Hamid (Petaling Jaya: Pelanduk Publications, 1993), p. 405.

112. Ahmad Sarji Abdul Hamid, ed. (1993, p. 404).

113. *The Star*, 11 September 1995.

114. *Time*, 9 December 1996.

115. For a critical analysis of Mahathir's Vision 2020 and the NDP, see Jomo K.S., *U-Turn? Malaysian Economic Development Policies After 1990* (Townsville: Center for East and Southeast Asian Studies, James Cook University of North Queensland, 1994).

116. See Democratic Action Party, *DAP Policies for Malaysia: Full Liberalization*, 3 October 1994.

117. Interview with Anuwar Ali, the Director of the Department of Higher Education in the Ministry of Education, Kuala Lumpur, 6 February 1998.

118. The survey was conducted in late 1996 with a graduate student of UPM (Universiti Pertanian Malaysia).

119. National-type school is a government or government-aided primary school using the Chinese or Tamil language as the main medium of instruction. Both the national language (Bahasa Melayu) and English are compulsory subjects in the national-type primary schools.

120. *NST*, 7 April 1995.

121. *Sixth Malaysia Plan 1991–1995*, p. 183, table 5.5.

122. See *Nanyang Siang Pau*, 20 May 1994.

123. For details of the continuing conflict between the MCA and *Dongjiaozong* for almost four decades, see Tan Liok Ee, "*Dongjiaozong* and the Challenge to Cultural Hegemony 1951–1987" in Joel S. Kahn and Francis Loh Kok Wah (1992, pp. 181–98).

124. For instance, see *FEER*, 12 December 1991 (Michael Vatikiotis, "A Question of Priorities"); 8 October 1992 (Michael Vatikiotis, "The Language Lobby"); and 11 November 1993 (Michael Vatikiotis, "Back to English").

125. For example, see Rustam A. Sani, *Politik dan Polemik Bahasa Melayu* (Kuala Lumpur: Utusan Publication and Distributors, 1993), pp. 105–50.

126. See the picture in Ling Liong Sik (1995, between p. 56 and p. 57). For other examples, see *FEER*, 10 February 1994 (Michael Vatikiotis, "Value Judgements"); *FEER*, 6 April 1995 (Jayasankaran, "Young Minds, Old Tool").

127. *FEER*, 8 September 1988.

128. *NST*, 14 November 1989.

129. *The Star*, 24 October 1990.

130. Interview with Lee Kim Sai, then deputy president of the MCA, Kajang, 25 February 1998.

131. Milne and Mauzy, 1999, p. 96.

132. Interview with Ong Tee Keat, an MP for Ampang Jaya and MCA Youth president, Kuala Lumpur, 5 February 1998.

133. Interview with Musa Hitam, Kuala Lumpur, 13 February 1998.

134. Interview with Lee Kim Sai, then deputy president of the MCA, Kajang, 25 February 1998.

135. There was a case for a deputy chief minister to be appointed in Penang in 1969 but the constitutional basis for the appointment was challenged. At that stage, no deputy chief minister had been appointed since the 1974 general election.

136. Interview with Ibrahim Saad, Kuala Lumpur, 19 February 1998.

137. See Edmund Terence Gomez and Jomo K.S., *Malaysia's Political Economy: Politics, Patronage and Profits* (Cambridge: Cambridge University Press, 1997), pp. 75–165.

138. See *Seventh Malaysia Plan 1996–2000*, p. 312 and p. 331.

139. Confidential interview, Kuala Lumpur, February 1998.

140. See Legal Research Board, *Private Higher Educational Institutions Act 1996* (Kuala Lumpur: International Law Book Services, 1996), clauses 42 and 43.

141. United Chinese School Committees Association of Malaysia et al., *Memorandum on the Education Bill 1995*, submitted by the seven major Chinese Associations to the Education Minister, 15 December 1995, p. 1. For more detail of the powers given to the Education Minister, see Legal Research Board, *Education Act 1996* (Kuala Lumpur: International Law Book Services, 1996), especially clauses 58, 59, 60, 61, 62, 67, 68, 69, 75, 76, 77, 85, and 126.

142. Emphases added. Section 28 states: "Subject to the provision of this Act, the Minister may establish national schools and national-type schools and shall maintain such schools."

143. See *Memorandum on the Education Bill 1995*, pp. 2–3.

144. Interview with Kua Kia Soong, academic director of *Dongjiaozong* Higher Learning Centre, Kajang, 20 January 1998.

145. See *Education Act 1996*, clause 71. Clause 72 specifies that the penalty for contravention of Clause 71 will be fined up to RM50,000 or imprisonment of up to five years.

146. For example, in September 1995, when Metro Vision, a private cable television station intended to air a famous Chinese mini-series "Justice Pao", promoting family values and loyalty to the country, it was initially stopped by the Information Ministry whose rationale was that "costume dramas" were not permitted to be screened over television. Although the decision was overturned following widespread objection by the Chinese community, the "Justice Pao" case is an example of recurring controversy over cultural policy. See *The Star*, 4 October 1995.

147. See *Nanyang Siang Pau*, 4 February 1996.

148. Interview with Saifuddin Nasution Ismail, then UMNO Youth secretary, Kuala Lumpur, 22 January 1998.

149. During the economic recession in 1998, there was a case illustrating this on a mini-scale. Anwar had urged the MCA to review the proposal to build a branch of the TARC in Bentong as this had generated concern among local Malay residents. Though UMNO had no intention of impeding the progress of TARC, such development projects should take into consideration the sensitivities of locals. Bentong division chief Adnan Yaakob had voiced concern over the setting up of

the branch campus of TARC, saying it would alter the area's racial composition. The proposal involved the development of 920 hectares to build 4,000 houses. It would create a new population, mainly Chinese, of 20,000. See *The Star*, 22 March 1998, 23 March 1998, and 25 March 1998.

150. Francis Loh (1998, pp. 14–17).

151. Gomez (1996, p. 45).

152. For the political developments towards the disintegration of Gagasan Rakyat, see Kua Kia Soong, *Inside the DAP 1990–1995* (Kuala Lumpur: Potensi Serentak, 1996), pp. 29–33.

153. See Gomez (1996, pp. 26–27, tables 6 and 7). The winning majority of Batu Lancang, the only state seat that DAP won in Penang, was just sixty-two votes. See *NST*, 27 April 1995.

154. Figures compiled from Gomez (1996, pp. 32–33, table 8). The other seven constituencies were introduced in the 1995 general election.

155. Interview with Lee Kim Sai, Kajang, 25 February 1998.

156. Confidential interview with a senior MCA official, Kuala Lumpur, January 1998.

157. Ling Liong Sik at the National Press Club in February 1999 for a talk on "The Malaysian Chinese: Crisis and Choice", quoted in Lim Kit Siang's press statement, 31 May 1999.

158. Seymour M. Lipset, *Political Man: The Social Bases of Politics* (Baltimore: Johns Hopkins University Press, 1981), p. 31.

159. Larry Diamond, "Economic Development and Democracy Reconsidered", in *Reexamining Democracy*, edited by G. Marks and Larry Diamond (Newbury Park, California: Sage Publications, 1992), p. 109.

7

The Rise of New Politics and Challenges to the Mahathir Regime

If any ruler puts a single one of his subjects to shame [*memberi' aib*], that shall be a sign that his kingdom will be destroyed by Almighty God. Similarly it has been granted by Almighty God to Malay subjects that they shall never be disloyal or treacherous to their rulers, even if their rulers behave evilly or inflict injustice upon them. (*Sejarah Melayu*)[1]

During my entire political career, when I visited every corner of the country, at any gathering, I felt confident of the support of the Malay society for UMNO. On the other hand, it was difficult to be certain of Chinese support or even be sure of their stand. Now the situation has changed. ... My experience was extremely peculiar, one that I had never experienced in my entire life. In Malay-majority areas, BN leaders and workers looked weary and exhausted as well as pressured. This was because in a very open, fearless and unhesitant manner, so many Malays — young, old, labourers, the learned, the rich, the poor — worked hard and earnestly for the opposition parties, no matter whether it was PAS, DAP, Parti Rakyat, or KeADILan. Only in Chinese-majority areas were the BN and UMNO leaders and workers relaxed. (Musa Hitam, 2000)[2]

The year 1998 marks a significant change in Malaysian political history. After several years of leadership conflict speculation within UMNO, Anwar Ibrahim was abruptly dismissed from office, expelled from the party, imprisoned under the ISA, beaten while in custody and eventually charged in court on five counts of sodomy and five counts of corruption. These events happened with Machiavellian ruthlessness in September 1998. Anwar sensed his time as Mahathir's deputy was about to end, but even he did not anticipate Mahathir acting in "such a despicable and shameless manner".[3] Interestingly, Mahathir claimed in an interview that he had not read Machiavelli's prescription on how to be a successful politician.[4] Anwar's abrupt dismissal and its aftermath, nonetheless, recall Machiavelli's famous dictum about cruelty, that a successful leader should not care about the infamy of cruelty in order to maintain power.

Anwar's sacking shocked the nation because such treatment of a deputy prime minister had never happened before. Even resignation was not part of Malaysian political culture until Mahathir came to power in 1981. During Tunku Abdul Rahman's era, Tun Abdul Razak was his deputy for the duration of his reign. It was only because of the death of his first deputy Ismail bin Abdul Rahman that two deputies served under Razak. Mahathir was Hussein Onn's deputy during his administration. To a much greater extent than in most other countries, leadership succession had been institutionalized as an important factor contributing to political stability in Malaysia. But up to 2002, Mahathir had four deputies and three of them resigned or were sacked. It is still uncertain whether the fourth deputy will succeed Mahathir as president. As Funston notes, it was under Mahathir's leadership that a certain degree of conflict within top levels of UMNO has become institutionalized.[5]

The Mahathir-Anwar leadership tussle is certainly not the first in Malaysian political history since there have been serious leadership struggles within UMNO circles. But unlike previous tussles, the Mahathir-Anwar conflict was something "unprecedented" in Malaysian politics. Its political, social, and even cultural consequences were not bounded by "Malay issues" or "UMNO affairs". In short, the Anwar episode has acted as a catalyst for a new political configuration, not just in Malay politics but in Malaysian politics as a whole.

Malaysia witnessed its most intense street protests since the 1960s, after the sacking of Anwar Ibrahim. At each public rally, Anwar attracted tens of thousands of Malaysians from all ethnic groups, though mainly Malays. Within a few weeks of Anwar's sacking, Mahathir's national image was tarnished and the expression of anti-Mahathir sentiment by Malays became commonplace. The harshness of the police in dispersing unarmed protesters shocked Malaysians, especially young middle-class Malays, who had accepted the political myth that only UMNO could protect them. Anwar's widely publicized appearance in court with a black eye reinforced the perception that this was not merely an internal Malay or UMNO affair but one of national significance. Thereafter, co-operation among non-government organizations and opposition parties, rallying on a variety of public issues, was enhanced. These developments culminated in the formation of an unprecedented united multi-ethnic opposition coalition, the Barisan Alternatif, which included PAS, DAP, PRM, and the newly formed KeADILan led by Anwar's wife Wan Azizah Wan Ismail, in anticipation of the 1999 general election.

To some extent, the circumstances and political manoeuvrings that surround the Mahathir-Anwar tussle resembled those of previous leadership conflicts, especially the situation preceding the split of the Mahathir-Musa leadership in 1986 and subsequent breakaway of UMNO in 1988. Musa believes that Anwar's problem was similar to his own with Mahathir, even though Mahathir's political handling of Anwar was much more refined, having learnt from experience in the mid-1980s.[6] Thus, the changing conflict configurations after September 1998 offer another opportunity to re-examine some of the same questions that were raised in the wake of the UMNO leadership crisis in 1987, in particular, the relationship between UMNO factionalism and the transition of authoritarian regimes. Specifically, to what extent does severe factional strife within the ruling UMNO circle transform the political system into a more open and responsive one in an ethnically fragmented society? In the new circumstances where UMNO has lost much of its traditional support from the Malay community, is Malaysia's single-party-dominant political landscape being realigned to a new multi-racial two-coalition party system?

This chapter aims to analyse the development and consequences of Anwar's downfall. It examines the context in which the leadership conflict took place and how Mahathir responded to a second crisis within the UMNO leadership. It asks the question: what were the consequences of Anwar's downfall for both Malaysian politics as a whole and Mahathir's political destiny in particular? In dealing with these issues, this chapter focuses, though indirectly, on a comparison of the two most recent UMNO factional splits: that of 1987 and of 1998 and their consequences for the transition of the Malaysian political system.

What Went Wrong?

What went wrong with the relationship between Mahathir and Anwar? Did it sour because Anwar was "morally unfit" to be a prime minister, as claimed by Mahathir? Or, was Anwar the victim of "a political conspiracy at the highest level", as alleged by Anwar? Was the leadership split the product of increasing differences in approach between Mahathir and Anwar in their handling of the economic crisis since mid-1997, as the foreign media assert? Or, was it another political crisis that had to happen after rumours of a power struggle between the two leaders? Several years after the Mahathir-Anwar leadership split, there is still speculation about the real reasons behind Anwar's abrupt downfall in September 1998.

Initially, Mahathir's official announcement was that Anwar's dismissal was because of his involvement in sexual impropriety, including affairs with prostitutes, and sodomy. Rumours had also been circulated that Anwar was the father of a child born to his private secretary's wife. In claiming this, Mahathir reiterated that he had "incontrovertible proof" of Anwar's indulgence in improper sexual activities.[7] Mahathir also claimed that Anwar's sacking and expulsion had nothing to do with differences over economic policies or a possible leadership challenge from his deputy.[8]

It is still a moot point whether Anwar committed acts of sodomy or not, while tests proved that it was his private secretary, not Anwar, who had fathered the child.[9] The unorthodox conduct of Anwar's trial cast doubt on its credibility and raised big questions about the impartiality of the court. Mahathir's accusations against Anwar then shifted into the political and economic realm as the public remained unconvinced of the sexual charges. In the middle of the trial, the original charges against him were amended. The revised charges shifted the focus to Anwar's interference in police investigations rather than the sexual allegations themselves.[10] This gave rise to a public perception that the issue of morality was not the real reason for Anwar's downfall. It was also argued that Mahathir, in fact, made the "incontrovertible" sexual allegations to kill Anwar politically. As a former senior government official put it, Mahathir's opponents had to fight against "the awesome power of incumbency". He mentioned that "if I resisted in leaving and if I were fighting against Mahathir, he might have produced ten men that I had sexual relations with".[11] It was reported that Mahathir offered Anwar the option of resigning several times to avoid the humiliation of having allegations of sexual indiscretion being brought out into the open. But, Anwar refused.[12]

Meanwhile, the foreign media gave prominence Mahathir's and Anwar's different handling of the economic crisis. Towards the middle of 1997, after almost a decade of high economic growth averaging more than 8 per cent annually, the Malaysian economic miracle had turned into a mirage, together with its ASEAN counterparts. Following the devaluation of the Thai baht on 2 July 1997, the Malaysian ringgit, the Philippine peso, and the Indonesian rupiah — together with the South Korean won, were in free fall. By the end of 1997, the Malaysian ringgit had depreciated by nearly 50 per cent to a value of about RM4.80 per U.S. dollar from around RM2.5 per U.S. dollar at the beginning of 1997. During the same period, the Kuala Lumpur Stock Exchange Composite Index (KLCI) also collapsed to just over 500 points from a high of 1,272 points on 25 February 1997, an astonishing 60 per cent drop in the average value of the shares listed on the main board of the KLSE in just ten months. Combined with the collapse of the currency and the stock market, real estate prices also dropped sharply from the middle of 1997. This triple disaster of ringgit, stock market, and real estate collapse left many Malaysians, especially those in the younger generation of middle-class Malaysians, in a state of confusion, shock, and frustration. And it was widely reported in foreign media that the breakup between the two leaders was closely related to the handling of the country's economic crisis.[13] To put it simply, Mahathir, by blaming external factors, favoured the loosening of monetary and fiscal policies aimed at stimulating growth and preventing the economy from sinking into recession.[14] On the contrary, Anwar, by focusing on internal problems, took the more conventional view of tightening monetary policies and austerity measures prescribed by the International Monetary

Fund (IMF). Anwar and his allies' criticism of "mega projects" and "the lack of transparency of privatized state patronage" was, of course, not pleasing to Mahathir. According to foreign media, the underlying differences in economic policies between the two leaders, especially since mid-1997, eventually led to Anwar's downfall in September 1998.

It was, indeed, well known that Mahathir and Anwar were at odds in certain areas of government policy even before the country faced economic recession. Perhaps what exacerbated the situation was Anwar's initial reluctance to bail out certain individuals or companies associated with Mahathir during the economic crisis. These differences, however, did not necessarily indicate that Anwar's approach to handling the economic crisis was in opposition to the wishes of Mahathir. According to Funston, "Mahathir's and Anwar's views on the international and domestic aspects of the crisis were not as far apart as has generally been argued". He argues that if there were any differences on certain policies, they received at least Mahathir's acquiescence.[15] Anwar also pointed out that the seemingly different attitudes to managing the economic crisis nevertheless arose from a team approach.[16] A senior UMNO leader, who was viewed as neither Mahathir's nor Anwar's ally, also stated that over the last ten to fifteen five years Mahathir schooled Anwar into his mode of thinking and Anwar subscribed, to a considerable degree, to "Mahathirism" after he joined UMNO.[17] Especially with the advent of UMNO (*Baru*), factional disputes themselves were largely limited to struggles for spoils rather than differences over policy or ideology.[18] In this regard, it would be an oversimplification to view the leadership split as directly caused by inherent differences in policies or leadership style between the two leaders.

What, then, went wrong with Anwar? Anwar believes that he was the victim of a high-level political conspiracy designed to finish his political future, a conspiracy that began more than one year before his downfall. Anwar's allies strongly believe that Mahathir's cronies, especially Daim Zainuddin, initiated the whole process of Anwar's destruction to protect or prolong their own political and economic interests because Anwar's ascendancy had increasingly threatened them.[19] These people allegedly kept telling Mahathir that Anwar was planning to challenge for the party presidency in the forthcoming party election of 1999 using the economic crisis as a spur. These allegations of leadership challenge made Mahathir paranoid. To kill Anwar politically, a close associate of Anwar says, Mahathir used the issue of immorality to cover the power struggle. This placed Anwar's supporters in a very defensive position.[20]

There is no doubt that the Mahathir faction conspired to remove Anwar from office. However, such factional rivalry is common in the conduct of party politics everywhere. In the case of Anwar, he was definitely seen by Mahathir's close associates as more and more dangerous as he was rapidly promoted as finance minister, deputy prime minister, and then acting prime minister. Anwar himself, like it or not, had to step on their toes to expand his power base. The more ground he gained, the more enemies he made within the government and the ruling party. Given this, there were plenty of reasons for conspiring to destroy Anwar and ensure Mahathir's cronies' continued hold on their political and economic interests. What, then, made Anwar's adversaries decide to topple him towards the end of 1990s? Musa Hitam comments on this question:

> What is splitting our party is the political culture in UMNO now — both the winning and losing side realize that there will be attempts to finish off the loser's political career. The loser will be cursed, condemned and obstructed not only in their political activities but also to the extent of threatening their rice-bowl. This fate is not limited to those who contest, but also extends to their supporters. His job is jeopardized; his business, his loans, his children's scholarships are also threatened. Not surprisingly, the contests are so intense and finally divisive. Hatred continues, animosity continues and purging continues. Under such conditions, contest within UMNO has truly become a matter of life and death.[21]

Prelude to the Deepening of the Mahathir-Anwar Leadership Struggle

With the advent of UMNO (*Baru*) in 1988, new guiding principles of behaviour appeared within the ruling party: "de-politicization" and/or "no-contest" for the party's top posts. Promotion of these "new traditions" was intended to protect Mahathir from a repeat of his experience in 1987. Consequently, the increasing competitiveness within UMNO during Mahathir's early leadership (1981–87) was gradually, but systematically, restricted with the creation of UMNO (*Baru*). Factional rivalries in the 1990s were always confined to competition between second-echelon leaders of the party.

However, immediately after the 1995 general election, these second-echelon rivalries were being transformed into proxy battles between Mahathir and his deputy, Anwar. Unhappily for Mahathir, these factional struggles were largely won by Anwar and his supporters. Since 1995, whenever Mahathir initiated political manoeuvres to assert his political authority, there were immediate and clear counter-attacks by Anwar and his followers which showed Mahathir's weakening grip on the party. Although Anwar did not mount a grand challenge against Mahathir, the way in which the likely successor and his allies were seemingly planning an eventual take-over of power was not welcomed by Mahathir and his people. Indeed, party unity towards the end of the 1990s had already exhibited cracks; it was just waiting for something to break it apart.

There were numerous indications of the deepening factional antagonism between Mahathir and Anwar after the 1995 general election. To begin with, Mahathir checked Anwar's growing influence by asserting the prime minister's prerogative to determine government posts. In the cabinet appointments of May 1995, Anwar's political allies were restricted to less influential ministries or to positions where Mahathir could monitor their activities, while Anwar's rivals or opponents were promoted to senior portfolios. Anwar saw the 1995 cabinet reshuffle as a case of Mahathir blocking any chance he had of establishing a power base in the government, despite his increasing popularity in the party.[22] Many of Anwar's allies also believed that Mahathir had learnt how dangerous it was to allow a repeat of the Musa case in which Musa was able to control almost half of the top positions in the government before the leadership tussle in the mid-1980s.

A few months later, however, UMNO's divisional elections in September 1995 brought a strong reaction from Anwar. Overall, the election results showed only thirty-four new faces, or about 22 per cent of the total, and not all of those were Anwar protégés. However, leaders who were personally identified with Mahathir faced difficulties in retaining their divisional chairmanships. Despite Mahathir's open support, some of his main allies failed to be re-elected as divisional heads, including Daim Zainuddin, Sanusi Junid, Ghafar Baba, and Rahim

Tamby Chik. In particular, Sanusi was defeated in Kedah, Mahathir's home state, despite Mahathir's open support for Sanusi. In Kedah, six of the fifteen divisional heads were replaced. This was a high ratio of replacement compared with the other states.[23] Meanwhile, Daim decided not to contest when he was challenged as divisional head. Earlier, Daim announced that he would stay as Merbok UMNO division head only if he were not challenged.[24] One of Anwar's closest allies states that the 1995 divisional election was a straight fight between Mahathir's and Anwar's factions. Although Anwar did not directly reveal his political ambitions at this time, his clear intention was to demonstrate his own influence and perhaps show Mahathir's declining influence in the party. The informant believed that Anwar's machinery was working very hard during the campaign period.[25] Indeed, the election results were a subtle message that Mahathir was losing his grip on the party. It was in this context that people saw Anwar as a possible challenger to Mahathir at the triennial party elections scheduled in 1996.

After that, "rumours of crisis" and a "denial syndrome" characterized UMNO's internal life as both leaders repeatedly attempted to deny rumours of conflict. This recalls the on-off speculations of a rift between Mahathir and Musa prior to the 2Ms leadership breach in 1986. Although Musa and Anwar repeatedly professed their loyalty to Mahathir, speculation of a leadership tussle and a possible leadership split had been ceaselessly spread inside and outside the ruling party. The more they denied the leadership problem, the more others believed that a leadership battle was imminent. Open pledges of loyalty were viewed as nothing more than a political *wayang kulit* (shadow play).

In these circumstances, a "no-contest" resolution for the top two posts was adopted in the party assembly, which was held a few months after the 1995 divisional elections.[26] It was reported that the "no-contest" resolution followed Anwar's open declaration on "no intention of challenging the Mahathir presidency" a few days earlier at the party's Youth meeting.[27] However, Anwar's tutelage argues that the original idea came directly from Mahathir and was endorsed at the supreme council meeting. In a very odd situation where he could not go against the so-called collective decision, Anwar had to openly support the "no-contest" idea.[28] This move was widely viewed as Mahathir's way of pre-empting a possible challenge for the party presidency at the party election scheduled in October 1996. Mahathir's presidency, therefore, was successfully entrenched for another four years, until 1999, and Mahathir's grip on the party seemed to be consolidated.[29] The "no-contest" resolution, in theory, was expected to bury the speculation of a purported rift between Mahathir and Anwar in the run-up to the 1996 party elections. However, ironically, the "proxy battles" between Mahathir and Anwar became increasingly furious after the "no-contest" decision. There was a further move by Mahathir's faction to expand the "no-contest" decision to other party posts but it was limited to the party president and its deputy.[30]

A few months later, Mahathir's authority was again seriously undermined by a strong move initiated by Anwar's supporters. In March 1996, twenty-two of the twenty-five Kedah UMNO assemblymen signed a memorandum declaring that they would oppose any move by Mahathir to replace Osman Aroff, the state's Menteri Besar and alleged Anwar ally, with Sanusi, a Mahathir loyalist and long-time rival of Anwar. The memorandum was described as "an act of defiance" against Mahathir's authority. Eventually, the "twenty-two Kedah rebels" were forced to make a public apology to Mahathir, but did not back down from their demands.[31] Later, in May 1996, Osman resigned after intense pressure from Mahathir who then named Sanusi as Kedah *menteri besar*. However, this happened only after Mahathir's grip on the party had been already seriously undermined. Anwar, of course, openly expressed his regret over the act of defiance by the twenty-two Kedah assemblymen. Nonetheless, he never forgot to stress the right of the party members to air their views on the position of *menteri besar* by emphasizing that their views in the memorandum "should not be taken lightly or ignored".[32] It was widely believed that the fight between Osman Aroff and Sanusi was a shadow power play between Anwar and Mahathir, though some of the Kedah assemblymen may have had their own reasons for rejecting Sanusi. According to a close confidant of Anwar, Anwar revealed his strong displeasure with Mahathir's move to replace Osman Aroff with Sanusi at that time.[33] Meanwhile, it was also reported that Mahathir asked the Kedah assemblymen whether their action was instigated by Anwar. This suggests that Mahathir was already very suspicious and uneasy with Anwar as early as 1996.

With the party elections only a few months away, speculation on the number two taking on the number one continued despite Mahathir's "no-contest" resolution. In spite of Anwar's support for the "no-contest" resolution, party delegates were aware of what had happened during the 1993 party elections when Anwar challenged Ghafar's deputy presidency. At that time too, Anwar had publicly announced, at least three times, that he had no intention of challenging Ghafar. This was why the Mahathir-chaired UMNO supreme council introduced a new party rule that further restricted the right to challenge incumbents, including the party president. According to the new rule, aspirants for the top party posts must declare their intentions by registering with UMNO headquarters by 7 May 1996. Only those who did so could be nominated by the divisions and those who failed to register would not be allowed to contest even if they had been nominated as candidates.[34] Although this new rule was introduced in the name of reducing excessive politicking, it was widely believed that one of the key motives behind the new rule was to stop a possible divisional nomination for Anwar as a candidate of the party president during the divisional meetings scheduled just before the UMNO elections of 1996, as had happened when Anwar took over the deputy presidency from Ghafar Baba in 1993. In July 1996, the supreme council even pushed through an unprecedented rule that banned all campaigning in its October 1996 triennial party election.[35] Without a doubt, the new rules limiting challenges to incumbents favoured those closely associated with Mahathir. Several party leaders were barred from standing as candidates for the supreme council for violating the "no campaign" rule. It cannot be coincidental that most of them were in the Anwar faction.

However, again, Anwar's supporters sent a clear signal to Mahathir that his time was running out during the triennial party elections in October 1996. On the first day of the elections, the two Anwar "endorsed candidates", Zahid Hamidi and Siti Zaharah Sulaiman, won the leadership of the Youth and Wanita wings respectively against the incumbents Rahim Tamby Chik and Rafidah Aziz who were strongly backed by Mahathir. It was, then, just before another vote commenced on the second day of the elections that Mahathir "had to" produce an emotional speech in which he wept in front of the party delegates while criticizing money politics. Largely owing to Mahathir's tearful speech, the second-round battle for the three vice-presidents and twenty-five members of the supreme council favoured Mahathir.[36] Indeed, as Milne and Mauzy point out, Mahathir might even have faced greater pressure for an early leadership succession if Anwar's first-round victories had continued.[37] Mahathir later admitted that his "unusual display of emotion" might have affected the results of the vice-presidency and supreme council on the second day.

At this juncture, it was difficult to tell if there was a serious leadership split between Mahathir and Anwar. There was no grand challenge by Anwar's faction to Mahathir's national leadership though he had ample opportunity in 1996. Nonetheless, it was quite clear that Anwar and his political allies tried to create a perception that Mahathir's end was approaching. Anwar has often been perceived as impatient for Mahathir's retirement, while Mahathir repeatedly reminded him that he would set the terms of his own retirement. Anwar's supporters, in particular, became more impatient about his ascendancy when Mahathir did not show any sign of voluntary retirement. This made Mahathir and his followers suspect Anwar of disloyal intentions, despite his repeated description of Mahathir as his "mentor" and "political father".

For the ten years after the leadership struggle of the mid-1980s, Mahathir had made great efforts to avoid a recurrence of the situation where the number two was seen as equal to number one. By pre-empting every possible challenge from his rivals or opponents, Mahathir was able to consolidate his political hold on the party as well as the government. Nonetheless, towards the end of the 1990s, Mahathir seemed to be confronted with a similar political dilemma to the one he had faced with Musa preceding the UMNO leadership crisis of 1987.

From the very beginning of Mahathir's administration, Musa had been part of the "2M" leadership rather than merely the deputy prime minister. Although the term connoted an ideal combination of the "Mahathir-Musa" leadership, this made Musa virtually Mahathir's equal. Musa believes that it was a big mistake that his supporters and the press continuously labelled his combination with Mahathir as the 2M leadership without considering Mahathir's uneasiness with the term. For Mahathir, number one is only one and number two still has to be second.[38] Indeed, Mahathir's sensitivities towards the connotation of the term "2M" were revealed in his claim that "2M" stood for "Mahathir Mohamad" rather than "Mahathir-Musa".[39] Towards the mid-1980s, Mahathir's uneasiness became more obvious as Musa's influence and popularity grew in and outside of UMNO. Musa was widely viewed in public as Malaysia's prime-minister-in-waiting although Mahathir did not show any intention of early retirement. What was even worse, Musa's liberal and flexible attitudes had often been contrasted with Mahathir's authoritarian and intransigent leadership style.

Mahathir thought Anwar, being only in his forties during the mid-1990s, would not be in such a hurry to take over from him. However, Anwar's rise within UMNO, and nation-wide popularity, went far beyond Mahathir's expectations.[40] To all public appearances, it was just a matter of time until Anwar took over the national leadership. Faced with Anwar's broadly based support, Mahathir, much sooner than expected, encountered a rapidly growing pressure for generational change. Again, Mahathir's leadership style was increasingly compared with that of Anwar, often less than favourably, bearing comparison with Musa's case in the mid-1980s. Especially after the 1995 general election, Anwar's rapid ascent posed a direct political threat to Mahathir's supremacy.

The Mid-1997 Economic Crisis: Whose Blessing in Disguise?

Meanwhile, mid-1997 marked a point of change in the to-ing and fro-ing of the UMNO leadership tussle. Firstly, it was at this time that Anwar's adversaries started an organized campaign to defame his high moral character which had assisted his meteoric rise in the party. A *surat layang* (literally: flying letter), alleging Anwar's philandering and homosexuality, was circulated widely among party members. The flying letters, or poison-pen letters, were circulated with the name *Surat Dari Kota* ("letter from the city") and it was widely believed that the writer was closely associated with Mahathir and Daim. According to the flying letters, Anwar had not only an adulterous relationship with the wife of his confidential secretary but also a homosexual relationship with his wife's former driver.[41] Even though it was not the first time that poison-pen letters had been written about Anwar, in his own words, this time it was a "most concerted, well-organized and well-orchestrated" effort to bring him down politically.[42] Incidentally, the case of the poison-pen letters against Anwar reminds us of an earlier defamatory book, *Challenger: Siapa Lawan Siapa*, that aimed to injure Musa's character just a month prior to the UMNO elections of 1987.[43]

Secondly, the relationship between Mahathir and Anwar shifted into a new phase as the country faced the mid-1997 economic recession. In short, occasional differences between Mahathir and Anwar were getting more and more irreconcilable. A serious schism between the two leaders fuelled renewed speculation that Anwar would resign as Mahathir's deputy as well as finance minister. Towards the middle of 1998, Mahathir's counter-attack on Anwar and his followers seemed to intensify. Similar to the 1987 UMNO leadership crisis, the economic crisis that struck Malaysia from mid-1997 highlighted the lines of fracture and deepened the power struggle between Mahathir and Anwar. However, as implied earlier, the regional economic crisis was only one contributing factor, and occurred at the end of the underlying political struggle or imagined split between Mahathir and Anwar.

Mahathir's support for an Anwar succession was still plausible at least until mid-1997, as shown in the appointment of Anwar as acting prime minister before Mahathir's two-month overseas leave in May 1997. Since Musa's acting premiership in September 1985, no Mahathir deputy has been designated acting prime minister, despite Mahathir's frequent absences from the country. It is still not clear whether Anwar's acting premiership was a major endorsement of Anwar by Mahathir or a probationary test to gauge his loyalty and capability as Mahathir's successor. Whatever the motives, Anwar's two-month tenure as acting prime minister proved him a capable leader and seemed to confirm his position as Malaysia's prime-minister-in-waiting. This worried Anwar's adversaries in the party and a group of politically well-connected corporate figures who had become fabulously wealthy with Mahathir's blessing. During Anwar's acting premiership in mid-1997, he launched one of the hottest issues on the national agenda, "the all-out war against corruption". In doing so, Anwar proposed the Anti-Corruption Bill 1997 to increase the powers of the Anti-Corruption Agency as well as enhancing penalties for corruption offences. Even though the new Anti-

Corruption Bill 1997 was endorsed by the Cabinet, it was alleged that some ministers had strong reservations. For them, Anwar's drive against corruption, by proposing the Anti-Corruption Bill 1997 in particular, was a threat to their futures. This was why the anti-Anwar forces were more determined than ever to undermine his ascendancy by circulating the allegations of sexual impropriety against him soon after Mahathir's return from leave. The poison-pen letters were later "upgraded" to a defamatory book, *50 Dalil: Mengapa Anwar Tidak Boleh Jadi PM* ("50 Reasons: Why Anwar Cannot Be Prime Minister") and widely distributed among party delegates during the June 1998 annual meeting of UMNO.

At an early stage, rumours of Anwar's philandering and homo-sexuality were confined to UMNO circles. It seems that Mahathir did not orchestrate the sexual conspiracy against Anwar. Indeed, in August 1997, it was Mahathir who got the police to carry out an investigation of the earlier allegations that showed the rumours were baseless.[44] Perhaps, the sex allegations against Anwar would have ended there. The mid-1997 economic crisis, however, triggered a series of developments that impacted adversely upon the Mahathir-Anwar relationship. Interestingly, it was none other than Mahathir's open statements on Anwar's sex scandal that publicized Anwar's sexual misconduct nation-wide.[45] Many of Anwar's allies thought that Mahathir's intermittent reminders of the sex allegations against Anwar were a very tactful way of keeping the issue of Anwar's alleged immorality alive, in order to put him in a vulnerable position if Mahathir's national leadership was weakened by the economic crisis.[46] They believe that the distribution of the book, "50 Reasons", during the UMNO general assembly of 1998 was a clear example of Mahathir's diabolical methods. Without Mahathir's endorsement, the book could not have been distributed among the delegates, especially by the party secretariat, despite Anwar having obtained a court injunction preventing its distribution, said his wife, Wan Azizah.[47] Hence, it was not surprising that the police began to investigate, according to Mahathir's directive, the contents of the book immediately after the party general assembly.

There is little evidence of any organized, or systematic, effort by Anwar and his followers to oust Mahathir after the mid-1997 economic recession. But it was quite clear that Anwar tried to create a perception inside and outside UMNO that Mahathir's style in running the country was not appropriate. Even though there was no grand challenge to Mahathir's leadership, there was no doubt that Anwar, or at least his associates, saw the worsening economic situation as a circumstantial advantage, if not a much awaited opportunity, to promote the idea of an early leadership succession, especially in circumstances where Anwar's adversaries had initiated a scurrilous character assassination on him by circulating the sex allegations.

Moreover, it was around this time that the foreign media began to highlight Mahathir's conspiratorial analysis as unproductive, incorrect, and even reckless as he frequently denounced foreign speculators as the main culprits behind the regional financial crisis and vowed to ban foreign currency trading in the country. The more he censured outside forces for the economic downturn, the more he became the target of criticism by the foreign media. During this period, some observers and the foreign media even suggested that Mahathir step down in favour of his deputy.[48] Towards the end of the year, as the country's economic situation deteriorated further, the general public also became more and more critical of Mahathir's controversial leadership. Subsequently, Mahathir's national leadership seemed to be very vulnerable at least for the first few months after the beginning of the mid-1997 economic downturn.

More unpleasantly for Mahathir, Anwar was thrust into the international spotlight as one of the leading younger generation of leaders in Asia. In particular, Anwar's more liberal and flexible approaches to the regional financial crisis were increasingly highlighted by the foreign media at Mahathir's expense. What was even worse, Anwar, on his part, seemed to try and cultivate an image as a modern and liberal leader by stressing all the big issues, such as democracy, human rights, civil society, and so on, that were popular in the Western countries but not with Mahathir.[49] Anwar's skilful use of image-making alienated Mahathir, as shown in his letter:

> As a high-ranking member of the administration, I often had to articulate and implement key policies [mega projects]. And when these were policies that I was personally unhappy with, I did so with great reluctance. But I took every opportunity to emphasize poverty eradication, low-cost housing, rural development, and small and medium-scale industries instead of mega projects.

And whenever the opportunity to be bold presented itself, I criticized bailouts and the avarice of big tycoons and I called for greater commitment to democratic practices and the development of civil society.[50]

Towards the end of 1997 in particular, with economic confidence sinking fast, Anwar seemed to reveal a reluctance to support Mahathir's unprofitable "mega projects" and certain bailouts associated with Mahathir, including Mahathir's eldest son Mirzan's KPB, the Bakun Dam project, and UEM's bailout of Renong. In fact, Anwar's apparent reluctance to support Mahathir-initiated mega projects was shown, on several occasions, even before the mid-1997 economic crisis. However, as the country faced economic downturn, Anwar frequently showed his unhappiness with a number of mega projects. Despite Mahathir's strong attachment to the mega projects even in the wake of the economic downturn, Anwar initiated the delay and the shelving of some of them, including Bakun Dam, the Northern Airport, and the KL Linear City. Again, Anwar made it clear that there would be no selective rescue nor bailout of an ailing private company by the government when he announced additional austerity measures on 5 December 1997. It should be noted that several of Mahathir's close associates were already facing serious financial problems at this time. It was also around this time that Anwar's allies claimed on a number of occasions that a small circle of Mahathir's cronies had benefited most from lucrative state patronage through privatization, though they did not criticize Mahathir directly.

For Mahathir's part, a series of developments from July 1997, such as differences in approach towards the economic crisis, the foreign media's growing criticism of him and Anwar's lukewarm attitude to the bailouts of his son and close allies, was clear indication of a well-considered move to undermine his national leadership and eventually to force him out of office. Mahathir was certainly none too pleased with various things Anwar had done in the wake of the economic crisis. It was in this light that Musa warned that the period towards the end of 1997 was a very risky time for Anwar's relationship with Mahathir as he was perceived as getting more impatient and preparing to take over power. As he pointed out:

By the end of 1997, the political leadership was already in a crisis mood. He [Anwar] was already touching on all the issues which I thought he should not with the PM, like what I did actually. It was basically based on my own experience. I knew what are the things that you need not and should not do when you are the DPM. And Anwar was repeating [what I did], but worse. … He has always been against the way Mahathir conducted himself and it showed the weakness of Mahathir's style. … I felt that Anwar should be more supportive rather than going off at a tangent and going somewhere else. … So, the line was so similar to my problem except it was more highlighted because of the high profile stand of Anwar.[51]

In particular, Anwar's unwillingness to save Mirzan's KPB was enough to convince Mahathir that Anwar was not prepared to protect his family and cronies' interests after his prime ministership.[52] In this context, a senior journalist asserted that Anwar had already exceeded Mahathir's own level of tolerance, by the end of 1997, by touching on the issues of cronyism and nepotism in particular.[53] Similarly, Musa made it clear that:

To put it in a very simple term, this is all about the search for the next leader who could ensure that the past leader and his cronies will not be in trouble … The more successors took action against predecessors, the more Mahathir [and his cronies] worried about their potential successor. … So he has to look for somebody whom he can absolutely trust. Musa was no, Ghafar was just temporary and Anwar became no.[54]

For the first few months after the mid-1997 economic crisis, Mahathir's strategy for political survival was not well co-ordinated. As mentioned earlier, Mahathir's initial response to the economic crisis was to blame foreign speculators, one of the conventional ways of consolidating national leadership by the Malay ruling élites. This time, however, such a strategy did not appear to be effective. On the contrary, though the economic crisis was largely due to external factors, Mahathir's frequent attacks upon foreign speculators rebounded not only in terms of the worsening economic situation but also as growing lack of confidence in his political leadership.

Mahathir's shrewdness as a political manipulator, however, should not be underestimated. At this point of his increasing unpopularity as leader, Mahathir raised an ethnic issue by singling out "the Jews" as the main culprits behind the economic crisis. Up to that point, even though he frequently blamed the economic downturn on the work of foreign speculators, his remarks were largely in code. However, on 10 October 1997, addressing a rally of about 10,000 Muslim villagers in Kuala

Terengganu, Mahathir directly criticized the Jews, like George Soros, for having a hidden agenda to block the progress of Muslims. Mahathir was quoted by the local press as well as the national news agency, Bernama, and his comments were then given extensive coverage in the international media, as saying:

> We may suspect that they, the Jews, have an agenda, but we do not want to accuse … incidentally, we are Muslims and the Jews are not happy to see the Muslims progress … the Jews robbed the Palestinians of everything, but in Malaysia they could not do so, hence they do this, depress the ringgit.[55]

A day later, Mahathir clarified that he merely stated that incidentally George Soros was a Jew and Malaysia is a Muslim-dominated country. Nonetheless, it was widely believed that Mahathir's anti-Semitic remarks were part of an elaborate attempt to divert the issue into a racial one to consolidate his leadership. As Musa mentioned, such racial tactics were nothing new in multi-ethnic Malaysian politics and, once again, Mahathir proved that his political career had been built on similar episodes of scapegoating, such as those demonstrated in the aftermath of the 1987 leadership crisis.[56] In 1987 the escalation of racial tension and subsequent ISA arrests, as a series of diversionary exercises in the midst of his leadership crisis, gave Mahathir a circumstantial advantage against internal challenges in the ruling party.[57] Whereas the Chinese were the main targets in 1987, this time "the Jews" were used as a diversionary card to get people to rally around him.

Mahathir's anti-Semitic remarks immediately escalated the foreign media's antagonism towards him. In particular, thirty-four U.S. congressmen drafted a resolution and sent a letter, dated 27 October, to demand Mahathir openly apologize or to resign as the Prime Minister of Malaysia. Perhaps more favourable to Mahathir, at this time tension had built up between Malaysia and the United States as the Clinton administration attempted to apply a U.S. domestic law, the Iran-Libya Sanctions Act 1996, to Malaysia because of Petronas's investment in the Iranian gas industry.[58] Subsequently, external pressures prompted Malaysian politicians, including opposition parties, and editorial writers of all stripes to denounce foreign interference in domestic political affairs and express full support for Mahathir. Public rallies, placards, car stickers, and badges expressing support for Mahathir were also widespread. Then,

Anwar announced that he would move an unprecedented parliamentary vote of confidence in Mahathir following all nine *menteri besar* and four chief ministers' vowing to support Mahathir's leadership.[59] The state leaders pledged their unconditional support for "*all actions that had been or would be taken by Dr Mahathir in handling the country's economic problems*".[60] As Mahathir himself believes, the well co-ordinated upsurge in nationalistic sentiment after mid-October provided him with advantageous conditions to recapture the ground that he had lost in the wake of economic crisis.[61]

Not surprisingly, it was just one day after the passing of the motion of confidence in Parliament that Mahathir took the political initiative by proposing the setting up of a National Economic Action Council (NEAC) to oversee the country's economic recovery. In recommending the council's formation, Mahathir implied that the proposed council could be compared with the National Operations Council (NOC), which suspended Malaysia's Constitution and ruled the country after the May 13 racial riots in 1969, by saying that "we will adopt a similar approach as we did during the Emergency even though we have not declared a state of emergency".[62] At this time, it was a moot point whether the proposed NEAC was to have executive powers or was merely advisory in nature. Nonetheless, some analysts argued that the formation of a trouble-shooting economic council was a clear move to protect, and/or bailout, a small group of corporate figures closely linked to the ruling party, and Mahathir in particular. It was also widely believed that the NEAC, as an *ad hoc* crisis council chaired by Mahathir, aimed to infringe Anwar's authority as finance minister in circumstances where Anwar showed differences in approach to handle the economic problems.

Meanwhile, Anwar also appeared to pre-empt the situation before the NEAC was fully established. On 5 December 1997, Anwar, as finance minister, announced a series of belt-tightening measures which were described as a "homegrown IMF program without the IMF".[63] Major austerity measures included: further cutbacks in 1998 government expenditure by 18 per cent, on top of the 3 per cent announced in the 1998 Budget on 17 October; revising 1998 growth to 4 to 5 per cent from 7 per cent previously; and reducing salaries of government ministers by 10 per cent. In addition, a number of mega projects were deferred.

Anwar also announced that there would be no government bailout of politically well-connected companies and corporate figures.[64] Anwar's announcement came after a cabinet meeting held in Langkawi on 3 December chaired by Mahathir, who approved the new economic measures. Some analysts believed that the December 3 cabinet meeting was the turning point of the Mahathir-Anwar relationship which was now on a collision course. Indeed, a series of developments after the December 3 cabinet meeting demonstrated the widening disagreement between Mahathir and Anwar. For example, on the day after the cabinet meeting, Mahathir openly affirmed that "the government will proceed with its plan for the RM10 billion land bridge project linking northern peninsular Malaysia and southern Thailand despite the ringgit's depreciation".[65] One day later, however, Anwar reversed Mahathir's stand by announcing that "neither Malaysia nor Thailand was in a position to start on the RM10 billion land bridge" when he unveiled the December 3 cabinet decision of the austerity package.[66] It took two days for Mahathir to break his silence and reluctantly endorse the-Anwar-initiated-austerity-measures as "necessary to restore confidence in the economy".[67]

A clear sign of Mahathir's effort to curb Anwar's capacity as Finance Minister was the appointment of former Finance Minister Daim Zainuddin, Mahathir's most trusted lieutenant, as executive director of the NEAC on 20 December 1997. Anwar was named as the council's deputy chairman with Mahathir as chairman. Mahathir made it clear that Daim would exercise full power to carry out the council's directives.[68] Though it was reported that Anwar viewed Daim as the right man for the NEAC executive director, Anwar was very upset about Daim's installation and confided in his close allies that "Mahathir is squeezing me".[69] Much later, Anwar wrote in a letter that he had suspected that Mahathir wished to remove him by December 1997.[70] Perhaps, at this time Mahathir was signalling Anwar to resign, in a similar way as he had to his former deputy Musa, who resigned in 1986. However, the signals in the mid-1980s were one-sided from Mahathir whereas in the Mahathir-Anwar case they were somewhat reciprocal. Therefore, it was not entirely surprising that the year 1998 saw the final rupture of the growing leadership conflict between Mahathir and Anwar.

Mahathir and Anwar: The Final Struggle

The UMNO supreme council elections were scheduled for mid-1999, and in March 1998 UMNO was to conduct elections in its 165 divisions. Given that each division elects eleven delegates to the general assembly that elects the supreme council, the March divisional elections, though local by nature, were regarded as a litmus test of the balance of power between Mahathir and Anwar. It was then widely anticipated that Anwar would receive very solid support at the upcoming divisional elections. Moreover, once the election campaign had begun, Anwar would be in an advantageous position because of the great turbulence and political change in neighbouring Asian countries at the time of the economic crisis. For these reasons, Anwar's camp expected to get a majority of votes. In particular, the Youth and Wanita wings were viewed as very solid Anwar strongholds.[71]

At the beginning of 1998, Mahathir's attempt to pre-empt a possible challenge to his presidency began. In his efforts to minimize so-called "internal politicking", Mahathir advised would-be challengers not to contest the incumbent divisional heads who were supreme council members during the divisional elections scheduled on 12 to 29 March. In the same way, supreme council members who were not divisional heads were also warned against contesting the divisional head posts.[72] And, ten days later, the "no-contest advice" was followed by a "no-contest directive", banning contest for incumbent divisional heads in Kelantan from the Mahathir-chaired Kelantan UMNO liaison committee. Though the "no-contest directive" supposedly only applied to Kelantan, Mahathir did not forget to "advise" other UMNO divisions to avoid disruptive contests through internal compromise in the run-up to the divisional elections.[73] As expected, the "no-contest directive" in Kelantan was followed by similar moves in other states, such as Selangor, Perlis, Terengganu, Pahang, and Sabah.

Without doubt, Mahathir's "advice" and the subsequent "directive" on "no-contest" were strategies for retaining the status quo by discouraging Anwar's supporters from challenging the incumbent divisional chiefs who presumably accepted the continuation of Mahathir's leadership. As for supreme council members who were mostly divisional chiefs, Mahathir was unwilling to see any changes in the council's composition in favour of Anwar. Owing to the "no-contest directive", a number of supreme council members who were facing possible challenges by Anwar's allies were able to retain their divisional head posts. Interestingly, it was alleged that the majority of supreme council members who were not divisional heads at this time were made up of close associates of Anwar. Their electoral eligibility was usurped by the "no-contest directive" although most of them were well-prepared to stand against pro-Mahathir incumbent divisional chiefs.[74]

The outcome of the divisional elections, in general terms, showed that the status quo had been maintained, especially for the posts of divisional chief. There were only twenty-four new divisional chiefs in the 165 divisions. In other words, more than 80 per cent of the incumbent leaders were retained during the elections. In particular, Perlis, Perak, Pahang, and Terengganu saw a 100 per cent success rate for the incumbent divisional chiefs, as shown in Table 7.1. Nonetheless, it was still arguable whether Mahathir's advice on no-contest had worked effectively in the run-up to the divisional elections, especially if one scrutinized the result of the other key divisional posts — the deputy and vice-chairmen, and the Youth and Wanita chiefs. For instance, 35 per cent of divisional deputies and 52 per cent of divisional vice-chairmen had changed. Especially for the Youth chief's post, nearly 60 per cent were new. In fact, considering about 40 per cent of the incumbent chiefs had exceeded the forty-year age limit, a great number of the changes had been widely expected before the elections. Nevertheless, the drastic turnover of almost 60 per cent of new UMNO Youth leadership was enough to suggest that Mahathir's advice of no-contest had been disregarded. In fact, before the elections, Anwar and his close allies indicated that Mahathir's advice should be confined to divisions held by supreme council members and not extended to all division chiefs or other division posts.[75] It was, then, an open secret that Anwar's electoral machinery worked very hard in the run-up to and during the divisional elections. Indeed, the divisional election results were only to confirm the growing discrepancy between the two leaders. The outcome of the divisional elections pointed to possible manoeuvring for the party presidency in the following year's UMNO supreme council elections.

TABLE 7.1
The Number of New Faces in the 1998 UMNO Divisional Elections

	Divisions	Chief	Deputy	Vice Chief	Youth Chief	Wanita Chief
Perlis	3	—	2	2	2	—
Kedah	15	2	3	8	7	1
Penang	11	2	4	8	5	3
Perak	23	—	1	8	13	4
Kelantan	14	3	7	8	7	2
Terengganu	8	—	—	3	5	2
Pahang	11	—	5	7	3	6
Selangor	17	2	2	8	13	2
Negeri Sembilan	7	2	3	2	4	2
Malacca	5	3	4	4	2	1
Johor	20	5	10	13	14	8
Sabah	20	1	8	7	11	2
FT, Labuan	11	4	8	7	7	4
Total	165	24	57	85	95	37
(percentage)		(14.5)	(34.5)	(51.5)	(57.6)	(22.4)

Source: *The Star*, 18 April 1998, p. 20.

It was therefore not surprising that, soon after the divisional elections, further steps were taken to insulate the Mahathir presidency from challenges. To begin with, as happened in the run-up to the 1995 UMNO annual assembly, yet another "no-contest" resolution for the top two posts — the party presidency and deputy presidency — was proposed by Mahathir's supporters. If the resolution was passed during the June 1998 UMNO annual assembly, Mahathir's presidency would be successfully entrenched for another four years up to 2002. In addition, several amendments to the UMNO constitution were proposed by Mahathir's allies. The proposed amendments included the tightening of qualifications for potential challengers running for division and high-level posts, by requiring a minimum 25 per cent of the total number of nominations cast, different from the existing constitution whereby one only needs two nominations from the divisions to make a challenge for any post.[76] Some even proposed the deferment of the scheduled 1999 supreme council elections until after the general election in 2000.[77] There is no doubt that these amendments were all aimed at consolidating Mahathir's presidency by preserving the incumbent party leadership. Interestingly, it was around this time that Mahathir resumed his attacks on foreign currency speculators after several months of relative silence.[78]

This time, however, party delegates were unlikely to endorse the "no-contest" resolution. On the contrary, there was already pressure on Mahathir to allow challengers from Anwar's camp. In particular, the UMNO Youth chief Zahid Hamidi, an Anwar backer, urged the Youth executive committee members not to table any proposal calling for "no-contest" for the movement's top two posts with a view "to ensure democracy remains fertile in UMNO".[79] Immediately after this, Anwar welcomed Zahid's willingness to face possible challenges in the 1999 UMNO supreme council elections as a way of preserving "the spirit of the constitution as well as the democracy and the healthy culture in the party".[80] Again, Zahid's remarks and Anwar's positive response fuelled renewed speculation on the possibility of Anwar challenging Mahathir in the 1999 UMNO supreme council elections.

As the rift between Mahathir and Anwar widened, yet another external factor began to impact upon their relationship. This was the explosive political situation in Indonesia which came to a head in May 1998. In the wake of the mid-1997 economic crisis, Soeharto became the main target of public fury over his involvement in *korupsi* (corruption), *kronisme* (cronyism), and *nepotisme* (nepotism). The Indonesian *reformasi* movement finally forced the once mighty Soeharto to step down on 21 May. Around May and early June, Mahathir became more paranoid as various political groups in and outside Malaysia began to draw parallels between him and Soeharto. Some of them openly suggested that the time had come for Mahathir, having been in power for seventeen years by July 1998, to step down and make way for a new generation of leaders. The general public, already critical of Mahathir's controversial leadership in handling the country's economic crisis, showed increasing support for an early Anwar succession. An informal survey over the Internet in mid-1998 showed that only 16.7 per cent of the respondents had confidence in Mahathir's handling of the economic crisis, whereas 64.6 per cent of them felt Anwar was the best person to lead Malaysia out of the crisis. The opinion poll also showed extravagant spending on unimportant projects, corruption, and nepotism were the most serious problems under the Mahathir government. In this regard, 65 per cent of the respondents felt the necessity of political reform if Malaysia were to emerge stronger from the crisis.[81]

It was around this time that Anwar himself publicly stressed the need to "reform" the Malaysian version of "corruption, cronyism, and nepotism" in order to avoid an Indonesian-style crisis. Anwar even talked about the positive elements of the economic crisis by emphasizing "creative destruction" to cleanse society of corruption, cronyism, and nepotism.[82] In particular, at a Johor UMNO convention on 8 June 1998, Anwar warned of the dangers of Malaysia facing a similar crisis to that of Indonesia where people demanded changes, if *reformasi* were not undertaken. Though Anwar's call for reform did not necessarily mean an early leadership succession, for Mahathir the *reformasi* slogan in Indonesia meant nothing more than the ousting of the Soeharto presidency. For Mahathir, the adoption of the same *reformasi* rhetoric and the anti-KKN (*korupsi, kronisme, nepotisme*) campaign by Anwar and his supporters was aimed at achieving the same result. The timing of Anwar's call for *reformasi* in particular, unveiled about a week before the upcoming UMNO general assembly, was transparently mischievous. Soon after Anwar's call for reform, a lot of noise was made about the question of cronyism and nepotism by Zahid and other like-minded members. Rumours of plans to "boo" Mahathir's opening speech and a subsequent "plot" by thirty-odd MPs planning to demand Mahathir's resignation during the party's general assembly were widely circulated at this time. All this was enough to convince Mahathir that there was an organized effort to force him out of office in the wake of Soeharto's downfall in Indonesia.

Having sensed the imminence of Anwar's attack upon his leadership, Mahathir took systematic steps to emasculate Anwar in the run-up to, and during, the UMNO general assembly. First of all, Mahathir gave a series of public warnings not to make "unsubstantiated" claims about nepotism and cronyism a few days before the assembly. Meanwhile, Daim called Zahid and advised him to step backward from his strong criticism on nepotism and cronyism for the sake of his own political future. This happened just eight hours before Zahid was supposed to deliver his speech. Then Zahid asked Saifuddin, then the Youth secretary, not to distribute the already-printed text of his speech because of some amendments to the context of the speech.[83] Defying a pre-assembly warning by Mahathir, Zahid brought up the issue of cronyism and nepotism as a top agenda item, but in a slightly more moderate manner. But it was, in fact, Anwar himself who asked Zahid to delete all the strong words against Mahathir from his speech. Anwar, however, gave his blessing to Zahid to raise the issue of nepotism and cronyism in a way that indirectly challenged Mahathir's leadership. Immediately after Zahid's speech, Mahathir retaliated against accusations of nepotism and cronyism by releasing a list of names which showed that Anwar's relatives and close associates, including Zahid himself, had also benefited substantially from privatized state contracts and special share allocations.[84] At the same time, 2,000 copies of the defamatory book, *50 Dalil: Mengapa Anwar Tidak Boleh Jadi PM*, were distributed to UMNO delegates by the party secretariat, despite Anwar having obtained an interim injunction preventing its distribution on 17 June. It was then no surprise that Mahathir ordered the police to re-investigate the "contents" of the book, although an earlier police investigation had revealed that the sexual allegations against Anwar were baseless.

No formal resolution prohibiting contests for the top two posts in the next year's supreme council elections was proposed during the party assembly. After successfully outmanoeuvring critics at the crucial assembly, however, Mahathir accelerated his counter-attack. Despite Anwar's repeated pledge of loyalty during and after the party assembly, Mahathir's distrust of his protégé became irreversible. On 24 June, three days after the assembly, Daim was named Special Functions Minister and given executive powers for co-ordinating efforts to oversee economic development. The appointment of Daim, as virtual finance minister, deliberately undermined Anwar's political future as finance minister and as heir apparent. Soon after Daim's return, the tight-fisted monetary and fiscal policies of Anwar were replaced by the more expansionary polices favoured by Mahathir.[85] Then, within a few weeks, two of Anwar's strongest allies, Johan Jaaffar and Ahmad Nazri Abdullah, were forced to resign as the chief editors of the two major Malay newspapers, *Utusan Melayu* and *Berita Harian*, respectively. This was followed by the resignation of the director general of TV3, the country's largest private television network. All three positions were later filled by pro-Mahathir figures. This was viewed as a pre-emptive move to limit the possibility of an Anwar counter-attack.

In the mean time, soon after the assembly, Mahathir shrewdly linked the issue of nepotism and cronyism with that of foreign machination to instigate Malaysians and eventually topple the government. It was not surprising, then, that Zahid changed his stance on the allegations of nepotism and cronyism by being forced to say that such practices did not exist in Malaysia.[86] Incidentally, it was around this time that Malaysia's relations with Singapore were troubled by the issue of the relocation of Malaysia's immigration checkpoint in Singapore. The relocation of Malaysia's Customs, Immigration, and Quarantine (CIQ) operation in Singapore had been a controversial issue as early as 1992. The issue, however, became a bitter one after early July 1998 as the scheduled date (1 August 1998) of relocation of Singapore's CIQ to the new Woodlands Train Checkpoint (WTCP) from Tanjong Pagar was approaching. The dispute with Singapore gave Mahathir an opportunity to mobilize nationalist emotion around his leadership. It was even argued that the issue would not have reached such an intense level if there were no serious internal politicking within UMNO. Throughout August, Mahathir made a series of official "meet-the-people" visits to all states. Officially, those tours were to explain to people the country's economic problems. It was, however, clear that the nation-wide trips were well-planned to reinforce Mahathir's popularity in the country by increasingly appealing to national solidarity.

In the midst of growing nationalistic sentiment, Mahathir appeared to consolidate his grip on power within UMNO circles. In early August, a special committee was set up under the instruction of the supreme council. The special committee, chaired by then UMNO secretary-general Sabaruddin Chik, was designed to propose several amendments to the UMNO constitution. The principal agenda of the committee was to review the "ten-bonus-votes" system which allows a candidate for the president or deputy president's post to gain ten votes automatically upon securing a divisional nomination. Anwar had used the ten-bonus-votes system to oust then UMNO deputy president Ghafar Baba in the run-up to the 1993 party elections. Other main agenda items of the special committee were a series of limitations preventing new party members from contesting senior party posts. Without doubt, these proposed amendments were to further institutionalize the incumbent's advantage in favour of Mahathir and his allies. Interestingly, a series of public pledges by state leaders around this time gave support only to Mahathir's leadership, unlike the simultaneous support for Anwar's leadership as in previous years.

Being well aware of impending political disaster, Anwar openly declared in Penang, where he was the UMNO liaison committee chairman, that he would ensure all eleven UMNO divisions to nominate Mahathir for party president. At this time, Anwar vowed that he would never challenge the party presidency and described himself as a student, whereas Mahathir was his teacher and someone who was more like a father to him. Anwar, however, did not forget to remind, in jest, UMNO members that they should make sure to nominate him for the number two post.[87] As an Anwar associate pointed out, this was a telling gesture of Anwar under siege attempting to secure Mahathir's assurance for his position as heir apparent in a reciprocal way.[88] Mahathir, however, paid but little attention to Anwar's request by sarcastically replying to Penang UMNO members not to forget to nominate "someone who wants to be deputy" in next year's party elections.[89]

Meanwhile on 31 July, Dato' S. Nallakaruppan, Anwar's occasional tennis partner, had been taken into police custody for questioning in connection with the defamatory book, "50 Reasons". Though Anwar obtained an interlocutory court injunction against the author and publisher on the same day, Nallakaruppan's arrest was aimed at Anwar and his allies. On 13 August, Nallakaruppan was charged under the ISA with unlawful possession of live ammunition, an offence carrying a mandatory death sentence upon conviction. It seemed that Nallakaruppan was detained in order to increase the pressure on Anwar. Then, the Attorney-General foreshadowed the possibility of further arrests in relation to the book, "50 Reasons".[90] After that, Bank Negara Governor and his deputy, Ahmad Mohd Don and Fong Weng Phak who were closely aligned with Anwar, were removed from their posts due to their differences with the government over the management of the economy.[91]

Their resignations, soon followed by currency control, were viewed as Anwar's final setback.[92] Mahathir's manoeuvrings finally led to Anwar's abrupt dismissal from office, expulsion from the party, ISA arrest, and trial in September 1998.

One day after Anwar's dismissal from government, a special UMNO supreme council was called to discuss the matter of Anwar's expulsion from UMNO. It is alleged that a few supreme council members suggested suspending Anwar from the party and waiting for the court's decision over Anwar's charges. However, as a supreme council member claimed, the meeting was already prepared for Anwar's expulsion. It was alleged that there was nothing the supreme council members could do to change Anwar's political destiny as the meeting had started with Mahathir's directive that he wanted Anwar expelled from UMNO. The supreme council member believed that if anyone were to object to Mahathir's directive during the supreme council meeting he or she would have shared the same fate as Anwar.[93]

Kamarudin Jaffar, Anwar's close confidant, believes that Anwar should have fought it out with Mahathir by raising the issue of nepotism and cronyism himself, not just through Zahid as he had done during the party assembly in June 1998. He argues that a direct challenge by Anwar would not have given Mahathir enough time or opportunity to plot to destroy Anwar politically by raising the question of Anwar's moral misconduct. Even if Mahathir had brought up the issue, it would not have been effective in his move to oust his deputy because the conflict would already be seen as a political challenge.[94] In addition, by launching an "all-out-war" at the June 1998 party assembly, the floating party delegates, or fence-sitters, would have been forced to side with Mahathir or Anwar. At least, Anwar's followers may have taken their chance to make their stand clear much earlier when they were still in a relatively strong position. Other close allies of Anwar said that they were willing to go for the "all-out-war" against Mahathir if an instruction had been given by Anwar at that time. And they believe that, if there had been a challenge, Mahathir's position would have been far more vulnerable, considering the leadership changes in neighbouring countries in the wake of the regional economic crisis.[95]

Yet, by re-affirming his loyalty to Mahathir during and after the party assembly, Anwar had left his camp completely bewildered. Furthermore, by distancing himself from Zahid, Anwar even lost a degree of loyalty from his own supporters. Again, as Kamarudin Jaffar points out, "Anwar was over-confident until it was too late and until power was taken away from him. It was because of his hesitation that Mahathir took an opportunity to go on the offensive to remove Anwar's power base".[96]

The nature of Anwar's sacking suggests that Mahathir had learnt from his past experience with Razaleigh, who had allowed the opportunity to continue to challenge him from within mainstream Malaysian politics. In the case of Anwar, Mahathir effectively pre-empted any possible challenge from him by sacking him from the ruling party as well as the government. Furthermore, the subsequent imprisonment of Anwar significantly eroded his supporters' hope of his making a political comeback. By doing this, Mahathir not only eliminated any prospect of Anwar's challenge to his national leadership but also demonstrated that he could guarantee the protection of his cronies. Consequently, the ousting of Anwar from the government and UMNO enabled Mahathir and his cronies to consolidate their political and economic revenues without the threat of Anwar and his followers.

The Rise of the New Politics of Multi-Ethnic Awareness

Anwar was dismissed as deputy prime minister and finance minister on 2 September 1998, the day following Mahathir's controversial decision on currency controls. The very next day Anwar was expelled from UMNO. No sooner had he been ejected from the ruling party than Anwar launched a *reformasi* movement, highlighting the abuse of power and corruption by Mahathir's government, and called for Mahathir's resignation as well. It was reported that Mahathir offered Anwar the options of resignation from his government posts or criminal charges. Anwar refused to resign. Some suggested that Anwar should have accepted Mahathir's demand and wait for a future opportunity for a political comeback. Then they remembered Musa's voluntary resignation after his years of uneasy cohabitation with Mahathir. Many of Anwar's allies, however, believed that his only option was to take his political struggle to the people and rally public support by highlighting the issues of reform in Malaysia. According to Kamarudin Jaffar, a close confidant of Anwar,

Musa's resignation was viewed as a tactical withdrawal of "one step backward to move two steps forward" as there was the possibility of a political comeback through majority support of the supreme council members. In Musa's case, it was Musa who was on the offensive. But, in Anwar's case, it was Mahathir who was on the offensive. Kamarudin argues that Anwar's resignation would have been regarded as a desperate political setback not only to the public but also within UMNO circles.[97] After initiating a series of nation-wide public rallies, Anwar was finally detained without trial under the ISA on 20 September until charged in court at a preliminary hearing on 29 September when he appeared with signs of beating while in police custody.[98] Many political observers within and outside the country saw Anwar's sacking, expulsion and the subsequent detention as the denouement of a long political battle between Mahathir and his chosen successor. Nonetheless, such drastic measures failed to bring an end to the political confrontation.

A Return to "Normalcy"?

For a while after Anwar's dismissal, very serious élite divisions within UMNO circles, between Anwar's supporters and detractors, were widely expected, as had occurred in the wake of the UMNO split of 1987 when Razaleigh secured defections of a significant section of the ruling political élites. This time, however, similar fractures did not happen. On the contrary, Mahathir actually strengthened his hold on power within UMNO by keeping the ruling political élite, including seasoned political figures and even many of Anwar's allies, collectively on his side. In so doing, as mentioned earlier, Mahathir ruthlessly eliminated Anwar from the ruling party through a well-orchestrated special UMNO supreme council meeting. By removing any possibility of Anwar's comeback into UMNO politics, Mahathir could secure almost unanimous support of UMNO leaders. Within a few day of Anwar's expulsion, all UMNO MPs, *menteri besar*, cabinet ministers and deputy ministers, parliamentary secretaries, and UMNO division leaders came out in full support of Mahathir's decision. Indeed, UMNO leaders, remembering events of a decade ago and the consequences of siding with the wrong leaders, did not want to put themselves in a difficult situation. They tended to choose the easier and safer way.

Unlike the aftermath of the UMNO leadership crisis of 1987, there were no serious political purges against Anwar's allies, especially at senior levels of the UMNO leadership. Nonetheless, this did not necessarily mean that Mahathir's adversaries within UMNO were free of political oppression. It was alleged that the UMNO supreme council used various types of action against Anwar's supporters especially at the divisional level. These included expulsions, show-cause letters, warnings and suspension of membership. A UKM social scientist claimed that over the year since Anwar's dismissal, an average of four out of eleven UMNO divisional delegates had been sacked or subjected to other pressures for supporting Anwar and his *reformasi* movement. He argues that the political purge after the "Battle Royal" of 1987 was top-down but after Anwar's dismissal it was more from the bottom-up. In other words, Mahathir removed Anwar's colonels and captains rather then his generals.[99] To some extent, this was because what happened after Anwar's dismissal was quite different from what Mahathir had forecast. In the wake of Anwar's dismissal, anti-Mahathir feelings continued to run high in the country, though Mahathir and his close allies had thought that the Anwar episode would die down within a few weeks. Given the sensitivity of the issue and Anwar's popularity, the removal of more of his supporters from UMNO may have further undermined Mahathir's image and weakened the ruling party. The experience of the leadership crisis of 1987, during which a significant number of UMNO leaders challenged Mahathir's leadership after a series of political purges, made Mahathir reluctant to remove senior associates of Anwar within the ruling party. As another general election was approaching, those who were to be ousted might turn against Mahathir's leadership as such a situation would give them a chance to stand against UMNO candidates at the election. Under Malaysia's Constitution, the next general election had to be held before mid-2000.

Meanwhile, as a way of keeping Anwar's allies on side, Mahathir used the impending general election card very effectively. A well-known aide of Anwar, who sided with Mahathir after Anwar's expulsion, privately admitted that the forthcoming general election was one of the reasons why Anwar's allies, especially MPs and division leaders, seemed to distance themselves from him and his *reformasi* movement prior to and after his detention. Specifically, those who associated with Anwar feared that even irresolute attitudes would be subject to censure by Mahathir and, thus, their names would be left out of the list of candidates for the impending general election.[100] Indeed, Mahathir's government had hinted at the possibility of an early general election immediately after Anwar's dismissal. At this time, for those of the "rice bowl" mindset in UMNO, siding with Anwar was political suicide.

Outside UMNO, there were no immediate or widespread arrests after Anwar's dismissal, unlike *Operasi Lalang* after the UMNO leadership crisis of 1987. However, this did not mean that after the Anwar episode Malaysian civil society enjoyed a more open political arena. Authorities reiterated the possibility of arrests practically every day following Anwar's launch of *reformasi*. Well before Anwar's detention on 20 September, a series of arrests of his friends and associates was made. First, Sukma Darmawan, Anwar's adopted brother, was arrested on 6 September for his alleged involvement in acts of sodomy with Anwar. Next, Munawar Anees, Anwar's speechwriter, was detained on 14 September under the ISA on similar charges. Then, on the same day, Anwar's former private secretary in the Finance Ministry, Mohamad Ahmad, was arrested under section 117 of the Penal Code. After that, on 15 September, another of Anwar's former private secretaries, Mohamed Azmin Ali, was detained under section 117 of the Penal Code. Following Anwar's arrest on 20 September, sixteen of his political associates were also detained under the ISA. The detainees included leaders of Muslim youth organizations, including Angkatan Belia Islam Malaysia (ABIM, Malaysian Islamic Youth Movement), who were perceived as having wide political influence in the Islamic student movement. In addition, on several occasions Mahathir implied that Anwar's wife, Wan Azizah Wan Ismail, would be arrested. The selective ISA arrests continued in October and November, but expanded from the original core of Anwar supporters to those who organized and participated in the *reformasi* movement. Though there were no widespread ISA arrests, a culture of fear had already spread. An opposition leader commented that "we, in fact, expect another *Operasi Lalang* will strike the nation if Mahathir cannot control the current political situation".[101] Towards mid-November as the wet season began and the Muslim fasting month approached in December, street protests eventually subsided.

At the end of 1998, having dealt with Anwar's closest allies, Mahathir again manoeuvred to consolidate his power within UMNO. About one month after Anwar's sacking, seventeen amendments to the UMNO constitution were proposed by the constitutional amendment committee chaired by the UMNO secretary-general.[102] Most of the proposed amendments were passed at the UMNO extraordinary general assembly held on 13 December 1998. The amendments included: the removal of the ten-bonus-votes system; the requirement of a minimum of 30 and 20 per cent divisional nominations respectively for candidates for the party president and deputy president; and the empowerment of the supreme council to postpone the triennial supreme council elections. The provision of expulsion for life of any party member who contests the elections as an independent or opposition candidate was also included in the UMNO constitution.[103] These changes showed Mahathir's determination not to allow any possible comeback for Anwar or his supporters into UMNO politics. On 8 January 1999, Mahathir announced the postponement, for up to eighteen months, of the triennial supreme council elections, scheduled to take place in June 1999.[104] This prevented Anwar's remaining supporters or Mahathir's potential adversaries from mounting a leadership challenge at least until the end of 2000.

On the same day, Mahathir named Abdullah Badawi as Deputy Prime Minister as well as Home Minister. Mahathir's other loyalist Daim was appointed as Finance Minister. Among the senior UMNO leaders, Abdullah Badawi and Daim were the most anti-Anwar political figures. Although Mahathir relinquished two key posts, there was no doubt that he would continue to dominate the Cabinet. As *FEER* reported, "[Abdullah Badawi's] government will be predictable, there will be no change in policy, no change in the vision. So when Abdullah [Badawi] takes over, the Mahathir legacy will be preserved".[105]

In the aftermath of Anwar's dismissal these changes to the political and constitutional configuration of UMNO allowed Mahathir to reassert his power and patronage within the ruling party. In this context, Case argued that politics beyond Anwar in Malaysia would remain almost unchanged as Mahathir appeared to have effectively managed the crisis. In his recent study of UMNO factionalism and its effects on the system, Case concludes that:

> ... while on first blush the struggle between Mahathir and Anwar evokes serious divisions in élite-level relations, this break has neither been complete nor without precedent. Specifically, by isolating Anwar, Mahathir has regained the loyalties — or at least ensured the passivity — of the rest of the élite collectivity. ... Thus, if one believes that élite-level relations forge the most critical arena in which any meaningful political change must take place, Mahathir's regime would appear less threatened today than it was during the late 1980s, with the UMNO then splitting evenly into rival élite "teams".[106]

From "De-Politicization" to "Re-Politicization" and the Decline of Ethnic Politics

However, what distinguishes the Mahathir-Anwar tussle from the 1987 UMNO leadership crisis was that the former was not simply an intra-élite schism. In the wake of the 1987 UMNO leadership crisis, the conflicts were all within the UMNO context and were perceived as fairly typical, but rather intense, internal UMNO rivalry. The Anwar episode, however, drew people's attention from very different levels of Malaysian society, especially from the new generation of Malays. Together with the growing generalized grievances against Mahathir's cronyism and nepotism during the economic crisis, the excessive handling of the Anwar case acted as a catalyst for an unprecedented political awakening in the Malay community at large. In short, what happened after Anwar's downfall can be seen as a transition from "de-politicization" to "re-politicization" not only in the Malay community but also in Malaysian society as a whole.

Many political observers believe that if Anwar had been sacked only for his disloyalty, the Anwar episode would have been perceived as no more than a normal power struggle within UMNO, regardless of how unfair and unjust Mahathir was in removing him. However, Mahathir's humiliating treatment of Anwar in public was perceived by many Malays as cruel, vindictive, and even un-Islamic. It has been argued that Malay culture expects rulers not to impose their authority by shaming their subjects.[107] As Chandra Muzaffar observes, many Malays believe that since the colonial period UMNO has performed the role of "protector" of the Malays. For the last half century, this belief in a "protector-protected relationship" has been behind unstinting Malay support for UMNO.[108] However, the manner in which Anwar was humiliated and the way in which the state apparatus, the supposed-protector of the Malays, was used against unarmed demonstrators, mostly Malays, awakened a new generation of Malays from "political hibernation" or "false consciousness".

What may be more significant is the extent to which the political awakening has penetrated the rural Malay heartland, UMNO's political power base. Musa believes that Anwar's humiliation incited strong emotions among Malays and that this emotion cut across social, class, and regional boundaries. The question of Anwar's innocence or guilt was virtually irrelevant and the two Malay words, *kezaliman* (cruelty) and *kasihan* (pity), were at the very heart of anti-Mahathir sentiment. At this point, it was still debatable whether the widespread anti-Mahathir mood would translate into the erosion of Malay support for UMNO. Musa, however, made it clear that there were enough signs that for the first time ever Malays were starting to distance themselves from UMNO after Anwar's humiliation. He saw this as a clear indication that "dislike for Mahathir was transforming into dislike for UMNO".[109] A survey, indeed, showed that about 70 per cent of Malays were unhappy with the way that the "old man" treated his chosen successor.[110] Even within UMNO and government circles, quite a few party members and civil servants privately revealed their dissatisfaction with Mahathir's persecution of Anwar while significant numbers of UMNO members defected to opposition parties. A senior PAS official said that PAS membership increased by at least 8,000 per month. Thus PAS membership jumped by 20 per cent in the ten months after Anwar's dismissal. He argued that these new members were mostly from UMNO and, more importantly, covered a variety of the Malay community, old, young, rich, poor, learned, and non-educated, whereas before the Anwar episode the party usually attracted only young Malays.[111] An opposition leader stressed that "never before in the political history of the nation has the legitimacy of UMNO as the undisputed representative of the Malays been so seriously questioned and challenged".[112]

In sum, the anti-Mahathir mood in the aftermath of Anwar's

dismissal was not limited to UMNO leadership circles, as was to some extent the case of the 1987 UMNO leadership crisis. This time anti-Mahathir sentiment was widespread among the Malay grassroots. UMNO, therefore, can no longer take Malay support for granted. A series of political upheavals that have occurred since Anwar's dismissal reminds us of Przeworski's conditions that lead to the breakdown of authoritarian regimes. In particular, he emphasizes that "one would expect to observe mass unrest or at least mass uncompliance *before* any liberalization occurs".[113] As Francis Loh argues:

> The hegemony or ideological control of the government over the public has been broken and fragmented. Fissures have occurred. Sycophants aside, *the previous unquestioning loyalty among the public to the executive or party leaders has all but disappeared.* ... As never before a wide spectrum of Malaysian society has lost faith in many of the institutions of our parliamentary system [including the police, the judiciary, and the mass media].[114]

In this context, political commentator Rustam Sani argues:

> What happened to him [Anwar] is *a blessing in disguise*. If there had been a smooth transition of power from Mahathir to Anwar, only the personalities would have changed and the old system would have continued.[115]

When Anwar launched the *reformasi* movement, the objectives of his reform movement were somewhat unclear and even self-contradictory. Many of Anwar's critics claimed that if he had succeeded Mahathir he would have lead the country with the same system of corruption, cronyism, and nepotism as Mahathir. The argument commonly used was that Anwar started to promote *reformasi* only after his sudden political marginalization and the *reformasi* movement itself was in fact manipulated for his own political ends. Only a few people took seriously the so-called *reformasi* demonstrations, despite increased mass gatherings around Anwar. Others believed that this was mainly a matter of curiosity and, indeed, these activities were largely localized around Kuala Lumpur.

Indeed, as Farish Noor acknowledges, the so-called reformers, including Anwar supporters, opposition politicians, and NGO activists, were articulating a vague and ambiguous concept of *reformasi* without setting forth concrete programmes for reform.[116] Nevertheless, it should also be noted that the discourse of *reformasi* became deeply entrenched "everyday social and political reality" of Malaysia and appeared to be a very effective tool for "political and ideological confrontation" in Malaysian politics after Anwar.[117] What was perhaps more noticeable about the Anwar issue and the momentum of the *reformasi* movement was its catalytic role in the "political institutionalization" of a multi-ethnic consciousness which took a common stand against the political hegemony of the ruling BN coalition.

To begin with, two major multi-racial coalitions were launched while Anwar was in police custody on 27 September 1998. First, NGOs, headed by Suara Rakyat Malaysia (Malaysian People's Voice, SUARAM), initiated the formation of a multi-racial coalition calling for political, economic, and social reform in the wake of Anwar's downfall.[118] This was called Gagasan Demokrasi Rakyat (Coalition for People's Democracy, GAGASAN), comprising main opposition parties, including PAS, DAP, and PRM, and fourteen NGOs, mostly human rights organizations. As a NGO-led coalition, GAGASAN was designed to provide a forum for disparate opposition parties and NGOs seeking alternative ideas and programmes to those of the ruling BN coalition. According to Tian Chua, GAGASAN pro-tem chairman, the idea of forming GAGASAN as a social movement was mooted even a year before Anwar's dismissal when the country encountered the economic crisis of mid-1997, though the Anwar issue acted as a catalyst for materialization of the idea.[119]

Secondly, PAS reacted quickly to take advantage of the Anwar episode. The same day GAGASAN was formed, PAS launched another coalition, called Majlis Gerakan Keadilan Rakyat Malaysia (Council of Malaysian People's Justice Movement, GERAK), whose membership was similar to that of GAGASAN — PAS, DAP, PRM, and a dozen mostly Islamic NGOs including ABIM. The PAS-led GERAK, however, had a rather distinct Malay-Muslim flavour in its activities in the rural Malay areas. While GAGASAN focused on much longer-term objectives, GERAK's agenda was centred on the abolition of the ISA. Despite similar membership components, the main activities of the two coalitions were distinctive and mutually supportive. According to Tian Chua, GAGASAN attracted the urban-based, multi-racial middle classes through closed-door meetings, and through its programmes and seminars. Meanwhile, GERAK, with its strong grassroots networks, aimed at mobilizing lower-income peoples, especially in rural Malay communities.[120] Neither coalition acknowledged formal links with Anwar, though in general terms the formation of both stemmed from the Anwar case. A senior PAS official Subky Latiff pointed out that GERAK had no formal link with the Anwar-led *reformasi* movement, though it had sympathy with Anwar and his family.[121] Tian Chua also mentioned that the idea of GAGASAN was not restricted to campaigning for Anwar, even though members actively participated in the public protests held in the wake of Anwar's dismissal.[122]

Apart from these two coalitions, an amorphous but broad mass-based *reformasi* (reform) movement emerged in support of Anwar. As Farish Noor observes, this movement was actively involved in most public rallies in the aftermath of Anwar's expulsion from UMNO.[123] Unlike GAGASAN and GERAK, it tended to focus sharply on the issue of Anwar's imprisonment and sought his restoration and Mahathir's resignation. This broadly based movement was led by Anwar's family and his strong supporters. For ten weeks after Anwar's arrest, the *reformasi* group continued as a large mass movement, mobilizing grassroots support for Anwar and promoting anti-Mahathir sentiment, especially among the urban-based Malay middle class.

It was only after the public rallies subsided in early December 1998 that the Anwar-led *reformasi* movement was transformed into a formal multi-racial organization. This was called ADIL (Pergerakan Keadilan Sosial or Movement for Social Justice) and was led by Wan Azizah Wan Ismail, Anwar's wife. The formation of ADIL was the first official step by Anwar and his supporters to transform the *reformasi* agenda from a narrowly pro-Anwar one to a broader one of political, economic, and social reform. As Wan Azizah stressed, the issue was no longer only about Anwar's political fate but had snowballed into something bigger that promotes the reformation of the whole system of Mahathir's authoritarianism.[124] For a while, ADIL remained a multi-racial social coalition. This was because ADIL wanted to attract the support of the disparate political and social groups representing different racial and religious backgrounds.

Along with the political institutionalization of social mobilization, the most distinctive characteristic of Malaysian politics after Anwar was the changing attitude of the Malay middle class. Bell and his co-authors generalize that the middle classes in Asian countries are actually beneficiaries, not adversaries, of authoritarianism and therefore less willing to promote liberal democratic values.[125] Gomez and Jomo also described the expanding Malaysian middle classes in the 1990s as highly "materialistic" and unlikely to take "the avoidable risks of seeking reforms" of authoritarian forms of governance.[126] Similarly, in his earlier study of the middle class in the 1980s, Crouch assumes that the relatively prosperous Malaysian middle class provided a solid base of support and principal justification for an authoritarian style of politics.[127] Crouch's observation on the close relation between the middle class and regime stability has been evidenced in a series of by-elections and general elections in the 1990s, as the growing middle classes became the prime sources of popular support for the Mahathir government, despite its growing tendency towards authoritarian forms of governance.[128] Most interestingly, Saravanamuttu's survey of the Malaysian middle classes' attitudes shows not only that a remarkably high proportion of the Malays were satisfied with Malaysian political system which they considered as "just" and "fair", but that a large proportion of non-Malays — although less than that of the Malays — also agreed that the system was "fair". In particular, 91 per cent of the Malay middle class "agree" or "very much agree" that the Malaysian electoral system is fair, whereas 59 per cent of the Chinese and 62 per cent of the Indians replied positively to the same question.[129]

The Malay middle classes' attitudes, however, changed drastically after the removal of Anwar. The middle classes were not the main forces of popular upsurge in the aftermath of Anwar's dismissal. Nonetheless, for the first time unprecedented numbers of the Malay middle class were deeply involved in the *reformasi* movement. As Francis Loh points out, it was because of the changing attitudes in this previously pro-government Malay middle class that "expectations ran high for a change of government" in the run-up to the 1999 general election, although, for reasons discussed later, the change did not occur.[130] Shabery Chik, special assistant to Razaleigh Hamzah, stresses that the change in attitude among the Malay middle class is not just a cyclic occurrence. Middle-class Malays have also influenced attitudes among lower-income peoples in rural Malay communities through personal contacts and organizations, like ABIM and JIM, during the *reformasi* period and up to the general election. Shabery believes that, unless UMNO gives serious consideration of the Malay middle classes' change in attitude and role, UMNO's loss of legitimacy among them will spill over into the whole of Malay society.[131]

Furthermore, a significant number of middle-class non-Malays were involved in the *reformasi* movement. Although their participation in street demonstrations was lacking, their voices were heard in promoting the issues of justice, human rights, and democratic values. Their involvement was more issue-based and multi-racial in character.[132] In short, a significant section of the non-Malay middle classes, many of whom had been quite apathetic to politics, followed political developments more closely and critically than before Anwar's expulsion, even if they had yet to translate their views into action. An obvious example of the increase in political participation among young or previously apathetic groups was the registration of 680,000 new voters during the 1999 registration period, held about six months after the detention of Anwar. This was almost half a million more than the usual 200,000 new voters registered per annum. Many believe that the increased number of new registrants was motivated by the Anwar issue and they probably would have voted for the opposition coalition, if given the chance.[133]

What further distinguishes the post-Anwar political situation from the post-1987 UMNO leadership crisis is that there was no serious racial tension. Obviously, fear of racial riots was widespread in the country as Malaysians witnessed the bloody racial killings in Indonesia. The possibility of racial rioting in Malaysia was also suggested by the main-stream media, especially during *reformasi* demonstrations. However, unlike the dangerous racial disputes which occurred after the 1987 UMNO leadership crisis, the post-Anwar situation showed little sign of growing racial tension. On the contrary, the *reformasi* demonstrations seemed to lower racial barriers between the Malay and non-Malay communities. Musa also observes that there has been a considerable decrease in racial politics during the *reformasi* phase. In the past, he had said:

... any demonstration of any nature in Kuala Lumpur or Penang would always turn racial. Even if they were against the government, they would burn the Chinese shops. If the *reformasi* movement and demonstrations could be given any significance in terms of Malaysian politics — if there is anything that I could unhesitatingly come to [consider] a positive conclusion — it never turns racial. It's amazing. In the old days, people would be afraid of it turning racial. To me the *reformasi* movement is significant. It is more issue-based than racial. I'm fascinated.[134]

What then made Malaysian politics after Anwar less racial in character? First, the general Malay perception towards the Chinese communities in the 1990s was not as antagonistic as it had been in the 1970s and 1980s. This was largely because of the impact of the New Economic Policy (NEP) over the past two decades and the country's high economic growth during the 1990s. This resulted in the creation of a large multi-racial middle class in Malaysian society, especially a large, well-educated, young urban Malay middle class, and considerably diluted economic barriers between Malays and Chinese. It is significant that young urban middle-class Malays were at the forefront of most of the *reformasi* demonstrations after Anwar's dismissal.

Besides, the non-Malay communities did not perceive the UMNO leadership crisis as an opportunity to pursue their own political and social rights, as they did in the aftermath of the UMMO leadership crisis of 1987. On the contrary, around this time the non-Malay communities were concerned with possible reversion to the politics of racialism from what is called the politics of "developmentalism" and "cultural liberalization".[135] This was also one of the main reasons why the Chinese communities and DAP leaders noticeably separated themselves from the *reformasi* movement. They viewed Anwar's sacking and expulsion as an internal UMNO affair, at least at the initial stages of the *reformasi* movement and, thus, did not become deeply involved in Anwar-led *reformasi* demonstrations. The possibility of collision between Malays and Chinese in 1998, therefore, was much less than in 1987. Furthermore, the main issues following the 1987 UMNO leadership crisis were largely racially sensitive matters, whereas after the more recent crisis the key issues were non-racial ones, such as the abuse of power, corruption, and transparency.

Several other particular factors also contributed to the decrease in racial politics at the time of the 1998 crisis. First, the case of Lim Guan Eng attracted wide sympathy not only among Chinese but also among many Malays because he had been imprisoned for defending the rights of a Malay girl who was an alleged victim of statutory-rape by then Melaka Chief Minister Rahim Tamby Chik. Lim Guan Eng, MP for Kota Melaka and deputy secretary-general of the DAP, went on trial in January 1996 and was sentenced in April 1998 to two concurrent eighteen-month jail terms for printing a political pamphlet, *Mangsa Dipenjarkan, Penjenayah Bebas* (Victim Imprisoned, Criminal Free), criticizing the government for not pressing statutory-rape charges against Rahim Tamby Chik.[136] As a way of promoting his multi-racial stance, Anwar often showed solidarity with Lim Guan Eng by recalling his concern and sympathy for the Lim Guan Eng case well before his own dismissal from the government. As a symbolic gesture, Anwar signed a DAP petition seeking a royal pardon for Lim Guan Eng on a visit to a DAP branch in Kajang during the *reformasi* movement.[137] The reduced significance of race was suggested when Malays joined Chinese and Indians to welcome Lim as he emerged from the prison on his release on 25 August 1999. Also, Tian Chua drew enormous Malay support for his active involvement in the Malay-dominated *reformasi* movement. During *reformasi* demonstrations, he was arrested at least four times and emerged as a hero among many Malays.[138] Despite the individual nature of these cases, they contributed to the bridging of the racial divide before and during the *reformasi* movement.

After the removal of Anwar, one of the main factors contributing to the decrease in racial politics was the changed attitude of Malaysians towards the mainstream media. Until recently, a majority of the Malaysian public depended heavily on mainstream media for general information and their understanding of political developments. Reporting in the mainstream media, however, was often grossly biased in favour of the government and, thus, reinforced and legitimized the established power structure. Moreover, the effects of media partisanship were even more serious given the relative weakness of, and restriction on, alternative mass media; that is, the organs of opposition parties and NGOs, weeklies, and monthlies. All these alternative sources were both financially weak and very limited in their circulation. The 1990 general election offered a good example of how far the government-controlled media would go to foster racial fear in the interests of the ruling political élites within the short period of three or four days before polling.[139]

This time around, however, public antagonism towards the mainstream media increased noticeably over the unfair coverage of the Anwar issue. The mainstream media's lack of credibility resulted in a dramatic increase in alternative media's popularity. In particular, *Harakah*, the biweekly organ of PAS, increased its circulation extraordinarily, from approximately 60,000 to 300,000 per issue, in the wake of Anwar's dismissal. The total sales of *Harakah* reached around RM700,000 per week. Considering the estimated 200,000 circulation of the two main English newspapers, *NST* and *The Star*, it could be said that *Harakah* became a *de facto* mainstream newspaper after Anwar's downfall.[140] *Aliran Monthly*, a more middle-class oriented critical publication, also more than doubled subscriptions and street sales during late 1998 and early 1999.[141] Besides these, several new political magazines, such as *Detik* and *Eksklusif*, were launched and circulated widely around this time. Other political material, such as videos, cassette tapes, and even VCDs were in high demand. Moreover, a significant number of Internet sites became very popular among Malaysians and played a crucial role in promoting pro-Anwar and pro-*reformasi* material.[142] These alternative sources provided serious competition to the pro-government mainstream media since the Malaysian public was very anxious to receive credible news and critical analyses of the political upheaval of the country.

In short, as mentioned earlier, UMNO leadership conflicts are nothing new in Malaysian politics; the removal of Anwar, however, acted as a catalyst for the resurrection of Malaysian civil society. First of all, what makes Malaysian politics after Anwar different from the previous UMNO leadership crisis of 1987 and its aftermath is the Malay community's unprecedented disenchantment with UMNO leadership. The other significant change in Malaysia's political life after Anwar's dismissal is the emergence of a new politics of multi-ethnic awareness in Malaysian civil society, especially among the young Malaysian middle classes. As Francis Loh stresses:

Whereas ethnicity previously dominated the discourse and practice of Malaysian politics, it no longer does so, or at least not to the same predictable extent. Recent developments especially those that occurred over the past two years suggest that *a new discourse and practice of participatory democracy, not merely electoral and procedural democracy, has gained ground among Malaysians of all ethnic groups.*[143]

The 1999 General Election and Its Implications

On 4 April 1999, with Anwar's endorsement and in anticipation of an early general election, ADIL turned into a political party, KeADILan (Parti KeADILan Nasional or National Justice Party), led by Wan Azizah. KeADILan is a multi-racial political party. Along with former UMNO members, key multi-racial reformers, like Chandra Muzaffar (JUST), Tian Chua (GAGASAN), Irene Fernandez (Tenaganita), and many ABIM leaders, were prominent within the KeADILan leadership. And it was widely expected that the multi-racial KeADILan would be situated as a middle group in the coming general election between the Malay-based PAS and the Chinese-dominated DAP, just as former UMNO-splinter party Semangat 46 was in 1990.[144]

Until the 1990s, elections in Malaysia, as Crouch observes, had been perceived as just a routine ritual-casting of a vote every four or five years to provide "a cloak of legitimacy for what is really authoritarian rule".[145] Certainly, the rules of electoral competition in Malaysia do not seem to be designed to allow the electorate to change the government, even though they allow an element of choice. Due partly to the delineation of electoral constituencies in favour of rural Malays, opposition parties have never been able to prevent the ruling coalition from securing its two-thirds majority in Parliament, except in 1969 when racial rioting led to the postponement of voting in East Malaysia. Even in 1969, the ruling coalition obtained 64.1 per cent of parliamentary seats in the peninsula with only 48.4 per cent of the total number of votes cast.[146] In 1990 the ruling coalition gained over 70 per cent of parliamentary seats with only 52 per cent of the total vote.[147] As long as elections in Malaysia are largely contests for ethnic support and opposition parties are divided along ethnic lines, the multi-ethnic ruling coalition's two-thirds majority in Parliament seems to be impregnable.

The 1999 general election, however, was not viewed as another ritualistic and orchestrated exercise legitimating the UMNO-led government's authoritarian rule.[148] Malaysia's four main opposition parties, PAS, DAP, PRM, and KeADILan, formed an unprecedented and better-than-expected multi-ethnic opposition coalition under the common banner of the Barisan Alternatif (Alternative Front or BA). After much deliberation, the allied opposition parties nominated Anwar as their candidate for prime minister, seeking to provide a "capable" and "collective" leadership as an alternative to the ruling BN government. On 20 September 1999, the BA issued a statement regarding its nomination of Anwar as opposition candidate for prime minister. Given Anwar's six-year jail sentence that began in April 1999, the BA announced that there would be an interim prime minister, if it came to power, and a fair judicial inquiry for Anwar regarding the alleged political conspiracy against him. The BA then proposed that it would allow Anwar to lead the country once justice was delivered.[149] Finally in October 1999, as the general election approached, the BA announced a common election manifesto and even an alternative budget.[150]

Indeed, it was not the first time that opposition parties had formed an electoral alliance, as the elections of 1969 and 1990 showed. There was an electoral alliance among the opposition parties in the west coast states of Peninsular Malaysia in the 1969 general election, involving DAP, PPP (People's Progressive Party), and the newly formed Gerakan Rakyat Malaysia.[151] For the first time in electoral history, however, PAS and DAP united as a multi-ethnic opposition coalition under one banner with a common election manifesto. In 1990, Razaleigh's Semangat 46 had to form two separate opposition coalitions; one with PAS and other Muslim-based parties (APU) and the other with DAP and other predominantly non-Malay parties (Gagasan Rakyat), due to the mutual distrust between PAS and DAP. There was no common ground at all, especially between PAS and DAP, except the need to avoid contests with each other and they used their own banners in campaigns. Even Semangat 46 and PAS could not come up with a common election manifesto due to their ideological differences over the establishment of an Islamic state. As Razaleigh admitted, the two separate opposition coalitions were formed in a hasty manner due to "the need of accommodation" as the election was very near.[152] It was even argued that the very reason Razaleigh combined with PAS and DAP was the "political convenience" of toppling Mahathir's government, without any long-term basis for accommodation within the opposition.[153] There were straight fights in more than 90 per cent of the constituencies in the 1990 elections. It was, however, widely reported that the opposition parties, PAS and DAP in particular, carried out their internecine fight even after nomination day. The voters' confidence in the opposition therefore eroded considerably during the election campaign. Such deep discord in the opposition was clearly stated in a senior DAP leader's remark as follows:

> The 1990 opposition coalition was not a tripartite arrangement. DAP had something to do with Semangat 46 and PAS had something to do with Semangat 46. However, DAP had nothing to do with PAS for political reasons. So, that was a terrible disadvantage of DAP to be seen on the same platform with PAS.[154]

The preparation for the 1999 general election, however, involved a much longer process of co-operation within the opposition, even before the removal of Anwar. Especially after Anwar's sacking and the subsequent upheaval, there was a greater commitment from the opposition to come up with a common platform. This was due to the strong pressure from the grassroots, especially among the young generation of Malays. According to Syed Husin Ali, there were a dozen meetings among the opposition parties before August 1999. But not one meeting was boycotted by any political party and at the meetings the same representatives were always present, except twice. He believes that there was a more sincere commitment in the opposition's preparation for the 1999 general election, compared with the "marriage of convenience" among the opposition parties in 1990.[155] Lim Kit Siang also admitted that the opposition groups faced much stronger pressure from the people to expand the limits of mere liberalization unleashed in September 1998.[156] In this regard, unlike 1990, the emergence of the opposition coalition came about not only because of the chance of a win in electoral terms, but as a response to the new political atmosphere which produced a greater commitment to a more open, accountable, and democratic government, among leaders and members of the opposition parties. Especially given the growing mass grievance over Mahathir's ruling style and widespread perceptions of the ruling coalition's corruption, political observers viewed the emergence of the multi-ethnic opposition coalition as a better opportunity, after the failure of 1990, to bring about a shift in Malaysian politics from one of single-party dominance to a two-coalition party system. At least, the BA anticipated obstructing the Mahathir government's authoritarian rule by depriving it of its two-thirds majority in Parliament.

The 1999 election results, however, did not meet the expectations of the BA. Although BN's popular vote declined significantly from the historically high level of 65.1 per cent in 1995 to a more normal 56.5 per cent in 1999, BN secured almost 77 per cent of parliamentary seats. On the surface at least, BN's convincing victory appeared to confirm yet again the hypothesis that electoral competition in Malaysia is little more than a ritual by which the UMNO-led government authenticates the legitimacy of its authoritarian rule.

Nonetheless, the opposition did not entirely fail to undermine the Malaysian political order of single-party dominance. A close scrutiny of the results demonstrates that considerable change has occurred in Malaysian politics. The 1999 general election revealed that a large number of voters were disenchanted with the ruling coalition, especially UMNO. First of all, BN's majority in parliamentary seats was reduced markedly from 166 to 148 out of 193. The opposition coalition was also able to decrease BN's state legislature seats from 350 to 281 out of 394, as shown in Table 7.2. More significant was the major shift in voting patterns among the Malays. Despite all the pre-election speculation about how much anti-Mahathir sentiment would be translated into real votes, UMNO's apprehensions were realized as the UMNO-led ruling coalition suffered serious losses in most of the Malay-dominated states of the north. As a result, BN lost another state, Terengganu, to the opposition, along with Kelantan. Barisan Nasional was all but wiped out in both states. Moreover, Malay votes went noticeably against the ruling coalition in Kedah, Perlis, and Pahang. This indicated a sharp erosion of Malay support for UMNO, which had been the main contributor to the ruling coalition's election victories for the last four decades.

As shown in the Table 7.2, UMNO lost twenty-first of its ninety-three parliamentary seats and sixty-six of its 242 state assembly seats respectively. For the first time, UMNO took less than half (seventy-two) of the total parliamentary seats (148) won by the ruling coalition. What is more disconcerting for UMNO, its winning margins in all but one of the fifty-nine parliamentary seats retained by UMNO in Peninsular Malaysia were greatly reduced, as shown in Table 7.3.

UMNO's top leaders, including Mahathir, Abdullah Badawi, Razaleigh, Rafidah, and Najib, showed declines in their winning majorities (see Table 7.3). Also, UMNO lost four ministers, six deputy ministers, one *menteri besar*, several state executive councillors, and

TABLE 7.2
**Parliamentary and State Assembly Seats
Won by Major Political Parties, 1995–99[a]**

	Parliament		State	
	1995	1999	1995	1999
UMNO	89 (93)	72	230 (242)	176
MCA	30	28	70	68
MIC	7	7	15	15
Gerakan	7	7	23	22
Others[b]	29	34	—	—
Total (BN)	162 (166)	148	338 (350)	281
DAP	9 (7)	10	11 (8)	11
PAS	7 (8)	27	33	98
Semangat 46[c]	6 (0)	—	12 (0)	—
KeADILan	— (1)	5	—	4
PBS	8 (6)	3	—	—
Others[d]	— (4)	—	— (1)	—
Total (BA)	30 (26)	45	56 (42)	113

[a] Figures within parentheses refer to the number of seats before the dissolution of Parliament.
[b] Includes the BN component parties in Sabah and Sarawak (PBB, SUPP, SNAP, PBDS, UPKO, SAPP, and LDP).
[c] Semangat 46 joined UMNO in 1996.
[d] Includes MDP, STAR, and Independent.
— = Data not available.

Source: Compiled from Zakaria Haji Ahmad, "The 1999 General Elections: A Preliminary Overview", in *Trends in Malaysia: Election Assessment*, Working Paper in the Trends in Southeast Asia series (Singapore: ISEAS, 2000), pp. 9–10.

parliamentary secretaries.[157] According to Francis Loh, UMNO's popular vote in constituencies where two-thirds of voters were Malay dropped significantly, from 62 per cent in 1995 to 49 per cent in 1999. Compared with the 1995 elections, UMNO's losses in its total vote in selected states were: Kelantan, −6 per cent; Terengganu, −14 per cent; Perlis, −12 per cent; Kedah, −9 per cent; Selangor, −31 per cent; Negeri Sembilan, −32 per cent; Penang, −25 per cent; and Malacca, −21 per cent. The losses in those last four states were even more serious than those of the states in the so-called Malay heartland in the north, though they did not result in seat losses for UMNO (see Table 7.6).[158]

The Muslim-based PAS registered major gains, though the election results were not favourable for other BA component parties, as shown in Table 7.2.[159] This was mainly because non-Malay voters largely supported BN candidates in contrast to the erosion of support among the Malays for UMNO and BN. Barisan Nasional's performance was outstanding in most multi-ethnic constituencies where no single ethnic group composed a majority. The BN won all but one of the sixty-one multi-ethnic constituencies where Malays comprised less than a two-thirds majority and the Chinese constituted less than half of voters in a constituency.[160] Indeed, the rally of non-Malay voters behind the ruling coalition did much to prolong Mahathir's eighteen-year rule.

The newly formed KeADILan obtained only a handful of seats in Parliament and the state assemblies. Yet, KeADILan candidates lost very narrowly in most multi-ethnic constituencies and the party's share of the popular vote was similar to the DAP's, as shown in Table 7.4. It was clear that KeADILan's multi-ethnic approach was well recognized in Malaysian politics, especially as no political space had been given for multi-ethnic parties in the past. DAP's performance in 1999 was no worse than in 1995, despite the losses of several of its prominent leaders. Indeed, what happened was that the party maintained its traditional stronghold but was unable to attract new support from the growing multi-racial Malaysian middle classes.

As Francis Loh observes, the figures demonstrated that the support among the Chinese for BN and BA was quite evenly distributed. For instance, in the twenty-four urban constituencies in the peninsula where Chinese comprised 50 per cent or more of the voters, the BN secured

TABLE 7.3
Winning Majorities in Parliamentary Seats Won by UMNO, 1995 versus 1999

State	Constituency[a]	Majority	
		1995	1999
Perlis	Padang Besar (82.57%)	10,070	4,519
	Kangar (78.05%)	11,000	4,049
	Arau (87.24%)	6,929	1,586
Kedah	Langkawi (90.63%)	8,425	6,547
	Kubang Pasu (83.71%) {Mahathir[b]}	17,226	10,138
	Merbok (55.71%)	22,201	15,376
	Sungai Petani (58.27%)	26,221	12,133
	Kulim Bandar Baharu (65.01%)	14,302	8,067
Kelantan	Gua Musang (91.1%) {Razaleigh[c]}	8,980	2,925
Penang	Kepala Batas (73%) {Badawi}	17,834	11,175
	Tasek Gelugor (76.6%)	12,651	4,236
	Balik Pulau (56%)	30,046	9,434
Perak	Larut (83.25%)	10,991*	4,009
	Bagan Serai (68.33%)	6,250	1,584
	Bukit Gantang (63.4%)	15,154	5,101
	Cenderoh (73.29%)	11,793	3,990
	Tambun (58.62%)	26,639	7,084
	Kuala Kangsar (64.69%) {Rafidah}	10,649	2,774
	Pasir Salak (78.29%)	17,115	5,045
	Bagan Datoh (56.29%)	14,830	4,617
Pahang	Lipis (53.91%)	10,113	6,356
	Jerantut (78.77%)	7,194	1,463
	Kuantan (54.5%)	23,096	7,361
	Paya Besar (81.93%)	16,759	3,563
	Pekan (90.88%) {Najib}	10,793	241
	Marah (90.31%)	14,046	3,748
	Temerluh (61.3%)	7,852	213
	Rompin (87.16%)	12,825	6,028
Selangor	Sabak Bernam (74.91%)	14,452	901
	Tanjung Karang (80.33%)	15,818	2,075
	Kuala Selangor (56.76%)	18,342	9,920
	Gombak (75.20%)	30,878	803
	Hulu Langat (59.45%)	30,812	3,866
	Shah Alam (60.54%)	40,715	1,440
	Kuala Langat (53.02%)	9,211	8,020
	Sepang (55.34%)	15,669	7,162

TABLE 7.3 (continued)
Winning Majorities in Parliamentary Seats Won by UMNO, 1995 versus 1999

State	Constituency[a]	Majority 1995	1999
Kuala Lumpur	Wangsa Maju (54.2%)	27,894	5,618
	Titiwangsa (60.4%)	18,966	1,513
	Lembah Pantai (54.1%)	13,389	1,454
Negeri Sembilan	Jelebu (62.15%)	2,940	7,119
	Jempol (56.46%)	15,704	11,919
	Tampin (62.99%)	23,452	9,979
	Kuala Pilah (75.47%)	20,600	2,818
Malacca	Alor Gajah (80.59%)	25,096	12,332
	Batu Berendam (53.61%)	22,325	7,288
	Jasin (67.09%)	22,128	10,691
Johor	Ledang (53.85%)	23,361	13,507
	Pagoh (60.05%)	17,599	12,857
	Mersing (68.49%)	13,525	10,861
	Parit Sulong (62.94%)	25,354	17,657
	Muar (63.46%)	9,483	7,182
	Sri Gading (67.71%)	26,350	17,558
	Batu Pahat (54.91%)	24,993	17,448
	Tenggara (56.61%)	24,518	20,817
	Sungai Benut (65.35%)	21,142	20,692
	Kota Tinggi (81.43%)	33,769	32,161
	Tebrau (50.82%)	39,140	35,485
	Johor Baru (47.8%)	34,118	24,558
	Pulai (57.75%)	29,403	24,568

[a] Percentage in constituency means the ratio of Malay population in the constituency.
[b] The winning majority of Mahathir in 1990 was 22,062.
[c] Razaleigh won as a Semangat 46 candidate in 1995.
* 1990.

Source: Kamarudin Jaffar (2000, pp. 24–25 and pp. 97–108).

only about 51 per cent of the popular vote cast, as shown in Table 7.5. And similar figures were found in the multi-ethnic constituencies in Peninsular Malaysia where no single ethnic group formed a majority.[161] Meanwhile, Francis Loh argues that BN polled only 45 per cent of the average popular vote and won only one of the nine Chinese-dominated

TABLE 7.4
Percentage of Votes and Number of Seats
Won by the BA in 1999
(Parliamentary, Peninsular Malaysia)

Party	% of Votes	No. of Seats
PAS	17.4	27
DAP	13.5	10
KeADILan	12.3	5
PRM	1.2	0

Sources: N.J. Funston, "Malaysia's Tenth Elections: Status Quo, *Reformasi* or Islamization?", *Contemporary Southeast Asia* 22, no. 1 (2000): 50.

constituencies where the Chinese comprised more than 80 per cent of the total number of votes.[162] Thus, it is a moot point whether the BN regained its two-thirds parliamentary majority because the Chinese deserted the opposition, though more Chinese did rally behind the ruling coalition. Barisan Alternatif's share of the popular parliamentary vote was 42.5 per cent in 1999.[163] Of this, only 23.3 per cent of the popular vote was reflected in Parliament (forty-five of 193 parliamentary seats) due to the first-past-the-post electoral system. Almost 35 per cent of parliamentary seats (fifty out of 144) in the peninsula were won with majorities of less than 10 per cent of the popular vote. The BN won twenty-nine of these seats. What is more important, the 680,000 new

TABLE 7.5
BN's Average Percentage Vote Polled in Malay-Majority[a] and
Chinese-Majority[b] Constituency in 1986, 1990, 1995, 1999 Elections

	1986	1990	1995	1999
Malay	61.18	54.86	59.25	48.80
Chinese	41.09	41.55	53.19	51.36

[a] Malays constitute more than or equal to two-thirds majority of voters in a constituency.
[b] Chinese constitute more than or equal to 50 per cent majority of voters in a constituency.

Source: Loh (2000).

registrants in 1999 who were not able to vote for dubious reasons constituted about 7.1 per cent of the 9,564,071 total registrants for the 1999 general election or 9.7 per cent of the 7,009,507 voters who actually voted in the parliamentary election.[164] As Francis Loh notes, the ratio of BN to BA parliamentary seats in Peninsular Malaysia would be seventy-three to seventy-one, if the BA had taken all the marginal seats through a 5 to 6 per cent swing in votes in favour of the opposition.[165]

Indeed, as shown in Table 7.6, the BN's support was noticeably concentrated in several states, especially Johor, Sabah, and Sarawak. The sixty-six seats gained from these three states account for almost 45 per cent of the total number of parliamentary seats won by the BN in the 1999 elections.

TABLE 7.6
Percentage of Votes in the 1999 Parliamentary Election (by State)

	Barisan Nasional[a]	Barisan Alternatif
Kelantan	38.9 (1/14)	61.1
Terengganu	41.2 (0/8)	58.8
Kuala Lumpur	50.2 (6/10)	49.8
Penang	51.4 (6/11)	48.6
Selangor	54.8 (17/17)	44.8
Perak	55.5 (20/23)	44.5
Kedah	55.8 (7/15)	44.2
Perlis	56.2 (3/3)	43.8
Melaka	56.6 (4/5)	43.4
Pahang	57.4 (11/11)	42.6
Negri Sembilan	59.2 (7/7)	40.8
Johor	72.9 (20/20)	27.1
Peninsular total	55.4 (102/144)	44.4
Sabah	59.4 (17/20)	4.9 (37.3)[b]
Sarawak	65.9 (28/28)	25.0
Labuan	71.3 (1/1)	10.8 (28.6)[b]
Grand total	56.5 (148/193)	40.3 (42.5)[b]

[a] Figures within parentheses refer to the number of seats won by the BN out of the total number of constituencies.
[b] Figures within parentheses included the PBS.

Source: Funston (2000, p. 50).

Summary

The survival of an authoritarian or semi-authoritarian regime may be threatened by conflicts within the ruling group. In Malaysia, therefore, a more responsive political system could be expected from factional splits in Malaysia's dominant political party, UMNO. There is, however, little evidence that the UMNO-led authoritarian regime became more democratic after the severe factional rivalries in 1987. Factional disputes within the ruling bloc, especially after Anwar's downfall in 1998, offer another opportunity to revisit the nexus between UMNO factionalism and the transition from authoritarian rule under Mahathir's leadership.

Superficially at least, learning from the experience of 1987, Mahathir made sure that Anwar was completely isolated from the mainstream of Malaysian politics. Anwar's legacies within UMNO appear to have petered out only a few weeks after his expulsion. The UMNO-led ruling coalition was then returned to power in the 1999 general election and retained its traditional two-thirds majority in Parliament. Barisan Nasional's victory, however, was won at a heavy price, especially for many in UMNO. The election results demonstrate a significant diminution of UMNO's domination of the popular Malay vote. UMNO could no longer take its traditional Malay allegiance and loyalty for granted. Indeed, the loss, or at least erosion, of support for UMNO from its traditional power base is really something new to Malaysian politics and goes beyond the similar crisis situation of 1987.

More importantly, the Anwar episode and its social, cultural, and political consequences disclosed a possible erosion of the politics of racialism. What distinguishes Malaysian politics after Anwar's dismissal from the previous UMNO leadership crisis of 1987 is the emergence of multi-ethnic awareness in Malaysian civil society, especially among the young Malaysian middle class. Unlike the previous elections, this time voting behaviour hinged more upon the question of leadership than ethnicity as the central issue: who could run the country with more accountable, more workable, and less corrupt processes. The 1999 election results also showed that the Barisan Alternatif, as a viable electoral proposition, has a reasonable chance of winning in a substantial number of multi-ethnic seats with only small swings in popular votes. It would be premature to conclude that Malay voters have abandoned UMNO and that cracks have begun to appear in the UMNO-led authoritarian regime. However, as Francis Loh argues, the ferment and fragmentation of Malaysian politics after Anwar makes a change of government a real possibility with only a small swing in voting behaviour — a far cry from the situation of the last few decades, when BN victory was ensured by the ritual casting of votes.[166] Shamsul also sees Malaysian politics beyond Anwar as the beginning of "new politics" of "resistance":

> Whatever the future holds, sooner or later Malaysia has to move on without Mahathir, even if Anwar is not at the helm. But nobody could deny that the "Anwar factor" has been critical in the making and consolidation of the "new" Malaysian politics, especially in building a democracy of which Malaysians can be proud of.[167]

It is, nonetheless, worth noting that UMNO has experienced several periods of severe factional strife but each time the party has retained its internal cohesion and re-emerged as strong as ever. Crouch also emphasizes that the dynamics of political competition can sometimes lead to a strengthening of authoritarian characteristics in the system, as the ruling élites are "not essentially [responding] to social and economic pressures", but "often motivated primarily by the quest for political power".[168] Meanwhile, a survey among UKM students, conducted by KeADILan before the 1999 election, showed that 80 per cent of the respondents were willing to vote for the opposition coalition, but only 11 per cent of this 80 per cent had confidence in BA's capacity to head the government.[169] As the survey implied, one of the key reasons the opposition parties were unable to turn their general support into real votes during the 1999 elections was not only due to external factors, but also to their own internal political weaknesses.

NOTES

1. *Sejarah Melayu (Malay Annals)*, quoted in Barbara Watson Andaya and Leonard Y. Andaya, *A History of Malaysia* (London: Macmillan Press, 1982), pp. 44–45.

2. Musa Hitam at the annual general meeting of UMNO branches in the Johor Baru division on 19 February 2000. Quoted in *Aliran Monthly* 20, no. 2 (2000): 8.

3. Anwar Ibrahim, "From the Halls of Power to the Labyrinths of Incarceration", a letter from Sungai Buloh prison on 3 November 1998.

4. *The Star*, 7 August 1996.

5. N.J. Funston, "Malaysia: A Fateful September", *Southeast Asian Affairs 1999*, p. 169.

6. Interview with Musa Hitam, former Deputy Prime Minister, Kuala Lumpur, 23 August 1999.

7. *Straits Times*, 23 September 1998.

8. *Straits Times*, 9 September 1998.

9. For a basic record of the Anwar trial, see *Asiaweek*, 13 November 1998 (Arjuna Ranawana, "Facts and Figures"). The background to, milestones and reports on, the Anwar trial can be traced at <http://straitstimes.asia1.com/anwar/anwarindex.html>.

10. For a record of the revised charges, see *Straits Times*, 14 January 1999.

11. Confidential interview in August 1999.

12. See *Straits Times*, 9 September 1999.

13. For a more detailed analysis of the economic crisis in Malaysia and the Southeast Asian countries, see Manuel F. Montes, *The Currency Crisis in Southeast Asia* (Singapore: Institute of Southeast Asian Studies, 1998); Ross H. McLeod and Ross Garnaut, eds., *East Asia in Crisis: From Being a Miracle to Needing One?* (London and New York: Routledge, 1998); and H.W. Arndt and Hal Hill, eds., *Southeast Asia's Economic Crisis: Origins, Lessons, and the Way Forward* (Singapore: Institute of Southeast Asian Studies, 1999).

14. Mahathir's view, that currency traders sparked the region's financial crisis, are well expounded in a book of Mahathir's speeches and articles. See Mahathir Mohamad, *In the Face of Attack: Currency Turmoil* (Petaling Jaya: Limkokwing Integrated, 1998).

15. See Funston (1999, especially pp. 167–68). According to a close associate of Daim, who asked not to be named, Daim also believed that the breakaway of the top two leaders had nothing to do with the economic situation (confidential interview on 21 August 1999, Kuala Lumpur).

16. An analysis of Mahathir's and Anwar's contradictory, but mutually supportive, approaches to the country's economic crisis can be found in Ranjit Gill, *Asia Under Siege: How the Asian Miracle Went Wrong* (Singapore: Epic Management Services, 1998).

17. Interview with Rais Yatim, Minister in Prime Minister's Department, Kuala Lumpur, 11 August 1999.

18. For more details on UMNO factionalism and money politics, see *Aliran Monthly* 15, no. 7 (1995): 2–9 ("Political Rivalry and Privatized Patronage"). See also E.T. Gomez and Jomo K.S., *Malaysia's Political Economy* (Cambridge: Cambridge University Press, 1997), especially pp. 124–30.

19. Anwar's letter to Mahathir dated 25 August 1998 in *Aliran Monthly* 18, no. 8 (1998): 12.

20. Interview with Kamarudin Jaffar, MP for Tumpat (PAS), Kuala Lumpur, 25 August 1999.

21. Musa Hitam's speech at the annual general meeting of UMNO branches in the Johor Baru division on 19 February 2000. Quoted in *Aliran Monthly* 20, no. 2 (2000): 10.

22. Interview with Kamarudin Jaffar, Kuala Lumpur, 25 August 1999. In 1995, Muyhiddin Yassin, the former *menteri besar* of Johor and an Anwar loyalist who had obtained the highest number of votes among the three vice-presidents in the 1993 party elections, was named Minister of Culture, Youth, and Sports (a relatively minor portfolio). Meanwhile, two other political confidants of Anwar, Nazri Aziz, then Acting Youth Chief, and Ibrahim Saad, the former Deputy Chief Minister of Penang, were made deputy ministers in the Prime Minister's Department. See *FEER*, 18 May 1995 (Jayasankaran, "Change and Continuity").

23. See the table in *The Star*, 5 October 1995 ("Polls See Eclipse of Some Big Guns").

24. *The Star*, 31 August 1995.

25. Interview with Saifuddin Nasution Ismail, Kuala Lumpur, 23 August 1999. Saifuddin was one of the leading figures who represented pro-Anwar Youth circles during the 1995 divisional elections.

26. *The Star*, 26 November 1995.

27. *The Star*, 24 November 1995 ("Anwar: Don't Nominate Me").

28. Interview with Saifuddin Nasution Ismail, Kuala Lumpur, 23 August 1999.

29. *FEER*, 7 December 1995 (Jayasankaran, "Still the Boss").

30. *The Star*, 30 September 1995 ("No Contest for Top *Wanita* UMNO Posts"); *The Star*, 19 March 1996 ("Zaharah: No Resolution Against Contest"); and *The Star*, 24 April 1996 ("Siti Zaharah: Contest Will Not Cause Split").

31. For more on the twenty-two Kedah assemblymen case, see *FEER*, 11 April 1996 (Jayasankaran, "Back Off"); *FEER*, 16 May 1996 (Jayasankaran, "Showing Who's Boss").

32. *The Star*, 27 March 1996.

33. Interview with Ibrahim Saad, former Deputy Chief Minister of Penang, 16 August 1999, Petaling Jaya.

34. For a fuller description of the new rule, see *The Star*, 7 April 1996.

35. *The Star*, 7 July 1996 ("Dr M: Ban to Ensure Fairness"). See also *FEER*, 25 July 1996 (Jayasankaran, "Equal Opportunity").

36. For details of the election results, see *FEER*, 24 October 1996 (Kulkarni, Murray

Hiebert, and Jayasankaran, "Succession Saga") and *Asiaweek*, 25 October 1996, pp. 27–28.

37. R.S. Milne and Diane K. Mauzy, *Malaysian Politics under Mahathir* (London and New York: Routledge, 1999), p. 155.

38. Interview with Musa Hitam, Kuala Lumpur, 23 August 1999.

39. Milne and Mauzy (1999, p. 40).

40. *Aliran Monthly* 13, no. 9 (1993): 2–6 ("Anwar Ibrahim: Prime Minister-to-Be").

41. More details on the flying letters, see *FEER*, 11 September 1997 (Jayasankaran, "Poison Pen").

42. *Business Times*, 26 August 1997.

43. Literally, "Challenger: Who's Fighting Whom?" For more on the defamatory book against Musa, see *The Star*, 17 April 1987 ("Musa Gets Order to Stop Sale of Book").

44. *NST*, 3 September 1997.

45. For the first open statement by Mahathir, see *The Star*, 25 August 1997.

46. Interview with Kamarudin Jaffar, Kuala Lumpur, 25 August 1999.

47. Interview with Wan Azizah Wan Ismail, President of KeADILan, Petaling Jaya, 26 August 1999.

48. *Time*, 6 October 1997 (Anthony Spaeth, "Man in the Middle").

49. See Anwar's interview with *Time* magazine on 6 October 1997 ("What Is Success Without Freedom?"). Also see Anwar Ibrahim, *The Asian Renaissance* (Singapore: Times Books International, 1996).

50. Anwar's letter from Sungai Buloh prison on 3 November 1998.

51. Interview with Musa Hitam, Kuala Lumpur, 23 August 1999.

52. In Mirzan Mahathir's case, it was reported that he had lost more than RM2 billion in his shipping company, Konsortium Perkapalan Berhad (KPB), in the wake of economic downturn (*Singapore Business Times*, 8 September 1997). Despite Anwar's "no bailout" announcement in December 1997, Petronas, wholly owned by the Malaysian government, eventually paid RM1.7 billion for Mirzan's KPB. See *Aliran Monthly* 18, no. 3 (1998): 2–5. However, there was a severe disagreement between Anwar and Mahathir over the amount of the bailout of Mirzan's KPB. According to Anwar, Mahathir was very displeased that Mirzan could not get the RM2.2 billion he wanted; instead, all he received was RM1.7 billion (see Anwar's letter from Sungai Buloh on 3 November 1998).

53. Interview with Shamsul Akmar Musakamal, then journalist of *The Star* and currently at *NST*, Petaling Jaya, 6 August 1999.

54. Interview with Musa Hitam, Kuala Lumpur, 23 August 1999.

55. *Bernama*, 11 October 1997.

56. Interview with Musa Hitam, Kuala Lumpur, 13 February 1998.

57. For more details, see Chapter 5.

58. In early October, it was reported that Total, a French energy company, and its consortium partners, Malaysia's national oil company Petronas and Russia's Gazprom, planned to invest US$2 billion to develop the Iranian gas industry, which the United States said defied U.S. sanctions legislation (*NST*, 1 October 1997). And, following Mahathir's anti-Semitic remarks and a U.S. congressman's draft resolution, the issue of possible U.S. sanctions on Malaysia was highlighted by the local Malaysian newspapers as interference with the sovereign rights of Malaysians.

59. The motion of confidence in Mahathir passed in Parliament on 19 November 1997. For the full text of the motion, see *NST*, 20 November 1997.

60. *NST*, 14 November 1997 ("State Leaders Denounce U.S. Congressmen's Move"), emphasis added.

61. See *NST*, 12 November 1997 ("PM: Quit Suggestion Made Me Stronger Instead"). For details of the political effect of external pressure on Mahathir's leadership, see *FEER*, 27 November 1997 (Jayasankaran, "Two-Edged Sword: Anti-American Mood Angers U.S. but Helps Mahathir").

62. *NST*, 21 November 1997 ("Economic Action Council Proposed").

63. *FEER*, 18 December 1997 (Jayasankaran, "Hit the Brakes").

64. For the full text of Anwar's announcement on new economic measures, see *NST*, 6 December 1997.

65. *NST*, 5 December 1997 ("Land Bridge Project Will Proceed, Says Dr Mahathir").

66. *NST*, 6 December 1997 ("Land Bridge Project Is Deferred, Says Anwar").

67. *NST*, 8 December 1997 ("PM: Tough Measures Necessary"). For more details of the December 3 cabinet decision and its consequence, see *FEER*, 18 December 1997 (Jayasankaran, "Hit the Brakes"); *Asiaweek*, 19 December 1997 (Assif Shameen, "Mahathir Shifts into Reverse").

68. *NST*, 21 December 1997 ("Daim Appointed NEAC Executive Director").

69. Interview with Saifuddin Nasution Ismail, Kuala Lumpur, 23 August 1999.

70. See Anwar's letter from Sungai Buloh prison, 3 November 1998.

71. According to one of Anwar's close allies, he had strong support in about seventy-five to eighty divisions out of 165 and substantial support in more. E-mail correspondence with Saifuddin Nasution Ismail on 25 April 2000.

72. *NST*, 16 January 1998 ("Let Supreme Council Members Retain Division Posts").

73. *NST*, 27 January 1998 ("No Contest for Top Kelantan Umno Posts") and *NST*, 7 February 1998 ("Dr M's Advice Seen as a Directive").

74. E-mail correspondence with Saifuddin Nasution Ismail on 25 April 2000.

75. Anwar and his close allies' unhappiness with Mahathir's "no-contest advice" had been intermittently, but openly, revealed in public. For example, see *NST*, 17 February 1998 ("Stay Neutral or Face Action, Anwar Warns Party Leaders"); *NST*, 10 February 1998 ("Ahmad Zahid: Allow Contests Where Changes Are Needed").

76. *Asiaweek*, 24 April 1998 (Sangwon Suh and Santha Oorjitham, "A Matter of Rejuvenation").

77. *NST*, 4 May 1998 ("Selangor Umno Wants Party Polls Postponed").

78. For more details, see *FEER*, 21 May 1998 (Murry Hiebert and Jayasankaran, "Mixed Signals").

79. *NST*, 9 May 1998 ("Umno Youth Posts Should be Contested"); *NST*, 20 May 1998 ("Ahmad Zahid Reiterates His Stand").

80. *The Star*, 11 May 1998 ("Anwar Backs Zahid's Call on Contests for Top Posts").

81. *Asiaweek*, 3 July 1998 (Sangwon Suh, "Speaking One's Mind").

82. In a confidential interview, a government official close to Daim claimed that Mahathir and his associates, Daim in particular, were even suspicious that Anwar and his allies might engage in economic sabotage in the wake of the Indonesian *reformasi* movement, by allowing the country's economy to deteriorate further for the purpose of ousting Mahathir. According to the official, around June and July 1998, Anwar's close allies met the Indonesian opposition leader, Amien Rais, to consult on how Malaysia might follow Indonesia's example. Mahathir was apparently furious with the Anwar group's close contacts with the Indonesian opposition.

83. Interview with Saifuddin Nasution Ismail, Kuala Lumpur, 23 August 1999.

84. *The Star*, 17 June 1998 ("Cronies All"); *The Star*, 22 June 1998 ("List on Show"). The full lists of the names can be found at <http://cnn.com/asianow/asiaweek/98/0703/nat_3_list.html>.

85. *Business Times*, 2 July 1998 ("DPM: RM5Bn to Revive Infrastructure Projects").

86. *NST*, 10 July 1998 ("Umno Youth Changes Stance on Allegation of Nepotism, Cronyism").

87. *NST*, 12 August 1998.

88. Interview with Ibrahim Saad, Deputy Minister in Prime Minister's Department, Petaling Jaya, 16 August 1999.

89. *NST*, 12 August 1998.

90. *NST*, 23 August 1998.

91. *NST*, 30 August 1998.

92. On 1 September 1998, the day before Anwar's sacking as Deputy Prime Minister and Finance Minister, Mahathir imposed capital controls and fixed the currency at RM3.80 to the U.S. dollar.

93. Interview with Ibrahim Saad, then UMNO supreme council member, Petaling Jaya, 16 August 1999.

94. Interview with Kamarudin Jaffar, Kuala Lumpur, 25 August 1999.

95. Interview with Saifuddin Nasution Ismail, Kuala Lumpur, 25 August 1999.

96. Interview with Kamarudin Jaffar, Kuala Lumpur, 25 August 1999.

97. Interview with Kamarudin Jaffar, Kuala Lumpur, 25 August 1999.

98. For eye-witness accounts of the public rallies in the run-up to the arrest of Anwar, see *Aliran Monthly* 18, no. 9 (1998): 19–30. A more comprehensive account and interpretation of the Anwar episode can be found at Fan Yew Teng, *Anwar Saga: Malaysia on Trial* (Selangor: Genting Raya Sdn. Bhd., 1999).

99. Interview with Shamsul A.B., Professor of Social Anthropology at Universiti Kebangsaan Malaysia, Bangi, 12 August 1999.

100. Confidential interview, Kuala Lumpur, August 1999.

101. E-mail correspondence with Teresa Kok, then a Central Committee member, and an MP from the DAP, 5 October 1998.

102. *Business Times*, 8 October 1998 ("Supreme Council Agrees to Amend Umno Constitution").

103. *NST*, 14 December 1998 ("15 Constitutional Amendments Passed").

104. *The Star*, 9 January 1999 ("Umno Polls Put Off to Next Year").

105. *FEER*, 21 January 1999 (Jayasankaran, "Tactical Retreat"). For further explanation of Mahathir's consolidation of power through the cabinet reshuffle, see *Asiaweek*, 22 January 1999, pp. 16–22.

106. William Case, "Politics Beyond Anwar: What's New?", *Asian Journal of Political Science* 7, no. 1 (June 1999): 15.

107. Andaya and Andaya (1982, pp. 44–50).

108. Chandra Muzaffar, *Protector? An Analysis of the Concept and Practice of Loyalty in Leader-Led Relationships within Malay Society* (Penang: Aliran, 1979), especially pp. 50–71 and 114–54.

109. Interview with Musa Hitam, Kuala Lumpur, 23 August 1999.

110. *FEER*, 29 October 1998 (Murray Hiebert, "A Single Spark").

111. Interview with Subky Latiff, PAS Central Committee Member, Kuala Lumpur, 9 August 1999.

112. Lim Kit Siang, "The Impact of the Anwar Ibrahim Case on Politics in Malaysia", paper presented at Griffith University, Brisbane, 4 May 2000.

113. Adam Przeworski, "Some Problems in the Study of the Transition to Democracy", in *Transition from Authoritarian Rule: Comparative Perspectives*, edited by Guillermo O'Donnell, Philippe C. Schmitter, and Laurence Whitehead (Baltimore and London: Johns Hopkins University Press, 1986), p. 50; italics in original.

114. Francis Loh, "A Nation on Trial", *Aliran Monthly* 18, no. 9 (1998): 7, italics added.

115. Interview with Rustam Sani, quoted in *Australian,* 28 December 1998, p. 6, italics added.

116. For a distinctive analysis of how the concept of *reformasi* was introduced, developed, and utilized in the Malaysian political arena, see Farish A. Noor, "Looking for Reformasi: The Discursive Dynamics of the Reformasi Movement and Its Prospects as a Political Project", *Indonesia and the Malay World* 27, no. 77 (1999): 5–18.

117. Farish A. Noor (1999, pp. 5–6).

118. SUARAM is a non-governmental organization committed to upholding human rights. It began as a campaign body for the abolition of the Internal Security Act (ISA) in 1989 after the 1987 *Operasi Lalang.*

119. Interview with Tian Chua, currently vice-president of KeADILan, Kuala Selangor, 24 August 1999.

120. Interview with Tian Chua, Kuala Lumpur, 10 August 1999.

121. Interview with Subky Latiff, Kuala Lumpur, 9 August 1999.

122. Interview with Tian Chua, Kuala Lumpur, 10 August 1999.

123. Farish A. Noor (1999, p. 11).

124. Interview with Wan Azizah Wan Ismail, Petaling Jaya, 26 August 1999.

125. Daniel A. Bell, David Brown, Kanishka Jayasuriya, and David Martin Jones, eds., *Towards Illiberal Democracy in Pacific Asia* (Oxford: St. Martin's Press, 1995).

126. For on analysis of why the middle class did not play a reforming role in Malaysia during the 1990s, see Edmund Terence Gomez and Jomo K.S., "Authoritarianism, Elections and Political Change in Malaysia", *Public Policy* 2, no. 3 (July to September 1998): 113–44.

127. Harold Crouch, *Domestic Political Structures and Regional Economic Cooperation* (Singapore: Institute of Southeast Asian Studies, 1984), especially pp. 5, 25–26.

128. For the specific results of the by-elections, see NSTP Research and Information Services, *Elections in Malaysia: A Handbook of Facts and Figures on the Elections 1955–1990* (Kuala Lumpur: NSTP, 1994), pp. 61–107.

129. For more details, see Johan Saravanamuttu, "The State, Ethnicity and the Middle Class Factor: Addressing Nonviolent, Democratic Change in Malaysia", in *Internal Conflict and Governance*, edited by Kumar Rupesinghe (New York: St. Martin's Press, 1992), p. 56.

130. Francis Loh Kok Wah, "Post-NEP Politics in Malaysia: Ferment and Fragmentation", paper presented at the Second Australia-Malaysia Conference, ANU, Canberra, 24–26 May 2000, p. 4.

131. Interview with Ahmad Shabery Chik, Special Assistant to former Semangat 46 president Razaleigh Hamzah, Canberra, 24 May 2000.

132. For more details of their activities, see Francis Loh (2000, pp. 3–4).

133. The 680,000 new registrants were not allowed to vote in the 1999 general election as the Election Commission (EC) claimed that their registration as eligible voters could not be processed until February 2000, due to the enormous increase in number of the new registrants.

134. Musa Hitam <http://www.malaysiakini.com/archives_news/2000/may/may6–7/news2.htm>. Weekend edition, 6–7 May 2000.

135. Francis Loh (2000).

136. For the details of the Lim Guan Eng case, see *Aliran Monthly* 18, no. 8 (1998): 32–37, 40 ("A Shameful Episode"); *FEER*, 18 June 1998 (Murray Hiebert, "Missed Opportunity"); and *The Rocket*, June 1999, pp. 43–47 ("Sedition Is a Serious Offence …").

137. For more correspondence between Anwar and Lim while in prison, see *Aliran Monthly* 19, no. 2 (1999): 4–7 ("Anwar Writes to Guan Eng" and "Guan Eng Replies to Anwar").

138. *Aliran Monthly* 18, no. 11–12 (1998): 24–25 ("Chua Detained … Again").

139. For details of the media's role in the 1990 general election, see Mustafa K. Anuar, "The Malaysian 1990 General Election: The Role of the BN Mass Media", in *Kajian Malaysia* 8, no. 2 (1990): 82–102.

140. Interview with Zulkifli Sulong, group editor of *Harakah*, Kuala Lumpur, 27 August 1999. *Harakah's* sale price per issue was then RM1.30.

141. E-mail correspondence with Francis Loh Kok Wah, Aliran Exco member, 17 June 2000.

142. For lists of pro-Anwar and pro-*reformasi* websites and analyses of the growing influence of the alternative media over the public after the Anwar episode, see *Aliran Monthly* 19, no. 5 (1999): 28–31 (Mustafa K. Anuar, "Turning Over?").

143. Francis Loh (2000, p. 1; emphasis added).

144. Interview with the KeADILan president Wan Azizah Wan Ismail and her deputy Chandra Muzaffar in *Asiaweek*, 16 April 1999 ("We Want to be a Bridge").

145. Harold Crouch, "Malaysia: Do Elections Make a Difference?" in *The Politics of Elections in Southeast Asia*, edited by R.H. Taylor (Cambridge: Cambridge University Press, 1996), p. 114.

146. R.K. Vasil, *The Malaysian General Election of 1969* (Kuala Lumpur: Oxford University Press, 1972), pp. 85–96.

147. Khong Kim Hoong, *Malaysia's General Election 1990: Continuity, Change, and Ethnic Politics* (Singapore: Institute of Southeast Asian Studies, 1991), p. 15.

148. Mahathir dissolved Parliament on 11 November 1999. The 1999 general election was held on 29 November 1999 after an eight-day-campaign period following nominations on 20 November 1999.

149. For the full text of the BA statement, see <http://members.tripod.com/~mahazalimd/220999x4.html>. Posted on 22 September 1999.

150. For the full text of the common election manifesto, see Kamarudin Jaffar, *Pilihanraya 1999 Dan Masa Depan Politik Malaysia* (Kuala Lumpur: IKDAS, 2000), pp. 71–94.

151. For more details, see Vasil (1972, pp. 21–24).

152. Interview with Razaleigh Hamzah, former Semangat 46 president and currently UMNO supreme council member, Kuala Lumpur, 23 February 1998.

153. Interview with Ibrahim Ali, former Semangat 46 Youth chief, Kuala Lumpur, 23 February 1998.

154. Interview with Tan Seng Giaw, vice-chairman of DAP, Petaling Jaya, 4 February 1998.

155. Interview with Syed Husin Ali, president of PRM, Petaling Jaya, 17 August 1999.

156. Interview with Lim Kit Siang, Petaling Jaya, 17 August 1999.

157. For detailed election results, see <http://www.spr.gov.my/election95.html>.

158. Francis Loh (2000, p. 6).

159. Many prominent opposition leaders of other BA component parties lost their seats or failed to win in the 1999 elections. These included: Lim Kit Siang, Karpal Singh, and Chen Man Hin (DAP); Chandra Muzaffar, Irene Fernandez, Tian Chua, and Marina Yusoff (KeADILan); and Syed Husin Ali (PRM).

160. Francis Loh (2000, p. 8).

161. For a detailed case study of vote distribution in a multi-ethnic constituency, see *Aliran Monthly* 19, no. 11–12 (1999): 24–26 (Jeyakumar Devaraj, "What Next for the Barisan Alternatif?").

162. Francis Loh (2000, p. 7).

163. N.J. Funston, "Malaysia's Tenth Elections: Status Quo, Reformasi or Islamization?" *Contemporary Southeast Asia* 22, no. 1 (2000): 50, table 2.

164. Figures from the public relations office of Malaysian Election Commission, via e-mail from Liew Chin Tong, political secretary to the MP for Seputeh, on 12 July 2000.

165. Francis Loh (2000, p. 11).

166. Francis Loh (2000, p. 13).

167. Shamsul A.B., "The Redefinition of Politics and the Transformation of Malaysian Pluralism", paper presented to the conference on Southeast Asian Pluralism, ISEC-Ford Project, Kuala Lumpur, 5–6 August 1999, p. 17.

168. Harold Crouch, "Malaysia: Neither Authoritarian nor Democratic", in *Southeast Asia in the 1990s: Authoritarianism, Democracy and Capitalism*, edited by Kevin Hewison, Richard Robison, and Garry Rodan (St. Leonards, NSW: Allen & Unwin, 1993), pp. 135–57.

169. Interview with Tian Chua, Kuala Lumpur, August 1999.

Whither Malaysia?

During the years after independence when ethnic conflict was perceived as the main threat to regime stability in Malaysia, inter-ethnic élite co-operation was the most crucial element in the maintenance of the dominant Malay ruling élite's power. Accordingly, the UMNO-led Malay ruling élite opted for political compromise with other communal leaders in coalition government to maintain its legitimate influence over the political process. Although the Malaysian political system did not fully conform to all features of consociationalism mentioned by Lijphart, it nonetheless involved the articulation of the key ones for the first twelve years of independence (1957–69). In particular, the presence of inter-ethnic élite co-operation in the Alliance government and sufficient rank-and-file support made Malaysian politics consociational during the earlier period of independence. Given the intense ethnic and societal cleavages in Malaysia, much writing on consociationalism has been oriented towards exploring how the various ethnic leaders were able to reach some measure of consensus to preserve their political legitimacy.

Towards the end of the 1960s, the Alliance-type of consociational compromise, however, became increasingly unfeasible for maintaining regime stability as Malaysian ethnic society became more and more politicized. In particular, the Alliance's disastrous outcome in the 1969 general election which triggered the subsequent May 13 racial riots demonstrated that consociational inter-ethnic compromises were less effective for the Malay ruling élite as a means of maintaining its own political power. This was one of the most crucial reasons for the Malay ruling élite seeking an alternative mode of regime maintenance and shifting towards more hegemonic control, which led to the unambiguous UMNO-led Malay dominance of the 1970s and 1980s. During this period, changes took place in almost every field of Malaysian society, the political, social, economic, legal, and even ideological spheres. The major anti-crisis strategies — the *Rukunegara* as a behaviour code for daily life, the amendment and enactment of repressive laws, a new development plan (NEP), and the realignment of a ruling scheme (BN) — necessarily led to the consolidation of UMNO's authoritarian rule within and outside the ruling coalition. To some extent, the rule of consociational bargaining continued to be utilized. However, during the 1970s and 1980s, the political configuration in Malaysia inclined more and more towards the control end of a control–consensus spectrum.

Towards the end of the 1980s, the nature of the conflict undermining the power and position of the dominant ruling élite changed again as UMNO, the dominant group in the government, underwent severe factional conflicts. Factionalism is a common feature of party organization, although political parties are often perceived as unitary actors in political theories. UMNO's recent experience of factionalism was, and still is, not all that distinctive because it had been common enough in the party since its formation in 1946. The internal life of UMNO underwent a series of quiet, but constant, struggles for the strengthening of factional allies during the 1960s and 1970s. The character of UMNO's factionalism, however, changed in the 1980s and even developed to the point where the essential unity of the party itself was at stake. Especially after the UMNO leadership crisis of 1987, factional rivalries within UMNO circles took an increasingly life-or-death quality and thus appeared to constitute a crucial threat to the Mahathir-led ruling élite. It was therefore a natural step for Mahathir to engage in a greater degree of conflict resolution to maintain his own grip on UMNO in a situation of deepening factional conflict.

Given the closeness and bitterness of the intra-élite schism within the ruling Malay élite in 1987, Malaysian politics was expected to be much more responsive and competitive. There might even have been a transition from "semi" to "full" democracy. There is, however, little evidence that the severe factionalism promoted political liberalization in Malaysia under Mahathir's new political party, UMNO (*Baru*), especially during the period of 1987–90. Indeed, what Mahathir actually did was destroy the existing ruling party and rebuild it around his dominant personality. First, Mahathir reduced the political space of civil society by using the Internal Security Act (ISA) as a repressive instrument in *Operasi Lalang* in October 1987, following the "self-created" racial tension. Mahathir then drove out all of his rivals within the new political configuration. With the advent of UMNO (*Baru*) in 1988, new guiding principles of behaviour appeared within the ruling party: "de-politicization" and/or "no-contest" for the party's top post to create UMNO (*Baru*) as a loyalist party. Promotion of these "new traditions" was in response to Mahathir's bitter experience of serious challenge to his leadership by well-organized factional alliances led by Razaleigh and Musa in 1987. The increasing electoral competitiveness during Mahathir's early leadership (1981–87) was gradually, but systematically, restricted when he rebuilt UMNO as UMNO (*Baru*). It was only after Mahathir had successfully driven out all his enemies and effectively quashed opposition within the new political configuration that he reverted to a traditional checks-and-balances approach, but without the risk of a leadership challenge. After 1990, with his rivals gone, Mahathir was able to further consolidate his grip on power within and outside the new ruling party.

The years after 1990 replayed some of the key features of the period 1987–90, especially in the political sphere. Throughout the 1990s, Mahathir's main concern was to centralize the processes of power within his personal domain. Mahathir seemed much less tolerant than pre-1987 in managing potential opponents in the ruling party. To a certain extent factional rivalries among the second-echelon leaders were permitted to counter the growing pressure of a generational shift in the party leadership. Nonetheless, whenever new factional forces attempted to increase their influence and thus undermine Mahathir's supremacy, tighter authoritarian rules were applied to strengthen Mahathir's centralized political control. The pace of constitutional amendments, including the UMNO (*Baru*) constitution, quickened and the reasons for the amendments increasingly reflected the Prime Minister's self-aggrandizing motives. The notion of a strong executive authority has long been enshrined in the Malaysian political system, especially after Mahathir took over in 1981. However, in the years after 1990 the key democratic features of Malaysian politics were eroded due to the growing concentration of power in Mahathir's hands at the expense of the legislature, the monarchy, and the judiciary. By the mid-1990s, there was scarcely any element remaining to check the growing authoritarian rule of the Mahathir government.

Perhaps paradoxically, the years after 1990 also demonstrated that inter-ethnic tolerance had increased dramatically in Malaysian society. This was largely because of the Mahathir government introducing a series of accommodative policies aimed at the non-Malay communities through so-called "cultural liberalization". Given that Malaysia's economy grew steadily from the late 1980s, UMNO leaders and members demonstrated more flexibility towards non-Malay communities' demands concerning language, education, religion, and cultural heritage. State-driven cultural liberalization, however, seemed not to stem from the Mahathir-led ruling élite's growing commitment to multi-ethnic nation-building. A better explanation for the shift of ethnic politics in the 1990s can be found in Mahathir's and UMNO leaders' increasing confidence in their dominant political and economic positions. It is, therefore, presumed that a U-turn involving the retraction of the so-called cultural liberalization would be quite likely if, in the near future, Mahathir and UMNO leaders were to face an increasingly insecure situation that threatened their political and economic hegemony.

Moreover, the climate of greater tolerance in Malaysia's ethnic politics was not necessarily accompanied by greater political liberalization. As mentioned above, the tolerance for political expression in the years after 1990 was increasingly limited. The Mahathir regime's ambivalence towards political and cultural expression characterized the post-1990 Malaysian political system as "repressive-responsive" along a continuum between liberal democracy and authoritarianism. These "repressive-responsive" elements in the Malaysian political system throughout the

1990s, however, were not necessarily contradictory but mutually supportive for regime maintenance.

The recent factional conflict within UMNO and subsequent downfall of Anwar in 1998 offer another opportunity to revisit the nexus between factionalism in the ruling bloc and political liberalization in authoritarian or semi-authoritarian regimes. The circumstances and political manoeuvrings that surround the Mahathir-Anwar tussle resembled, to a very large extent, those of the earlier factional disputes in UMMO during the mid-1980s and subsequent breakaway of UMNO in 1988. But unlike the previous factional conflicts, the Mahathir-Anwar clash and its socio-political and cultural consequences were something unprecedented in Malaysian politics, because the Anwar episode was not simply circumscribed as an intra-Malay or UMNO's internal affair.

Unlike the situation just after the 1987 leadership crisis when very serious élite divisions occurred within UMNO circles, Anwar's legacies appear to have petered out relatively quickly. Learning from the experience of 1987, Mahathir swiftly pre-empted any possible challenge from Anwar by sacking and ousting him from the ruling party. Anwar's subsequent imprisonment effectively eroded his followers' hopes of his comeback into mainstream Malaysian politics. By doing this, Mahathir was able to keep the ruling political élite, including seasoned political figures and many of Anwar's allies, on his side. Again, Mahathir retained his grip on power and the authoritarian political landscape of Malaysia remained almost the same.

The Anwar episode, however, affected Malaysians from very different levels of society. One of the most significant impacts of the upheaval was its catalytic role in the resurrection of Malaysian civil society from "de-politicization" to "re-politicization". Mahathir's public humiliation of Anwar caused a political awakening especially among Malays of the young generation. Unlike the previous power struggle of 1987, anti-Mahathir sentiment was widespread not only within UMNO circles, but also among the whole Malay community. Indeed, the most distinctive characteristic of Malaysian politics after Anwar was the Malay community's unprecedented disenchantment with UMNO's leadership. The 1999 general election demonstrated the extent to which a major shift in voting patterns within the rural Malay heartland had occurred.

There was intense pre-election pessimism about how much anti-Mahathir sentiment would be translated into real votes. UMNO's apprehensions, however, were realized as it suffered serious losses in most Malay-dominated constituencies.

The other significant change in Malaysia's political life after Anwar was the emergence of a new politics of multi-ethnic awareness in Malaysian civil society which took a common stand against the political hegemony of the ruling BN coalition. For the first time in Malaysia's political history, unprecedented numbers of the multi-ethnic middle class, especially among the Malay middle class, were deeply involved in a reform movement seeking more open, accountable, and democratic governance. What further distinguishes Malaysia's political configuration post-1998 from the post-1987 UMNO leadership crisis was a considerable decline of ethnicity as the central issue. The decrease in racial politics, then, enabled the main opposition parties, PAS, DAP, PRM, and KeADILan, to come together for the first time under the opposition coalition, Barisan Alternatif, in 1999. The opposition coalition could not entirely satisfy the newly emerging multi-ethnic civil society's aspirations for a breakdown of the single-party dominant ruling coalition's political hegemony. The emergence of the multi-ethnic opposition coalition and its strong electoral performances in 1999, however, prompted a reconsideration of the decades-old hypothesis about the ritual exercise of elections in Malaysia, as electoral competition in post-1999 was no longer simply perceived as a ceremonial procedure for legitimizing the UMNO-led government's authoritarian rule.

The question then arises, how will UMNO react to this situation to restore its predominant political position in Malaysian politics? Will Mahathir's UMNO be more adaptive to the changing expectations of the Malay community and prioritize issues such as the abuse of centralized power, the reform of the ruling party, and change of leadership? Or, will the new multi-racial political configuration and the resurrection of Malaysian civil society continue and eventually lead to a transition from UMNO-led authoritarian rule to democracy?

Some have argued that the ruling élite sometimes concede "functional needs" to transform, or at least modify, certain forms of authoritarian rule into more responsive modes, not because of a change in their primary concerns towards openness and/or good governance but for their own political survival. In this regard, many political analysts, and even some UMNO leaders, suggested that the UMNO-led government and UMNO itself needed to be more responsive, if not be reinvented, to meet the challenge of the 1999 general election.

Post-election developments, however, suggest that Mahathir is not prepared to respond positively to the changing expectations of Malaysian civil society. Mahathir continues to rely on the same harsh methods of authoritarian control in handling his political opponents and critics. A series of crackdowns on the opposition came within a few weeks of the 1999 elections. Following the Home Ministry's letters threatening to ban five alternative publications, *Harakah, Detik, Eksklusif, Wasilah,* and *Tamadun,* several leaders from the three main opposition parties were arrested for sedition under the Official Secrets Act. Karpal Singh, deputy chairman of the DAP and Anwar's lawyer, was arrested for sedition in connection with his defence of Anwar in court. Marina Yusoff, vice-president of KeADILan, was also charged for sedition for comments in a speech about UMNO's initiating role in the May 13 racial riots of 1969. Mohamed Ezam Mohd. Noor, KeADILan Youth chief, was charged under the Official Secrets Act for disclosing classified government documents involving anti-corruption investigations of top UMNO leaders. Zulkifli Sulong, group editor of *Harakah,* and Chea Lim Thye, the owner of the firm that prints *Harakah,* were arrested for sedition for publishing an article which suggested there was a government conspiracy to frame Anwar.[1] A few weeks later, *Harakah,* the political organ of PAS, was allowed to print only twice monthly instead of twice weekly.[2] In addition, the annual permits of *Detik* and *Eksklusif* were not renewed by the Home Ministry.[3]

As for Anwar, he was found guilty in August 2000 of sodomy and sentenced to nine years of imprisonment, to be served consecutively to the six-year jail term he is serving for four corruption convictions relating to abuse of power while he was Deputy Prime Minister. The sentence effectively removes Anwar, fifty-three, from contesting at least the next three general elections for up to the year 2015, even though he could be free in 2010 after serving two-thirds of his fifteen-year jail term. This is because, under Malaysian law, he would still be disqualified from holding any public office for another five years. If Anwar is not granted remission, he would only be released in fifteen years and this will deny him twenty years of political life and activity. To many observers, even UMNO leaders and members, Anwar's sodomy verdict was perceived as "cruel and harsh" and, therefore, the severity of the sentence may inspire a reform movement led by the multi-racial opposition forces.

It was in these circumstances that Mahathir fanned a sensitive issue surrounding the provision of Malay special rights. In his National Day speech on 30 August 2000, Mahathir criticized the Malaysian Chinese Organizations Election Appeals Committee (*suqiu*)'s seventeen-point pre-election memorandum and slammed *suqiu* as "communists" and "extremists".[4] *Suqiu*'s seventeen-point appeal had been publicly endorsed by the BN component parties and subsequently accepted in principle by the Cabinet prior to the 1999 general election. Mahathir, however, alleged that the Cabinet had earlier accepted *suqiu*'s seventeen-point election memorandum "under pressure" in circumstances where the government headed by UMNO had become weaker in the wake of economic and political crises before the general election.[5] Indeed, during the last general election, the ruling coalition adapted the strategy of winning over the non-Malays, especially the Chinese, and Chinese votes helped provide the Mahathir government with another five-year term in power. However, the Mahathir-led UMNO, sensing that it was losing traditional support from the Malays, U-turned to the politics of ethnicity to win back the Malays. A Chinese political commentator believes that the *suqiu* issue was used by Mahathir and UMNO leaders to create a sense of crisis for the Malays in circumstances where the severity of the Anwar verdict may have energized multi-ethnic opposition.[6] Far from introducing political and democratic adaptations, post-election developments indicate that Mahathir appears to be banking on the same iron-fisted control and the racial politics he has used in the past.

This continuing authoritarian trend is directed not only against the opposition but also operates within UMNO. Mahathir seems to refuse to recognize the need to rejuvenate the ruling party and heed his critics. During the UMNO supreme council elections in May 2000, Mahathir consolidated his power even further by effectively sidelining Razaleigh, his only remaining serious challenger, not only for the top two posts but even for the vice-presidency. As for the top two posts, any room for challenge was contracted as contests were prevented through Mahathir's no-contest "advice" and a subsequent no-contest "resolution" of the supreme council, despite the party constitution's provision for contests. Razaleigh was even put out of the race for the vice-presidency as his eligibility to stand as a candidate was rejected by the supreme council. Under the newly amended UMNO constitution, an aspiring candidate for the vice-presidency must secure 10 per cent of nominations from the 165 divisions, that is, at least seventeen nominations, to be eligible to stand as a candidate. Razaleigh had received the required seventeen nominations to contest the vice-presidency but his candidacy was rejected by the supreme council as the nomination from the Gua Musang division was declared invalid. Gua Musang nominated Razaleigh as a vice-presidential candidate at the division's committee with the endorsement of the divisional delegates' meeting rather than directly by the divisional delegates' meeting, resulting in a controversial debate over the interpretation of the UMNO constitution.[7] Nonetheless, it is believed that the disqualification of Razaleigh's candidacy was a reflection of Mahathir's own wish not to allow any room for individual threats to the incumbent party leadership.

Many UMNO officials worry in private that if UMNO does not change and respond positively to the changing circumstances of the Malay community, the party will lose the strength and values which have enabled it to remain the dominant political force in the country. A senior official stressed that UMNO's problems have become much more serious than outsiders have observed, especially after the party's supreme council elections in May 2000. He believes that there is no "will" within the current Mahathir-led UMNO leadership to reform the party. But what is even worse, the newly elected UMNO leadership shows neither "credibility" nor "will" to reform the party after the leadership succession. Abdullah Badawi's unopposed ascendancy to the deputy presidency has yet to be endorsed by the party delegates while the election of the three vice-presidents was not the result of the delegates' confidence in them, but rather a "protest vote" against Mahathir's leadership.[8] The three elected vice-presidents are Najib, Muhammad Taib, and Muhyiddin Yassin. Interestingly, they were in the *Wawasan* team that Anwar had forged in the 1993 UMNO elections, though the 2000 election results did not necessarily reflect support for Anwar.[9] Indeed, Najib's convincing victory with the highest number of votes in the UMNO elections, compared with his 241-vote margin in the 1999 general election, suggests that UMNO supreme council elections do not reflect Malay grassroots sentiment.

After the supreme council elections in May, UMNO, again, prepared to amend its constitution during a special assembly in November 2000. Initial proposals included extending the term of the supreme council from three to five years. Rafidah Aziz, head of Wanita UMNO, even proposed that the post of the three vice-presidents be scrapped. If the proposals were to be adopted by the party, UMNO supreme council elections due in 2003 would be postponed up to 2005 to synchronize with current parliamentary terms — meaning that Mahathir and the incumbent UMNO leaders would not face another leadership test for the next five years. None of these controversial proposals were accepted. Nonetheless, this is another example of the UMNO leadership failing to meet the reformist demands of most ordinary party members for fear of losing its own grip on power.

The Lunas state assembly by-election, held just a few weeks after the UMNO special assembly in November 2000, showed that the ruling coalition, especially UMNO, was unable to recover the ground it lost at the 1999 general election. Lunas is an ethnically mixed constituency (43 per cent Malays, 37 per cent Chinese, and 19 per cent Indians) in Kedah, Mahathir's home state. Although the KeADILan candidate, Saifuddin Nasution, won with a narrow majority of 530 votes, he managed to reduce the 1999 election margin between the BN and the opposition by more than 5,000. This was the first time the ruling coalition had been defeated in Lunas since independence in 1957. The opposition's victory also cost the ruling coalition a two-thirds majority in the state assembly. More importantly, the repudiation of Mahathir in his own home state was perceived as an indication that Anwar was still a potential rallying point and that his "cause" was not waning. During the election campaign, KeADILan tried to draw the battle line between Mahathir and Anwar and Anwar's "black-eyed" posters were distributed widely. In this regard, an UMNO supreme council member, Shahrir Samad, attributed the BN's defeat to "the character of our leader, Dr Mahathir".[10] Similarly, the KeADILan candidate Saifuddin mentioned that the Mahathir factor, which had been considered a crucial asset to the BN for the last decade, turned out to be an advantage for the opposition in the Lunas by-election. He stressed that "we just have to wait for our enemy to commit a mistake, and Mahathir did it".[11]

Consequently, the BN's loss in Lunas raised public criticism of Mahathir's authoritarian leadership again. What was even worse, this time the accusations came mainly from within UMNO circles. In addition to Shahrir's criticism of Mahathir shortly after the by-election, it was reported that many other UMNO leaders and members openly questioned Mahathir's leadership and governance.[12] This led to Mahathir's conciliatory gesture, in January 2001, to seek a tripartite dialogue on Malay unity with two other Malay-based opposition parties, PAS and KeADILan. The Malay unity talks did not take place as KeADILan immediately turned down Mahathir's invitation and PAS eventually decided not to participate as well. In explaining KeADILan's decision not to attend, a high-ranking official argued that the main issues faced by UMNO were not merely questions of Malay unity but more seriously the abuse of power, corruption, and a crisis of confidence in leadership and governance. He believed that Malay supporters would have been very disappointed with PAS leaders if they had had dealings with UMNO. He stressed that the Mahathir-led UMNO's problems were much more serious than many observers thought and it would take a long time to repair the erosion of UMNO's support.[13]

What, then, can be said about the role of the newly formed opposition coalition in responding to a more politicized Malaysian civil society and transforming the UMNO-led authoritarian rule into a more democratic one? Many political observers were doubtful of the sustainability of BA at the time of the 1999 general election. On the surface, however, BA appears to be holding together and institutionalizing co-operative mechanisms among component parties. KeADILan's political future appears to be different from Semangat 46 as it is seeking to merge with PRM, another multi-ethnic BA component party.[14] It is fair to say that, at least for a year or so after the 1999 general election, relations within BA have stabilized compared with before the election.

For instance, the institution in which the BA component parties discussed their common election manifesto and seat allocation before the 1999 general election continues. This body, called the "BA Secretariat", was chaired by Chandra Muzaffar, and met almost weekly, or at least fortnightly, to consolidate the relationships among the BA opposition parties. The BA's top leaders also continued their irregular meetings, as the "Presidents Council". There has always been a "pre-council meeting", or at least communication, among the BA MPs before Parliament sits, too. Moreover, about twenty policy bureaus, called "Barisan Alternatif Bureaus", have been formed to assist the BA MPs. The BA Bureaus are perceived as *de facto* shadow cabinets drawn from BA's component members. Similar local BA committees, called "Shadow Local Authorities", have subsequently been formed in some constituencies. A series of "inter-civilization dialogues" has also been organized by PAS and DAP to foster mutual understanding at the grassroots level. These post-election developments were quite different from the relationships that had been maintained among the opposition parties in Gagasan Rakyat and APU in the aftermath of the 1990 general election.

Nonetheless, the extent to which the opposition parties have overcome their perceived credibility problem remains hard to gauge. It is too early to use the 1999 election result to indicate the direction in which Malay voters are swinging. PAS's defeat in the Sanggang state assembly by-election in April 2000 makes observers cautious about assuming that the Malay swing away from UMNO in 1999 will be continued in the next general election. UMNO retained the seat with an increased majority (from 1,038 to 1,963), despite a slight increase in Chinese votes for PAS in this Malay-dominated Sanggang seat. The results showed that, to some extent, Malays had moved back to UMNO. On the other hand, the Teluk Kemang by-election which followed Sanggang showed that the BA component parties could still mobilize a considerable vote for each other. For KeADILan particularly, the by-election result was regarded as "a victory in defeat" as it sharply reduced the BN's winning margin from 9,942 in the 1999 general election to 5,972 in the typical multi-ethnic parliamentary seat of Teluk Kemang.[15] Perhaps more importantly, KeADILan's victory in the Lunas by-election signalled to the Mahathir government that opposition forces were capable of capturing ethnically mixed constituencies which have, over last few decades, constituted the core of the ruling coalition support.

The serious rift between DAP and KeADILan over the right to contest the Teluk Kemang and Lunas seats, however, illustrated that considerable pre-election credibility problems and mutual distrust among the BA component parties were still evident. In the process of selecting the opposition candidate for the Teluk Kemang by-election, DAP wanted to run a candidate exclusively. According to DAP, Teluk Kemang is a traditional DAP seat and the KeADILan candidate who had contested the 1999 election using the DAP banner during the campaign had acknowledged the DAP's influence in the area. However, KeADILan insisted the seat now belonged to them according to the new arrangements made by leaders of the BA's four component parties before the 1999 general election. In the end, KeADILan ran a candidate in the by-election. There were, however, rumours that KeADILan had threatened to withdraw from BA if it failed to be nominated in Teluk Kemang, though KeADILan leadership has denied this.[16] The rift between DAP and KeADILan widened during the Lunas by-election with the DAP declaring its virtual boycott of the campaign following the BA presidents council dropping the DAP's candidate for one of KeADILan's. Party grassroots also mounted pressure on DAP leadership to pull out of the opposition coalition. Although the DAP decided to stay in the BA, it was widely believed that the party leadership, especially among the younger leaders, had become more vulnerable and even embittered by the apparent emergence of KeADILan as a viable alternative opposition force.

The Anwar episode and its social, cultural, and political consequences helped to create a more promising climate for the emergence of a third force in Malaysian politics. However, the question of whether PAS and DAP will allow KeADILan to extend its influence as a third political force remains to be seen. It is well known that the two main opposition parties were reluctant to see the emergence of the multi-ethnic KeADILan as a viable alternative opposition force. Previously, Malays had only PAS as an alternative to UMNO, whereas the Chinese had to accept the DAP when they supported the opposition. In 1990, Razaleigh's Semangat 46 was regarded as an alternative for the Malays but not the Chinese.

However, the formation of KeADILan with its strong multi-ethnic character seemed to provide both Malays and Chinese with an alternative. Especially for young urban-based Chinese, KeADILan was viewed as a viable alternative. Given that the DAP was facing problems attracting support from the younger generation, the emergence of KeADILan as a third opposition party posed a long-term threat to the DAP. The situation was more or less the same with PAS. In fact, PAS was not really happy with the formation of KeADILan from the very beginning. This was why both DAP and PAS were so reluctant to give any promising seats to KeADILan when BA negotiated seat allocations in the run-up to the 1999 general election. Since then, PAS and DAP have tended to sideline or ignore KeADILan in various ways.[17] It can be argued that the two existing parties perceive KeADILan as a bigger enemy than the ruling coalition in the longer term if KeADILan survives with its multi-ethnic character. Some even believe that the two parties, or at least their top leaders, were more interested in consolidating their power bases within the current system of racial politics than changing the structure of the Malaysian political system itself towards a new politics of multi-racialism.

Also, there was a lack of confidence, or even mutual suspicion, among BA's component parties. In particular, many political analysts doubted whether DAP and PAS would co-operate with one another on a long-term basis. It is fair to say that DAP and PAS have enjoyed a better relationship with each other than with KeADILan and PRM since the 1999 general election. Nonetheless, it was not long after the 1999 elections that the two main opposition parties started serious arguments over some of PAS's policies on the issue of an "Islamic state". The ruling coalition-controlled mainstream media also highlighted and exaggerated examples of PAS's strict religious enforcement in Kelantan and Terengganu. Additionally, PAS leaders' divergent views, particularly over the establishment of an Islamic state and the role of Islam, exacerbated the perception of mutual suspicion within the opposition coalition. DAP leaders often demanded that PAS drop its Islamic state concept and adhere to the BA 1999 general election common manifesto.[18] In responding to this, PAS reiterated that no party should ask another to abandon its political ideology. According to PAS leaders, this is why PAS has never asked DAP to abandon its "Malaysian Malaysia" concept.[19]

Escalating arguments over the Islamic state issue between DAP and PAS continued for a few months to mid-2001. Finally, in September 2001, DAP decided to leave the opposition coalition five days before the Sarawak state assembly elections.

It has become clear that the social, political, and circumstantial conditions induced by the Anwar episode have put the sustainability of authoritarian forms of governance in Malaysia in doubt. Case notes that the "resurrection of civil society, a promise of popular upsurge, and the enhanced prospects for democracy will constitute the most important changes in Malaysia's political life after the removal of Anwar".[20] However, as O'Donnell and Schmitter emphasize, enhanced favourable circumstances for a new political order are "by no means a constant". The euphoria of a transition can easily subside when a majority of the people become keener on a "new social order".[21] Furthermore, the discourse for a new social or political order has often become a principal justification for imposition of a new authoritarian form of governance in many previously authoritarian or semi-authoritarian countries.

Until recently, Mahathir has challenged the discourse of political liberalization by arguing that Western-style democratic values are inappropriate in the socio-political cultures of Asian countries that stress conformity, consensus, and communal loyalty over confrontational forms of politics. Such arguments about "Asian values" place Malaysia's political system as a form of "semi-democracy", "quasi-democracy, "soft-authoritarianism", or "state-led democracy". However, the Mahathir government is now facing increasing challenges to expand the boundaries of liberalization and limited democracy. There is no denying that the sharp erosion of Malay support for UMNO creates high expectations of a shift away from Mahathir's style of authoritarian rule. Many political observers inside and outside UMNO caution that UMNO should take the resurrection of civil society and its pressures for *reformasi* seriously. Failing that, the possibility of breakdown of the ruling bloc could become a reality.

The Anwar episode and subsequent political upheaval, indeed, stimulated some of the favourable conditions for a transition from authoritarian to democratic rule in Malaysia. However, successful democratic transition in any society cannot be explained merely by a context favourable to democratization. Furthermore, the breakdown of an authoritarian regime does not necessarily lead to the establishment of certain democratic forms of governance. Rather, the regime can often be transformed into an "uncertain something else". Transitions can develop into "the instauration of a political democracy", but can also give way to "the restoration of a new, and possibly more severe, form of authoritarian rule".[22] It is worth noting that, in Malaysia, the ruling political élite has shown considerable capacity to make effective political adaptations, through both coercive and co-optive means, in order to safeguard their own political survival despite crisis situations. For the past few decades, UMNO, in particular, has successfully adapted to a series of internal and external crises and had continued to re-emerge as strong as ever at the national and state levels. The crucial questions for the future of the opposition parties, both individually and collectively, are how to overcome their mutual suspicion, or defensive mentalities, and develop convincing alternative political programmes to promote voters' confidence in them in the foreseeable future.

NOTES

1. For more details, see *Aliran Monthly* 19, no. 11–12 (1999): 2–6 (Anil Netto, "A Y2K Crackdown"); *AWSJ*, 17 January 2000 (Chandra Muzaffar, "Mahathir's Clampdown"); and *FEER*, 27 January 2000 (S. Jayasankaran and Simon Elegant, "Rules for Rulers").

2. For more details on the publication limits placed on *Harakah*, see *FEER*, 13 January 2000 (Simon Elegant, "Press Alarm"); *FEER*, 16 March 2000 (Simon Elegant, "Net Gains"); and *Aliran Monthly* 20, no. 2 (2000): 13–14 (Mustafa K. Anuar, "The Forbidden Fruit Called: *Harakah*").

3. *The Star*, 26 April 2000 ("Publication of Weekly Tabloid Suspended").

4. *Suqiu* was formed by eleven Chinese organizations a few months before the 1999 general election. The *suqiu's* seventeen-point pre-election appeal, however, was endorsed by 2,089 Chinese organizations nation-wide. For the full text of *suqiu's* memorandum, see <http://suqiu.org/Suqiu_english.htm>.

5. John Funston, "Malaysia: UMNO's Search for Relevance", *Southeast Asian Affairs 2001*, p. 196.

6. Interview with Wong Chin Huat, executive secretary to the Malaysian Chinese Organizations Election Appeals Committee (*suqiu*), Kuala Lumpur, 6 April 2001.

7. For more information on the Gua Musang nomination issue, see *The Star*, 14 April 2000 ("Ku Li Gets Ticket for Vice Presidency Race"); 14 April 2000 ("Ku Li Poser Still a Hot Topic"); 18 April 2000 ("Gua Musang Nominations Declared Invalid"); and 19 April 2000 ("Ku Li: It's a Game Where Players Are Also Referees").

8. Interview with Rais Yatim, Canberra, 26 May 2000.

9. It is claimed that Mahathir wanted Ghani Othman, Menteri Besar of Johor, and Osu Sukam, Chief Minister of Sabah, to be elected but both failed to win.

10. Cited in Zakiah Koya, "Dr M to Blame for Lunas Defeat: UMNO Veteran", *Malaysiakini*, 30 November 2000.

11. E-mail correspondence with Saifuddin Nasution Ismail dated 1 December 2000.

12. Funston, *Southeast Asian Affairs 2001*, p. 198 and *FEER*, 14 December 2000 (S. Jayasankaran, "Rude Wake-Up for Mahathir").

13. Interview with Tian Chua, Vice-President of KeADILan, Kuala Lumpur, 5 April 2001.

14. *NST*, 22 March 2000 ("Keadilan and Parti Rakyat Agree to Merge").

15. The Teluk Kemang parliamentary constituency consists of 45.4 per cent Malays, 33.2 per cent Chinese, and 20.6 per cent Indians. For an analysis of the by-election results, see *The Star*, 12 June 2000 (A. Letchumanan, "Bittersweet Result for Both Sides").

16. For more details, see Ng Boon Hooi, "KeADILan, Not DAP, to Contest Teluk Kemang", *Malaysiakini*, 16 May 2000.

17. For example, it is claimed that DAP sometimes bypassed the BA structure and sent its officials to meet the Terengganu and Kelantan state government leaders to discuss the latter's policies on non-Muslims. And the two main inter-civilization dialogues were organized in January and March 2000 only between DAP and PAS, excluding KeADILan.

18. For more details of DAP's stand on the Islamic state issue, see Lim Kit Siang, *BA & Islamic State* (Petaling Jaya: Democratic Action Party, 2001).

19. Susan Loone and Kevin Tan, "Islamic State: DAP Throws Out PAS Compromise", *Malaysiakini*, 26 July 2001.

20. William Case, "Politics Beyond Anwar: What's New?" *Asian Journal of Political Science* 7, no. 1 (1999): 7.

21. Guillermo O'Donnell and Philippe C. Schmitter, *Transition from Authoritarian Rule: Tentative Conclusions about Uncertain Democracies* (Balimore and London: Johns Hopkins University Press, 1986), p. 54.

22. O'Donnell and Schmitter (1986, p. 3).

References

Books, Journals, and Chapters

Ahmad Fauzi Abdul Hamid. "Political Dimensions of Religious Conflict in Malaysia: State Response to an Islamic Movement". *Indonesia and the Malay World* 28, no. 80 (2000): 32–65.

Abdul Rahman Putra, Tunku. *May 13: Before and After*. Kuala Lumpur: Utusan Melayu Press, 1969.

Abraham, Collin E.R. *Divide and Rule: The Roots of Race Relations in Malaysia*. Kuala Lumpur: INSAN, 1997.

Ahmad Sarji Abdul Hamid, ed. *Malaysia's Vision 2020: Understanding the Concept, Implications and Challenges*. Petaling Jaya: Pelanduk Publications, 1993.

Alias Mohamed. *PAS's Platform: Development and Change 1951–1986*. Petaling Jaya: Gateway Publishing House, 1994.

Allen, J.D.V. *The Malayan Union*. New Haven: Yale University Press, 1967.

Allen, Richard Hugh Sedley. *Malaysia, Prospect and Retrospect: The Impact and Aftermath of Colonial Rule*. London: Oxford University Press, 1968.

Andaya, B.W. and L.Y. Andaya. *A History of Malaysia*. London: Macmillan Press, 1982.

Anwar Ibrahim. *The Asian Renaissance*. Singapore: Times Books International, 1996.

Arndt, H.W. and Hal Hill, eds. *Southeast Asia's Economic Crisis: Origins, Lessons, and the Way Forward*. Singapore: Institute of Southeast Asian Studies, 1999.

Aziz Addruse, Raja. *Conduct Unbecoming*. Kuala Lumpur: Walrus Books, 1990.

Aziz Zariza Ahmad. *Mahathir's Paradigm Shift: The Man Behind the Vision*. Taiping: Firma Malaysia Publishing, 1997.

Barraclough, Simon. "The Dynamics of Coercion in the Malaysian Political Process". *Modern Asian Studies* 19, no. 4 (1985): 797–822.

―――. "Political Participation and Its Regulation in Malaysia: Opposition to the Societies (Amendment) Act 1981". *Pacific Affairs* 57, no. 3 (1984): 450–61.

Barry, Brian. "Consociational Model and Its Dangers". *European Journal of Political Research* 3 (1975): 393–412.

Beaglehole, J.H. "Malay Participation in Commerce and Industry: The Role of RIDA and MARA". *Journal of Commonwealth Political Studies* 7, no. 3 (1969): 216–45.

Bell, Daniel A., David Brown, Kanishka Jayasuriya, and David Martin Jones, eds. *Towards Illiberal Democracy in Pacific Asia*. New York: St. Martin's Press, 1995.

Boo Cheng Hau. *Quotas versus Affirmative Action: A Malaysian Perspective*. Kuala Lumpur: Oriengroup, 1998.

Bowen, John R. "The Myth of Global Ethnic Conflict". *Journal of Democracy* 7, no. 4 (1996): 3–14.

Brown, David. *The State and Ethnic Politics in Southeast Asia*. London: Routledge, 1994.

Brown, Michael E. and Sumit Ganguly. *Government Policies and Ethnic*

Relations in Asia and the Pacific. Cambridge, Massachusetts: MIT Press, 1997.

Camroux, D. "State Responses to Islamic Resurgence in Malaysia: Accommodation, Co-option and Confrontation". *Asian Survey* 36, no. 9 (1996): 863–65.

Carnell, Francis G. "The Malayan Elections". *Pacific Affairs* 28, no. 4 (1955): 315–30.

Case, William. "Politics Beyond Anwar: What's New?" *Asian Journal of Political Science* 7, no. 1 (1999): 1–19.

————. *Elites and Regimes in Malaysia: Revisiting a Consociational Democracy.* Clayton: Monash Asia Institute, 1996.

————. "Semi-Democracy in Malaysia: Withstanding the Pressures for Regime Change". *Pacific Affairs* 66, no. 2 (1993): 183–205.

Chandra Muzaffar. *Freedom in Fetters: An Analysis of the State of Democracy in Malaysia.* Penang: Aliran, 1986.

————. *Protector? An Analysis of the Concept and Practice of Loyalty in Leader-Led Relationships within Malay Society.*Penang: Aliran, 1979.

Chandrasekaran Pillay. *The 1974 General Elections in Malaysia: A Post Mortem.*Singapore: Institute of Southeast Asian Studies, 1974.

Cheah Boon Kheng. "The Social Impact of the Japanese Occupation of Malaya (1942–1945)". In *Southeast Asia under Japanese Occupation,* edited by Alfred W. McCoy. New Haven: Yale University Press, 1980.

Chin, James. "The Sabah State Election of 1994". *Asian Survey* 34, no. 10 (1994): 904–15.

Clutterbuck, Richard. *Conflict and Violence in Singapore and Malaysia 1945–1983.* Boulder: Westview Press, 1985.

Coats, Howard and Frances Dyer. *The Print and Broadcasting Media in Malaysia.*Kuala Lumpur: South East Asia Press Center, 1972.

Comber, Leon. *13 May 1969: A Historical Survey of Sino-Malay Relations.* Kuala Lumpur: Heinemann Asia, 1983.

Crouch, Harold. "Malaysia: Do Elections Make a Difference?" In *The Politics of Elections in Southeast Asia,* edited by R.H. Taylor, pp.

114–35. Cambridge: Woodrow Wilson Center Press and Cambridge University Press, 1996.

————. *Government and Society in Malaysia*. Ithaca and London: Cornell University Press, 1996.

————. "Malaysia: Neither Authoritarian nor Democratic". In *Southeast Asia in the 1990s: Authoritarianism, Democracy and Capitalism*, edited by Kevin Hewison, Richard Robison, and Garry Rodan, pp. 135–57. St. Leonards, NSW: Allen & Unwin, 1993.

————. *Domestic Political Structures and Regional Economic Cooperation*. Singapore: Institute of Southeast Asian Studies, 1984.

————. *Malaysia's 1982 General Election*. Singapore: Institute of Southeast Asian Studies, 1982.

————. "The UMNO Crisis: 1975–77". In *Malaysian Politics and the 1978 Election*, edited by Harold Crouch, Lee Kam Hing, and Michael Ong. Kuala Lumpur: Oxford University Press, 1980.

Crouch, Harold, Lee Kam Hing, and Michael Ong, eds. *Malaysian Politics and the 1978 Elections*. Kuala Lumpur: Oxford University Press, 1980.

Diamond, Larry. *Developing Democracy: Toward Consolidation*. Baltimore and London: Johns Hopkins University Press, 1999.

————. "Economic Development and Democracy Reconsidered". In *Reexamining Democracy*, edited by G. Marks and Larry Diamond, pp. 93–139. Newbury Park, California: Sage Publications, 1992.

Diamond, Larry, Juan J. Linz, and Seymour Martin Lipset, eds. *Politics in Developing Countries: Comparing Experiences with Democracy*. Boulder and London: Lynne Rienner Publishers, 1990.

————. *Democracy in Developing Countries: Asia*. Boulder, Colorado: Lynne Rienner Publishers, 1989.

Emerson, Rupert. *Malaysia: A Study in Direct and Indirect Rule*. Kuala Lumpur: University of Malaya Press, 1964.

Esman, Milton J. "The Management of Communal Conflict". *Public Policy* 21 (1973): 49–78.

_____ . *Administration and Development in Malaysia: Institution Building and Reform in a Plural Society*. Ithaca and London: Cornell University Press, 1972.

Faaland, Just, J.R. Parkinson, and Rais Saniman, eds. *Growth and Ethnic Inequality: Malaysia's New Economic Policy*. Kuala Lumpur: Dewan Bahasa dan Pustaka, 1990.

Fan Yew Teng. *Anwar Saga: Malaysia on Trial*. Selangor: Genting Raya Sdn. Bhd., 1999.

Farish A. Noor. "Looking for Reformasi: The Discursive Dynamics of the Reformasi Movement and Its Prospects as a Political Project". *Indonesia and the Malay World* 27, no. 77 (1999): 5–18.

Fishman, Robert M. "Rethinking State and Regime: Southern Europe's Transition to Democracy". *World Politics* 42, no. 3 (1990): 422–40.

Funston, N.J. "Malaysia's Tenth Elections: Status Quo, Reformasi or Islamization?" *Contemporary Southeast Asia* 22, no. 1 (2000): 23–59.

_____ . "Malaysia: A Fateful September". *Southeast Asian Affairs 1999*, pp. 165–84. Singapore: Institute of Southeast Asian Studies, 1999.

_____ . *Malay Politics in Malaysia: A Study of the United Malays National Organisation and Party Islam*. Kuala Lumpur: Heinemann Educational Books, 1980.

Furnivall, J.S. *Netherlands India: A Study of Plural Economy*. Cambridge: Cambridge University Press, 1939.

Gill, Ranjit. *Asia Under Siege: How the Asian Miracle Went Wrong*. Singapore: Epic Management Services, 1998.

_____ . *The UMNO Crisis*. Singapore: Sterling Corporate Services, 1988.

Goh Cheng Teik. *The May Thirteenth Incident and Democracy in Malaysia*. Kuala Lumpur: Oxford University Press, 1971.

Gomez, Edmund Terence. *The 1995 Malaysian General Elections: A Report and Commentary*. Singapore: Institute of Southeast Asian Studies, 1996.

_____ . "Electoral Funding of General, State and Party Elections in Malaysia". *Journal of Contemporary Asia* 26, no. 1 (1996): 81–99.

_____ . *Political Business: Corporate Involvement of Malaysian Political Parties.* Townsville: Centre for East and Southeast Asian Studies, James Cook University of North Queensland, 1994.

_____ . *Politics in Business: UMNO's Corporate Investments.* Kuala Lumpur: FORUM, 1990.

Gomez, Edmund Terence and Jomo K.S. "Authoritarianism, Elections and Political Change in Malaysia". *Public Policy* 2, no. 3 (July–September 1998): 113–44.

_____ . *Malaysia's Political Economy: Politics, Patronage and Profits.* Cambridge: Cambridge University Press, 1997.

Gullick, J.M. *Malaysia: Economic Expansion and National Unity.* London: Ernest Benn, 1981.

_____ . *Malaya.* London: Longmans, 1964.

Hall, D.G.E. *A History of South-East Asia.* Fourth edition. London: Macmillan Press, 1981.

Halpern, Sue M. "The Disorderly Universe of Consociational Democracy". *West European Politics* 9, no. 4 (1986): 181–97.

Hanna, Willard A. "The Separation of Singapore from Malaysia". *American Universities Field Staff* 13, no. 21 (1965): 12–14.

Hari Singh. "UMNO Leaders and Malay Rulers: The Erosion of a Special Relationship". *Pacific Affairs* 68, no. 2 (Summer 1995): 187–205.

Heng Pek Koon. *Chinese Politics in Malaysia: A History of the Malaysian Chinese Association.* Singapore: Oxford University Press, 1988.

Hewison, Kevin, Richard Robison, and Garry Rodan, eds. *Southeast Asia in the 1990s: Authoritarianism, Democracy and Capitalism.* St. Leonards, NSW: Allen & Unwin, 1993.

Hodder, B.W. *Man in Malaya.* London: University of London Press, 1959.

Horowitz, Donald L. *Ethnic Groups in Conflict.* Berkeley: University of California Press, 1985.

Hua Wu Yin. *Class and Communalism in Malaysia: Politics in a Dependent Capitalist State.* London: Zed Books Ltd., 1983.

Huntington, Samuel P. *Political Order in Changing Societies.* New Haven: Yale University Press, 1968.

Jackson, R.N. *Pickering, Protector of Chinese.* Kuala Lumpur: Oxford University Press, 1965.

Jackson, Robert. *The Malayan Emergency.* London: Routledge, 1991.

Jesudason, J.V. *Ethnicity and the Economy: The State, Chinese Business, and the Multinationals in Malaysia.* Singapore: Oxford University Press, 1989.

Joginder Singh Jessy. *History of South-East Asia (1824–1965).* Kedah: Penerbitan Darulaman, 1983.

Jomo K.S. and Ahmad Shabery Chik. "Malaysia's Islamic Movements". In *Fragmented Vision: Culture and Politics in Contemporary Malaysia,* edited by J.S. Kahn and Francis Loh, pp. 79–106. Sydney: Allen & Unwin, 1992.

Jomo K.S. "Deepening Malaysian Democracy with More Checks and Balances". In *Malaysia Critical Perspectives,* edited by Muhammad Ikmal Said and Zahid Emby, pp. 74–95. Petaling Jaya: Persatuan Sains Sosial Malaysia, 1996*a*.

_____ . "Election's Janus Face: Limitations and Potential in Malaysia". In *The Politics of Elections in Southeast Asia,* edited by R.H. Taylor, pp. 90–113. Cambridge: Woodrow Wilson Center Press and Cambridge University Press, 1996*b*.

_____ . *U-Turn? Malaysian Economic Development Policies After 1990* Townsville: Center for East and Southeast Asian Studies, James Cook University of North Queensland, 1994.

_____ . *A Question of Class: Capital, the State, and Uneven Development in Malaya.* New York: Monthly Review Press, 1988.

Kahin, Audrey. "Crisis on the Periphery: The Rift between Kuala Lumpur and Sabah". *Pacific Affairs* 65, no. 1 (Spring 1992): 30–49.

Kahn, Joel S. and Francis Loh Kok Wah, eds. *Fragmented Vision: Culture and Politics in Contemporary Malaysia.* Sydney: Allen & Unwin, 1992.

Kamarudin Jaffar. *Pilihanraya 1999 Dan Masa Depan Politik Malaysia.* Kuala Lumpur: IKDAS, 2000.

Kessler, Clive. *Islam and Politics in a Malay State: Kelantan 1838–1969.* Ithaca: Cornell University Press, 1978.

Khong Kim Hoong. *Malaysia's General Election 1990: Continuity, Change, and Ethnic Politics.* Singapore: Institute of Southeast Asian Studies, 1991.

Khoo Boo Teik. *Paradoxes of Mahathirism: An Intellectual Biography of Mahathir Mohamad.* Kuala Lumpur: Oxford University Press, 1995.

Kua Kia Soong. *Inside the DAP 1990–1995.* Kuala Lumpur: Potensi Serentak, 1996.

————. *A Protean Saga: The Chinese Schools of Malaysia.* Kuala Lumpur: Resource and Research Center, 1990.

Kumar Rupesinghe, ed. *Internal Conflict and Governance.* New York: St. Martin's Press, 1992.

Lee H.P. *Constitutional Conflicts in Contemporary Malaysia.* Kuala Lumpur: Oxford University Press, 1995.

Lee Kam Hing. *Politics in Perak, 1969–1974: Some Preliminary Observations with Reference to the Non-Malay Political Parties.* Kuala Lumpur: Department of History, University of Malaya, 1977.

Lee Kuan Yew. *Towards a Malaysian Malaysia.* Singapore: Ministry of Culture, 1965.

Lehmbruch, Gerhard. "Consociational Democracy in the International System". *European Journal of Political Research* 3 (1975): 377–91.

Leifer, Michael. "Singapore in Malaysia: The Politics of Federation". *Journal of Southeast Asian History* 6, no. 2 (1965): 54–70.

Lijphart, Arend. *Democracy in Plural Societies: A Comparative Exploration.* New Haven and London: Yale University Press, 1977.

————. "Cultural Diversity and Theories of Political Integration". *Canadian Journal of Political Science* 4 (1971): 1–14.

_____ . "Consociational Democracy". *World Politics* 21, no. 2 (1969): 207–25.

Lim Kit Siang. *BA and Islamic State.* Petaling Jaya: Democratic Action Party, 2001.

_____ . *The Dirtiest General Elections in the History of Malaysia.* Petaling Jaya: Oriengroup Sdn. Bhd., 1991.

_____ . *The $62 Billion North-South Highway Scandal.* Petaling Jaya: Democratic Action Party, 1987.

Lim M.H. "Affirmative Action, Ethnicity and Integration: The Case of Malaysia". *Ethnic and Racial Studies* 8, no. 2 (1985): 250–76.

Lipset, Seymour M. *Political Man: The Social Bases of Politics.* Baltimore: Johns Hopkins University Press, 1981.

Loh, Francis Kok Wah. "Modernization, Cultural Revival and Counter-Hegemony: The Kadazans of Sabah in the 1980s". In *Fragmented Vision: Culture and Politics in Contemporary Malaysia,* edited by Joel S. Kahn and Francis Loh Kok Wah, pp. 225–53. Sydney: Allen & Unwin, 1992.

_____ . *The Politics of Chinese Unity in Malaysia.* Singapore: Maruzen Asia, 1982.

Lustick, Ian. "Lijphart, Lakatos, and Consociationalism". *World Politics* 50, no. 1 (1997): 88–117.

_____ . "Stability in Deeply Divided Societies: Consociationalism versus Control". *World Politics* 31, no. 3 (1979): 325–44.

Mahathir Mohamad. *In the Face of Attack: Currency Turmoil.* Petaling Jaya: Limkokwing Integrated, 1998.

_____ . "Malaysia: The Way Forward". In *Malaysia's Vision 2020: Understanding the Concept, Implications and Challenges,* edited by Ahmad Sarji Abdul Hamid, pp. 401–20. Petaling Jaya: Pelanduk Publications, 1993.

_____ . "The Second Outline Perspective Plan, 1991–2000". In *Malaysia's Vision 2020: Understanding the Concept, Implications and Challenges,* edited by Ahmad Sarji Abdul Hamid, pp. 421–47. Petaling Jaya: Pelanduk Publications, 1993.

_____. *The Malay Dilemma*. Kuala Lumpur: Times Books International, 1970.

Mansfield, Harvey C., trans. *Niccolo Machiavelli, The Prince*. Chicago and London: University of Chicago Press, 1998.

Marks, G. and Larry Diamond, eds. *Reexamining Democracy*. Newbury Park, California: Sage Publications, 1992.

Mauzy, Diane K. "Malay Political Hegemony and Coercive Consociationalism". In *The Politics of Ethnic Conflict Regulation,* edited by John McGarry and Brendan O'Leary, pp. 106–27. London: Routledge, 1993.

_____. *Barisan Nasional: Coalition Government in Malaysia*. Kuala Lumpur: Marican & Sons Sdn. Bhd., 1983.

McCoy, Alfred W., ed. *Southeast Asia under Japanese Occupation*. New Haven: Yale University Press, 1980.

McGarry, John and Brendan O'Leary, eds. *The Politics of Ethnic Conflict Regulation*. London: Routledge, 1993.

McLeod, Ross H. and Ross Garnaut, eds. *East Asia in Crisis: From Being a Miracle to Needing One?* London and New York: Routledge, 1998.

McRae, Kenneth, ed. *Consociational Democracy: Political Accommodation in Segmented Societies*. Toronto: McClelland & Stewart, 1974.

Mead, Richard. *Malaysia's National Language Policy and the Legal System*. New Haven, Yale University Southeast Asia Studies, 1988.

Means, Gordon. *Malaysian Politics: The Second Generation*. Singapore: Oxford University Press, 1991.

_____. *Malaysian Politics*. London: Hodder and Stoughton, 1976.

_____. "Special Rights as a Strategy for Development: The Case of Malaysia". *Comparative Politics* 5, no. 1 (1972): 29–61.

Milne, R.S. "Bicommunal Systems: Guyana, Malaysia, Fiji". *Publius* 18, no. 2 (1988): 101–14.

_____ . *Government and Politics in Malaysia*. Boston: Houghton Mifflin, 1967.

Milne, R.S. and Diane K. Mauzy. *Malaysian Politics under Mahathir*. London and New York: Routledge, 1999.

_____ . *Politics and Government in Malaysia*. Singapore: Times Books International, 1978.

Milne, R.S. and K.J. Ratnam. "Politics and Finance in Malaya". *Journal of Commonwealth Political Studies* 1, no. 3 (1965), pp. 182–98.

Mohamed Noordin Sopiee. *From Malayan Union to Singapore Separation: Political Unification in the Malaysia Region 1945–1965*. Kuala Lumpur: Penerbit Universiti Malaya, 1974.

Mohamed Suffian (Tun), H.P. Lee, and F.A. Trindade, eds. *The Constitution of Malaysia, Its Development: 1957–1977*. Kuala Lumpur: Oxford University Press, 1978.

Mohammad Agus Yusoff. *Consociational Politics: The Malaysian Experience*. Kuala Lumpur: Perikatan Pemuda Enterprise, 1992.

Montes, Manuel F. *The Currency Crisis in Southeast Asia*. Singapore: Institute of Southeast Asian Studies, 1998.

Morgenthau, Hans. *Politics Among Nations: The Struggle for Power and Peace*. New York: Alfred A. Knopf, 1985.

Muhammad Ikmal Said and Zahid Emby, eds. *Malaysia Critical Perspectives*. Petaling Jaya: Persatuan Sains Sosial Malaysia, 1996.

Muhammad Syukri Salleh. *An Islamic Approach to Rural Development: The Arqam Way*. London: Asoib International, 1992.

Munro-Kua, Anne. *Authoritarian Populism in Malaysia*. London: Macmillan Press, 1996.

Mustafa K. Anuar. "The Malaysian 1990 General Election: The Role of the BN Mass Media". *Kajian Malaysia* 8, no. 2 (1990): 82–102.

Nordlinger, Eric A. *Conflict Regulation in Divided Societies*. Cambridge, Mass.: Center for International Affairs, Harvard University, 1972.

NSTP Research and Information Services. *Elections in Malaysia: A Handbook of Facts and Figures on the Elections 1955–1990.* Kuala Lumpur: NSTP, 1994.

_____ . *Elections in Malaysia: Facts and Figures.* Kuala Lumpur: NSTP, 1990.

O'Donnell, Guillermo and Philippe C. Schmitter. *Transition from Authoritarian Rule: Tentative Conclusions about Uncertain Democracies.* Baltimore and London: Johns Hopkins University Press, 1986.

Ongkili, James P. *Nation-Building in Malaysia, 1946–1974.* Singapore: Oxford University Press, 1985.

Parkinson, C.N. *A Short History of Malaya.* Singapore: D. Moore, 1954.

Parmer, J.N. *Colonial Labor Policy and Administration.* New York: Association for Asian Studies, 1960.

Phang Siew Nooi. *Financing Local Government in Malaysia.* Kuala Lumpur: University of Malaya Press, 1997.

Przeworski, Adam. "Some Problems in the Study of the Transition to Democracy". In *Transition from Authoritarian Rule: Comparative Perspectives,* edited by Guillermo O'Donnell, Philippe C. Schmitter, and Laurence Whitehead, pp. 47–63. Baltimore and London: Johns Hopkins University Press, 1986.

Purcell, Victor. *Malaya: Communist or Free?* London: Victor Gollancz, 1954.

_____ . *The Chinese in Malaya.* London: Oxford University Press, 1948.

PUTERA and AMCJA. *The People's Constitution for Malaya.* Kuala Lumpur: Ta Chong Press, 1947.

Rabushka, Alvin and Kenneth A. Shepsle. *Politics in Plural Societies: A Theory of Democratic Instability.* Columbus, Ohio: Charles E. Merrill Publishing Company, 1972.

Rais Yatim. *Freedom under Executive Power in Malaysia.* Kuala Lumpur: Endowment Sdn. Bhd., 1995.

Ramanathan, Sankaran and Mohd. Hamdan Adnan. *Malaysia's 1986 General Election: The Urban-Rural Dichotomy.* Singapore: Institute of Southeast Asian Studies, 1988.

Ratnam, K.J. and R.S. Milne. *The Malaysian Parliamentary Election of 1964.* Singapore: University of Malaya Press, 1967.

Ratnam, K.J. *Communalism and the Political Process in Malaya.* Singapore: University of Malaya Press, 1965.

Reid, Anthony. "The Kuala Lumpur Riots and the Malaysian Political System". *Australian Outlook* 23, no. 3 (1969): 258–78.

Roff, Margaret. "The Politics of Language in Malaya". *Asian Survey* 7, no. 5 (1967): 316–28.

Roff, William. *The Origins of Malay Nationalism.* New Haven: Yale University Press, 1967.

Rothchild, Donald. *Managing Ethnic Conflict in Africa: Pressures and Incentives for Cooperation.* Washington, DC: Brookings Institution Press, 1997.

_____ . "Review Article: Ethnicity and Conflict Resolution". *World Politics* 22, no. 4 (1970): 597–616.

Rustam A. Sani. *Politik dan Polemik Bahasa Melayu.* Kuala Lumpur: Utusan Publication and Distributors, 1993.

Salleh Abas. *The Role of the Independent Judiciary.* Kuala Lumpur: Percetakan A-Z Sdn. Bhd., 1989.

Salleh Abas and K. Das. *May Day for Justice: The Lord President's Version.* Kuala Lumpur: Magnus Books, 1989.

Saravanamuttu, Johan. "The State, Ethnicity and the Middle Class Factor: Addressing Nonviolent, Democratic Change in Malaysia". In *Internal Conflict and Governance,* edited by Kumar Rupesinghe, pp. 63–70. New York: St. Martin's Press, 1992.

Searle, Peter. *The Riddle of Malaysian Capitalism: Rent-Seekers or Real Capitalists?* St. Leonards, NSW: Allen & Unwin, 1999.

Shafruddin B.H. *The Federal Factor in the Government and Politics of Peninsular Malaysia.* Singapore: Oxford University Press, 1987.

Sharma, Archana. *British Policy towards Malaysia, 1957–1967.* London: Sangam Books Limited, 1993.

Sheridan, L.A. *The Federation of Malaya Constitution.* Singapore: University of Malaya Law Review, 1961.

Slimming, John. *Malaysia: Death of a Democracy.* London: John Murray, 1969.

Smith, M.G. *The Plural Society in the British West Indies.* Berkeley and Los Angeles: University of California Press, 1965.

Soenarno, Radin. "Malay Nationalism, 1896–1941". *Journal of Southeast Asian History* 1, no. 1 (1960): 1–28.

Steinberg, D.J., ed. *In Search of Southeast Asia: A Modern History.* Sydney: Allen & Unwin, 1987.

Steiner, Jurg. "The Principles of Majority and Proportionality". *British Journal of Political Science* 1, no. 1 (1971): 63–70.

Stockwell, A.J. *British Policy and Malay Politics during the Malayan Union Experiment, 1945–1948.* Kuala Lumpur: Malayan Branch of the Royal Asiatic Society, 1979.

Stockwell, A.J., ed. *Malaya, Part I: The Malayan Union Experiment 1942–1948.* London: HMSO, 1995.

————. *Malaya, Part II: The Communist Insurrection 1948–1953.* London: HMSO, 1995.

————. *Malaya, Part III: The Alliance Route to Independence 1953–1957.* London: HMSO, 1995.

SUARAM. *Malaysian Human Rights Report.* Petaling Jaya: SUARAM Komunikasi, 1998.

SUARAM and K. Das. *The White Paper on the October Affair and The Why? Papers.* Kelana Jaya: SUARAM Kommunikasi, 1989.

Suryadinata, Leo, ed. *Ethnic Chinese as Southeast Asians.* Singapore: Institute of Southeast Asian Studies, 1997.

Tan Liok Ee. "*Dongjiaozong* and the Challenge to Cultural Hegemony 1951–1987". In *Fragmented Vision: Culture and Politics in Contemporary Malaysia,* edited by Joel S. Kahn and Francis Loh Kok Wah, pp. 181–98. Sydney: Allen & Unwin, 1992.

Tarling, Nicholas. "Intervention and Non-Intervention in Malaya". *Journal of Asian Studies* 21, no. 4 (1962): 523–27.

Taylor, R.H., ed. *The Politics of Elections in Southeast Asia.* Cambridge: Cambridge University Press, 1996.

Tregonning, K.G. *A History of Modern Malaya.* London: Eastern Universities Press, 1964.

Trindade, F.A. and H.P. Lee, eds. *The Constitution of Malaysia: Further Perspectives and Developments.* Petaling Jaya: Penerbit Fajar Bakti, 1986.

Tweedie, M.W.F. "The Stone Age in Malaya". *Journal of the Malayan Branch of the Royal Asiatic Society* 26, part 2 (1953): 1–100.

Vasil, R.K. *Ethnic Politics in Malaysia.* New Delhi: Radiant Publishers, 1980.

_____ . *The Malaysian General Election of 1969.* Kuala Lumpur: Oxford University Press, 1972.

_____ . "The 1964 General Elections in Malaya". *International Studies* 7, no. 1 (1965): 39–56.

von Vorys, Karl. *Democracy Without Consensus: Communalism and Political Stability in Malaysia.* New Jersey: Princeton University Press, 1975.

Walker, Leslie J., trans. *The Discourses of Niccolo Machiavelli*, vol. I. London: Routledge, 1991.

Williams, Louise and Roland Rich, eds. *Losing Control: Freedom of the Press in Asia.* Canberra: Asia Pacific Press, Australian National University, 2000.

Williams, Peter Alderidge. *Judicial Misconduct.* Petaling Jaya: Pelanduk Publications, 1990.

Wilson, Samuel Herbert. *Report of Brigadier-General Sir Samuel Wilson, Permanent Under-Secretary of State for the Colonies on His Visit to Malaya 1932.* London: His Majesty's Office, 1933.

Wong, C.S. *A Gallery of Chinese Kapitans.* Singapore: Dewan Bahasa dan Kebudayaan Kebangsaan, Ministry of Culture, 1963.

Zainal Abidin bin Abdul Wahid. "The Japanese Occupation and Nationalism". In *Glimpses of Malaysian History,* edited by Zainal Abidin bin Abdul Wahid. Kuala Lumpur: Dewan Bahasa dan Pustaka, 1970.

Zainuddin Maidin. *The Other Side of Mahathir.* Kuala Lumpur: Utusan Publication & Distributors Sdn. Bhd., 1994.

Zakaria Haji Ahmad. "Malaysia: Quasi Democracy in a Divided Society". In *Democracy in Developing Countries: Asia,* edited by Larry Diamond, Juan J. Linz, and Seymour Martin Lipset, pp. 347–81. Boulder, Colorado: Lynne Rienner Publishers, 1989.

Zakaria, F. "The Rise of Illiberal Democracy". *Foreign Affairs,* November–December 1997, pp. 22–43.

Zakry Zbadi. *Why Anwar? Political Games of UMNO's Leadership.* Kuala Lumpur: Gelanggang Publishing, 1993.

Monographs, Papers, Theses, and Documents

Amnesty International. *Malaysia: Human Rights Undermined — Restrictive Laws in a Parliamentary Democracy,* 1 September 1999.

————. *The Trial of Opposition Parliamentarian Lim Guan Eng: An Update,* 28 March 1997.

Anwar Ibrahim. "From the Halls of Power to the Labyrinths of Incarceration". Letter from Sungai Buloh prison on 3 November 1998.

Bass, J. "Malaysian Politics, 1968–1970: Crisis and Response". Ph.D. thesis, University of California, 1973.

British Malaya. *A Report on the 1947 Census of Population.* London: Crown Agents for the Colonies, 1949.

————. *A Report on the 1931 Census and on Certain Problems of Vital Statistics.* Westminster: Crown Agents for the Colonies, 1932.

Case, William. "Pseudo-Democracy in Southeast Asia: Uncovering State Leaders and the Business Connection". Paper presented at the Asia in Global Context Conference, University of New South Wales, 28 September to 1 October 1998.

_____ . "Semi-Democracy in Malaysia: Pressures and Prospects for Change". In *Regime Change and Regime Maintenance in Asia and the Pacific*. Discussion Paper Series Number 8. Canberra: Research School of Pacific and Asian Studies, Australian National University, 1992.

Chin, James. *'Kataks', Kadazan-Dusun Nationalism and Development: The 1999 Sabah State Election*. Discussion Paper Series Number 24, Regime Change and Regime Maintenance in Asia and the Pacific. Canberra: Research School of Pacific and Asian Studies, Australian National University, 1999.

_____ . "Politics of Federal Intervention in Malaysia with Reference to Sarawak, Sabah and Kelantan". Paper presented at the First International Malaysian Studies Conference, University of Malaya, 11–13 August 1997.

Commonwealth Secretariat. *General Elections in Malaysia 20–21 October 1990: The Report of the Commonwealth Observer Group*, 1990.

Democratic Action Party. *DAP Policies for Malaysia: Full Liberalization*, 3 October 1994 <http://www.malaysia.net/dap/poll-1.htm>.

Enloe, Cynthia H. *Multi-Ethnic Politics: The Case of Malaysia*. Research Monograph No. 2. California: Center for South and Southeast Asia Studies, University of California Berkeley, 1970.

Federation of Malaysia. *Malaysia Population Statistics, Estimated Population by Races and Sex as at 31st December 1964*. Kuala Lumpur: Department of Statistics, 1965.

_____ . *The 1957 Population Census of the Federation of Malaya*. Report No. 14. Kuala Lumpur: Department of Statistics, 1960.

_____ . *Malayan Constitutional Documents*. Kuala Lumpur: Government Press, 1958.

_____ . *The Federation of Malaya Agreement, 1948 As Amended*. Kuala Lumpur: Government Press, 1956.

_____ . *The Federation of Malaya Agreement (Amendment) Ordinance*. Kuala Lumpur: Government Press, 1952.

Federation of Malaya Constitutional Commission. *Report of the Federation of Malaya Constitutional Commission 1957.* Rome: Food and Agriculture Organization of the United Nations, 1957.

Government of Malaysia. *Seventh Malaysia Plan 1996–2000.* Kuala Lumpur: Percetakan Nasional Malaysia Berhad, 1996.

―――. *Sixth Malaysia Plan 1991–1995.* Kuala Lumpur: National Printing Department, 1991.

―――. *Mid-Term Review of the Fifth Malaysia Plan 1986–1990.* Kuala Lumpur: National Printing Department, 1989.

―――. *Fifth Malaysia Plan 1986–1990.* Kuala Lumpur: National Printing Department, 1986.

―――. *Mid-Term Review of the Fourth Malaysian Plan 1981–1985* Kuala Lumpur: National Printing Department, 1984.

―――. *Fourth Malaysia Plan 1981–1985.* Kuala Lumpur: National Printing Department, 1981.

―――. *Third Malaysia Plan 1976–1980.* Kuala Lumpur: Government Press, 1976.

―――. *Mid-Term Review of the Second Malaysia Plan 1971–1975.* Kuala Lumpur: Government Press, 1973.

―――. *Parliamentary Debates on the Constitution Amendment Bill 1971.* Kuala Lumpur: Government Printer, 1972.

―――. *Second Malaysia Plan 1971–1975.* Kuala Lumpur: Government Press, 1971.

―――. *Towards National Harmony.* Kuala Lumpur: Government Press, 1971.

―――. *Rukunegara.* Kuala Lumpur: Jabatan Chetak Kerajaan, 1970.

Great Britain. *Malayan Union and Singapore: Summary of Proposed Constitutional Arrangement.* London: HMSO, 1946.

Lawson, Stephanie. "Some Conceptual and Empirical Issues in the Study of Regime Change". In *Regime Change and Regime Maintenance in Asia and the Pacific.* Discussion Paper Series Number 3. Canberra:

Research School of Pacific and Asian Studies, Australian National University, 1991.

Legal Research Board. *Private Higher Educational Institutions Act 1996*. Kuala Lumpur: International Law Book Services, 1996.

_____ . *Sedition Act 1948*. Kuala Lumpur: International Law Book Services, 1996.

_____ . *Education Act 1996*. Kuala Lumpur: International Law Book Services, 1996.

_____ . *Federal Constitution*. Kuala Lumpur: International Law Book Services, 1995.

_____ . *Official Secrets Act 1972*. Kuala Lumpur: International Law Book Services, 1994.

_____ . *Education Act 1961*. Kuala Lumpur: International Law Book Services, 1993.

_____ . *Internal Security Act 1960*. Kuala Lumpur: International Law Book Services, 1988.

Lim Kit Siang. "The Impact of the Anwar Ibrahim Case on Politics in Malaysia". Paper presented at Griffith University, Brisbane, 4 May 2000.

Loh, Francis Kok Wah. "Post-NEP Politics in Malaysia: Ferment and Fragmentation". Paper presented at the Second Australia-Malaysia Conference, Australian National University, Canberra, 24–26 May 2000.

_____ . "Pluralism and Democracy in Malaysia: Political, Cultural and Social Challenges". Paper presented at Islam, Culture, and Democracy: A Regional Roundtable, Kuala Lumpur, 17–18 August 1998.

Ministry of Home Affairs. *The Government White Paper: Towards Preserving National Security*, 14 March 1988.

National Operations Council. *The May 13 Tragedy: A Report of the National Operations Council*. Kuala Lumpur: Government Press, 1969.

Shamsul A.B. "The Redefinition of Politics and the Transformation of Malaysian Pluralism". Paper presented to conference on Southeast Asian Pluralism, ISEC-Ford Project, Kuala Lumpur, 5–6 August 1999.

Tan Chee Beng. "Baba and Nyonya: A Study of the Ethnic Identity of the Chinese Peranakan in Malacca". Ph.D. thesis, Cornell University, 1979.

Treasury Malaysia. *Economic Report 1975–76.* Kuala Lumpur: Treasury's Economics Division, 1975.

United Chinese School Committees Association of Malaysia et al. *Memorandum on the Education Bill 1995*, submitted by the seven major Chinese Associations to the Education Minister, 15 December 1995.

Newspapers and Periodicals

Aliran Monthly, Malaysia

Aliran Quarterly, Malaysia

Asian Wall Street Journal (AWSJ), Hong Kong

Asiaweek, Hong Kong

Berita Harian, Malaysia

Business Times, Malaysia

Far Eastern Economic Review (FEER), Hong Kong

Harakah, Malaysia

Malaysian Business, Malaysia

Malaysian Digest, Malaysia

Nanyang Siang Pao, Malaysia

New Straits Times (NST), Malaysia

Sin Chew Jit Poh, Malaysia

Straits Times, Singapore

Sydney Morning Herald, Australia

The Nation, Thailand

The Rocket, Malaysia

The Star, Malaysia

Time, United States

Utusan Malaysia, Malaysia

Utusan Melayu, Malaysia

Interviews*

Ahmad Shabery Chik, special assistant to former Semangat 46 president Razaleigh Hamzah (January 1998; August 1999; May 2000).

Anuwar Ali, director of the Department of Higher Education in the Ministry of Education (February 1998).

Chong Eng, former state assembly member and MP from DAP (February 1998).

Chor Chee Heung, former parliamentary secretary to the Minister of Transport and Deputy Minister of Home Affairs (February 1998).

Chua Tian Chang (Tian Chua), vice-president of KeADILan (February 1998; August 1999; April 2001).

Elizabeth Wong, former co-ordinator of SUARAM (January 1998).

Hatta Ramli, political secretary to PAS president Fadzil Noor (May 2000).

Hew Kuan Yau, political secretary to the secretary-general of DAP (August 1999).

Hishammuddin Hussein, UMNO Youth chief (February 1998).

Ibrahim Ali, former Semangat 46 Youth chief and UMNO supreme council member (February 1998).

Ibrahim Saad, former deputy minister in the Prime Minister's Department and UMNO supreme council member (February 1998; August 1999).

---

* Official positions held at time of interview. Names of confidential interviewees omitted.

Jayasankaran, *Far Eastern Economic Review* correspondent (August 1999).

Jomo Kwame Sundaram, former president of Malaysian Social Science Association (August 1999).

Kamarudin Jaffar, MP from PAS (August 1999; May 2000).

Kua Kia Soong, academic director of *Dongjiaozong* Higher Learning Centre (January 1998).

Lee Ban Chen, former deputy director of Planning and Development Bureau in United Chinese School Committees' Association of Malaysia (January 1998).

Lee Kim Sai, former deputy president of MCA (February 1998).

Liew Chin Tong, former political secretary to the MP for Seputeh, DAP (August 1999).

Lim Guan Eng, former MP and vice-chairman of DAP (January 1998).

Lim Kit Siang, former parliamentary opposition leader and chairman of DAP (February 1998, August 1999, April 2000).

M.G.G. Pillai, journalist (February 1998).

Mohamed Ezam Mohd. Nor, KeADILan Youth chief (April 2001).

Mohd Anuar Tahir, secretary-general of KeADILan (April 2001).

Muhammad Asri Mohd. Ali, UM academic (August 1999).

Musa Hitam, former Deputy Prime Minister of Malaysia (February 1998, August 1999).

Nasir Hashim, pro-tem chairman of Malaysian Socialist Party, Kuala Lumpur (January 1998).

Ong Tee Keat, MP and MCA Youth chairman (February 1998).

Palanisamy Ramasamy, UKM academic (January 1998).

Rais Yatim, former deputy president of Semangat 46 and minister in the Prime Minister's Department (February 1998; August 1999; May 2000).

Razaleigh Hamzah, former Semangat 46 president and currently UMNO supreme council member (February 1998).

Rustam Sani, former deputy president of Malaysian Social Science Association and vice-president of PRM (February 1998).

Saifuddin Nasution Ismail, former UMNO Youth secretary and state assembly member from KeADILan (January 1998; August 1999; April 2000; December 2000).

Shamsul A.B., UKM academic (August 1999).

Shamsul Akmar Musakamal, journalist (February 1998; August 1999).

Subky Latiff, former PAS information chief and PAS Central Committee member (August 1999).

Syed Husin Ali, president of PRM (February 1998; August 1999).

Tan Seng Giaw, vice-chairman of DAP and MP (February 1998).

Teresa Kok Suh Sim, MP from DAP (October 1998; August 1999; May 2000).

Wan Azizah Wan Ismail, president of KeADILan (August 1999).

Wee Choo Keong, former MP from DAP and secretary-general of Malaysian Democratic Party (February 1998; August 1999).

Wong Chin Huat, executive secretary to the Malaysian Chinese Organizations' Election Appeals Committee (Suqiu Committee) (April 2001).

Zulkifli Sulong, group editor of *Harakah* (August 1999).

Index

ABOUT THE AUTHOR

In-Won Hwang is a Research Fellow at the Institute for East Asian Studies, Sogang University, Korea. Before that he was Visiting Professor in the Faculty of International Relations, Ritsumeikan University, Kyoto, Japan. His areas of research interest are democratization and consolidation in Malaysia; regime change and regime maintenance in Southeast Asian countries.